A Short History of
Ireland

A Short History of
Ireland

Second edition

JOHN O'BEIRNE RANELAGH

CAMBRIDGE
UNIVERSITY PRESS

Published by the Press Syndicate of the University of Cambridge
The Pitt Building, Trumpington Street, Cambridge CB2 1RP
40 West 20th Street, New York, NY 10011-4211 USA
10 Stamford Road, Oakleigh, Melbourne 3166, Australia

First edition © Telstore Ltd 1983
Second edition © Cambridge Publishing Ltd 1994

First published 1983
Second edition 1994
Reprinted 1995 (twice)

Printed in Great Britain at the University Press, Cambridge

A catalogue record for this book is available from the British Library

A catalogue record for this book is available from the Library of Congress

ISBN 0 521 47548 1 hardback
ISBN 0 521 46944 9 paperback
ISBN 0 521 24685 7 first edition hardback
ISBN 0 521 28889 4 first edition paperback

CE/WD

Contents

Preface to first edition

Ireland's history is distinguished by two special characteristics. First, a recognizable Irish nation, of course over time itself a conglomerate of many 'nations', distinct from a British nation, with its own language, customs and lore dating back to the iron age, survived right into the nineteenth century. This gave Irish nationalism a particular force. Secondly, over the centuries of increasingly powerful and centralized British government, ruling social and political pressures combined first to make Irish people feel and then to believe that they were inferior. This is one of the worst things that any nation or race can do to another. It results in the most terrible of paradoxes where in practical matters there is a desire equally to welcome and to oppose, thus ensuring that failure accompanies success, and despair and a sense of futility underlie the whole of life. As many Irishmen were government spies, agents and informers as were national heroes; emigration became almost the only way of escaping depression. To the present day many Irish writers find it somehow necessary to practise their art away from home.

In modern times the complexities of economic development, international arrangements and the rejection of Irish nationalism in Northern Ireland have begun to change traditional attitudes. The very concept of a unitary Irish nation has been challenged, and the reality of Ireland's connections with Britain has begun to be faced honestly for the first time by politicians. In the last quarter of the twentieth century we can, I think say that Ireland's people are at last considering themselves in relation to an Irish world for which they themselves accept responsibility.

I would like to thank Charles Davidson, Sean Dowling, Susannah Johnson, Joseph Lee, Deirdre McMahon, Victor Price, David Rose, Richard Rose, A. T. Q. Stewart and Norman Stone who have all helped me most generously with their knowledge and advice. I owe them all a great debt: my accuracies are their achievement; any inaccuracies are mine. To my wife, Elizabeth, I owe most thanks of all.

Grantchester, 1982

Preface to second edition

Since I wrote this book twelve years ago, there has been a great change in mainstream Irish nationalism and in the awarenesses of the Republic. Roman Catholic moral and social teaching, militating against contraception, divorce, abortion, pushing Ireland apart from the liberal values at the heart of the European Union, have given way to a more secular sensibility. American Catholic attitudes have replaced traditional Irish ones: there is hostility to Church leadership and control. There is a general indifference to traditional Gaelic culture. Terror has become a way of life for malcontents in the North, of which terrorists are a part. They have confirmed their debasement of a struggle that was noble and have fundamentally conditioned Irish nationalism and unionism for most Irishmen. Very few of the men and women involved in the Irish fight for freedom in the 1916–21 period could identify with those who act in the name of the IRA and its splinter groups today. Unionists of the same period would undoubtedly reject those 'loyalists' who have also chosen terror as a weapon.

The balance of this book is weighted to the period after 1800 in which modern Ireland has been formed. Terrorism and its attendant horrors in Northern Ireland, spilling at times into England and the Republic – and even occasionally further afield – have forced the Republic effectively to moderate its claims to the whole island of Ireland. At the same time, the less organic, federal and provisional nature of the union between Northern Ireland and Britain (i.e., England, Scotland and Wales) has become steadily clear as United Kingdom (i.e., Britain and Northern Ireland) governments have committed themselves to observe only majority verdicts by voters within the North on the future of the province, and not to consider the views of British voters on the matter. Indeed, Westminster governments and the people of Britain by no means crave possession of Northern Ireland: unionists in the North are acutely conscious of this. Assertions to the contrary are a combination of misrepresentation and misappreciation that now suits terrorists and their supporters. Similarly, in the Republic, people are conscious that Irish unity will involve terrible costs that they are by no means certain they wish to pay. The fact that IRA terror has not been applied in the Republic indicates that the IRA knows that they cannot play with politics in the South, and that any tolerance they may enjoy there would be jeopardized by the least activity. The United Kingdom's resolve to combat terrorism and, with some exceptions, the tempered way in which the resolve has been discharged, consistently demonstrated by successive governments and the security forces over the last quarter century, commands respect, not least in the South.

I am conscious of sometimes using the terms Catholic and Protestant to distinguish between the two principal communities in Northern Ireland. In doing this, I am in line with journalists and commentators over the last twenty-five years who have formed the appreciation of most people. And it has been the case that local politics in the North have reflected religious divisions more than anything else. But to promote religious background as *the* dividing element in the North is inaccurate. It is certainly one of the main classifications, but economic, social and political distinctions are equally important and cut across religion: a religious war is not taking place in the North. About 40 per cent of the population of Northern Ireland is Catholic; about 33 per cent of Northern Ireland Roman Catholic voters support Sinn Fein, the political arm of the IRA: the rest vote for anti-Sinn Fein Parties; some vote for Unionists. The probability is that there would have to be much more than a simple Catholic majority in the North before a majority of voters would endorse unification with the Republic: being Catholic does not mean being a supporter of immediate unity with the South. It is the case today that Northern Protestants are overwhelmingly unionist, but some have been among Ireland's foremost nationalists and radicals. Michael Farrell, one of the founders of the People's Democracy movement in the late 1960s that energised the civil rights campaign beginning the present troubles, was a Protestant.

Neither the United Kingdom nor the United States fills the imagination of Irish people any more. The other countries of Europe are ever more real to them today. They see the United Kingdom as a clapped-out old place, and not a threatening imperial presence: Charles Haughey, Irish taoiseach in the 1980s, was the last political leader who perceived the United Kingdom in imperial terms. Irish people have recognized that they cannot live off memories forever.

Finally, it should be remembered that politicians, whom we elect yet love to disparage, have been called by terrorism to put their safety, their families' safety, and their lives on the line time and again. The Conservative Party spokesman on Northern Ireland, Airey Neave, was killed by a bomb in his car at the House of Commons in 1979. Anne Wakeham, the wife of the Conservative chief whip, and Sir Anthony Berry, MP, were killed in a bomb explosion in the Grand Hotel, Brighton, during the Conservative Party conference in 1984. In the same explosion, Norman Tebbit, a Cabinet Minister, was severely injured and his wife, Margaret, permanently crippled. Ian Gow, MP, who had been a junior Minister in Northern Ireland, was killed by a bomb in his car at his home in 1990. The men and women in the security forces and many individuals in all walks of life in Northern Ireland have been called constantly to risk injury, and their lives, every day. At the end of this edition, I have provided a table of some of the deaths and injuries terrorism has inflicted in the North: space prevents a full account.

I am indebted to all those who made suggestions and corrections to the first edition of this book, for any mistakes that remain and any that may be new, I am responsible.

Grantchester and Bergen,
November 1993   JOHN O'BEIRNE RANELAGH

Map 1 Ireland

1

Prehistory and legends

Human bones found in a cave in Co. Waterford in 1928 indicate that the first Irishmen may have lived before 9000 BC. But the evidence is unreliable, and in any case they would not have survived the last cold spell which ended the ice age around 7000 BC. The first significant human habitation dates from the middle of the seventh millennium BC. In the previous 25,000 years a variety of animal life flourished, notably the giant Irish deer with antlers spanning up to ten feet; elephant-like hairy mammoths, hyenas, wolves and foxes. As temperatures changed, Ireland variously experienced tropical forests, tundra and open vegetation. Earlier still, the landscape of the country was formed. The Mountains of Mourne and other famous land forms were created some seventy-five million years ago as molten lava cooled. Drumlins and deep valleys like the Gap of Dunloe were sculpted and gouged by the gigantic force of ice 200,000 years ago.

Until about 9,000 years ago, Ireland was attached to Britain. As the world's climate warmed the ice melted, sea levels rose, and Ireland lost its land link with Britain and became an island on the north-western corner of the European continental shelf, separated from her neighbours by shallow seas. A fall in sea-level of 350 feet (106 metres) would once again connect south-east Ireland and Wales, while a fall of about 600 feet (182 metres) would lay bare the sea floor to France as well as the continental shelf 150 miles out into the Atlantic, west of the provinces of Munster and Connaught. Britain retained her land connections much longer with the European mainland across the southern reaches of the North Sea to Belgium, the Netherlands and north-western Germany. This explains why Britain, unlike Ireland, has snakes: by the time they reached west Britain after the ice age, Ireland was already an island

1

(although legend has it instead that St Patrick, Ireland's patron saint, banished the reptiles).

However, before the rising sea submerged these land bridges, the first humans to settle in the British Isles came across them, probably reaching Ireland on a land connection from Scotland. When this too had been submerged, around 6700 BC, Ireland was left alone facing the Atlantic. The first settlers found a country whose principal geographical characteristics had been formed. Of the country's twenty million acres, an eighth were hills and mountains with inhospitable rocks bared by ice, wind and rain. Much of the rest was wooded, but by 3000 BC another eighth had become bog as trees and other vegetation collapsed into lakes and streams. Of the remaining fifteen million acres, most of it good productive land, not until the twentieth century has it been exploited fully with improving agricultural efficiency and afforestation policies. But eight and a half thousand years ago, before mass human habitation, Ireland like Britain was covered by dense deciduous forests, with only lakes, mountains, streams and rivers breaking the cover. Thus was provided the habitat for animal life and food and shelter for the first Irishmen.

The first communities in Ireland were composed of mesolithic (middle stone age) people. There are conflicting opinions about their origins and first settlements. They did not live by farming, but instead collected food and hunted wild life. For the most part, they seem to have lived by the sea shore or lake and river banks. It is likely that they did undertake sea voyages, but in very primitive craft, probably skin-clad coracles similar to those that survive to the present day in the west of Ireland. Their primitive economy lasted undisturbed for over two thousand years until the knowledge of domestication of animals and plants arrived in Ireland during the fourth millennium BC. Even then, mesolithic ways of life continued for perhaps two thousand years after the first farmers began to settle in the country.

Little is known of mesolithic man in Ireland. No mesolithic graves (one of the principal sources of evidence for archaeologists) have been discovered, and significant traces of only one mesolithic community have been found at Mount Sandel in Co. Londonderry. Excavations there have revealed the post holes of round huts, approximately 20 feet (6 metres) across, with central hearths and associated pits. The Mount Sandel site is likely to have been a winter residence, more substantial than those used at other times of the year. The other main source of information about these people comes from the large number of their rubbish dumps that have been found. They contain the remnants of sea food – molluscs, crustaceans and fish – birds and sometimes mammals, together with flint and stone implements and chippings produced in the course of tool-making. But there is no direct evidence of the linguistic and religious culture, let alone the ethnic composition of these Irishmen. What is clear from these excavations, however, is that from about 3500 BC neolithic (late stone age) farmers began to arrive and to assimilate the mesolithic hunter–gatherers.

In comparison to mesolithic settlers, neolithic farmers were sophisticated and technically advanced. They also had a major impact on the natural landscape, clearing large tracts of land, using polished stone tools to till and plant the soil with crops. Herds of sheep and cattle were kept, and neolithic communities penetrated far inland. Their agricultural way of life, with domestication of animals, complemented the coastal fishing and hunting economy of their mesolithic predecessors, and this is the probable reason why both ways of life co-existed for so long.

The neolithic settlers in Ireland originated in the Middle East from where they were gradually forced to emigrate as expanding population in their homelands increased the pressure for new farming lands. By about 5000 BC they had moved through the Balkans, pushing along the Mediterranean coast into France and Spain, and then northwards to the Low Countries and Britain. Bringing their own crops and livestock, they probably sailed in coracles to Ireland across the sea from Spain, Portugal and Brittany. The evidence is unclear, but they may have also introduced the art of pottery, decorating and shaping pots with round bottoms for storing food, and heavier flat bottoms for cooking. The most impressive neolithic site in Ireland so far discovered was at Lough Gur on the Knockadoon Peninsula, about 12 miles (19.7 km) south of Limerick city. Excavated mainly in the 1930s and 1940s, the domestic structures of an early Irish farming community were revealed. Houses were built with stone foundations, some round, some rectangular, with wooden frame walls filled with earthen turves. Polished stone axes with wooden handles and picks made from the antlers of deer were used by these people. Bones were shaped as needles, awls and other domestic implements for spinning wool and making clothing and material for warmth. Flint arrow and spearheads provide clear indication that the new settlers hunted as well as farmed. Bone and stone bead bracelets and ornaments demonstrate that they were probably as interested in their appearance as we are today. They even set up factories to produce their stone axes, but the most striking remains of the neolithic farmers are the massive stone megaliths and dolmens they raised for their dead.

There are several different types of neolithic burial sites in Ireland, suggesting that these settlers arrived from a variety of places and in successive waves. There is some evidence that the first neolithic mortuary monuments may have been constructed of timber, only to be superseded by those of stone construction. Whether of stone or wood, these monuments all consisted of a central chamber or gallery which was covered with earth to form a mound. The earliest stone tombs dating from around 3000 BC are reckoned to be those known as 'court cairns' which are especially numerous in the northern half of the country, suggesting that a particular neolithic immigrant group was associated with them. A long, straight-sided stone gallery with a stone slab roof covered with earth, incorporating an open court – sometimes in the middle of the gallery but more often at one end – characterizes these buildings. The tombs were collective, with the dead, sometimes cremated, sometimes buried, being placed in the galleries with personal artifacts, thus indicating that their religion involved belief in an after-life. The court was apparently used for burial and doubtless religious rites. Tombs of other traditions also abound. 'Passage graves' are especially numerous in the north and east of Ireland, forming some of the most spectacular illustrations of stone age architecture. These graves are usually found on hilltop sites, grouped in cemeteries, with a stone passage leading to a burial chamber, all covered in an earth cairn. The earliest date from about 2800 BC and the leading example of a passage grave site, and one of the most significant in western Europe, is on the river Boyne, at Newgrange, Knowth and Dowth, near Drogheda, Co. Meath, dating from 2500 BC. Here, as with other passage graves, the stone walls of the burial chamber are decorated with elaborate spiral, zig-zag and meandering carvings. The dead were cremated and, as with the court cairn people, were placed in the chamber together with pottery, beads and tools. At Newgrange, the extent and intricacy of the carvings suggest that some of the patterns may have had a religious significance, possibly even depicting highly stylized human faces and figures. Newgrange was designed by its builders so that the sun could enter the chamber only once a year, around midwinter day, suggesting that the passage grave people may have had a knowledge of astronomy and involved the sun in their worship.

The existence of passage graves and similar artwork outside Ireland – notably in Brittany and the Iberian peninsula – supports the observation that these people in Ireland belonged to a group of sea-borne immigrants enjoying ancestral traditions and connections with the developing urban civilizations of the Mediterranean. More than this, from the size and positioning of passage grave sites, archaeologists have been able to suggest something of the society of their constructors. While the graves are grouped in cemeteries and used communally, the larger ones seem to have been the repositories of chieftains and their families, with smaller graves being grouped around them: evidence of an hierarchic social order preserved in death.

Another sort of chambered tomb, 'dolmens', built during the neolithic era, probably derived from the court cairn people. They were single-chamber tombs, with standing stones acting as a support for a large capstone which was then covered with earth to form a mound. Concentrated in the north and east of the country, they tend to be further inland than court and passage graves, suggesting that their builders had penetrated woodland further and were thus later than the court and passage peoples. Some dolmens have capstones weighing perhaps 100 tons: stark testimony to the ingenuity and engineering ability of these stone age people.

The fourth type of megalithic tomb, and broadly a later one, is the 'wedge' type consisting of a single main chamber with walls and ceiling formed of stone slabs in a rectangular shape, narrowed at one end to produce a wedge-like effect. Almost 40 have been found, predominantly in the south-west, often close to metal deposits, indicating that they represent bronze age rather than neolithic people. It may well be that the wedge tomb builders were among the first groups in Ireland to use metal, and that their farming economy was more dependent upon cattle and grazing than their neolithic predecessors since these graves are usually found on light, well-drained soil. Bodies, cremated or, if whole, in a crouched position, were placed inside the wedge stone box along with pots, ornaments or other equipment. Tombs were used individually, not collectively, although often clustered together.

Metal working of copper, gold, silver and lead developed in the Near East around 3500 BC, and experimentation with alloys led to the discovery of bronze in the latter third millennium BC. The toughness of bronze made complex casting possible and also provided a harder cutting edge for tools and weapons. In the period before 2000 BC new migrations took place in Europe, ultimately reaching the British isles.

The group who brought the bronze age to Ireland are known as the 'beaker people' from their distinctive beaker-like pots, and probably came from Britain to the north and East of Ireland around the end of the third millennium BC. As with neolithic immigrants, it seems the beaker people supplemented rather than supplanted the existing peoples of the country: the continuation of megalithic burial practices after the arrival of the beaker people suggests this as well as a continuation in the traditions and patterns of life. Their burial practices were not as elaborate as the neolithic farmers', although they often used the same sites. They employed cist-like graves, often grouped in cemeteries, usually scooped in the flat earth. Little evidence remains of how bronze age people in Ireland lived, although we know more about them than their neolithic and mesolithic precursors. While their burials employed stone, their dwellings were less permanent, usually constructed of wood and earth. But in Lough Gara, on the borders of counties Sligo and Roscommon, draining revealed a concentration of lake island buildings – *crannogs* – dating from the bronze age. They were artificial islands built in or near the edge of a lake, forming platforms for wooden buildings surrounded by a defensive wooden fence. Crannogs were built from these early times – indeed, there is some evidence that they date from neolithic times – and lived in right into the seventeenth century AD.

Stone circles also date predominantly from the bronze age which lasted in Ireland until around 700 BC. While there are no circles which compare with Stonehenge in England, or as extensive as the stone works at Carnac in Brittany, there are a number that are monumental in scale. At Grange, near Lough Gur, Co. Limerick, for example, a circle surrounded by a massive outer bank has a standing stone ring of 150 feet (45 metres) in diameter. The circles probably varied in purpose, some being for religious and ritualistic use, others perhaps to facilitate astronomical measurements. Single standing stones were also first erected during the bronze age, sometimes as grave markers and sometimes perhaps as territorial markers. Such stones continued to be erected into the early Christian era some thirteen hundred years later, many being 'converted' to Christian use with the addition of carved crosses and *ogham* inscriptions.

Ogham is the first written form of the Irish language, dating from a very early period of Irish Christianity. The letters, based on the Roman alphabet, are represented by lines, up to five in number, set at various angles on either side of a stem line. Frequently found in southern Ireland, *ogham* stones are rare in the rest of the country. Those that have survived usually tell us the name of a person followed by the name of an ancestor, and it is clear that the script was used for epitaphs and memorials. But before the arrival of Christianity, the Celts came to Ireland.

The Celts came to Ireland from Europe, and probably originally from the lands around the Caspian Sea from which they emigrated in all directions. Sociologists and linguists have detected important similarities between Celtic language, laws, customs and religion and those of the Hindus in India. Two groups populated the British Isles, the Gaels and the Brythoni. The Brythoni settled in Britain and the Gaels occupied Ireland and some of Scotland. The Gaelic language, related to British and Gaulish, was the direct forebear of the Irish language today. Exactly when the Celts arrived is not clear, but by 500 BC Ireland seems to have been a completely Celtic country. They brought with them the iron age culture which had come to central and eastern Europe around 800 BC. Iron was stronger than bronze, and iron ploughs dug deep and were long-lasting. Bronze age settlers had traditionally adopted new metallurgical discoveries, and thus no clear break between the two cultures can be determined.

More is known about the Celts than about any other prehistoric people outside Greece and Italy. In Ireland alone, the archaeological information is vast: over 30,000 Celtic ring forts and sites can still be seen today. From Greek and Roman sources, we have vivid descriptions of ancient Celtic society. Since the Celts themselves transmitted knowledge orally, not until the advent of Christianity in Ireland, which also brought the skill of writing to the country, did

Celtic Irishmen transcribe their tales and sagas, laws and annals. Through these writings, however, a detailed picture of iron age life is available.

The first recorded mention of the Celts dates from the sixth century BC and places them in France and Spain. Herodotus, writing in the fifth century BC, described the Celts as one of two western European peripheral peoples living along the Danube and in the Pyrenees. Because the Celts came to live on the periphery of Europe, particularly in Ireland, they avoided assimilation into the Roman Empire and the later turmoil of the Huns, Goths and Vandals in the Dark Ages after the fall of Rome. Consequently, two special features characterize Irish Celtic heritage. First, more Irish Celtic artifacts survive than for any other Celtic group. Secondly, Irish Celtic language and culture survived right up to modern times, remaining widespread to the end of the nineteenth century. Gaelic, in fact, is the oldest living vernacular in the West. It took the famines of the 1840s and 1850s, together with emigration and English-language educational policies, to bring the general use of the Irish language to an end. And, since oral tradition was a strong element in this culture, a consistent Irish historical consciousness was maintained. It is now a joke that Cromwell is still 'remembered' in Ireland, but for over 200 years after his death, amongst millions of Irishmen memory of him was no joke at all.

The earliest written evidence of Ireland and its people can be dated from the ninth century BC when Homer in *The Iliad* described the north-west of Europe as 'A land of fog and gloom . . . Beyond it is the Sea of Death, where Hell begins.' About 400 years later a Carthaginian sailor, Himilco, left a record of a voyage through the Pillars of Hercules (Straits of Gibraltar), northwards up the coast of Portugal to the Bay of Biscay and along the coast of France. He saw Celts sailing 'at high speed' in coracles and learnt of 'the Sacred Island (so the ancients called it). This lies amid the waves, abounding in verdure, and the race of the Hierni dwell there widespread.' Several centuries later, in the first-century BC, an unflattering picture was again recorded by the Greek geographer Strabo. Sensibly noting that 'We relate these things, perhaps, without having trustworthy authorities', Strabo portrayed the Irish Celts as 'More savage than the Britons, [they] feed on human flesh and are enormous eaters. They deem it commendable to devour their deceased fathers as well as openly to be connected not only with other women but also with their own mothers and sisters ... The natives are wholly savage and lead a wretched existence because of the cold.'

In fact, the Celtic Gaels of Ireland possessed a highly sophisticated society. Their massive stone forts, built along the coast of Ireland (or 'Erin' as they called it) and in the interior on hills, suggest a warlike and dangerous society. Inside the forts – some of which encompassed as much as forty acres – lived whole communities, largely dependent upon cattle grazing on the land and fields spread around. Smaller communities and isolated homesteads also abounded, often – as with the stone forts – on or near Bronze Age sites, thus indicating that the Gaels accepted and, perhaps, assimilated older religious customs. They enjoyed a tribal social organization without any political unity but having in common a language, religion and culture. Independent tribal chiefs and kings were dominant in their own areas. Only once, at the beginning of the eleventh century AD, were most Gaelic tribes united under one high king, Brian Boru, and then only for his lifetime. The Gaels were different from other Celtic groups in maintaining the system of kingship for so long, but in most other respects they were similar to the Celts of France, the Gauls.

In his *History of the Gallic Wars*, Julius Caesar provides one of the most detailed accounts of Celtic society. He distinguished three broad social groups, druids, warriors and farmers. Druids were both the repository of Celtic knowledge and wisdom and the teachers of succeeding generations. Since the Celts did not write, druids underwent up to twenty years of study, learning the sagas, laws and religious practices of their people, and accurate recitation was demanded:

It is said that they commit to memory immense amounts of poetry, and so some of them continue their studies for twenty years. They consider it improper to commit their studies to writing...They also have much knowledge of the stars and their motion, of the size of the world and of the earth, of natural philosophy, and of the powers and spheres of action of the immortal gods, which they discuss and hand down to their young students.

Celtic religion taught of an after-life and an immortal soul which passed into another body after death. Their god of the underworld, Dis, was also regarded as the common father of mankind. Human and animal sacrifices were conducted by the druids who were also the priests.

Over 400 different Celtic gods are known. Most can be identified as local or tribal deities, but about 100 appear to have been generally worshipped. The Roman poet Lucan noted that the Celts worshipped three gods in particular: Esus, the god of arts and crafts, the patron of traders and travellers, whose Greek equivalent was Hermes and, by all accounts, was the most popular; Taranis, probably the equivalent of Zeus (the Irish word *torann*, meaning 'thunder', comes from Taranis), and Teutatis, probably a different, named god of each tribe. *Tuath*, the Irish for 'tribe', comes from the same linguistic root as Teutatis, and in the Gaelic sagas, warriors frequently pledge themselves, swearing 'by the god by whom my tribe swears'. Lug was another important deity, probably of harvests and fertility, and has lived on in the place names Laon, Leon, Loudon and Lyons in France, Leiden in the Netherlands and Leignitz in Germany (now Legnica in Poland). Lug was celebrated in Ireland by the Gaels on 1 August, from which Garland Sunday today can be traced.

Streams, rivers, springs and trees were also incorporated in Celtic religion. Some rivers, like the Boyne, were even regarded as divine. The earth itself was worshipped, in female form, as a mother, defender and provider. Bulls, bears, boars and horses enjoyed divine representation. In the great Gaelic sage, *The Tain*, the supernaturally endowed brown and white bulls can be seen as the vestiges of a bull-god.

From about 400 BC, the Celts competed with the forces of Rome, sacking the city itself in 387 BC. In the centuries which followed, however, Roman legions gradually conquered the Celts in Spain, France, England and central Europe, though even then Celtic tribes continued to harass their oppressors. Strabo, writing of the Gauls, described them as 'madly fond of war, high-spirited and quick to battle, but otherwise straightforward and not of evil character'. Diodorus Siculus, a first-century BC Greek historian, in his history of the world, noted:

Physically the Gauls are terrifying in appearance with deep-sounding and very harsh voices. In conversation they use few words and speak in riddles . . . They are boasters and threateners and given to bombastic self-dramatization, and yet they are quick of mind with good natural ability for learning. . .When the armies are drawn up in battle array they are wont to advance before the battle-line and to challenge the bravest of their opponents to single combat, at the same time brandishing before them their arms so as to terrify their foe. And when someone accepts their challenge to battle, they loudly recite the deeds of valour of their ancestors and proclaim their own valorous quality, at the same time abusing and making little of their opponent and generally attempting to rob him beforehand of his fighting spirit. They cut off the heads of their enemies slain in battle and attach them to the necks of their horses. . .and they nail up these first fruits upon their houses.

Diodorus' account is remarkably similar to descriptions of battle in the Gaelic sagas, and highlights the importance Celts gave to qualities of courage and bravery in the individual.

The particular customs of the Celtic Gaels of Ireland were first recorded by Gaelic Christian monks in the seventh century AD. The monks overcame their abhorrence of paganism and set down in writing the records of their forebears, providing scholars with an extensive account of the political and cultural organization of Ireland in the centuries before and during the Dark Ages. Along with the artistic wealth of the Gaels, attested by the surviving volume of golden objects and ornaments. Gaelic Christianity with its piety, learning and artwork, not only made Ireland legendary throughout the world, but also has provided Irishmen with a source of profound pleasure and pride.

Gaelic society, in common with its time, had rigid hierarchic order. There were three broad social groups, the aristocrats, the freemen and the slaves. Aristocrats included not only tribal kings (*ri*), but also warriors (*flaithi*), judges (*breitheamh* or berhons), druids (*draci*), poets (*fili*), historians (*seanchaidhe*) and a number of professional advisers (*aos dana*) who shared with the king the duties of guarding the well-being of the tribe (*tuath*), organizing feasts and sacred occasions and applying the law. Poet and historians had a particularly honoured place in society, and a poet's satire was an especially powerful sanction since (it was believed) it could bring disgrace, physical disfigurement and even death to its victim. By the fourth century AD there were five leading Gaelic kingdoms which, despite fluctuating fortunes, remained ascendant for 800 years. Roughly, they corresponded to the present provinces of Ulster, Leinster, Munster and Connaught with the fifth and smallest in the counties of Meath and Westmeath. Each of these kingdoms was dominated by one or two families. In Munster, it was the Eoganachta clan; in Ulster the Ui Neill; in Leinster the Ui Muiredaig and Ui

Faelain; in Connaught the Ui Briuin and in Meath the southern Ui Neill family. Within these kingdoms, about 150 lesser ones were grouped. There was no central control in the country, unlike the Roman system where rulers exercised power from capitals, and kings depended upon their own personal qualities for authority. Even when particularly mighty kings sought recognition as high king (*Ard ri*), all that could be expected was respect – sometimes with tribute, sometimes with fealty – from other provincial kings, and political and military alliances against an enemy. High kings would take hostages to secure loyalty or as a token of dependence, and would expect help in time of war. From the ninth century AD, some high kings tried to claim sovereignty over the whole country, but before this such claims were unknown.

The distinguishing feature of the Gaelic aristocratic class (apart from its 'academic' groups) was that its members possessed (or belonged to families that possessed) clients and vassals, with all the authority and influence involved. The highest grade of nobleman was the chief (*toisech*, from which comes the modern *taoiseach*, the Irish prime minister) of a large number of other nobles for whom he was responsible to the king or overlord.

The class of freemen (*cele*) had at least twenty-seven subdivisions consisting of grades of farmers, merchants and tradesmen, and was the foundation of Gaelic society. Cattle provided the calculation of wealth, and the basic unit of value was a young heifer. The highest grade of freeman was a cattle man (*boaire*), precisely described in a Gaelic law tract:

All his household goods are in their proper place: a cauldron with its spit and handles; a vat in which a measure of ale may be brewed; a cauldron for everyday use; small vessels – iron pots and wooden kneading-boards and mugs, so that he does not need to borrow them – a sink; a bath... [His larder] is capable of receiving a king or a bishop or a scholar or a brehon from the road, prepared for the arrival of any guest...He owns seven buildings: a kiln; a barn and a share in a mill so that it grinds for him; a house of twenty-seven feet; an outhouse of seventeen feet; a pigsty; a shelter for calves and a shelter for sheep. He owns twenty cows; two bulls; six oxen; twenty pigs; twenty sheep; four domestic boars; two sows; a riding horse...He has pasture which sustains sheep without need to change ground. He and his wife have four suits of clothes.

Freeman were the clients of nobles, paying rent in return for protection and cattle. Property ownership was vested in family groups (*fine*) which included all relations in the male line of descent for five generations. This was the case for members of the aristocracy as well as for freemen and explains the basis for the most serious crime in Gaelic law: if one branch of a family monopolized the kingship for four generations, then other branches risked losing their royal status and thus descending in the social order, and so might be tempted to murder their own kinsfolk – the crime of *fingal*. To avoid this, heirs were often elected during a king's lifetime. As long as a man was a member of the royal family group and sound in limb and mind, he was eligible for kingship. In practice, the most powerful family member was usually elected.

Slaves (*mug*) were usually those unfortunates captured in war or placed in bondage as criminals. It was possible for slaves to obtain freedom by practising a skilled profession, such as a smith or a physician. A female slave could be valued as equal to six heifers.

The two principal centres of Gaelic Ireland were Emain Macha, recorded as the city 'Isamnion' on the map of Ireland drawn by Ptolemy of Alexandria in the second century AD, and now known as Navan Fort, near Armagh, and Tara in the valley of the river Boyne in Co. Meath. Both were ancient sites upon which the Gaels erected massive ring forts: at Emain Macha the huge 40-feet wide circular earthwork encloses eighteen acres of ground; at Tara the central earthwork alone encloses over twelve acres. Emain Macha, political centre of the Ulster kingdom, was probably abandoned after being destroyed in the middle of the fifth century AD during a war between Ulster and Connaught, coinciding with the advent of Christianity in Ireland and the foundation of the primacy of Armagh. Tara lasted as a political and pagan centre for longer – until about 560 when it was abandoned. Later it enjoyed a revival as the royal seat of the kings of Meath and ultimately of the high king of Ireland. By the time of St Patrick, Tara was principally a religious centre with an established hold on the imagination of the Irish people – a hold which remained powerful up to modern times. In 1798 Irish rebels gathered at Tara spontaneously, as if possessed of some ancestral memory. In 1843, Daniel O'Connell organized one of the largest assemblies in Irish history at Tara, clearly calculating that the folk knowledge of the site was an important additional weapon in his campaign for Irish home rule.

The Irish Sea protected Gaelic society, providing a barrier first against the legions of Rome and then against the vandalizing European tribes of the Dark Ages. As a result, uniquely in Ireland was preserved an iron age culture removed, museum-like, from the mainstream of European development. Gaelic society, based as it was on a system of local allegiances, remained a series of tribal monarchies right into the Middle Ages, its longevity due in no small part to the stability provided by the Brehon Laws.

Gaelic law was carefully devised and was interpreted by the brehons who held an exalted social position. The Brehon Laws stipulated in exact detail the rules, penalties and privileges governing social and political intercourse. No one was above the law. The great books of early Christian Ireland record the legend of St Patrick in 438 AD ordering that the laws and customs of Gaelic Ireland be written down. But for some considerable time after St Patrick, brehons continued to learn and pass on the laws orally from one generation to the next. Nothing escaped their jurisdiction. They enumerated the duties, obligations, rights and privileges of each class of person, from the king to the slave. The principles governing property management were specified, as were detailed rules affecting building, brewing, bee-keeping and milling, as well as complex, sophisticated rules for the relations between fathers and sons, masters and servants, rulers and subjects, husbands and wives. In addition, the Laws specified the characteristics of each rung of the social ladder down to how many vessels of milk and ale and how many sheep and cattle were required to qualify for each one.

The brehons themselves received a fee for their judgements from those in dispute. Fair and careful judgements were, in turn, secured by the laws which made brehons personally liable for damages, besides forfeiting fees, in the case of a false or unfair judgement. 'Every brehon', says the collection of third-century AD laws in the (later) *Book of Acaill*, 'is punishable for his neglect: he is to pay money-fine for his false judgement.' The laws and brehons were held in great respect, and their influence obviously permeated the whole of life. 'There are three periods of evil for the world', we learn from the Seanchus Mor, the collection of fifth-century AD civil laws, 'the period of a plague, of a general war, and the dissolution of verbal contracts...The world would be evilly situated if express contracts were not binding.' Three principles were embedded in the laws. First, every freeman had a right to the use of communal land: to be deprived of this right constituted a grave injustice. Secondly, every freeman who failed to meet his obligations to his lord or king would face the same process as any other debtor, and so would not be arbitrarily penalized. Thirdly, the right to compensation or retribution ultimately lay with the injured person.

The Brehon Law of Compensation provides an example of the intricacy of the Gaelic administration of justice. In the earliest times, the Law of Retaliation prevailed, but was gradually replaced by Compensation. The person injured sued and, if the offender responded, the case was heard by a brehon according to the law. Penalties took the form of fines. If an offender refused to submit to this process, or if he refused to pay a fine or a debt, then the process of Distress came into effect whereby the injured person could seize the offender's property – almost always his cattle – after giving notice of his intention (and so providing some days' grace for the offender to meet his obligation). Property was seized in three stages. First, the injured person, accompanied by witnesses, claimed but did not remove the property. This was then followed by the second stage of a formal stay of a day or some days, during which the offender had to give a pledge – usually valuable goods or a member of his family as hostage – that he would meet his debt at the end of the stay when his pledge would also be returned. The final stage followed the stay when the injured person actually removed property to the value originally stipulated by the brehon. If the offender refused to give a pledge, then there was no stay and the property was removed immediately. If, after a pledge was given, an offender still refused to pay, then his pledge was kept which, if a hostage, could be sold or used as a slave or a bondsman until the debt was worked off. If an offender defied all the injured person's proceedings, then the old rule of direct retaliation could be employed.

In cases where an offender or debtor was superior in rank to the creditor or injured person, then the plaintiff could secure the right to arbitration by fasting outside the defendant's door. This procedure was held in some awe, and it is clear that great dishonour fell upon a defendant who refused to submit to it: 'He that does not give a pledge to fasting is an evader of all; he who disregards all things shall not be paid by God or man.'

From the Brehon Laws comes our knowledge of the system of fosterage. Children were often placed in the care of foster parents, sometimes because of friendship, more often accompanied by a payment varying with the social ranks of those concerned. Boys were fostered until the age of seventeen and girls until fourteen. Foster parents had the duty of teaching boys the martial arts, how to ride and to swim, and how to play board games. Fostered children had the duty of supporting their foster parents in old age. The system was employed to maintain harmony between neighbours and between tribes, and the ties of fosterage remained close. When the legendary Gaelic hero, Cuchulain, in single combat slew his foster-brother Ferdia, the event is one of the tragic climaxes of the saga of the *Tain*.

The Laws rarely resorted to capital punishment, preferring instead an elaborate compensation system, which also had the benefit of preventing long vendettas and establishing the law as the preferred arbitration procedure. Victims of physical injury were entitled to 'sick maintenance' from the culprit, which involved the payment of a fine as well as the costs – lodging, food, medical – of the cure. In cases of murder, a fine was paid to the dead man's family, double that required for manslaughter. Many modifying circumstances had to be taken into account: the reason for the murder; provocation; social rank etc., so the brehon making judgement had to possess diplomatic skills on top of legal erudition. The murderer of a freeman, for example, faced a fine (payable in cattle) which could be from one to thirty head depending upon his own social position, plus twenty-one head if the murder was not malicious or forty-two head if it was. If the culprit did not pay, then his family were held responsible: if they did not pay the fine, then they had to hand the culprit over to the victim's family. Only then could the offender be executed, but he could also be used or sold as a slave. Failing this, an offender's family had to expel him and accept a levy on their property to free them from responsibility. Expelled persons had to leave their tribe or clan as well, becoming outlaws upon whom their victims' families were free to exact revenge, or if not outlaws, joining another tribe in return for protection.

The position of women under the laws compared with that of men, and was honourable. Divorce was allowed freely, and marriages could be ended by common consent with wives enjoying most of the same rights as their husbands. For an aristocrat, 'To his wife belongs the right to be consulted on every subject', and more generally, husbands did not own wives: 'It is only contract that is between them.' Property was shared by wives and could not be disposed of without consent. But while husbands could take secondary wives, a wife who committed adultery could customarily be burnt alive. Women were also expected to become warriors, and were only exempted from martial duty in 697 AD by the Synod of Tara. They had the right to pursue a case at law and to recover debts equally with men, and they could inherit property although primacy in this respect was accorded to men. But if a man had no sons, then his daughter inherited, and in any event, daughters were always entitled to a dowry out of the general estate.

Other modes of punishment also operated, although not before brehons whose judgements involved penalties only of compensation. Blinding was one of the most common. From the records it seems that blinding was usually the consequence for a king or chief defeated in battle. It was done by jabbing a needle into the eye, and one of the principal reasons for the practice was because a disfigured person was not eligible for election as a king or chief, so blinding ensured the complete subjection of a defeated rival or enemy.

The power of the Brehon Laws, and the enduring loyalty of the Irish people to them was demonstrated by their extraordinary survival through centuries of warfare and conquering invasion in Ireland. Four centuries after the Norman–English first set foot in the country, their descendants often adopted Irish forms, customs and language, much to the anger of Anglo-Irish governments. The Irish State Papers of the sixteenth century were peppered with laws and complaints against the continuing widespread use of brehons and their law. From 1919 to 1921 the nationalist dail courts even attempted to revive the Brehon code as a native Irish answer to British law.

Together with the laws, Gaelic sagas have reached through the centuries as a source of inspiration to generations of Irishmen. Those that have come to us were transmitted orally, often for periods of over one thousand years, before being written down. Most that survive were recorded by Christian monks from the seventh to the twelfth centuries. They provide us with a fascinating picture of the way of life and the values of the Gaels, and can be compared to the Homeric epics of Greece. Indeed, only the classics of Greece and Rome give a more complete account of pre-Christian European societies. Unlike the classics, however, the tales of Gaelic Ireland were not collected or recounted by any single author, and the styles of different storytellers can still be discerned in versions of the same tale.

Four great collections or 'cycles' of the sagas have survived: the Mythological cycle, which gives an account of pre-Christian times; the Ulster or Red Branch cycle, which roughly covers the first two centuries AD; the Fenian cycle, which deals with the period from the third century AD to around the seventh century, and the King cycle, which recounts the history of Ireland in the first millennium AD. The earliest manuscripts of the sagas are later in date than the tales they tell: the story of the encounter between Oisin, the last of the Fenians, and St Patrick, for example, was not written down until 1750.

The sagas are, of course, myth not history. However, they provided a romantic vision of early Ireland which was at the heart of the Gaelic revival at the end of the nineteenth century, when scholars like Douglas Hyde translated and publicized them, providing heroic models for modern Irish nationalism. Their tales of magic and mystery, of heroes overcoming difficulties, delighted Matthew Arnold and are thought by some scholars to have inspired the French romances about the Holy Grail. In the sagas, the Fomorians were the first inhabitants of Ireland, dark and evil, always sinister. After them came Partholon and a small group of followers who were credited with clearing land for farming and forming lakes and rivers. Three hundred years to the day after their arrival, Partholon's followers died of a mysterious illness. They were succeeded by the Nemedians who cleared more land and formed more lakes, but eventually left the country for lands in northern Europe. Next came the Firbolgs whom the tales credit with the establishment of Tara and the division of Ireland into five kingdoms. They only lived in peace for thirty-six years until the Danaans arrived in a great fleet of ships which they burned on the shore after disembarking and defeated the Firbolgs in a great battle near Cong, Co. Mayo. The Danaans were said to have come from the northern islands of the world. They brought with them four treasures: the Lia Fail, a stone which cried out when each new king was inaugurated (a 5-foot tall granite stone at Tara and the Stone of Scone in Westminster Abbey presently compete for recognition as the original); Dagda's Cauldron, an inexhaustible vessel named after their ancient chief; the magical sword of their king, Nuada; and the spear of their god-hero, Lug.

Scholars have speculated that the Danaans may have represented the original Gaels. Lug and Dagda were also Gaelic gods – Lug even became the prototype of the Arthurian Lancelot – and the sagas, despite being recorded by pious Christian monks possessing a horror of pagans, consistently favour the Danaans and present their successors and the last race of invaders to take possession of Ireland, the Milesians, in the same terms. It could be that the Milesians were a late invention designed to distinguish between Christian and pagan Ireland. However, all this is an attempt to extract history from myth.

According to the sagas, the Milesians came from Spain and, overcoming magic spells cast against them, defeated the Danaans in two great battles. They divided Ireland into two kingdoms, one in the north and the other in the south. With the Milesians were the great poet, Cir, who went to the northern kingdom, and the great harpist, Cennfinn, who went to the south. In this way the sagas explained why in later centuries northern Ireland was noted for its poetry and southern Ireland for its music. The Milesians were also credited by the sagas with providing Ireland with its names – 'Banba', 'Fodla' and 'Eriu' (the dative case of which is 'Erin') – originally the names of three queens they met when they first landed in the country and whom they promised to name the country after.

The sagas, while not history, nevertheless present the quality of Gaelic society and enable scholars both to judge other evidence more easily and to gain insight into the character of the age. More than this, some tales actually deal with historical figures while others have historical significance. The tale of the *Voyage of Bran* in an eighth-century text from the Red Branch cycle, for example, provides evidence of the Gaels' involvement with the sea and possible voyages of exploration.

One of the greatest of the tales, the *Táin Bó Cúailgne* – the *Cattle Raid of Cooley* – has historical roots, reflecting the struggle that probably took place between rival gaelic tribes in Connaught and Ulster. It comes from the Red Branch cycle and had been forgotten for generations until revived in the late nineteenth century by scholars and poets, fired by the *Tain*'s epic quality. The hero of the saga, Cuchulain, was the personification of Gaelic warriors' virtues. He is presented as always fighting honourably, and in him can be seen the Gaelic ideal of a warrior aristocracy with their attributes of bravery, honesty, learning and martial prowess. In death, Cuchulain remained true to these qualities as, mortally wounded, he tied himself (so the saga tells us) to a high stone by a lake, where, gripping his sword, he died facing his enemies. This scene not only inspired the leadership of the 1916 rising against British rule, but also the Irish artist, Oliver Sheppard, who in 1936 used the figure of Cuchulain in death for his statue in Dublin's General Post Office to commemorate that rising.

For several hundred years in the early Christian era, Gaelic warriors dominated much of Britain, becoming known as the *Scotti* to the Romans and thus, ultimately, giving Scotland its name. Irish Gaelic kingdoms were established in Wales, Cornwall, England north-west of the Pennines, and in Scotland. In turn, the Irish took the name *Goidil* (Gaels) for themselves, from the Welsh Celtic *Gwyddyl*, during the fourth century AD. The Fenian cycle of tales relates to this period, illustrating the sophisticated nature of Gaelic society on the eve of Christianity arriving in Ireland. The tales concern Finn MacCool and his followers, the Fenian warrior band, who were analogous to one of the great Celtic legacies to the modern world: the legendary cycle of King Arthur and the Knights of the Round Table. To become a Fenian, a warrior had to know the laws of poetry. He also had to accept four rules: always to choose a woman for a wife on the grounds of her good manners and virtue rather than because of her wealth; never to be violent towards a woman; always to accede to requests for help, and never to flee from fewer than ten champion warriors. A Fenian's family and tribe also had to agree not to seek revenge should he be killed. The Gaels' concern for the arts, for chivalry, for law and their knowledge of the nature of mankind are all apparent. Their interest in history (as well as drama) is clearly attested in the King and Fenian cycles where historical figures are often woven into the narrative. Together, the sagas give us a window on the Gaelic world. They also provide us with prototypes and analogues for some of the most famous stories of Western literature: the tale of Diarmuid and Grainne in the Fenian cycle, for example, is at least an analogue if not the prototype for the tragic European romance of Tristram and Iseult.

Much of the history and mythology of the Gaels was forgotten with the coming of Christianity, and much that survived that coming was forgotten over the ensuing millennium. Sometimes, this was because the gods and customs of the Gaels became devils and forbidden rites in Christianity. Sometimes – particularly in the seventeenth, eighteenth and nineteenth centuries – this was because the ancient lore only existed with the spoken Gaelic word, which itself was persecuted and diminished by law and by famine. Sometimes, no doubt, tales and deeds were lost to posterity because a Christian monk could not bring himself to record pagan practices. One monk who did overcome such scruples, penned at the end of the saga of the *Tain* which he had helped to write down, 'I who have written this history, or rather fable, am doubtful about many things ...For some of them are figments of demons, some are poetic imaginings, some true, some not, and some for the delight of fools.'

Christianity probably came to Ireland first through trade with Britain and Gaul (France) at the end of the fourth century. By 431 there were sufficient Christians in Ireland for Pope Celestine to send to them a deacon, Palladius, at the request of the Church of Gaul. Nothing is known of Palladius' mission except that Palladius himself was killed shortly after his arrival. The following year, according to the usually received chronology, St Patrick, with a few companions, came as a missionary to Ireland.

2

Invaders

A great deal of controversy surrounds St Patrick, 'the Apostle of Ireland' and the country's patron saint. In the first place, there is some debate about the dates of his life. He wrote a partial autobiography, his *Confessions*, the earliest (although incomplete) version of which dates from the ninth century *Book of Armagh*, which indicates that he was born around 390. However, some of his disciples lived well into the sixth century, suggesting that he arrived in Ireland around 456 and died around 490. This extended time-span may mean that there were, in fact, two or even three Patricks, but it is a problem that remains unsolved. The traditional day of his death, 17 March, has become Ireland's national day and despite uncertainty, 461 popularly agreed as the year in which the patron Saint died.

In the *Confessions*, Patrick tells us he was born in a town which he named as 'Bannavem Taberniae', and speaks in general of Britain as his birthplace and the home of his parents. It was in western Britain, probably near Bristol and the river Severn. Sean Dowling has made an interesting case for the town of Avonmouth, near Bristol and on the river Severn, as Patrick's place of origin. Arguing that 'Bannavem Taberniae' is Patrick's Latin version of the Gaelic translation of 'Avonmouth', Dowling writes:

To anyone familiar with Irish, the word 'Bannavem' should instantly suggest 'Bun-abhann', or 'Rivermouth'. The present English name of 'Avonmouth' is the Saxon or Old English translation or half-translation of the original Celtic name. Similar half-translations are 'Dartmouth', 'Weymouth', 'Exmouth', 'Falmouth' etc. All these occur in southern England. The Roman name for the Severn was Sabrina, corresponding to a Celtic word 'Sabarn' or 'Sabh(v)arn'. In modern Irish the whole name would be 'Bunabhann an tSabhrainne'.

From his *Confessions* we also learn that Patrick's father was named Calpurnius and was not only a decurion, a member of the Roman British ruling group, but also a deacon of the Christian Church and a landowner. He and others like him suffered at the hands of raiding Irishmen, and Patrick himself and his two sisters were taken captive in one such raid. From the age of sixteen for six years, Patrick was a slave herdsman in Co. Antrim, which occupation gave him plenty of time for contemplation. 'Every day was spent in frequent prayer', he says, going on to reveal that the love of God increased in him so much, that he would recite one hundred prayers a day, and almost as many each night. 'I felt no evil', he adds, 'nor was there any laziness in me because, as I now see, the Spirit was burning within me.' At the age of twenty-three, Patrick escaped back to England and his home a convinced Christian. He probably would have stayed at home with his family were it not for a vision:

I saw in the night the vision of a man whose name was Victoricus, coming as it were from Ireland, with countless letters. And he gave me one of them and I read the opening words of the letter which were 'The voice of the Irish' and as I read the beginning of the letter, I thought that at the same moment I heard their voice...: 'We ask thee, boy, come and walk among us once more.'

He left home after this vision. He may have travelled to the south of France to be received and ordained as a priest, but he may instead have travelled north in England to be ordained by Germanus of Auxerre, a soldier–bishop evangelizing in Britain around 430. At any rate it seems clear that Patrick was properly ordained a priest, but more than that is problematical. One of the scribes of the *Book of Armagh* tells us:

In the thirteenth year of the Emperor Theodosius, the Bishop Patrick was sent by Celestine, Bishop and Pope of Rome, to instruct the Irish. Bishop Palladius was first sent, who was also called Patrick by a second name, and he was martyred among the Irish, as the old saints have said. Then the second Patrick was sent by the Angel of God Victor and by Pope Celestine. All Ireland believed, and nearly all were baptised by him.

Against this, however, is the whole nature of Patrick's *Confessions* which were written as his defence against charges, brought in an ecclesiastical court in Britain, which – almost certainly – concerned his claim to be a bishop and his authority for journeying to Ireland as a missionary. The internal evidence of the *Confessions* and of Patrick's one other documentary account of his mission, his *Letter to Coroticus*, clearly indicate that Patrick was never consecrated a bishop, but had to claim the position once in Ireland in order to ordain priests himself to help carry out his work. In addition, it also seems that Patrick applied to his British superiors (i.e. bishops) for permission to undertake his mission to Ireland, was refused, and nevertheless went ahead thus forcing an ecclesiastical court to judge his actions. In the *Confessions*, Patrick even implies that he was found guilty:

Accordingly, on the day I was condemned, as related above, on that night I saw a writing – it was before my image without honour – and at the same time I heard the Divine voice saying to me 'With displeasure we have seen the image of a chosen one stripped of title', nor did he say 'I have seen' but 'We have seen' as if He joined Himself with me as if He said 'Who touches you touches, as it were, the apple of my eye.'

Throughout, Patrick was certain of his defence: that in all his actions he enjoyed the sanction of the highest source of all, of God himself 'who is greater than all'. The natural reluctance of later Irish Christian monks, claiming descent and legitimacy from Patrick's mission, to admit that the mission was not legitimate is the simplest explanation of the confusion about Patrick's status.

The Irish Church, founded by Patrick who established its centre at Armagh, rapidly adapted to the circumstances of the country. At first, Patrick succeeded in introducing the concept of bishoprics, as existed in France, with their hierarchy of ecclesiastical authority. Soon, however, the geography and political experience of the country – without towns and roads and without central political unity – demonstrated that Patrick's plan was completely unsuitable. So, instead of having a number of city-based bishop and archbishoprics, Ireland developed – in opposition to Patrick's intentions – a monastic Church more in keeping with Gaelic society. While Patrick 'baptised thousands, ordained clerics everywhere' and 'gave presents to kings', his colleagues and successors concentrated more upon converting the leaders of Gaelic society, not attempting to interfere with Gaelic social structure, thus meshing their evangelism with native custom and practice. Pagan Gaelic celebrations were tolerated and sometimes – like the Feast of All Saints – adopted for Christian purposes. The forts and encampments of Gaelic kings and chiefs were chosen as the sites for churches, abbeys and monasteries, although Tara remained a pagan centre well into the sixth century.

Legends rapidly accumulated around Patrick's life. He is credited with having banished snakes from Ireland from the summit of Croagh Patrick in Co. Mayo, and to have established the shamrock as one of Ireland's national symbols by using the three leaves of the plant to explain the mystery of the Trinity to the high king at Tara. The undoubted success of his mission accounts for the central place he came to hold in Irish tradition. In 1932 the Eucharistic Congress in Dublin, on the fifteenth centenary of the saint's commencement of his mission, witnessed the largest crowds ever assembled in the city until Pope John Paul II's visit in 1979.

A century after Patrick's arrival, Irish monks began evangelizing abroad themselves. Pagan Gaels' veneration of learning, and the Gaelic class of learned men – the brehons, poets, historians and druids – found a natural place within the Christian order and lent the Irish Church a special quality. St Ninian, an Ulsterman, the first major missionary and teacher after Patrick, established early in the fifth century the monastery of Candida Casa at Whithorn in western Scotland where many more missionaries studied. By the first quarter of the sixth century, Patrick's episcopal organization was succumbing to monasticism with abbots supplanting bishops as the principal churchmen in Ireland. One such abbot, St Finnian, went on to found the monastic school at Clonard, Co. Meath, where he emphasized study and scholarship to a group of followers known as the 'Twelve Apostles of Ireland'. Two of them, St Ciaran and St Colmcille (also known as St Columba), were to establish monasticism and scholarship as the hallmarks of the Irish Church. St Ciaran founded the church and monastery of Clonmacnois on the river Shannon. St Colmcille founded the monasteries of Derry, Swords, Durrow and Kells before sailing with twelve followers to Iona on the west coast of Scotland, where he built one of the greatest early Christian monastic schools before he died in 597. *The annals of Clonmacnois* state that Colmcille wrote three hundred books in his own hand, and by tradition he is held to be the scribe of the *Cathach*, the oldest surviving Irish manuscript. From his foundation at Iona, Irish monks converted Scotland and much of England and, as the seventh-century English monk and historian, the Venerable Bede, was always anxious to point out, Colmcille and the monks from Iona also played a large part in maintaining Christianity among their converts.

The combination of evangelism, asceticism and scholarship epitomized by monks like Colmcille provided the Irish Church with its golden age. Their missionary fervour and complete dedication to Christianity carried Irish monks outside the British isles to Italy, France, Spain, Germany and central Europe. From 500 to 800, the Irish Church had no compare in the Christian world. After 800 its missionary work did not stop, but it became increasingly involved in the Roman controversy about the date of Easter and the ever-increasing claims of the papacy, and at home Viking raids destroyed domestic stability. Yet the achievement of the early Irish Church produced a lasting influence on the development of Christianity. In the three hundred years before the ninth century, expatriate Irish missionaries reintroduced Christianity to areas which had been overrun by the tribes which completed the collapse of the Roman Empire. They replaced the custom of public absolution with the Irish Church's practice of private confession, used by the Catholic Church to the present day. The most prominent of these expatriates was St Columbanus, born in the province of Leinster around 543, who with his followers founded the monasteries of Annegray, Luxeuil and Fontaines in France, St Gall in Switzerland, Wurzburg in Germany, Vienna in Austria, possibly one at Prague in Czechoslovakia, and Bobbio in Piedmont in northern Italy where Columbanus died in 615.

After the fall of Rome in the fifth century, the Dark Ages became set in Europe. Marauding Teutonic tribes ravaged the European continent, and the Jutes, Angles and Saxons overran England. In the whole of Europe, Ireland alone remained unscathed, providing a refuge to Christian scholars, more and more of whom escaped there with lasting effect. By the time of the Emperor Charlemagne in the eighth century, if a man knew Greek it was simply assumed he was Irish. Alcuin, the leading scholar at the court of Charlemagne, and Scotus Eriugena ('Scotus' meaning 'Irish'), Europe's foremost philosopher in the ninth century, both studied at Clonmacnois where they learned not only the Bible and Christian theology, but also the language and the works of the writers and poets of ancient Greece and Rome. 'Almost all Ireland, disregarding the sea, is migrating to our shores with a flock of philosophers' complained Heiric of Auxerre in 870 observing the sheer multitude of Irishmen in the kingdoms of Europe.

The first Viking raids on Irish monasteries occurred in 795 when Iona was sacked and the grave of St Colmcille desecrated. That same year Vikings also landed on Lambay Island, off the coast of Dublin. These first raids were conducted by Vikings from Norway, but they were by no means the first pillagers of Irish religious sites.

Between the time of Patrick and the arrival of the Vikings, Ireland had developed considerably politically. By the late eighth century two high kingdoms dominated the many small kingdoms and tribes of the country. In the north the Ui Neill ruled from Tara, while in the south the Eoganachta ruled from the Rock of Cashel. Between them lay a third, small province of Leinster around Dublin. In the eighth century and throughout the ninth century, the Ui Neill and Eoganachta struggled for supremacy, in the process destroying more monasteries, churches and abbeys than the Vikings ever did. As a result, there was no united Irish resistance to the Vikings, and many Irish kings and chiefs allied with the invaders. By the late eighth century the outstanding artistic achievement of the early Christian era, the Irish illuminated manuscripts, was already perceived as being too vulnerable to political violence, and the perfection of the more sturdy stone and metal religious work began to absorb the artistic energies of Irish monks.

The finest, though not the earliest, illuminated manuscript is the eighth-century copy of the Gospels, the *Book of Kells*, now the pride of the Library of Trinity College, Dublin. By the time the three scribes who copied the *Book* started writing, Vikings had already landed in Britain. Indeed, it is likely that the *Book* was begun on Iona and transferred for safety and completion to Kells. The first illustration in it is the earliest representation of the Virgin and Child in a western manuscript. Written in Latin, the language of the Church which St Patrick introduced to Ireland, it employs a script which is the recognizable precursor of Irish script today. Each page of the *Book of Kells*, and of every other Irish manuscript of the period, is testimony to a fantastic amount of painstaking work and skill. For the scribes, it was another way of communing with God.

Metalwork flourished beside the art of illumination in Ireland during the Dark Ages and later. There was a much longer history of making exquisite metal objects in Ireland than there was of writing and illumination. Christian Irish metalworkers were able to draw upon countless generations of knowledge, skill and experience to make the croziers, chalices, pestles, crosses and other religious artifacts which the Vikings prized so much. From the ninth century onwards, as Viking raids increased, the skills of the calligrapher and the metalworker combined in the third great Irish art form, the stone high crosses. While churches and monasteries could have their manuscript and metal treasures plundered and destroyed, the craftsmen of the crosses must have realized that their stone work would not attract the Vikings in the same way.

Stone crosses of simple design date from the eighth century, but by the ninth century complex configurations of biblical scenes – usually of the crucifixion and the disciples and Christ – were incorporated within the shape of the cross. During the ninth century, however, the high cross itself developed, and the designs became more intricate. At Moone, Co. Kildare, the high cross is 17 feet tall and contains scenes which include Daniel in the Lion's Den and Adam and Eve on the point of eating the apple.

In the face of ever-increasing violent Viking incursions and domestic anarchy, and as Christianity became established, stone began to be used in building construction as well. Small, boat-shaped churches and beehive-shaped stone cells began to be built in the eighth century, and many can still be seen in the south-west of Ireland. Stone round towers were built on religious sites from about 900 until 1150. Tall, thin, with conical roofs and doorways some distance from the ground, these probably fulfilled the dual function of bell- and watch-towers. No other buildings are so unmistakably Irish: only two – both in Scotland – have been discovered outside Ireland. Put together, the change from inflammable manuscripts and wood to durable stone crosses and buildings reflected the great terror the Vikings inspired. One Irish monk wrote thankfully in the margin of his manuscript one stormy night:

> The wind is fierce tonight
> Ploughing the wild white ocean;
> I need not dread fierce Vikings
> Crossing the Irish Sea.

For two hundred years the Viking raids lasted. They attacked not only Ireland, but also Britain and the rest of Europe as far afield as Paris, Sicily and Constantinople. Christianity, which had with difficulty in western Europe survived the fall of Rome, now found itself faced with severe attack again. Had it not been for the Viking urge to settle and willingness to adopt Christianity, Christian Gaelic society might have been completely lost. Viking kingdoms were founded in Normandy, southern Italy, eastern England and in Ireland in Leinster where in 841 the Norse king Thurgesius founded Ireland's first city, Dublin, at the mouth of the river Liffey. In 851 after a great naval battle at Carlingford Lough, the Norwegian Vikings were replaced in Ireland by their Danish kinsmen, who proved just as anxious as their predecessors to relieve monasteries of their treasures.

The Vikings were not a purely destructive force in Irish history. By the second half of the ninth century, Viking raids had given way to Viking settlement, intermarrying and trading with the Irish, and even giving us the name 'Ireland' – the old Gaelic of 'Erin' or 'Eire' with the Scandinavian word 'land' added. As the struggle between the Eoganachta and Ui Neill for dominance in Ireland progressed, Viking settlers began to be drawn into the fabric of Irish politics. By the early years of the tenth century, the Ui Neill had defeated the Eoganachta (at the battle of Ballaghmoon in 908) and subdued the Viking settlements in all but Dublin, where the Vikings found common cause with the men of Leinster and allied for their independence against the Ui Neill. This was the high point of Ui Neill success. Before they could extend their domination in the east of the country, in 914 a great Viking fleet landed a new wave of invaders at Waterford. Within six years they had established themselves in Dublin and had founded towns at Limerick, Cork and Wexford. In 977 the Viking King Olaf of the Sandals defeated the Ui Neill high king Domnall and extended his kingdom from Dublin to the Shannon, placing the Irish in Meath under an oppression so severe they called it a 'Babylonish captivity'.

As the end of the tenth century approached, however, two important events had taken place. The Vikings in Ireland, despite their fierceness, had in the main accepted Christianity, and Brian Boru had become high king of southern Ireland.

Brian Boru has been compared to Alfred the Great, and his twelfth-century biographer made Alfred the model for his hero. His outstanding achievement was that he enforced his authority in varying degrees over all the people of Ireland – Viking settlers included – and defeated the Danes. The extent of his authority was not unusual – the greatest of the Ui Neill kings in the three previous centuries had enjoyed comparable power – but he overthrew Ui Neill hegemony and made the high kingship a sought-after prize in the eleventh and twelfth centuries. He did not make a national monarchy or a nationhood, but his career sparked the subsequent theory of an all-powerful high kingship for which later leaders fought. Brian was born around 940 into the Cenneidigh clan of north Munster, and took the name 'Boru' from the town of Borime, near Killaloe in Co. Clare. He rapidly proved himself an able warrior and strategist in countless battles against the Danes who had conquered much of Munster. In 968 he won a notable victory which regained Cashel, re-establishing it as the seat of the Munster kings. From 976 Brian ruled southern Ireland as king of Munster, and from 1002 he was acknowledged as the first absolute high king of all Ireland. He re-asserted the ecclesiastical primacy of Armagh, and in 1004 he demonstrated his own supremacy by conducting a grand tour of the country, marching northwards from his palace at Kincora (near Killaloe), always keeping the sea to his left, through Connaught and Ulster to Armagh, south through Meath to Dublin which he entered in triumph and where he received homage from the Viking residents, and then through Leinster and Munster back to Cashel.

Despite his successes and his claims, however, Brian always faced resistance to his authority. The families of Leinster had always been reluctant vassals to the Ui Neill and found Brian no different. During the ninth and tenth centuries they had frequently allied with the Danes of Dublin against the hegemony of the Ui Neill, and by 1014 Brian faced a serious challenge to his authority in the shape of a Leinster–Dublin–Viking alliance. On Good Friday, 23 April 1014, the two sides joined battle at Clontarf, outside Dublin. They were evenly matched, but the Danes were eventually driven back to the beach at Clontarf where an exceptionally high tide drowned hundreds of them before they could reach the safety of their ships. During the battle, Brian himself was killed at the moment of his victory. As the Vikings themselves admitted in *Njal's saga*: 'Brian fell, but won at last.' After his death, no other high king ever attained the complete supremacy he enjoyed. Indeed, not until the reign of Queen Elizabeth I did any ruler compare with Brian in authority in Ireland.

The battle of Clontarf was not fought by Brian or the Leinstermen and their allies for the sovereignty of Ireland, although in subsequent nationalist tradition it was portrayed as such a battle. It was really an episode in the constant internal struggle for provincial and regional sovereignty.

As a result of Brian's victory, the Boru dynasty established itself and Brian's descendants ruled Munster and much of Ireland for the following 150 years. There was another consequence of his victory as well: in contrast to Britain at this time, where the Danish King Canute had established his dominance, in Ireland the Danes now firmly opted for a commercial life. By 1014, the Danes were a minor political force in Ireland, and Brian's victory at Clontarf confirmed this. Danes in their towns of Dublin, Wexford, Waterford, Cork and Limerick controlled Ireland's wine trade, and their trading ties not only began to concentrate the wealth of Ireland on the east coast in Leinster, but also to maintain a quality of separateness from the rest of the country. This was particularly manifested in two ways. First, Danes in Ireland naturally felt strong connections with Danes nearby in Britain. Secondly, and as a corollary, Danes in Ireland followed the practices of the Roman Church which acknowledged the primacy of bishops and held sway in Britain and western Europe, rather than of the Irish Church which was dominated by abbots. Thus the Church in Britain was interested in reforming the Irish Church and in extending its influence to Ireland directly. Together, these elements were to fuel conflicts and eventually were to involve Britain directly in Irish affairs. But before this happened, Irish art and architecture flowered again.

In Irish monasteries, in the eleventh and twelfth centuries, monks and scribes began to record old Gaelic poems and sagas in manuscripts like the *Book of Leinster* and the *Book of Armagh*. Before this, they had concentrated upon Latin transcriptions of religious texts, but with the passing of the first flush of enthusiasm for asceticism and evangelizing which had characterized the early Irish Church, Irish monks had become more worldly and their monasteries more secular. In this way, ancient Gaelic heritage was preserved in the monasteries. In addition, Irish versions of the Trojan Wars and the Roman Civil War were written as the scribes experimented with their new-found freedom. The art of the high cross reached its climax with refined, sophisticated carving, and metalwork attained a new mastery with the extraordinarily fine

Cross of Cong, commissioned in about 1123 by Turloch O'Connor, King of Connaught, to enshrine a relic of the True Cross. Church building became more elaborate: the splendid Hiberno-Romanesque Cormac's Chapel on the Rock of Cashel was begun by King Cormac MacCarthy of Munster in 1127. It incorporated rib-vaulting in the roof of the chancel, a technique which the Crusaders had brought back to Europe from the Near East, and which was first used in the choir of Durham Cathedral which was completed in 1093. The use of this technique at Cashel within forty years was a testimony to Irish adventurousness at this time, as well as to wide-flung contacts. The Romanesque style soon came to govern ecclesiastical building throughout the country, culminating with Clonfert Cathedral in Co. Galway, completed in 1164.

However, the Irish Church with its secularization and rejection of episcopal authority was becoming increasingly anomalous. Between 640 and 1080 there was no written correspondence between the Irish Church and the papacy; no Irish armies took part in the Crusades. Both these facts reflect the way in which Ireland was removed from the mainstream of European politics and society. While this preserved Gaelic culture, it also meant that Gaelic culture influenced the Irish Church. By the eighth century, before the Viking onslaughts, Gaelic customs had given rise to lay abbots, married clergy, pluralism and family succession to ecclesiastical office in the Irish Church. In the Roman Church, which by the twelfth century had succeeded in establishing its dominance in Britain and the rest of Europe, reforms had ended similar abuses and had created an episcopal hierarchy recognizing papal authority in Church affairs. Pope Gregory VII (1073–85) in the programme 'Unity and Purity' included Ireland as being within his jurisdiction and, to carry out papal wishes, the Norman archbishops of Canterbury revived their claim to be supreme over Ireland.

Canterbury's claim over Ireland dated from the sixth century when St Augustine was appointed first archbishop of Canterbury by Pope Gregory I with authority over the British isles as a whole. This authority remained nominal until, after their conversion, Danes in Ireland chose to join Danes in England and recognize Canterbury's ecclesiastical primacy over Armagh or local Irish abbots. Thus there was a constant pull from England exerted upon Leinster, Dublin and the other towns of Ireland's eastern seaboard, and on occasion archbishops of Canterbury used their claim to press the case for reform of the Irish Church upon Irish high kings. Recognizing the need for reform, Irish Church leaders set about reorganizing the Irish Church on Roman lines and sought papal approval for their efforts. In 1150 an Italian, Cardinal Paparo, was appointed first papal legate to Ireland, and in 1152 he attended a synod at Kells, Co. Meath, convened by the abbots and bishops of the Irish Church. At this synod Paparo, with his papal authority, ratified an episcopal organization for the Irish Church consisting of thirty-six bishoprics and four archbishoprics at Cashel, Tuam, Dublin and the primacy at Armagh. In return for selecting Dublin as the metropolitan see for Leinster, churchmen there at last accepted Armagh's authority instead of Canterbury's. However, in order for the reforms to succeed against generations of different practice, the support of a powerful, central political authority was required. Such an authority did not exist in Ireland – at any one time there were at least three leading kings with competing claims – and so in 1155, by the papal bull 'Laudabiliter', Pope Adrian IV granted the lordship of Ireland to the powerful King Henry II of England 'to reveal the truth of the Christian faith to peoples still untaught and barbarous'.

In the middle of the twelfth century, Ireland while constantly warring internally was not 'untaught and barbarous', and it was Christian. Statements to the contrary in 'Laudabiliter', however, were designed to sustain papal requirements for reform of the Irish Church and to justify the selection of Henry II as a papal agent in this respect. Pope Adrian IV was also the only English Pope in history – he was born Nicholas Breakspear at Abbot's Langley, near St Albans – and held high notions of the papal supremacy over all other rulers. No doubt he saw that if Henry II expanded his power to Ireland, then there would be an opportunity to secure firm control of the Church there too. The Pope's right to grand such an authority derived from the 'Donation of Constantine', supposedly of 325 but subsequently shown to have been an eighty-century forgery, whereby the papacy claimed to have assigned temporal sovereignty over all islands converted to Christianity. In 'Laudabiliter' Pope Adrian IV refers to this while neatly stating papal supremacy: 'Ireland, and indeed all islands on which Christ, the sun of justice, has shed His rays, and which have received the teachings of the Christian faith, belong to the jurisdiction of blessed Peter and the holy Roman Church is a fact beyond doubt, and one which Your Majesty recognizes'. In return for papal support in entering Ireland, Henry II was required 'to pay to St Peter the annual tax of one penny from each household, and to preserve the rights of the churches of that land intact and unimpaired'. The Pope's blessing was clear:

We regard it as pleasing and acceptable to us that you should enter that island for the purpose of enlarging the boundaries of the Church, checking the descent into wickedness, correcting morals and implanting virtues, and encouraging the growth of the faith of Christ; that you pursue policies directed towards the honour of God and the well-being of that land, and that the people of that land receive you honourable and respect you as their lord.

This was the start of England's formal claim to Ireland; a claim which, if the Irish were obedient to the head of the Church, was to be accepted without opposition.

Controversy has raged as to whether 'Laudabiliter', like the 'Donation of Constantine', was a forgery or a later invention of Norman–English kings to justify their Irish exploits. No copy of the bull is in the Vatican Library, and the only existing text comes from the Norman–English Giraldus Cambrensis' untrustworthy *Conquest of Ireland* written between 1186 and 1189. However, there is other contemporary evidence for 'Laudabiliter' and it is now generally accepted that it was not a forgery. Most important, the Irish accepted it without question at the time.

A year after the Pope had granted Henry II the lordship of Ireland, the high king, Turloch O'Connor, died. The O'Connor family had ruled Connaught for several generations before becoming dominant throughout Ireland during the twelfth century. Ten years later, in 1166, Turloch's son Rory became high king. Before he could properly establish his authority, however, Henry II, fourteen years after he had been granted them, decided to claim the rights set down in 'Laudabiliter'. He was prompted to do so by Diarmuid MacMurrough, king of Leinster.

MacMurrough has been remembered only as a villain, the man singly responsible for Ireland's domination by Britain. He was a villain, but he was more besides. Under his auspices the *Book of Leinster* was written, a great anthology of literature and history. He built churches and monasteries (he also destroyed some), and was a master of Irish politics and position. He was ruthlessly cruel: in 1132 in an attempt to place a relation of his as abbess of the convent at

Kildare, he had the rival abbess raped by a common soldier to render her unfit to continue office. He was also a man of passion, and therein lay his own and Ireland's undoing. In 1152 he ran off with the wife of a rival king, Tiernan O'Rourke, prince of Breffny. O'Rourke never forgave Diarmuid for this and plotted his revenge. In 1166 he managed to gather the other sub-kings and chiefs of Leinster in his support and succeeded in forcing Diarmuid to flee Ireland, little realizing that Diarmuid's implacable determination to retain his kingship matched O'Rourke's hatred of him.

Diarmuid travelled to Bristol where he had religious and trading friends and there learnt that Henry II was in France. In the early spring of 1167, Diarmuid caught up with the roving Henry II in Acquitaine, sought his support to regain his kingdom, swore fealty to him and, if he did not already know, learned about 'Laudabiliter'. For Henry II, the Irish exile's request for help no doubt presented an opportunity to distract his own unruly subjects in Wales and the Welsh Marches from causing him trouble (underemployed knights, Henry had found, generated lawlessness), and so he gave Diarmuid money and authority to recruit support in England and Wales. Diarmuid returned to Bristol, but was disappointed with the local response to his cause. Then he was approached by Richard FitzGilbert de Clare, earl of Pembroke, known today as Strongbow. Strongbow was sulking and restless because Henry II had not confirmed his title of earl of Pembroke and had given to others some lands to which Strongbow thought he was entitled. He agreed to support Diarmuid in Ireland, and in return Diarmuid promised Strongbow his daughter in marriage and the succession to the kingdom of Leinster over the rights of Diarmuid's sons. Men whose surnames are now amongst the most common in Ireland joined the enterprise. Robert FitzStephen, a Norman–Welsh adventurer whose mother through a succession of husbands and lovers made him related to a host of connections in Wales and at Henry II's court, was the next to throw in with Diarmuid, together with many of his relations. Strongbow's first cousin and FitzStephen's half-brother, Maurice FitzGerald, agreed to join in return for Diarmuid's promise that he would share with FitzStephen the town of Wexford and some surrounding lands. Diarmuid also managed to secure the services of a group of Flemish mercenaries led by Richard Fitzgodebert de Roche, and they accompanied him when he returned to Ireland in the summer of 1167. In this piecemeal fashion began the Norman invasion of Ireland, the consequences of which are still with us today.

In Ireland, Diarmuid rallied support in south Leinster, and then bided his time for nearly two years, all the while urging his new allies to come and intervene on his behalf. On 1 May 1169 or thereabouts, the first of Strongbow's expeditionary forces landed at Bannow Bay, Co. Wexford, consisting of about ninety horsemen and three hundred archers and men-at-arms, led by FitzStephen. Within a day another strong force landed at Bannow Bay under the command of Maurice de Prendergast, who was (apparently) from a Flemish colony in Pembrokeshire and not related to the Strongbow/ FitzStephen family. Under FitzStephen, the Normans first captured Wexford town, using the longbow and cavalry – both new to Ireland – to great effect. Naturally alarmed by this new invasion which, although small in number, was obviously militarily formidable, the high king Rory O'Connor marched against Diarmuid. Events played into O'Connor's hands. De Prendergast and two hundred of his men, faced by the prospect of being overwhelmed by O'Connor's army, asked Diarmuid for passage back to Wales. Diarmuid arranged for no ships to be available, and so de Prendergast promptly changed sides. Diarmuid then chose prudence and recognized O'Connor as high king in return for freedom of action in south Leinster, and O'Connor left unaware of the strength of the Norman threat. Diarmuid immediately wrote to Strongbow to send reinforcements, and so brought about the battle which later generations of Irishmen were to regard as crucial. Strongbow sent an advance guard under the command of Raymond Carew ('le Gros'), another FitzStephen/ FitzGerald/Strongbow relation, with ten knights and seventy archers. In May 1170 they landed at Baginbun on the Wexford coast and quickly defeated a local Irish army that marched against them, securing their bridgehead. They were joined on 23 August by Strongbow himself who landed at Crook, near Waterford, with a major force of 200 knights and 1,000 soldiers. Together with Carew, two days later Strongbow in one day successfully besieged Waterford, pausing in the town's Cathedral to marry Diarmuid's daughter as had been agreed three years earlier. Within a month, on 21 September, Diarmuid and Strongbow had captured Dublin, and Leinster, Ireland's richest province, was completely in their hands.

The superior weaponry of the Normans played a large part in their success, but so did the personal courage and military skill of their leaders: at Baginbun, Carew had stampeded a herd of cattle against his enemies, thus routing them and securing victory for his own miniscule force. They used to great effect the longbow, which 245 years later was to destroy the flower of French chivalry on the field of Agincourt. The Irish, accustomed to fighting on foot, without armour, had no real defence against the arrows and cavalry of the Normans.

Ironically, because of his success, Strongbow now found his whole enterprise at risk. Henry II, alarmed that his vassal might secure sufficient wealth and power in Ireland to challenge his authority, simply ordered Strongbow and the other adventurers to return to their homes by Easter 1171, and in order to prevent further reinforcements reaching them, he also placed an embargo on all sailings from England and Wales to Ireland. For any who refused to obey, the penalty was to be forfeiture of their lands in England, Wales and France. Strongbow and his colleagues tried to change Henry II's mind by promising to hold their newly won lands in the king's name. While waiting for Henry II's reply, however, in May 1171 Diarmuid MacMurrough died and Strongbow had to undertake a new campaign in Leinster – because of Henry II's embargo, without hope of reinforcements – to force acceptance of his claim to the kingship. He found himself under such severe pressure from Rory O'Connor, who laid siege to Strongbow in Dublin during the summer of 1171, that he offered to submit to him, 'to become his man and hold Leinster of him'. O'Connor would only agree to the Normans keeping the towns of Dublin, Waterford and Wexford, and Strongbow refused to accept these terms. He was saved from defeat only by the courage and skill of one of his lieutenants who, with a surprise attack, routed O'Connor's army and lifted the siege. In September, Strongbow heard from Henry II that he could, after all, keep his new lands on condition that he held them in the king's name and that the king himself would have Dublin, Waterford, Wexford and extensive tracts of land in Leinster. Henry II, forced by Strongbow's success to intervene in Ireland, found that the Norman conquest of Ireland was now underway.

On 17 October 1171, Henry II himself landed at Waterford with 500 knights and over 3,500 men-at-arms and archers. It was a formidable army, calculated to impress not only Strongbow, but also the native Irish. The following day Strongbow did homage, and most of the kings and chiefs of Leinster and Munster followed suit as Henry travelled to Lismore and then to Cashel where he arranged for a synod which, while dealing with matters of Church practice, also secured the recognition by each Irish bishop to Henry's overlordship of Ireland. The synod also helped Henry make peace with the papacy which, since the murder of Thomas à Becket, archbishop of Canterbury, in 1170, had threatened him with excommunication. Pope Alexander III, Adrian IV's successor, as a result of the synod of Cashel, wrote congratulating Henry personally, conferring on him the title 'Lord of Ireland'; congratulating the Irish bishops for accepting Henry, and congratulating the Irish leaders who had sworn him fealty. It was almost inevitable that in 1175, three years after Henry himself had returned home, Rory O'Connor should travel to England and, with the Treaty of Windsor, swear allegiance to Henry. By 1250, less than eighty years after Strongbow first landed in Ireland, three-quarters of the country was under Norman control, with only the rock lands of Connaught and west Ulster not penetrated. Within a generation of the conquest, most of the leading churchmen in Ireland were Normans, and they secured the wishes of the papacy, decreed by the synod of Cashel, that 'the divine offices shall be celebrated according to the usage of the Church of England'. They also ensured that the Church in Ireland would be loyal to the British crown. This loyalty, even in the centuries after the Reformation, remained in the Irish Church. After the Reformation, popes often support British Protestant monarchs because they recognized, as the British Empire expanded, the usefulness of having an influence on those who ran the Empire through the ever-faithful Catholic Irish.

The Normans brought to Ireland not only a strong military tradition, but also a different Anglo-Norman legal structure of Common Law based upon the personal ownership or land and not, as in Irish Brehon Law, ownership vested in an extended family or clan. To protect their lands, and to enforce their laws, they built castles, at first with earth and timber, but in a short space of time with stone and mortar. Dublin Castle, which was to become the seat of Anglo-Norman government in Ireland, was begun in 1204 on the site of the old Norse fort which dominated the city from the southern banks of the river Liffey. The walled towns of Galway, New Ross,

Athenry and Drogheda were founded, and other towns built all over Ireland. The fortified nature of Norman buildings testified to their own warlike qualities as well as to the fact that they were clearly conquerors, surrounded by hostile and resentful Irishmen. Gerald de Barry, known as Giraldus Cambrensis, one of Strongbow's cousins, chronicled the Norman conquest in a work of brilliant propaganda designed to cast a rosy glow on the exploits of his relatives while castigating the native Irish as immoral and undisciplined and thus of no real threat to upright, courageous and ever-vigilant Normans:

For this hostile race is always plotting some kind of treachery under cover of peace. . .This wily race must be feared far more for its guile than its capacity to fight, for its pretended quiescence than for its fiery passions, for its honeyed flattery than for its bitter abuse, for its venom than for its prowess in battle, for its treachery than for its readiness to attack, and for its feigned friendship than for its contemptible hostility.

Perceptions such as this were to colour English views of the Irish for centuries afterwards, and still find an echo today.

Giraldus Cambrensis, with some perspicacity, stated what he thought was necessary for effective government in Ireland:

Since in such matters an excess of caution does no harm, and indeed even the most elaborate precautions are scarcely adequate, as soon as this race has fully submitted to the yoke of obedience, then like the people of Sicily it should be completely forbidden the use of every sort of arms by public edict, and a severe penalty should be laid down for any contravention of this law. . .Ireland should pay tribute to Britain in the form of gold, or the birds which are so plentiful there.

The yoke of obedience was never properly positioned by the Normans in Ireland, but at several times Norman–Irish legislators attempted to impose penal laws of the type suggested by Giraldus. The first Irish parliament was recorded in 1264, established on the English model, with Norman–Irish representatives coming from every part of the country except Connaught and west Ulster. By 1300 some towns and boroughs were also represented, but with the exception of brief periods in the seventeenth century, not until 1922 did an Irish parliament represent the mass of the native Irish people.

One of the first laws passed by the thirteenth-century Irish parliament prohibited the Norman–Irish from wearing Gaelic dress because it confused relationships between the governors and the governed. The relationship that parliament established with the bulk of the Irish people was to last five centuries. It was a parliament of and for the ruling group in Ireland and, unlike England where parliament came to represent wider and wider interests, in Ireland parliament remained the possession of narrow interests always conscious of their fragile position. There were not enough Norman–Irish every to release them from dependence upon the political disorganization of the native kings and chiefs they lived amongst, and from time to time this dependence itself was challenged. In 1258 the leading native Irish leaders united behind Brian O'Neill, the senior member of the great Ulster family, and declared him king of Ireland. This unity was short-lived, but in 1263 a number of Irish leaders invited King Haakon IV of Norway to lead them against the Normans. One of the most severe threats to Norman–Irish security came in 1315 from Scotland after the defeat the previous year of King Edward II of England by Robert the Bruce at Bannockburn. Conquest of Ireland was a natural step in the Scottish king's dream of a Celtic kingdom. His brother, Edward Bruce, landed at Larne in September 1315 and within a year controlled most of Ireland north of Dublin. Had Edward Bruce and his troops been less rapacious, the invasion would probably have received widespread Irish support and succeeded. As it was, the Bruces lost their early Irish allies and when in 1317 Pope John XXII supported Edward II by excommunicating Bruce's clerical allies, the back of the invasion was broken. Edward Bruce was defeated and killed at Dundalk the following year by a Norman–Irish army reinforced from England.

In the first two hundred years after the conquest, the Norman–Irish were able to look, *in extremis*, to support from England. But when in 1337 the Hundred Years' War between France and England began, Norman–Irishmen had no choice but to accept and make the best of their minority position. This was not too difficult since willingness to compromise was one of their attributes, and since the conquest also brought some benefits. They offered peace and stability to those who submitted to them, in contrast to the feuding which had characterized the relationships between native Irish kings like MacMurrough and O'Brien. They did not, in general, attempt to dismember Gaelic society, preferring instead to encourage native Irishmen to continue to farm and herd as before. Only the Gaelic nobility was displaced, and then only because they challenged the Norman–Irish for power. Individual Gaelic leaders who accepted

Norman–Irish sovereignty were treated as equals, and intermarriage was common. As the years went past, succeeding generations of Norman–Irishmen became more and more Gaelicized in their ways, adopting the Brehon Laws and customs of the country. Just as in previous centuries with previous invaders, the Gaels assimilated the Norman–Irish too. A measure of the extent of this process is illustrated by the Statutes of Kilkenny, promulgated by the government in 1366, which decreed that the two races, Norman and Gaelic, should remain separate: marriage between the races was made a capital offence, and Norman–Irishmen were forbidden to play the Irish harp or speak Gaelic. The fears underlying these edicts were largely justified, and the Statutes themselves were a confession of defeat.

The government responsible for the Statutes was effective only in an area of Leinster around Dublin that was coming to be known as the English Pale. The wealth of the province and of the city had attracted the attention of most of the Norman settlers as well as of the English crown. Thus it naturally became a haven for English immigrants and of English law and practice. The Statutes, which remained in force until 1613, were part of a constant effort to prevent the English Pale from being assimilated in the same way as the Norman–Irish. As the Statutes of Kilkenny explained:

Whereas at the conquest of the land of Ireland and for a long time after, the English of the said land used the English language. . .Now many English of the said land, forsaking the English language, fashion, mode of riding, laws and usages, live and govern themselves according to the manners, fashion and language of the Irish enemies, and also have made divers marriages and alliances between themselves and the Irish enemies.

By the close of the fourteenth century, the Norman–Irish had become more Irish than English, and many of them contributed to the revival of Gaelic literature and culture that took place during the period 1200 to 1400. Gerald FitzMaurice, third earl of Desmond, who from 1367 to 1369 served as justiciar (the king's deputy) of Ireland, was known to his contemporaries as 'Gerald the Poet' for his Gaelic compositions (he is credited with being the originator of Gaelic love poetry) and, as the *Annals of the Four Masters* later declared, he 'excelled all the English and many of the Irish in knowledge of the Irish language, poetry and history'. Resurgent Gaelic chieftains, often with the support of Gaelicized Norman families, gained control of more and more land. Art MacMurrough in 1376 was able to re-establish a Gaelic kingdom of his own in Leinster. The cost of defending the Pale and of buying off neighbouring chiefs and warlords like MacMurrough, began to tell heavily upon the royal exchequer. King Richard II during a lull in the Hundred Years' War came to Ireland to reassert royal authority with a large army in 1394. He was the first English king to set foot in Ireland since Henry II in 1171–2. MacMurrough submitted to him, only to rebel immediately after Richard's departure, killing in battle Roger Mortimer, the childless king's heir. Richard returned to Ireland in 1399 to bring MacMurrough to terms, but instead found his own crown challenged in England by Henry Bolingbroke, duke of Lancaster. The king sailed back to England to meet deposition and death in the Tower of London. For the next hundred years, English rule in Ireland was in practice confined to the area of the Pale.

3

From the Tudors to Cromwell

The Church from the fourteenth to the seventeenth centuries, like the Norman–Irish, also became more and more removed from English influence and control. The religious orders – the Cistercians, Dominicans, Franciscans and Augustinians – which had arrived at the time of the Norman invasion, had been instrumental in reforming the Irish Church, helping to enforce the payment of tithes and establishing a diocesan episcopate and a parochial system. However, by the early thirteenth century, the discipline and practices of the Irish Church degenerated, and the Synod of Kells' acceptance of papal authority had associated the Irish Church with the papacy at the most sordid period in the history of the popes. As early as 1221 a visiting French monk noted, 'In the abbeys of this country the severity of Cistercian discipline and order is observed in scarcely anything but the wearing of the habit.' The Irish clergy were noted for the hereditary character of their profession. In 1250 the bishop of Ossory complained to the Pope about hereditary succession in the churches of his diocese. Decrees from the primate of Armagh (always from the Pale, a foreigner or an Englishman) and from various provincial synods in the fifteenth century had little effect. A visitation made in 1546 to the rural deanery of Tullaghoge, Co. Tyrone, revealed some of the clergy as 'concubinary'. Bishop Turlough O'Brien of Killaloe (1483–1526) had a son. Mahon, who became bishop of Kilmacduagh (1503–32), and married a cousin. Their son, Turlough, also became bishop of Killaloe (1556–69) like his grandfather, and like his father also married a cousin, the daughter of the first earl of Thomond.

Amongst the laity, Gaelic customs predominated. Divorce, secular marriage, fosterage and common property ownership remained widespread, among native Irishmen and the Norman–Irish outside

43

the Pale as well. Amongst the laity, two great Norman–Irish (from the fourteenth century onwards known as 'Old English') families dominated the scene: the Butlers in their earldom of Ormond, who remained substantially loyal to the crown, and the FitzGeralds in their earldoms of Desmond and Kildare who came to resist the crown and government unless it was their own. They conducted their affairs like the Irish chieftains around them, according to the Brehon Laws and private agreements, with little reference to any outside authority. Like the O'Neills and O'Donnells of Ulster, who regained supremacy in their areas, this state of affairs remained unchallenged until the Reformation. They all built fortified tower houses as strongholds, the ruins of over two thousand of which still dot Ireland. During the same period in England, windowed manor houses were the order of the day, reflecting the contrast in the political and social condition of the two countries.

The turmoil of the times in Ireland inevitably affected England. In September 1447, King Henry VI appointed Richard, duke of York, his lieutenant in Ireland in an attempt to divert the duke's ambitions to take Henry's crown. Richard proved a wonderfully skilled politician. Landing at Nowth, near Dublin, with a large army, he acknowledged his Norman and Irish ancestors including Brian Boru, and made plain his wish to secure the support of all Irishmen in his coming struggle for the throne. Accordingly, he promoted and favoured those – regardless of ancestry – who submitted to him. As one contemporary observer put it, 'ere twelve months come to an end, the wildest Irishman in Ireland shall be sworn English'. His son, George, afterwards duke of Clarence, born in Dublin three months after Richard's arrival there, was baptized in the capital. The event was celebrated by the ordinary people of Dublin, and thereafter the white rose of York always attracted Irish support. In 1487 the imposter Lambert Simnel was crowned king of England in Dublin in the belief he was George's son. When Richard returned to England in September 1450, he left behind a country broadly united in loyalty to him. When he was forced to flee to Ireland after his defeat at the battle of Ludlow, the second major battle of the Wars of the Roses, his supporters controlled the country, and the Irish parliament not only ordered the arrest and execution of a royal messenger who arrived with writs against Richard, but also went so far as to give the first clear statement of Irish independence. It was a Norman–Irish parliament, not a Gaelic one, but it reflected an Irish perception:

The land of Ireland is, and at all times had been, corporate of itself by the ancient laws and customs used in the same, freed of the burden of any special law of the realm of England, save only such laws as the lords spiritual and temporal and the commons of the said land had been in great council or parliament there held admitted, accepted, affirmed and proclaimed.

Only the personal line of the crown was now considered to connect Ireland with England: the Irish parliament was claiming sovereignty in Ireland. Richard left Ireland in 1460, only to be killed at the battle of Wakefield. In March the following year the Yorkist cause triumphed, and Richard's eldest son became King Edward IV of England.

Loyalty to York continued after the first Tudor, Henry VII, became king in 1485. The justiciar, Garret More FitzGerald, eighth earl of Kildare, supported the claims of Lambert Simnel and subsequently in 1491 of Perkin Warbeck to be the Yorkist pretenders to the throne. FitzGerald, king of Ireland in all but name, persistently fought for Norman–Irish freedom. Generations of English neglect had forced the Norman–Irish to become self-sufficient and to compromise in a multitude of ways with Gaelic Ireland. They never became completely Gaelicized, but by the end of the fifteenth century, Norman–Irishmen could count on general support whenever they challenged English rule: there was a sufficient strength of common identity gradually to make the crown aware of the need to subdue and eventually to re-colonize the country.

Henry VII took the first steps to re-establish the authority of the English crown in Ireland outside the Pale. In 1494 he appointed as his deputy in Ireland Sir Edward Poynings to bring the country to 'whole and perfect obedience'. Poynings was completely loyal to his king. He was also an able soldier and administrator (FitzGerald wrote to a northern Gaelic chieftain that Poynings 'is a better man than I') and he quickly set about reducing the power of the Norman–Irish. He called a parliament of picked men at Drogheda which early in 1495 passed 'Poynings' Law'. This law, which remained in force until repealed in 1782, declared that an Irish parliament could only meet with the king's permission, and then could only pass laws previously approved by the king and his English Council. Poynings' immediate purpose was to prevent another Simnel or Warbeck securing the blessings of an Irish legislature, or of another more proper pretender finding in Ireland the protection and support Richard of York had found in 1459. The financial pressure on the royal exchequer, however, in supporting Poynings' Irish administration, began to tell. When FitzGerald swore to Henry VII that he would not support threats to the Tudor dynasty, the king decided that 'since all Ireland cannot rule this man, this man must rule all Ireland' and in 1496 FitzGerald succeeded Poynings as deputy. For the next thirty-eight years, the FitzGeralds ('Geraldines') ruled Ireland on the unwritten understanding that as long as there was no Irish threat to the English crown, and as long as the expense of Irish government was defrayed from Irish sources, kings of England were prepared to leave the country alone. Had Henry VII's Tudor successors maintained this policy, even Poynings' Law, administered by men like Fitzgerald, might have secured a degree of Irish freedom and an acceptance of English claims to Irish lordship which would have averted the strife and bitterness of the next four hundred years.

Henry VIII and his chancellor, Cardinal Wolsey, in contrast viewed Ireland as an untapped resource. Refusing to accept previous experience that the country was always a net cost to the exchequer (£16,000 in 1520) whenever the crown actively tried to run the government there, they viewed Ireland instead as being full of 'the King's decayed rents and embezzled lands'. The earl of Surrey, appointed lieutenant in 1519, was recalled two years later after reporting that he would need an army of over five thousand with munitions, fortifications and supplies to match in order to bring Ireland firmly under royal control. The Pale-dominated Council of Ireland (the small group of peers who ruled Ireland in consultation with the deputy) send regular reports to the king describing the activities of the Geraldines in terms of threat, and warning that the Pale was shrinking quickly. In 1534, the eldest son of the earl of Kildare, 'Silken' Thomas FitzGerald, Lord Offaly, rebelled against the king, sending for aid to Pope Paul III at the very moment Henry VIII had broken with the Church. A royal army quickly defeated Silken Thomas, who, together with five of his uncles, was executed at Tyburn in 1537. But while Silken Thomas had sought only to take advantage of the schism for immediate political purposes, nevertheless by his appeal to foreign power and the pope he established what was to become the traditional pattern of Irish nationalism. England's difficulty was henceforth seen as Ireland's opportunity; England's enemies were to be Ireland's friends. And while Catholicism was certainly a common denominator between Ireland and many of

England's enemies, it was always the national appeal, not the religious, which motivated Irishmen: in 1919 Irish nationalists despatched an envoy to the new, avowedly anti-Catholic communist government of Russia to request 'sympathetic recognition for Ireland as a sister state', simply because Britain was supporting that government's opponents.

Henry VIII's breach with Rome marked the beginning of this international element in Irish nationalism. The institution of the Anglican Church, after the Anglo-Norman conquest, was also to be the single most revolutionary event in Anglo-Irish relations. By the end of the sixteenth century, Ireland was a persistent source of anxiety to English government as England's Catholic European enemies proved again and again willing to fuel the flames of Irish nationalism with religious antagonism. Ireland's siting both in relation to the British mainland and to England's maritime links with her growing Empire, meant that even if England could not fully exploit Ireland's wealth, her strategic importance could not be overlooked. In 1579 Pope Gregory XIII and Philip II of Spain launched an expedition announced as a crusade which landed at Dingle, Co. Kerry. The following year a papal force landed at Smerwick, Co. Kerry. In 1601 over 3,000 Spaniards landed at Kinsale, Co. Cork, to help an Irish rebellion. In 1690, Louis XIV of France sent a 7,000-strong army to Cork which later fought for James II at the Battle of the Boyne. In 1798 over 4,000 French soldiers landed in Ireland to help another rebellion. During the Second World War, one of the principal fears of the British Admiralty was that German U-boats might find an Irish refuge.

Another consequence of the Henrician Reformation was that the continuation of Catholicism in Ireland added a further element to those of language, culture, geography and tradition which separated her from England. This was not, however, immediately the case. The Reformation at first took as much hold in Ireland as in England. The Act of Supremacy which in 1534 declared Henry VIII supreme head of the Church in England did not extend to Ireland. Three years later, in December 1537, after some opposition the Irish parliament passed its own Act declaring Henry to be 'the only Supreme Head on Earth of the whole Church of Ireland'.

The great age of Irish Christianity had been over for some time. The Church in Ireland was kept alive largely by the efforts of the

friars: the episcopal hierarchy was more concerned with accumu-
lating wealth and the politics of Tudor government than with
proselytizing. One observer reported in 1515, 'There is no
archbishop, no bishop, abbot or prior, parson nor vicar, nor any
other person of the Church, high or low, great or small, English or
Irish, that is accustomed to preach the word of God, saving the poor
friars beggars'. By 1517 the great cathedrals of Clonmacnois and
Ardagh were in ruins. When Henry VIII in 1536 appointed, as
archbishop of Dublin, George Browne, the English Augustinian
who had performed the marriage ceremony between the king and
Ann Boleyn, the Irish bishops welcomed him. They also accepted
with little resistance the claims to religious supremacy advanced by
Henry. When the monasteries were suppressed in Ireland, as in
England, Irish bishops, nobles and chiefs proved just as willing as
their English counterparts to despoil them. Over four hundred Irish
monasteries and abbeys were sold to laymen during the reigns of
Henry and his daughter Elizabeth I. The Ulster Irish chief, Turlough
Luineach O'Neill, for example, in 1575 personally insisted upon
securing the right to 'all the lands of monasteries, abbacies and of
other spiritual buildings' within lands granted to him by the crown.
And in Ireland, in contrast to England, there was no popular
resistance to the Reformation: there was no Pilgrimage of Grace, no
martyrs, no Sir Thomas More. In 1541 when the Irish parliament
passed an Act declaring Henry VIII to be king of Ireland, there was
no opposition. From that time to the present day, English monarchs
were to claim their Irish title as of right endorsed by parliament and
not, as the previous claim to the 'Lordship of Ireland' had been,
derived from the papal grant to Henry II four hundred years earlier.

The Irish Reformation parliament did not represent more than
about nine counties and between twenty and thirty boroughs, and
only the Anglo-Irish ruling group therein. In 1515 Henry VIII had
a governmental investigation carried out, 'The State of Ireland and
Plan for its Reformation', which described the nature of the
country and the problem of governing outside the Pale:

And first of all to make his Grace understand that there may be more than
sixty countries, called regions in Ireland, inhabited with the King's Irish
enemies; some regions as big as a shire, some more, some less, unto a little;
some as big as half a shire and some a little less; where reigneth more than
sixty chief captains wherein some call themselves Kings, some Princes,
some Dukes, some Archdukes, that liveth only by the sword and obeyeth to

no other temporal persons, but only to himself that is strong, and every of the said captains maketh war and peace for himself. . .Also there be thirty great captains of the English folk that follow the same Irish order. . .and every of them maketh war and peace for himself without any licence of the King.

In 1541 the king took steps to rectify this state of affairs and to extend his authority by securing the enactment by the Irish parliament of Surrender and Regrant legislation. As a result, all land in Ireland was considered to belong to the king who would 'regrant' it to those loyal to him. This was a final body-blow to the Gaelic customs of Brehon Law and the common ownership of property. In return for surrendering their lands to the king and swearing fealty, Irish chiefs would have their lands regranted to them personally. The chief of the Ulster O'Neills, Con, submitted on this basis in December 1541, taking the title earl of Tyrone and having his eldest son recognized as successor rather than his other son, Shane, or his nephews who had traditional Gaelic claims to be considered as successors. As a result of Surrender and Regrant, Con's grandson, Hugh, was to find that after a failed rebellion his rights to his lands and his authority within them were at the disposal of the crown.

Under Edward VI (1537–53) and Mary (1516–58), Henry VIII's son and daughter and successors in 1547 and 1553 respectively, the area in which royal government was effective was extended. In a series of military campaigns, launched from the Pale against the chiefs of Leix and Offaly who resisted the Surrender and Regrant legislation, royal armies established the first modern forts at Maryborough (now Portlaoise, Co. Leix, and Philipstown (now Daingean). Co. Offaly, which were to become springboards of a new Tudor policy: plantation.

In 1521, the lieutenant, the earl of Surrey, first suggested plantation as a means of subduing Ireland by replacing disloyal Irishmen with loyal English immigrants as colonists. In June 1550, in the middle of Edward VI's reign, the English privy council decided 'that Leix and Offaly, being the countries late of the O'Connors and O'Moores, should be let out to the King's subjects at convenient rents, to the intent it may both be inhabited and also a more strength for the King's Majesty'. The first planters, however, found that those they attempted to dispossess could fight back, and the government decided in the face of persistent and effective Irish resistance that too great a military presence was required to sustain the plantation, and this first attempt failed. It was under the devoutly Catholic Mary Tudor (1516–58) that the first effective plantations took place.

When Mary came to the throne in 1553, Protestantism was already waning in Ireland. This was partly because of the small number of towns and the lack of a strong and numerous middle class, which elsewhere in Europe provided the foundation congregation of Protestantism. It was also because of Tudor insensitivity and shortsightedness in attacking Gaelic society while simultaneously attempting a governmental and religious revolution. The Irish Reformation parliament in 1536 had also passed a law to promote 'English Order, Habit and Language', essentially re-affirming the Statutes of Kilkenny of 1366. The Gaelic language was prohibited along with Gaelic dress – saffron-dyed clothing, moustaches, long hair and forelocks. The Brehons and Gaelic poets and harpists were banned. Intermarriage between the native Irish and the English was again forbidden, and was made treasonable in certain circumstances. In 1549 the Mass was banned. The English-language *Book of common prayer*, drawn up by the Protestant archbishop of Canterbury, Thomas Cranmer, was foisted upon the Irish Church, the overwhelming majority of whose members spoke nothing but Gaelic. Irishmen found that on top of the English view of them as an inferior race, British government had found a new method of oppression through religion. It was not that there was any particular Irish wish to remain Catholic, but there was a wish for Christian rites which in practice was denied by the banning of the Mass and the prohibition of Gaelic. There was no rejoicing when the Catholic Mary came to power. Dowdall, the Catholic archbishop of Armagh appointed by Mary, urged plantation as a policy, writing to the queen that the solution to the problem of the rebellious Irish – his own flock – was to drive out or kill them, settling their lands with Englishmen instead. In its search for power, Tudor government was not swayed by religious distinctions. Mary's plantations, which were also in Leix and Offaly – renamed King's and Queen's counties – were conducted on military lines and were of a military nature, with planters being left in no doubt that their presence in Ireland was designed to secure royal authority and to defend it in arms whenever called upon to do so.

Tudor government, however, while being ruthless in exacting its requirements, for good political purposes also had a conciliatory side. In 1520 Henry VIII sent a dispatch to the lieutenant, Surrey, which stated an approach to Irish government that, despite some lapses, was to underpin the rationale of English administration ever afterwards.

The King expects to get lands back which he had wrongfully lost, he does not wish to oppose injustice by injustice. . .Like as we being their sovereign lord and prince though of our absolute power we be above the laws yet we will in no wise take anything from them that righteously appertains to them so of good congruence they be bound both by law fidelities and allegiance to restore unto us our own.

What successive English governments never properly understood was that, to the Irish, to accept English fair play, no matter how fair, was to accept English claims and the assumption of British rights in Ireland.

A successful measure of conciliation was the creation by Queen Elizabeth I in 1592 of Ireland's first university, in Dublin of which only one college, Trinity, was every founded. The decision to set up Trinity College was part of an attempt to counteract the growing tendency for young Irishmen to journey to universities in European countries hostile to England. For the first thirty years of its existence, the university, although Protestant, was able freely to accept Catholics and to teach Irish language and literature, and in its whole existence the College never banned Catholics *per se*.

The ruthless side of Tudor government, however, left a far more vivid memory. From 1566 to 1583, the Munster FitzGeralds, earls of Desmond, maintained a more or less constant guerrilla war against the government and its agents. They received help from Spain and, in 1580, from Pope Gregory XIII. Coercion and martial law became the regime in Munster during this period. One of the English commanders, Sir Walter Raleigh, put to the sword every member of a Spanish invasion force (they were Italians in the service of Spain) in 1580. His half-brother, Sir Humphrey Gilbert, frankly described 'putting man, woman and child to the sword'. Sir William Pelham, lord justice of Ireland, explained to the queen in 1579 his tactics. 'I keep them from their harvest, and have taken great preys of cattle from them, by which it seemeth the poor people . . . offer themselves with their wives and children rather to be slain by the army than to suffer the famine that now in extremity beginneth to pinch them.' The poet Edmund Spenser, author of *The faerie queen*, who had come to Ireland as secretary to the deputy in

1580, pictured Munster after the rebellion had ended with the capture and execution of the fourteenth earl of Desmond in 1583:

Out of every corner of the woods and glens they came creeping forth upon their hands, for their legs would not bear them. They looked like anatomies of death; they spake like ghosts crying out of their graves; they did eat of the dead carrions, happy were they if they could find them, yea, and one after another soon after, insomuch as the very carcasses they spared not to scrape out of their graves. And if they found a plot of watercresses or shamrocks, they flocked there as if to a feast.

Following the Desmond rebellion, in 1584 over 500,000 acres of FitzGerald land in Munster was confiscated by the crown and regranted to 'undertakers'. They brought a new twist to the scheme of plantation. Where previously English planters were expected to control their native Irish tenants, the undertakers agreed to repopulate their lands with English settlers, driving out the natives. Raleigh was given forty thousand acres; Spenser four thousand. However, the plantation was only partly successful: it faced the perennial problem of attracting settlers in sufficient numbers to defend themselves from the angry and vengeful dispossessed Irish around them. In 1591 when The MacMahon of Monaghan was charged with treason and his lands confiscated, Elizabeth rejected a plantation settlement in favour of dividing MacMahon's lands amongst his neighbours.

The most serious Irish rebellion since the Anglo-Norman conquest was generated directly by Elizabeth's determination to establish Tudor government throughout the country. Hugh O'Neill, the leader of the Ulster family, had been brought up at Elizabeth's court and was an unexpected rebel. He had served in the armies which put down the Desmond rebellion. In 1582 his loyalty was rewarded with the title earl of Tyrone and the grant of the O'Neill lands. Then, in 1588 he helped survivors of the Spanish Armada wrecked on the Ulster coast and in 1591 organized the escape of Red Hugh O'Donnell and of his cousins, Henry and Art O'Neill, from Dublin Castle where they were being held hostage for the good behaviour of the O'Donnells and O'Neills in Ulster. In 1593, Red Hugh organized a confederation of Irish chiefs in revolt and, like the FitzGeralds in Munster some years previously, sought foreign aid with a religious appeal to the forces of the counter-Reformation. In 1595, Hugh O'Neill joined with O'Donnell and came out in open revolt, adopting the role of champion of 'Christ's Catholic religion' and calling for a national rising. This was a watershed in Irish history: for the first time since Rory O'Connor had attempted to expel the Normans, the glimmerings of a national Irish resistance were stirred by O'Neill. In addition, the appeal for and expectation of foreign support on religious grounds, demonstrated that a Catholic Ireland could have powerful allies and that Anglo-Irish relations would never again be a purely bilateral affair.

O'Neill's rebellion was marked by early success. In 1598 at the Battle of Yellow Ford on the Blackwater river near Armagh, he ambushed and defeated a government force of over 4,000, killing more than half the number, including the commander. He began to be spoken of as 'Prince of Ireland', a harking back to his family's ancient claims to the Gaelic high kingship. In the winter of 1599–1600 he made what amounted to a royal progress through Munster. To combat him, Elizabeth appointed Charles Blount, Lord Mountjoy, as deputy. He arrived in Ireland in February 1600 and immediately proposed to defeat O'Neill by ringing Ulster with forts and using famine 'as the chief instrument of reducing this kingdom'. O'Neill appealed to Spain for help, stressing the religious aspect of his struggle by sending to the pope for recognition of his war as a Catholic crusade. In September 1601 about 3,500 Spaniards landed unopposed at Kinsale, Co. Cork. In November, O'Neill and O'Donnell marched south to meet them, and on Christmas Day the Irish army met Mountjoy as he besieged the Spanish army in Kinsale. Within hours O'Neill was defeated. It was a crucial defeat, marking the end of the war and the beginning of the end of Gaelic Ireland. Red Hugh went to Spain to canvass further support, but died there in September 1602, probably poisoned by an Irish agent of Mountjoy's. Hugh O'Neill returned to Ulster, finally submitting to Mountjoy on 23 March 1603, one day before Queen Elizabeth died. Ulster, the last unconquered province of Ireland, was thrown open to English rule, and at her death Elizabeth was the first English monarch who could properly claim control of most of the crown's second kingdom.

The legacy of Elizabeth's Irish wars, however, was long and bitter on both sides. After his submission, O'Neill journeyed to London where he was received by the new Scottish Stuart King James I. Sir John Harington, an English commander who had fought against

O'Neill for years, spoke for many after seeing O'Neill's reception. 'How did I labour after that knave's destruction. I adventured perils by land and sea, was near starving, ate horse flesh in Munster, and all to quell that man who now smileth in peace with those that did hazard their lives to destroy him.' For some time, the king and deputy Mountjoy pursued a liberal policy in Ireland and towards O'Neill, going so far as to tolerate Catholicism. But, in 1605, with the fears of a Catholic coup inspired by Guy Fawkes and the gunpowder plot, the pressures on James at home to prove that he was not a closet Catholic himself forced a tougher line. Religious toleration was ended and a new deputy, Sir Arthur Chichester, used Surrender and Regrant to whittle away the O'Neill and O'Donnell lands. O'Neill was on the point of arguing his case in London when Red Hugh's younger brother, Rory O'Donnell, earl of Tyrconnell, pre-empted O'Neill by plotting a secret flight to France. O'Neill realized that Chichester and the government would believe this to be another plot for war and would implicate him, and thus felt he had no option but to join the flight. On 4 September 1607 the two earls with ninety-nine followers set sail in a French ship from Rathmullan, Co. Donegal, never to return. O'Donnell died in Rome the following year and was buried in the Franciscan church of San Pietro di Montorio on the Janiculum hill. Eight years later O'Neill was laid to rest beside him with royal honours. British agents who had kept an eye on the great earl during his last years reported that in the evenings after dinner he had only one subject of conversation: 'his face would glow, he would strike the table, he would say that they would yet have a good day in Ireland'. Sir John Davies, attorney general of Ireland, saw O'Neill's exile as enabling the government to complete the work of St Patrick, 'for St Patrick did only banish the poisonous worms, but suffered the men full of poison to inhabit the land still'. To Irishmen, however, the 'Flight of the Earls', as it soon became known, represented a despairing determination never to accept defeat at the hands of Britain. Over the next two centuries it fell largely to Irish exiles to keep the flame of an Irish independence alight. At home, Irishmen found that if they did not abide by British law and custom, their future was limited. As the nineteenth-century Irish unionist historian, William Lecky, explained, to Tudors and Stuarts, 'the slaughter of Irishmen was looked upon as literally the slaughter of wild beasts'.

The flight of the earls had an immediate consequence: their lands were seized by the crown and designated in 1608 the new counties of Armagh, Cavan, Coleraine (later re-named Londonderry), Donegal, Fermanagh and Tyrone. A committee was appointed in London to prepare a detailed scheme of plantation, and in January 1609 it reported back recommending that the planters should outnumber the native Irish. The following year its proposals were put into effect, and Scottish and English settlers were invited to colonize the seized lands. As in the earlier Munster plantations, undertakers were granted lands for which they paid rent to the crown and agreed to populate with imported tenants. Lands were cleared completely of their native inhabitants, and evicted Irishmen were only allowed to live in certain areas. The most striking development, however, was the creation of twenty-three new towns including Belfast, each designed on a grid pattern with a central square or 'diamond'. The guilds of the City of London were granted the towns of Derry and Coleraine and the lands around. Both Derry and the county were re-named Londonderry after the city guilds' investment there (the use of the older 'Derry' still signifies nationalist sentiment opposed to London's 'theft' of their town). By September 1610 the reorganization was complete, and within three years most of the settlers had arrived. The counties of Down and Antrim had been settled privately and for the most part before the great Ulster plantation of James I, providing an adult English population of about 7,500 in 1622. To this was added a new, largely Scottish group of about 13,000 settlers by the Ulster plantation, bringing the Anglo-Scottish population of Ulster to over 20,000 in the early 1620s.

While more planters settled in Ulster within a shorter space of time than in any other plantation, still there were not enough to make the settlement viable without native labour and therefore tenants. The settlers' fear of the natives also contributed to their feelings of insecurity. 'Although there be no apparent enemy', an observer wrote in 1610, 'nor any visible main force, yet the wood-kern and many other (who have now put on the smiling countenance of contentment) do threaten every house, if opportunity of time and place doth serve.' In Londonderry settlers worked 'as it were with the sword in one hand and the axe in the other'.

Two developments flowed from this state of affairs. Many undertakers defaulted in their payments to the exchequer because

their expected rent income did not materialize as the settlement fell
below its planned numerical strength; and many native Irishmen
quickly came back as tenants and labourers for desperate landlords
on lands they had themselves once owned. To the Irish, the
slaughters and plantations of the sixteenth and seventeenth centuries,
and the attack on gaelic society, could only be explained in racist
terms. To the planters and the government, however, the Irish were
traitors who refused to accept the rights of conquest. O'Neill's
rebellion encouraged them simply to regard every Irishman as a
traitor, and so brutal measures were felt to be justified. At the same
time it must be pointed out that the crown dealt as harshly with
British traitors and opponents who had to face the tortures of the
Star Chamber. British martyrs (there were few Irish ones) were
burnt alive at the stake or hanged, drawn and quartered. Outside
the British Isles, the ave was even more severe. In South America the
Conquistadores indulged in an orgy of plunder and slaughter which
makes Ireland's experience minor in comparison. The Roman
Catholic Inquisition, instituted in 1229, was in full flood with the
counter-Reformation. On St Bartholomew's Day, 24 August 1582,
in France the government and mobs murdered thousands of
Huguenots. British government in Ireland during the sixteenth and
seventeenth centuries has to be seen in relation to the age.

Throughout this period, and despite their Gaelicization, the Old
English families had ultimately always regarded themselves as the
conquerors (and therefore the owners) of Ireland. The Anglo–
Normans who had conducted the conquest were their forbears and,
as Henry II had been quick to realize, the enterprise had been undertaken for selfish purposes, not in the interests of the crown. As lord
of Ireland, the British king had exercised authority in the country by
papal gift. Once Henry VIII, however, determined to be king of
Ireland in his own right, fundamental questions were raised. Old
English families like the FitzGeralds, and Gaelic families like the
O'Neills, saw that by maintaining their Catholic faith they could
advance logical and legalistic arguments against royal authority and
thus secure their lands in the face of the exercise of Surrender and
Regrant legislation which underpinned the Ulster plantation. The
Catholic Church, by a diplomatic policy of appointing native
Irishmen to native and Old English to Old English sees, successfully
encouraged a perception in which the cause of Catholicism came to

be identified with the cause of a 'free' Ireland during the seventeenth century. The first demonstration of this new development came with the Irish parliament which assembled in 1613.

Since 1543, the Irish parliament had met only four times (compared to the English parliament meeting in the same period approximately twenty times with many sessions), and there had been a twenty-five year gap by the time the 1613 parliament met. It was different from its Tudor predecessors in several respects. Unlike the English parliament which banned Catholics, the Irish parliament still accepted them and, of the 232 members, 100 were Catholic. Most were Old English, although eighteen native Irishmen had seats. Insecurity over land titles in the face of royal claims had generated a (largely Catholic) parliamentary opposition to the crown, which while loudly protesting about religious and constitutional issues was concerned to establish claims to property and ownership and not to seek religious change. Since the parliament had been summoned to ratify the Ulster plantation, this opposition and the reasons for it marked a significant change in the politics of the Old English. As was to be shown during the reign of Charles I, the Old English were to identify more and more with native Irish in resisting British administration in Ireland, appealing directly to the king over the heads of Dublin administrators. Thus despite their qualms about their security to their lands, after the flight of the earls Irish landlords, both Old English and native, reconciled their position by accepting royal claims in theory while resisting them in practice. In the 1613 parliament this was demonstrated by a boycott of the parliament while they appealed to James I for satisfaction, leaving the parliament to legalise the seizure of the Ulster lands, and to attaint the earls of Tyrone and Tyrconnell formally for treason. The Brehon Laws were declared abolished, and the whole panoply of British law – juries, assizes, and common law – was introduced instead. However, even this opposition in the Irish parliament was representative only of the governing group, and the parliament's legislation simply meant that the persecution of Gaelic Ireland was backed by more law. Gaelic customs remained, and the Brehon Laws continued to be used by Irishmen remote from central government for generations to come. The Irish people were to find that apparent conformity with governmental regulations was the simple way of getting by, keeping their Gaelic sensibility hidden and secret and for themselves. 'Hedge schools' developed during the eighteenth century where the successors to the Gaelic brehons, storytellers and musicians secretly taught young Irish boys and girls the history, traditions and tales of their ancestors.

Faced with the obvious resistance of the Old English and the surreptitious opposition of the Irish to their government, the Stuarts increasingly placed the Irish administration in the hands of men sent from England. Thomas Wentworth, earl of Strafford, who was sent by Charles I in August 1633 to be his lord deputy, did more than any other administrator to emphasize the differences between the governors and the governed in Ireland. He came determined to establish an Irish administration independent of local influence and controlled by himself alone as the king's representative. At the same time he faced the perennial problem of the cost of the Irish administration, made heavy by the constant need for a large army in Ireland both to subdue rebels and to repel potential invaders. By 1625, the year in which Charles I became king, the cost of this army was in the region of £70,000 per annum and the government began to cast about for money-raising schemes to meet this cost. The Old English were no longer trusted with the defence of the country: they had become too closely identified with the native Irish and their loyalties to each other rather than to the crown. So, Charles I in 1628 had intimated his willingness to grant his royal 'Grace and Bounty' to them, making concessions to the Old English on religious, constitutional and property issues, in return for their financial support of his army and administration. The 'Graces' were important to the Old English, seeming to be a statement that they enjoyed a special position and special favour in the eyes of the crown. Of course, if they really did enjoy such a position, then the crown would not have needed to bargain concessions with them to pay for an army. One of Wentworth's first acts was to summon an Irish parliament of picked members which he manipulated to secure parliamentary subsidies, and then refused to confirm the Graces. The position of the Old English was clearly revealed as helpless. They might grumble and complain, but they did not alone have sufficient strength to defy the government, let alone Wentworth's single-minded and unscrupulous purpose of achieving effective government – the policy of 'Thorough' which Archbishop Laud was to employ with disastrous results in England. To Wentworth,

'Thorough' was a function of government's financial strength and independence. In pursuing this policy, he managed to alienate every group in Ireland.

Wentworth's investigations convinced him that Ireland could produce much greater revenues for the crown. The weakness of land titles (the most important element in the Graces) was an obvious source of potential income. Landlords and tenants with weak titles could be expected to pay for security, or their lands could be taken and sold by the crown. The whole province of Connaught was claimed in this way, with between half and one-quarter of the land designated for plantation, and the remainder for a considerable fee confirmed to existing landowners. Old English and native Irish were treated alike, being fined and property being confiscated on the least excuse, and sometimes with forged documents. The earl of Cork was forced to surrender some Church lands and was fined £15,000 for not fulfilling the terms of the original grant. The City of London guilds had to pay a fine of £70,000 and lost their charters in Ulster for similar reasons. Wentworth allowed religious toleration to Catholics in return for a payment of £20,000, although in 1634 for the first time Roman Catholic students at Trinity College were asked to take the oath of Supremacy. Those who refused could still attend the University, but would not receive degrees, scholarships or fellowships. When Charles I went to war with the Scottish Presbyterians in 1639, Wentworth forced Scottish Protestants in Ulster to take the hated 'Black Oath' swearing allegiance to the king. Puritan and Presbyterian clergymen were replaced and dismissed as the deputy sought to extend royal authority and to increase royal revenue through the Anglican Church of Ireland by first establishing uniform discipline with the Church of England and then securing the ecclesiastical dues previously belonging to the Catholic Church before the Reformation. In these ways, Wentworth succeeded in increasing royal revenues, but he also forced into opposition every powerful group in the country and some, like the London guilds, in England too. After he was recalled by Charles in November 1639, Catholic Old English, the native Irish, and Protestant New English (the Tudor and Stuart landlords, planters and administrators) combined with English Puritans at Westminster in the revolutionary Long parliament to throw off Wentworth's controls, to attaint him, and to see him executed in May 1641. It was only when the Puritans began to press for an end to Catholic toleration in 1641 that this strange alliance dissolved.

By consistently acting as if he regarded people in Ireland as papists who would be prepared to pay for toleration, or potentially rebellious Scots who could be coerced through fear of native Irish revolt, Wentworth achieved the worst fears of his predecessors: an Ireland broadly united against the government. However, once Wentworth, the common enemy, had been executed, the alliance began to dissolve both in the Long parliament and in Ireland. What did not dissolve was the Catholic–Irish coherence that Wentworth had presumed and so had precipitated.

Irish exiles in Europe had maintained their contacts with their homeland and had proved willing to accept their Old English co-religionists as allies. The growing conflict in England between king and parliament, and the growing strength of Puritanism suggested that the moment for revolt to regain their lands was opportune. So it happened. An all-Ireland revolt was planned only to be betrayed on the eve of its commencement on 23 October 1641. Nevertheless, in Ulster where many of the former landowners lived in the woods and mountains, it went ahead under the leadership of Sir Phelim O'Neill, a leading member of the dispossessed Ulster family. The rebels captured Dundalk and besieged Drogheda. The Irish administration found itself in a quandary, not knowing whether to turn to the king or to parliament to suppress the rebellion. Within a year of the rebellion, however, it became clear that the rebels not only recognized the crown's authority (but not its officers) and claimed that their rebellion was against the actions of administrators like Wentworth, but were prepared to support the king in return for recognition of their claims. In addition, since Puritan and Presbyterian Scots in Ulster suffered the brunt of the rebellion and were offered support from Scotland and the Long parliament, the divisions of the English Civil War were naturally reflected in Ireland. Of note is the singular fact that even native Irish rebels from the outset of the rebellion (which was to last over eight years) accepted the theoretical right of the British crown to rule in Ireland. Not until the mid nineteenth century were Irishmen to rebel for a completely free and independent Ireland.

Under James I Catholic priests had been banned from travelling to Ireland, and fines had been imposed for non-attendance at Church of

Ireland services. Thus toleration for Catholics and the participation of Catholic clergymen were natural to the rebellion. The general English view that Catholics were natural traitors because the papal claim to the right to approve or depose rulers meant that they could not be equally loyal to two centres of authority, the pope and the king, seemed to be vindicated. But the rebellion was not religious, revolving simply around the question of the ownership of land. In May 1642 Catholic clergymen, the native Irish and the Old English leaders met and formed the 'Confederation of Kilkenny'. The Catholic primate of Ireland, Archbishop O'Reilly of Armagh, had taken the lead in forming the Confederation, giving the rebellion a moral and parliamentary framework, and declaring that they were waging a just war against Puritans 'who have always, but especially in recent years, plotted the destruction of the Catholics, the destruction of the Irish, and the abolition of the King's prerogatives'. A supreme council was set up in Kilkenny which acted as the rebels' government, and a general assembly – a parliament in all but name – was organized and met in October 1642, taking an oath to defend the Catholic faith and rights of the crown, and asserting that they were upholding the royal authority against the British parliament. The Confederation was plagued by internal arguments between the Old English who were worried about their security of title; the native Irish exiles who were worried that they had no lands at all, and the Catholic clergy who hoped for a religious war. Nevertheless, the Confederation maintained itself in common loyalty to the king and in military opposition to the Long parliament. And despite clerical pressure, the Kilkenny assembly consistently refused to discriminate against Protestants, preferring instead to concern itself with land ownership. Owen Roe O'Neill who had fled with his uncle Hugh O'Neill, the great earl of Tyrone, in 1607, and subsequently risen high in the service of Spain, returned to Ireland in the summer of 1642 to lead the Confederate forces. By the autumn of the year he controlled the whole country apart from Dublin, parts of Ulster and a handful of towns.

In Ulster, the outbreak of the rebellion in 1641 had been marked by the massacre or death from privation of about 12,000 Scottish and English planters. This was the result of indiscipline and the wreaking of private vengeance, not of policy; Sir Phelim O'Neill punished those of his soldiers found guilty of murder, and many times Catholic priests intervened to save planters' lives. Lurid accounts of atrocities soon circulated, and northern Irish Protestants felt justified in their siege mentality, of being surrounded and infiltrated by enemies. The myth that the wholesale extermination of Ulster Protestants was the purpose of the 1641 rebellion is still proclaimed in pulpits and platforms in Northern Ireland today. In 1646 a pamphleteer, Sir John Temple, claimed 300,000 people had been slaughtered – about three times more than the total Protestant population at the time – and his estimate rapidly entered Ulster Protestant folk memory. Twenty-eight years later, the founder of the Quakers, George Fox, visited Ireland and believed he could smell the victims' blood in the atmosphere: 'The earth and air smelt methought of the corruption of the nation, so that it yielded another smell to me than England did; which I imputed to be Popish massacres that had been committed, and the blood that had been spilt – from which a foulness ascended.' The historian Lecky over two hundred years later concluded that 'the Irish massacre of 1641 seems to me one of the great fictions of history, though a great number of murders were committee. The consensus of modern English historians, however, about it is so great that it is hardly possible to shake the belief in the English mind.'

The facts of massacre and the rumours of its extent and associated atrocities were seized upon by both sides in the developing English Civil War to raise money, to gain support and to justify the confiscation of more property. The Long parliament passed the Act for Adventurers in March 1641 which made available for purchase for plantation two and a half million acres of land all over Ireland. The idea of selling the rights to land in Ireland was also attractive to the king, desperately trying to raise money for his army. He had indicated his interest on several occasions by using the Confederate army against the English parliamentary army in Ireland, but after the Irish parliament had expelled Catholic MPs as rebels in June 1642, and the Confederation in reply demanded that the king repeal Poynings' Law and grant religious toleration, Charles I's options were limited and commercial exploitation of Irish land seemed to him, as it did to his opponents, a way of profiting from events in Ireland. It soon became clear, however, that investors had more faith in parliament's ability to fulfil its promises than in the king's, and so Charles instead chose to try and meet the Confederates' demands. He showed himself willing to compromise on nearly all the differences that lay between the Confederates and the crown, but found the intransigence of the increasingly clergy-dominated Confederates impossible to overcome. In February 1647 Charles' proposals for a settlement were rejected by the Kilkenny assembly, and the royal deputy, the earl of Ormond, decided to surrender Dublin (practically the only area under outright royal control) to the parliamentary forces preferring, as he said, 'English rebels to Irish rebels'. In 1649, after the English rebels had executed the king, the pacification of Ireland and the defeat of the Confederates was given priority by parliament, now dominated by Oliver Cromwell.

The presence of royalist garrisons, the Confederation of Kilkenny's royalist sympathies, and its antagonism to Protestantism, made the subduing of Ireland a priority in the eyes of Cromwell. Owen Roe O'Neill's army had proved at the battle of Benburb in 1646 that it was a formidable military force. During the battle, O'Neill's forces had killed over 3,000 Scottish soldiers of a parliamentary army, and had routed the remainder, winning a major victory which secured Ireland (temporarily) for the Confederates. On 15 August 1649, Cromwell, accompanied by 12,000 men of the New Model Army, landed at Ringsend, Dublin, to join the 8,000-strong parliamentary army which had successfully defended the city for over two and a half years. A month later on 11 September, he stormed the royalist stronghold of Drogheda, entering both the town and history with a vengeance.

The stories of enormous slaughter and of horrible atrocities at the outbreak of the Irish rebellion in Ulster in 1641 deeply impressed Cromwell and he apparently accepted the most evil motivations on the part of the rebels. He came to Ireland determined to establish the authority and government of the Long parliament's English 'Commonwealth' over Ireland; to enforce the 1642 Act for Adventurers by repaying investors with Irish lands, and to avenge the Ulster massacre of 1641. This last purpose seems to have dominated his thoughts at Drogheda where, having successfully besieged the town, on his orders the 2,600 men of the royalist garrison were put to the sword. Townspeople were also slaughtered. Cromwell reported that 'We put to the sword the whole number of defendants. I do not think thirty of the whole number escaped with their lives.' He went on to justify his action as 'a righteous judgement of God upon those barbarous wretches who have imbrued their hands in so much innocent blood' and argued that 'it will tend to prevent the effusion of blood for the future'.

Seventeenth-century rules of warfare allowed the slaughter of garrisons who unsuccessfully defended a town after refusing to surrender. This had happened during the English Civil War, although it was rare. But the killings at Drogheda were recognised by all as excessive. By his own testimony, supported by many others, Cromwell admitted that the slaughter was indiscriminate. He even made a convoluted attempt to blame the Irish themselves for his excesses, stating in a broadsheet he had printed in Cork in January 1650, 'You, unprovoked, put the English to the most unheard of and most barbarous massacre (without respect of sex or age) that ever the sun beheld.'

From Drogheda, Cromwell went on to Wexford (the royalist garrisons of Trim and Dundalk deserted their posts as soon as they heard what had happened at Drogheda) and on 11 October 1649 conducted another slaughter as ferocious as the first. Terror worked. New Ross surrendered to him without a fight on 19 October, followed by most of the towns in Munster. Owen Roe O'Neill, realizing that a united Confederate–royalist resistance was the only hope of defeating Cromwell, was attempting to make an alliance with the Irish royalist commander, the earl of Ormond, when he died in November. O'Neill's death removed the only military leader who might have faced Cromwell with any hope of success. By July 1650, Commonwealth armies were in command of all Ireland except Connaught.

The ferocious and ruthless slaughter that Cromwell conducted at Drogheda and Wexford was an act of policy. It was fundamentally different from the 1641 Ulster massacre which was the result of indiscipline. In the Irish popular memory, where myths are often as important as facts, in contrast to the events of 1641 Cromwell's activities need no embellishment.

Cromwell returned to England in May 1650 and next tackled Ireland legislatively. Three years later, on 2 March 1653, the British 'Rump parliament' voted to unify Ireland with Britain, abolished the Irish parliament and allowed for thirty Irish members in a new British parliament of 460 MPs. Further acts decreed the transplantation of Irish landowners to the inhospitable terrain of Connaught and Co. Clare. Their lands were sequestered for adventurers and demobilized parliamentary soldiers. Over eleven million acres were confiscated in the interests of about 1,000 adventurers and 35,000 soldiers. Irish landowners found east of the river Shannon after 1 May 1654 faced the death penalty or slavery in the West Indies and Barbados. About 44,000 people moved west into Connaught in the winter of 1653–4. It was not an exodus of the entire native population: as in previous plantations and confiscations, many stayed behind to become labourers and brigands (or 'Tories' as they were called). Still, 'To Hell or Connaught' became a proverbial phrase among later generations of Irishmen as a result of the Cromwellian plantations. In 1685, at the accession of King James II, only 22 per cent of the land of Ireland was owned by Catholic Irishmen.

The new settlers faced the same problems as previous planters and adventurers. It is thought that less than a quarter of the soldiers granted lands actually settled in Ireland: most preferred to sell their rights instead. The need for native labour to sustain the plantation meant that in practice there was a drift east of cheap Irish labour, back across the Shannon from Connaught. As with previous settlers, the Cromwellian planters were gradually to become Irishmen themselves. Only in the north where there was a considerable number of settlers from earlier plantations did differences remain, sustained by strong anti-Catholic Protestantism, the result of the Calvinistic quality of Cromwellians augmented by the powerful myths of the 1641 massacres.

4

Penal times

When the monarchy was restored in Britain in 1660, there was a general expectation that Cromwell's land settlement would be reversed. The Irish parliament was re-established, and the union between Ireland and England ended. Some royalists like Ormond had their lands returned, but Charles II refused substantially to alter the Cromwellian plantations. He realized that he owed his throne to those who had been leaders under Cromwell, and he rewarded them with promotions and security. In 1672, mid-way through Charles II's reign, Cromwellian settlers owned four and a half million of the twelve million profitable acres Ireland then had. Catholics owned three and a half million, and pre-Cromwellian settlers (mostly in Ulster) the rest. When the professedly Catholic James II succeeded his brother in 1685, many Catholics in Ireland thought that at last there would be a settlement of land-ownership in their favour. Instead, James' insistence upon his prerogative at the expense of parliament generated another English civil war. William, Prince of Orange and ruler of the Netherlands, the grandson of Charles I of England as well as James II's son-in-law, a Protestant, in 1688 was invited with his wife, Mary, to become joint sovereign of Britain by James' ecclesiastical and parliamentary opponents. He accepted, invaded England and defeated James who, after the defeat of the Scots loyalists at the battle of Killiecrankie in June 1689, only could look to his Irish kingdom and King Louis XIV of France for help.

In March 1689 James landed at Kinsale with a small French army, and was greeted throughout the country as the lawful monarch. He soon assembled an Irish army composed of loyalists, Catholic and Protestant, prepared to face a British Protestant government. For the first time since Hugh O'Neill's rebellion a century earlier, Irishmen of all sorts were acting together as a nation. This time, however, they were not in rebellion: they were supporting an English king in his attempt to regain his throne. This placed settlers in Ulster in particular in a dilemma. As devout Protestants, they were frightened by the Catholic James whose arrival in Ireland raised the spectre of the 1641 massacres again. On the other hand, they were also loyal to the crown and recognized that James was their legitimate king. When James sent a garrison north to Londonderry, the town's leading men, including the Protestant Church of Ireland bishop of Londonderry and the military commander, Colonel Robert Lundy, decided that the king's forces should be allowed in. However, some of the townspeople were more alarmed than their leaders by the prospect of a Catholic (although royalist) garrison taking over. The apprentice boys – youths and young men apprenticed to trades – were often Presbyterians, not conforming to the Anglican Church of Ireland, and thus on the counts of age and inclination more likely to disregard established authority. Just before James' troops arrived, thirteen apprentice boys took matters into their own hands and slammed the gates of Londonderry shut on 7 December 1688. By the boldness of their action they swung opinion in their favour. Colonel Lundy had to escape from the town in disguise, and his name has been a word of derision in northern Ireland ever since. From April the following year, James laid siege to the town, cutting it off completely. Finally, on 28 July 1689 a Williamite fleet led by the ship *Mountjoy* breached the boom placed across the river Foyle by James' men, and relieved the town in the nick of time since starvation was forcing its surrender. 'No Surrender' had been the apprentice boys' cry, and 'No Surrender' has remained the Protestant watchword in northern Ireland ever since.

In May 1689, two months before Londonderry was relieved, James had summoned what has become known as the 'Patriot parliament' in Dublin. It was the last Irish parliament until 1921 to have Catholic members (224 out of the 230 members of the Irish house of commons were Catholic), and its main concern was to legislate in the interests of those landlords who had been expropriated by Cromwell. It was an Anglo-Irish assembly defending the Anglo-Irish Catholic governing class penalized by the Cromwellian settlement; it was not concerned to seek redress for the poorer native Irish classes labouring on the farms and estates of landlords and planters. However, the parliament's activities were overtaken by events. James and William met in battle on the banks of the river Boyne on 1 July 1690 (which became 12 July when the calendar was changed in the eighteenth century). James was defeated and fled to France where he died in 1701, never setting foot in the British Isles again.

Irish resistance to William continued for over a year after the battle of the Boyne. An Irish army, 14,000 strong, commanded by some French generals sent by Louis XIV, and Patrick Sarsfield, an Irish soldier trained in France who had served in James II's Life Guards, continued to harry Williamite forces in the south. At Limerick in October 1691, Sarsfield and his colleagues surrendered with the Treaty of Limerick. It was an honourable Treaty, guaranteeing the rights and property of the men of the defeated army in return for their loyalty to King William and Queen Mary. Those who wished were allowed to sail into exile. Along with 11,000 officers and men, Sarsfield chose exile. There were already 5,000 Irish soldiers in France in the Irish Brigade of the French army, exiles from previous campaigns, and Sarsfield and his followers joined them. James created Sarsfield earl of Lucan in 1691, and Louis XIV appointed him a marshal of the French army. Two years later he was mortally wounded fighting for France against William of Orange at the battle of Landen in Flanders. 'Oh, that this were for Ireland!' he is reported to have said as he watched himself bleeding to death.

The Irish Brigade was soon christened the 'Wild Geese', and for generations to come Irishmen were to flock to the Brigade's colours as opportunities were denied them at home. Irish Brigades were formed in other European armies too. Fourteen Irishmen became field marshals in the Austrian army. It has been estimated that nearly one million Irishmen left their country to join these Brigades in the century after 1691. Count Peter de Lacy (1678–1751), born in Limerick, became a general in the Russian army and governor of Livonia. Don Alexander O'Reilly (1725–94), born in Ireland, became a Spanish field marshal and governor of Spanish Louisiana. The nineteenth-century President MacMahon of France traced his descent directly to an eighteenth-century Irish exile.

William's victory placed power in Ireland firmly in the hands of the Anglican 'Ascendancy' governing class. They were the group with governmental experience in Ireland, and they also enjoyed the most powerful connections with political and ecclesiastical leaders in

England. In addition, within their number were the richest land-lords in Ireland. By the close of the seventeenth century, Catholics in Ireland had had their landholdings reduced to 14 per cent of the useful land – a third less than when James II had come to the throne. The Ascendancy were to prove as anxious as Cromwell to secure the Protestant religion and to obtain more land.

In 1695 the Ascendancy-dominated Irish parliament began the legislation against Catholics known as the Penal Laws. Completed in 1727, the laws lasted for over a century. They were similar to anti-Catholic legislation in Britain, and were modelled on the anti-Protestant legislation of Louis XIV in France. But unlike Britain and France where the persecuted group was a minority, in Ireland they were the majority. Religion was used as a cloak for economic expropriation. In this, the Irish parliament was supported fully by the Westminster parliament which employed Poynings' Law to confirm its supremacy, making parliament in Dublin an adjunct of its power. At first, Irish MPs were satisfied with this relationship. They were colonists and, just like colonists in America, all they wanted of Britain was military and legal support for their schemes of exploitation. Later on, just as in America, Irish parliamentarians were to resent their subservience to Britain as their financial successes were perceived at Westminster as threatening British merchants' and landowners' interests. When that time came, what was rarely admitted was that they owed their wealth to the economic licence granted by the Penal Laws.

By 1701, Ireland had been effectively conquered. Wars, military campaigns and plantations affected most of the country and had succeeded in establishing British law and British government in all areas. Hugh O'Neill's rebellion had been the last stand of Gaelic Ireland which began to wither with his defeat. By 1641 Irish rebels possessed a different perspective: the Confederation of Kilkenny accepted the right of the crown to govern Ireland, complaining only about the nature of the government. After the Treaty of Limerick, the majority of Irishmen who still regarded themselves as Gaelic left their country for good. A large part of the Wild Geese was composed of native Irish and Old English noble families: thousands left Ireland between 1690 and 1730, removing the last barrier between the Irish people and their foreign rulers. The eighteenth century in Ireland completed the process of subjugation as the Penal

Laws witnessed the end of the ancient Gaelic order and the reduction to peasanthood of the Irish nation.

The first Penal Law ordered that no Catholic could have 'gun, pistol or sword, or any other weapon of offence or defence under penalty of fine, imprisonment, pillory or public whipping'. Over the next thirty years, a host of such laws were passed by the Irish parliament. The 1697 Banishment Act ordered all Catholic bishops and clergymen to leave Ireland. Catholics were forbidden to inherit land from Protestants; from taking leases of more than thirty-one years; from buying land or enjoying mortgages. Catholic land-owners were required to will their lands to all their sons equally unless one of them became a Church of Ireland Anglican, in which case he would inherit all the land. The 1704 Registration Act required priests to be registered, only one to each parish, and to take an oath of allegiance to the crown. The Irish privy council even attempted to secure legislation to castrate unregistered priests 'which they are persuaded will be the most effectual remedy', an indication of the virulent anti-Catholicism that held sway in Protestant Ireland. Other Acts were passed which prevented Catholics entering a profession or receiving a formal education. In 1727 they were denied the vote in parliamentary elections. Together, the laws worked through religion to suppress the Irish nation, clearly stating the Ascendancy's identification of Catholicism with nationalism in Ireland. Edmund Burke, in a famous phrase, described the laws as 'a machine of wise and elaborate contrivance, as well fitted for the oppression, impoverishment and degradation of a people, and the debasement in them of human nature itself, as ever proceeded from the perverted ingenuity of man'. By the reign of George I, the Irish lord chancellor was able to say 'The law does not suppose any such person to exist as an Irish Roman Catholic.'

It was one thing to pass laws; it was another to enforce them. The main purpose of the Penal Laws was to prevent any Catholic Irish challenge to the Ascendancy's control, so they were only really invoked when there were signs of trouble. This happened in 1714 when Louis XIV recognized James II's son as King James III of England, Scotland and Ireland, and in 1715 when there was a Stuart rebellion in Scotland. By the time George III came to the throne in 1760, however, it was clear that there would be no Stuart restoration, and the laws had fallen into general disuse. In 1766, Bonnie Prince Charles, the successor of James 'III', was denied recognition as king by the pope. In 1774 the unstitching of the laws began with an act allowing Catholics to take an oath of allegiance. By then, the laws had succeeded in reducing the land owned by avowedly Catholic landowners to 5 per cent.

There had been another effect as well. The Penal Laws had discriminated against all those who were not members of the Anglican Church of Ireland, so Dissenters suffered together with Catholics. Thus Presbyterian ministers, like Catholic priests, were unable to perform legal marriage ceremonies. Like everyone else in Ireland, they also had to pay the tithe to the Church of Ireland. The 1704 Act against popery had included a clause requiring government office-holders and members of parliament to belong to the Church of Ireland, thus debarring Dissenters as well as Catholics from office and from politics. Dissenters were, however, able to inherit land and property and take part in most of the activities of the state. During the eighteenth century, the industrious and numerous Presbyterians in Ulster became wealthy and influential as they developed their agricultural holdings and textile industries, and increasingly resented their second-class status. Thousands of Ulster Dissenters – an average of 4,000 a year throughout the eighteenth century – preferred to emigrate to America or back to Britain, providing the first wave of transatlantic Irish immigrants. Catholic emigration remained small because until 1780 they faced discrimination on religious grounds in the colonies too. 'The Presbyterians of the North', wrote the viceroy, Lord Harcourt in 1775, 'are in their hearts Americans.' Ten presidents of the United States and various legendary frontiersmen have been descended from Ulster Protestant stock, including Davy Crockett, Stonewall Jackson, Ulysses S. Grant and Woodrow Wilson.

The Irish Dissenters who did not emigrate gradually came as the eighteenth century progressed to identify more with their Catholic countrymen than with their British governors. By the end of the eighteenth century, as a result of this common political and religious discrimination (and because of free-thinking non-conformist traditions), many of the leaders of Irish nationalist movements were northern Irish Presbyterians. This continued even into the nineteenth century as well, changing only when the currents of religious and economic differences were exploited for political purposes, returning northern Protestants to their separate identity in Ireland.

William III was always more moderate than his parliaments in his attitude towards the Irish and religion. He had personally taken steps to ensure that the Treaty of Limerick was implemented fairly, and he resisted penal legislation. During the reign of his successor and sister-in-law, Anne (1702–14), however, the Anglican Ascendancy in Ireland secured the harsh discriminatory legislation they wanted to protect their political and economic supremacy against what they saw as the resentful, Catholic and pro-Stuart Irish. The determination with which they pursued their security was, however, undermined by parliament at Westminster. The British parliament since the early seventeenth century had set itself the purpose of protecting British agricultural, commercial and mercantile interests against both the crown and foreign and colonial competition. It was a parliament of lawyers, landowners and businessmen. In 1696 despite Irish Ascendancy protests, an Act was passed prohibiting goods from the colonies being exported directly to Ireland. In 1699 an Act placed heavy duties on Irish woollen goods and allowed them only to be exported to England, thus forcing a monopoly buyer. Since the English wool industry was threatened by Irish wool, this legislation effectively crushed the Irish industry. Linen weaving was allowed because it did not compete with any English counterpart. In 1719 a Declaratory Act complemented Poynings' Law and confirmed the right of the British parliament to legislate for Ireland, thus stripping the Irish parliament of any real power. These Acts were not the consequence of official British policy towards Ireland, but of particular economic interests at Westminster. Nevertheless, the significance of these measures of economic and political discrimination against Ascendancy interests in Ireland was constitutional, stirring an awareness amongst all sections in Ireland that their status was inferior to their counterparts in England. William Molyneux (1656–98), an Irish Anglican philosopher and friend of John Locke, as MP for Trinity College, Dublin, published his famous *The case of Ireland's being bound by Acts of Parliament in England stated*. Molyneux anticipated later Ascendancy (and American) politicians who applied his observations rather more widely than he intended. He argued that England and Ireland were separate kingdoms bound by a common crown, and that therefore Ireland had as much right as England to legislative and commercial independence. 'I have no other notion of slavery', he wrote, 'but being bound by a law to which I do not consent.' By order of the Westminster house of commons, his pamphlet was burned in public by the common hangman.

The Anglican Church of Ireland was a minority faith, ministering to only about one-sixth of the population and completely identified with the ruling Ascendancy class. It made very little effort to proselytize until the nineteenth century, and its members proved content to remain in a minority as long as they ruled the country. The Church itself and its clergy were made comfortable by the tithe, and the appointment to an Irish bishopric could make an Anglican clergyman wealthy. At the same time, the supremacy of Irish Anglicans was fragile. Some like William King (1650–1729), Church of Ireland archbishop of Dublin, were conscious of the faults and weaknesses of their position. 'The world', King wrote, 'begins to look on us as a parcel of men who have invented a trade for our easy and convenient living.' But even Archbishop King, while striving to make his Church popular, still supported Penal Laws as the best means of securing the Ascendancy's political and economic position.

The fears of the Ascendancy for their position in Ireland could be justified. The Stuart pretenders to the British crown provided a rallying point for Catholics and the prospect of French and Spanish intervention in support of the Stuarts. Mindful of this danger, during the Scottish campaign of Charles Edward Stuart, Bonnie Prince Charlie, in 1745 and 1746, the Irish government suspended some of the Penal Laws as a way of encouraging popular opinion in Ireland against him. There was also the constant reminder in the French army's Irish Brigade of native Irish antipathy to Britain and the Ascendancy. The Brigade enjoyed a constant supply of Irish recruits throughout the eighteenth century. At the Battle of Fontenoy on 11 May 1745 during the War of the Austrian Succession, the Brigade led by Lord Clare, shouting 'Remember Limerick', led the successful counterattack on the Coldstream Guards and turned the battle into a French victory. In 1756, revealing the fear that the Irish Brigade might one day fight in Ireland, the Ascendancy Irish parliament passed an Act imposing the death penalty on any native-born Irishmen who returned to Ireland after fighting for France. This had no effect on Irish emigrants seeking military service in the French army. A regiment of the Irish Brigade under Count Dillon fought for George Washington during the American Revolution. During the French revolution, the Brigade sided with the crown. Count Daniel O'Connell, the last commander of the Brigade, even offered its services against the Revolution to King George III. After Napoleon's defeat at Waterloo, Louis XVIII of France dissolved the Brigade.

Irish exiles served in other armies too. Ambrose O'Higgins, born in Co. Meath in 1720, entered Spanish military service and became viceroy of Peru where he died in 1801. His natural son, Bernardo O'Higgins, became the liberator and national hero of Chile and its first president. John Barry (1745–1803), born in Co. Wexford, emigrated to the American colonies and founded the American navy. In command of the brig *Lexington* in 1776 he captured the navy's first warship, HMS *Edward*. Richard Hennessy (1720–1800), born in Co. Cork, fought at Fontenoy, settled in Cognac and founded the famous Hennessy distillery. The success of men like these contrasted with the poverty, lethargy and suppression of their kinsmen in Ireland. They also showed that Irishmen were naturally capable of effective and enterprising organization, and were not necessarily inferior to the Ascendancy. Jonathan Swift drew attention to this contrast, commenting upon the achievements of Irishmen in foreign armies, 'which ought to make the English ashamed of the reproaches they cast on the ignorance, the dullness and the want of courage of the Irish natives; those defects, wherever they happen, arising only from the poverty and slavery they suffer from their inhuman neighbours'. The Ascendancy's 'inhuman' attitudes, reflected in the Penal Laws, also governed their behaviour.

The nobility and gentry of England provided a model for the Ascendancy. The elegant Georgian architecture of so many Irish towns and cities, and the beautiful country mansions like Castletown House and Carton House, of which Ireland today is justly proud, were all built during the eighteenth century by Ascendancy land-lords. The duke of Leinster, with an income of £20,000 a year from his Irish estates, built a town house in Dublin – Leinster House – with grounds so large that it now contains both houses of the Irish parliament – Dail and Seanad Eireann – the National Library, the National Museum and the National Gallery of Ireland. The Ascendancy middle class also prospered. Arthur Guinness (1725–1803) made a fortune by introducing 'Guinness's black Protestant porter', making his name and symbol, the harp, synonymous today with Ireland. Throughout, however, the Ascendancy remained a colonial class which unlike previous British ruling classes in Ireland never came fully to identify with the country. Jealous and nervous of their position, they soon developed distinctions of their own. Sir Jonah Barrington, writing in 1827, sharply observed Ascendancy Ireland, perceiving three sorts of Irish gentry: 'half-mounted gentlemen', 'gentlemen every inch of them', and 'gentlemen to the backbone'. The 'half-mounted', according to Sir Jonah, were on familiar terms with their servants and tended to carry lead-weighted whips with which they beat incautious peasants. The other categories of gentlemen tended to leave the professions and trade to the middle classes, and concentrated on farming their estates. Arthur Young, the essayist, agricultural experimenter and surveyor, spent from 1776 to 1778 in Ireland, noting:

A landlord in Ireland can scarcely invent an order which a servant, labourer, or cottier dares to refuse to execute. Disrespect or anything tending towards sauciness he may punish with his cane or his horsewhip with the most perfect security. . .Landlords of consequence have assured me that many of their cottiers would think themselves honoured by having their wives or daughters sent for to the bed of their masters, a mark of slavery that proves the oppression under which such people live.

The conditions of life for the vast majority of people in Ireland varied considerably. Many lived in squalor, while others were more prosperous. But there were gross disparities which, together with the restrictive Westminster legislation offending Ascendancy sensibilities, combined to produce not only a sense of separateness on the part of the Ascendancy, but also devastating criticism from within the ruling class. One man, more than any other, is identified with this critical voice: Jonathan Swift (1667–1745), Anglican dean of St Patrick's Cathedral, Dublin.

Swift was an unexpected critic and lampooner of his own class. Born in Dublin, he graduated from Trinity College and became secretary to the Williamite statesman, Sir William Temple. In 1694 he was ordained a clergyman in the Church of England, and over the next two decades developed a reputation in London as a wit and conversationalist. In 1704 he published two books anonymously, *A tale of a tub* and *The battle of the books*. He came to support the pro-Stuart faction in British politics – the Tories – writing broadsheets and articles in their cause. He also made the mistake of not hiding from his contemporaries his brilliant intellect and biting wit, with the consequence that he was not trusted. When his patron,

Robert Harley, became chancellor of the exchequer in 1710, Swift hoped for advancement and even a bishopric, but was disappointed, and in 1713 he accepted the best offer that was made to him and became dean of St Patrick's. He regarded this as banishment. With the eclipse of the Tories by the Whigs at Queen Anne's death the following year, Swift's hopes for recognition ended, and he spent the rest of his life in Ireland. As a result of his disappointment, but also because of his experience as dean, Swift became the arch exponent of anti-governmental political satire in Ireland. Two years before his appointment as dean, he wrote to a correspondent, 'You are in the right as to my indifference to Irish affairs, which is not occasioned by my absence but contempt of them.' By 1720 he was acutely interested in Irish affairs, publishing anonymously a pamphlet opposing the 1719 Declaratory Act and advocating resistance to it by boycotting English imports and buying only Irish goods. In 1724 he wrote the *Drapier's letters* – his authorship was an open secret – which played a large part in preventing 'Wood's Halfpence', the corrupt introduction of a new copper coinage to Ireland, arguing that 'government without the consent of the governed is the very definition of slavery'. Three years later in *A short view of the present state of Ireland* he singled out the practice of absentee landlordism, estimating that half the net revenues of Ireland were taken out of the country and spent in Britain. Ever increasing rents, the source of most revenue, Swift declared, 'is squeezed out of the very blood, and vitals, and clothes, and dwellings of the tenants, who live worse than English beggars'.

In 1729 Swift published his classical masterpiece of savage irony, *A modest proposal for preventing the children of poor people from being a burden to their parents or the country, and for making them beneficial to the public.* In this pamphlet he suggested that poor and rich alike might benefit by the sale of poor children as food for the rich, 'a most delicious, nourishing and wholesome food'. His most famous work, *Gulliver's travels*, which he wrote in his own name and published in 1726, was a thinly disguised political satire. It gained him celebrity and popularity, and while it does not deal with Ireland, its rage at misery and depravity must have been culled from Swift's Irish experiences, and analogies with Lilliput and Brobding-nag are to be found in early Irish folktales. Swift, no doubt to his own amusement, has rightly been regarded as an Irish patriot.

A contemporary and friend of Swift, the philosopher George

Berkeley (1685–1753), born near Kilkenny, became Church of Ireland bishop of Cloyne and a leading spokesman for reform in Ireland. In 1736 in the *Querist* journal he published articles in which he rhetorically wondered 'whether a foreigner could imagine that one half of the people were starving in a country which sent out such plenty of provisions?' and 'whether it be not a vain attempt to project the flourishing of our Protestant gentry, exclusive of the bulk of the natives?'. He had lived for some years in the American colony of Rhode Island where he had owned Negro slaves. 'The negroes', he wrote, 'in our Plantations have a saying "If negro was not a negro, Irishman would be negro." And it may be affirmed with truth that the very savages of America are better clad and better lodged than the Irish cottagers.'

Ascendancy Ireland produced other noted literary and political figures during the eighteenth century. Edmund Burke (1729–97), born in Dublin to a Protestant solicitor and a Catholic mother, educated in a Quaker school in Co. Kildare and at Trinity College, Dublin, where he was a founder of the college's historical society, eventually became a Whig member of the Westminster parliament for various English constituencies, making his home in London. Between 1780 and 1792 he wrote three pamphlets on Ireland, arguing for conciliation rather than coercion, drawing parallels with the revolt of the American colonists, and stating that insensitive handling of colonial aspirations by Britain was the cause of opposition to the British government in both places. His most famous work, *Reflections on the revolution in France*, published in 1790 towards the end of his life, argued for more reactionary policies. It also provoked Thomas Paine to write his *Rights of man* in reply. Burke's political thought, together with Benjamin Disraeli's, was to become the philosophy of modern British conservatism. Two playwrights, Oliver Goldsmith (1728–74) and Richard Brinsley Sheridan (1751–1816), both born in Ireland and, like Burke, graduates of Trinity College, Dublin, also made their careers in London. Goldsmith's *She stoops to conquer* (1773) and Sheridan's *The school for scandal* (1777) are amongst the most frequently performed plays in the English language. Sheridan served as a Whit MP for Stafford for thirty-two years from 1780. Unlike Burke, he admired the principles of the French Revolution. He eloquently opposed the Act of Union between Britain and Ireland in 1800.

Beneath the surface of privileged, wealthy Ascendancy society, a vibrant but hidden Gaelic Ireland survived. No longer enjoying political power, and denied its natural leaders through emigration, Gaelic Ireland clung to what it could: its language, customs and lore. When scrutinized by its rulers, it would seem to conform to the rules and regulations which bound its submission, but when alone it maintained its self-awareness and essential independence of spirit. The successors to the ancient brehons, bards and scholars – the Gaelic poets of the seventeenth and eighteenth centuries – were vital to the survival of a Gaelic world after the Flight of the Earls. They developed the 'aisling' form of poetry (all in the Irish language, difficult to capture in English translation). Couched in terms of lament, reflecting the Gaelic perception of their condition compared to their exploits in the past and the achievements of contemporary exiles, aisling poetry generally presents a vision of a beautiful maiden (symbolizing Ireland) pining for the return of her lover who will rescue her from her sorrow (a reflection of the state of Ireland under foreign rule). Eogan O'Rahilly (1670–1726) is one of the few Gaelic poets of this period whose name has come down to us. His poems, and those of others, possess a quality which places them on a par with the metaphysical and romantic poetry of Britain. O'Rahilly's 'The reverie', superbly translated by Frank O'Connor, is a masterpiece of the aisling art:

> One morning before Titan thought of stirring his feet
> I climbed alone to a hill where the air was kind,
> And saw a throng of magical girls go by
> That had lived to the north in Croghan time out of mind.
>
> All over the land from Galway to Cork of the ships,
> It seemed that a bright enchanted mist came down,
> Acorns on oaks and clear cold honey on stones,
> Fruit upon every tree from root to crown.
>
> They lit three candles that shone in the mist like stars
> On a high hilltop in Connello and then were gone,
> But I followed through Thomond the track of the hooded Queens
> And asked them the cause of the zeal of their office at dawn.
>
> The tall Queen, Euvul, so bright of countenance, said
> 'The reason we light three candles on every strand
> Is to guide the king that will come to us over the sea
> And make us happy and reign in a fortunate land.'

And then, so suddenly did I start from my sleep,
They seemed to be true, and the words that had been so sweet –
It was just that my soul was sick and spent with grief
One morning before Titan thought of stirring his feet.

Nationalistic themes provided the material for all these poets. In bardic schools in the seventeenth century, and in their smaller successors, the courts of poetry in the first half of the eighteenth century, native Irish poets met and determined the style and subject-matter of poems to be submitted to the next school or court. This gave Gaelic poems a special coherence, centring on personal and national misfortunes, extolling the virtues of native pride.

An Irish Romantic poet of another tradition, Thomas Moore (1779–1852), was as popular during his lifetime as his friend Lord Byron. His poems – which included 'The minstrel boy', 'The harp that once through Tara's Halls' and 'The meeting of the waters' – gained him recognition as the national poet of Ireland, and remain favourite expressions of Irish feeling.

The other principal expression of Irish feeling apart from poetry during the eighteenth century took the form of agrarian unrest. A great deal of misconstruction has surrounded the landlord–tenant relationship in Ireland, and too much significance has often been given to absentee landlordism. The simple fact is that the mass of the people – the peasantry – remembered that their ancestors had owned the land themselves relatively recently, and so there was always pressure for improvement. Estates were often well managed and profitable: between the 1720s and 1770s rent income perhaps trebled. Rents to absentees, as a proportion of the total, fell in the same period from between a fourth and a sixth to an eighth. Professional estate managers were frequently concerned with the welfare of tenants, and did much to prevent a state of suppressed land war throughout the country. Tenants with farms of one hundred to one hundred and fifty acres were common, and some tenants had four thousand and even ten thousand acres. As a result, while there was still a great deal of agrarian violence, it was usually prompted by specific causes: demands for tenant-right by name did not occur. Only in the nineteenth century did tenants' rights become the main feature of agrarian agitation, with demands for security of tenure and compensation for improvements at the fore.

Secret, oathbound peasant/tenant societies sprang up as the

instruments of agrarian unrest during the later eighteenth century. The Munster 'Whiteboys', formed around 1760, were the earliest such group, motivated by the enclosure of common lands. Named after their white shirts, the Whiteboys terrorized landlords in the south and west, murdering, robbing, burning crops and houses and maiming cattle. The 'Oakboys' in the north in the 1760s and their successors, the 'Steelboys' in the 1770s, were Presbyterian societies, similar to the Whiteboys and using the same methods, formed to resist increased rent and rate demands. Common to all these societies was opposition to the tithe paid to the Anglican, Established Church of Ireland. But because they lacked coordination and educated leadership, and were formed to resist specific, regional complaints, these societies never gained the dignity of national movements. What was important, however, was that through common distress, Catholics and Dissenters became aware of common objectives which were to help form the alliance which attempted national revolt in 1798.

The American (1775) and then the French (1789) Revolutions fused popular complaints in Ireland to political agitation, sparking a renewed national resurgence. The debates and arguments surrounding both revolutions had an electric effect on the British and Irish political and intellectual worlds. Many of the complaints of the American colonists were echoed by the Ascendancy in Ireland, neatly summed up by Jonathan Swift:

Were not the people of Ireland born as free as those of England? Is not their Parliament as fair and as representative of the people as that of England? Are they subjects of the same King? Does not the same sun shine on them? And have they not the same God for their protector? Am I a free man in England, and do I become a slave in six hours by crossing the Channel?

Military requirements presented the first opportunity for political reform in Ireland. The removal of Irish regiments to the American colonies in the 1770s means that the government had fewer resources to call upon, and thus forced a more conciliatory approach to calls for reform. In 1778 the American privateer, Paul Jones, raided Belfast Lough and seized a Royal Navy ship. All the viceroy could offer to Belfast citizens who appealed for protection was half a troop of unmounted cavalry and half a company of invalids. Merchants and industrialists wanted an end to the trading restrictions they had faced since the reign of William III. The Ascendancy wanted the freedom to govern Ireland without Westminster interference, and

Catholics and Dissenters wanted religious toleration. In 1779, George III's government agreed to the removal of many of the duties which hampered Irish trade. At the same time, the Irish parliament decided that the government's military weakness in Ireland made relaxation of the Penal Laws advisable. The Irish parliament's 'Gardiner's' Act of 1778 allowed Catholics to buy land freely for the first time in nearly a century. In 1780 the Test Acts preventing Dissenters taking part in politics were repealed. In 1782 the Ascendancy won their principal demand and obtained Westminster's agreement to repeal Poynings' Law and the 1719 Declaratory Act, thus obtaining for the Irish parliament the right to legislate for Ireland directly. In 1783 parliament at Westminster passed a Renunciation Act giving up its claims to legislate for Ireland.

The Ascendancy's demands had been spearheaded by the Irish Volunteers, a militia formed in 1779 nominally to defend Ireland against French invasion, but also to press the British government and Westminster for reform. They were led by three Anglican Irish parliamentarians, Henry Grattan (1746–1820), Henry Flood (1732–91) and the earl of Charlemont (1728–99); all three also led a 'Patriot Party' in the Irish parliament demanding greater rights for the Ascendancy. Within a year of their formation, forty thousand Irish Volunteers (all Protestants: Catholics were still not allowed to carry arms) – 'the armed property of the nation' as Grattan called them – were drilling in public. After securing the independence of the Irish parliament in 1782, Grattan hailed the 'King, Lords and Commons' of Ireland in national terms:

I found Ireland on her knees. I watched over her with an eternal solicitude; I have traced her progress from injuries to arms and from arms to liberty. Spirit of Swift! Spirit of Molyneux! Your genius has prevailed! Ireland is now a nation. In that new character I hail her!

He spoke accurately both for himself and for the Ascendancy, but his perception was not shared by the mass of the Irish people. They still faced economic, social, political and religious discrimination, and the Irish parliament for which Grattan and his Patriots campaigned was the institution of Ascendancy domination. As Gustave de Beaumont was to note some decades later about the Ascendancy: 'They said that they were Ireland and they ended by believing it.' Grattan himself realized that the Irish nation consisted of far more than the Ascendancy, and he urged both religious toleration and political representation for Catholics. 'The Irish Protestant', he declared, 'could never be free till the Irish Catholic had ceased to be a slave . . . I should be ashamed of giving freedom to but six hundred thousand of my fellow-countrymen when I could extend it to two million more.' In 1796 he proposed in the Irish house of commons to allow Catholics to become MPs, but was defeated by 143 votes to 19. Dejected and in bad health, he resigned his seat the following year. He returned to politics to oppose the union of Britain and Ireland, and spent the rest of his life campaigning for Catholic emancipation. His career was a testament to the fact that Irish history cannot be seen as purely Catholic versus Protestant, but is another example of nationalist sentiment coming from the advantaged side.

Unlike Grattan, most of the Ascendancy were concerned simply to strengthen their position as the rulers and owners of the country. Henry Flood in 1783 defended the Penal Laws on the grounds that 'ninety years ago four-fifths of Ireland were for King James. They were defeated. I rejoice in that defeat. The laws that followed were not laws of persecution; they were a political necessity', and argued against political toleration for Catholics on the grounds that Catholic Ireland would use political power to undermine the constitutional link with Britain.

The refusal of the Ascendancy to extend the rights they claimed for themselves to their Catholic and Dissenting countrymen – at a time when American and French cries for 'Liberty, Equality and Fraternity' filled the intellectual and political air – generated popular rebellion led from an unexpected quarter: a combination of radical Anglicans and northern Irish Dissenters. The leader of this new nationalism was a young man, Theobald Wolfe Tone (1763–98), the son of a Dublin Anglican coachmaker. He graduated from Trinity College and was called to the Irish Bar in 1789. He quickly tired of law, and fired with enthusiasm for the principles of the American and French Revolutions, he turned to politics instead. In Belfast in 1791 he formed the Society of the United Irishmen aiming for religious equality for all and political reform, and published a pamphlet, *An argument on behalf of the Catholics of Ireland*, in which he elaborated the Society's objectives in an effort to convert Dissenters to his views. In his *Autobiography* he explained:

To subvert the tyranny of our execrable government, to break the connection with England, the never failing source of all our political evils and to assert the independence of my country – these were my objects. To unite the whole people of Ireland, to abolish the memory of all past dissensions, and to substitute the common name of Irishman in place of the denominations of Protestant, Catholic and Dissenter – these were my means.

His supporters included men like Henry Joy McCracken, a Belfast Presbyterian textile manufacturer, and Lord Edward Fitzgerald, who was cashiered from the British army for proposing a republican toast at a Paris banquet in 1792. In 1792 Tone organized a Catholic Convention of elected delegates which petitioned for political and religious toleration. The prime minister, William Pitt the younger (1759–1806), faced by the looming threat of war with France, decided that conciliation was necessary in Ireland, and pressured the Irish parliament to pass a Catholic Relief Act in January 1793 giving propertied Catholics the right to vote and to enter the professions, but not to become MPs. Shortly after the Act was passed, Revolutionary France declared war upon Britain on 1 February, and proclaimed its promise to help the people of any nation to overthrow their rulers. Tone and the United Irishmen determined to take advantage of this promise and plotted rebellion. Discovered by the authorities, they were forced underground. Tone managed to leave Ireland, making his way to France to seek help. In the winter of 1796 at Bantry Bay he returned with a French fleet of forty-three ships carrying 15,000 soldiers, only to be prevented from landing, forced by storm to return to France. Leonard McNally, an Irish barrister, playwright, founder-member of the United Irishmen, and a spy for the government, correctly warned his employers that they had had a close shave:

The whole body of the peasantry would join the French in case of an invasion ...The sufferings of the common people from high rents and low wages, from oppressions of their landlords...and tithes are not the only causes of disaffection to Government and hatred of England; for though these have long kept the Irish peasant in a state of slavery and indigence, yet another cause, more dangerous, pervaded them all...This cause is an attachment to French principles in politics and religion, and an ardent desire for a republican government.

Since its foundation in Belfast, the United Irishmen had grown. Its founder membership was drawn from northern Irish Dissenters excited by Tone's ideals, resentful of discrimination, and armed as a result of their days in the Irish Volunteers. By 1795, government spies reported between 2,000 and 3,000 illegal United Irishmen groups all over the country, characterized by a new belligerence reflecting French revolutionary slogans. Tone indicated the lengths to which they were prepared to go in their demand for political independence from Britain, threatening the Ascendancy (whom he hoped to persuade to his point of view): 'If the men of property will not help us they must fall; we will free ourselves by the aid of that large and respectable class of the community – the men of no property.' In a free Ireland, he would accept the Ascendancy's economic position, but if they did not support him in achieving this freedom, then he was prepared to challenge their position too.

In the middle of May 1798, warned by its spies that a United Irishmen rebellion was planned for the 23rd of the month, the government cracked down. The leaders of the Society were nearly all arrested. The government-controlled yeomanry and militia forces, formed by loyal landlords, tenants and small farmers in 1796 when the danger of French invasion seemed great, roamed the country torturing and flogging suspected United Irishmen. As a direct consequence of the savage attempt to prevent rebellion, it happened. On 23 May, despite the loss of their leaders, thousands of United Irishmen, especially in the counties of Wexford, Wicklow and Mayo, took up their pikes and scythes, ambushed government forces, and killed officials and landlords. Most of the rebels were soon put to flight or captured by the yeomanry and militia. Without leaders, the rising which lasted for three weeks in Wexford quickly degenerated into a vengeful slaughter, with massacres of Protestants in the towns of Wexford and Enniscorthy. Captured gentry were often spitted upon pikes, and near New Ross 184 Protestant men, women and children were slaughtered. There was an equally grim retribution for the rebels after their defeat at Vinegar Hill on 13 June. In northern Ireland, news of the sectarian killings in Wexford alienated many Protestant United Irishmen, but others rose in defence of their original ideals. Henry Joy McCracken led an attack on Antrim town on 7 June where the rebels sang the 'Marseillaise', but was captured some days later and hanged in Belfast. By the middle of June the rebellion was over.

In France, Wolfe Tone learnt of these developments and feverishly organized an expeditionary force. On 22 August, a force of 1,000 men under the French General Humbert landed at Killala, Co. Mayo, but surrendered after some skirmishes. The following month, James Napper Tandy, who had been in France with Tone during May and June, landed with a small force on Rutland island off the Donegal coast, but sailed away upon learning of Humbert's surrender. On 12 October, Tone himself was captured after his fleet of nine ships was defeated by the Royal Navy off the coast of Donegal. Brought to Dublin, he was tried by court martial and sentenced to hang. He pleaded to be shot like a soldier, and when his execution was stayed he slit his throat with a penknife, dying by his own hand.

The 1798 rising was wrongly seen by the Ascendancy as a Catholic one. The Viceroy, Lord Cornwallis, who had surrendered to George Washington at Yorktown in 1781, and whose generalship had defeated Humbert, was quick to denounce 'the folly' he saw in 'substituting Catholic instead of Jacobin as the foundation of the present rebellion'. Sir Hercules Langrishe, an independent conservative Irish MP, was quite clear that 1798 was 'French politics and French success, it was the jargon of equality which had been diffused through a deluded multitude by designing men'. The Catholic Church, despite the fact that priests had led the sectarian Wexford revolt, was directly opposed to the rebellion, seeing in it the hand of anti-clerical and anti-papal revolutionary France. Within a week of the outbreak of the rising, the president of the Catholic seminary at Maynooth and twenty-eight prelates signed a public address condemning the rebellion and calling for the defence of 'our constitution, the social order and the Christian religion'. And while in the whole of Ireland, sixty priests were implicated in the revolt, fifteen Presbyterian ministers and nine licentiates or probationers were also arrested, and of these one Presbyterian minister and one licentiate were executed. 'The spirit of plunder and popular domination', in the words of Sir Hercules Langrishe, combined with 'French politics' not religious feeling, had led the attempt 'to break the bonds of society and set up the capriciousness of the popular will against the stability of settled government.' Wolf Tone's United Irishmen became the model for later Irish nationalists. Their colour, green, became established as the national colour. Tone's grave at Bodenstown, Co. Kildare, is to the present day the site of annual pilgrimages and demonstrations by nationalist groups, determined, in his words, 'to break the connection with England'. Unfortunately, the United Irishmen's attempt to transcend religious differences has not survived. Tone's rational republicanism was anti-clerical: he himself rejoiced when Pope Pius VI was captured by the French in the spring of 1798, writing in his diary that this was 'an opportunity to destroy for ever the papal tyranny'. Many of his Irish nationalist successors, however, were prepared to accept the identification of nationalism with Catholicism sought as an explanation of 1798 by the Ascendancy and first achieved by Daniel O'Connell, 'The Liberator'.

5

Union and emancipation

The Penal Laws had helped make a natural connection between Catholicism and reform in Ireland. In 1791 a Catholic Committee – first formed in 1759 – was revived to petition for relief measures. It enjoyed a measure of success, notably with the Catholic Convention of 1792 which Wolfe Tone had organized and which had played an important part in securing the Catholic Relief Act. The Catholics who took part in the Convention and who formed the Committee were, for the most part, wealthy Cork and Dublin merchants who shared many of the aspirations and commercial objectives of the Ascendancy. The great Catholic mass of Irishmen (in common with the mass of people in Britain) were not represented anywhere. And while the Ascendancy ruling class was connected to the governing classes in Britain, before the Industrial Revolution attracted Irish labourers to British cities, ordinary people in both countries had little contact with one another. Writers and travellers like Bishop Berkeley, Arthur Young and Jonathan Swift were actually describing to their English readers an Irish way and condition of life quite unlike that which obtained in England. The Catholicism of Ireland was simply the highlight of a separate cultural (and by 1800 an increasingly separate national) identity.

With the Stuart, Cromwellian and Williamite plantations of the seventeenth century, Gaelic culture became the property of the peasantry, with only a few old Gaelic noble families like the O'Byrnes of Wicklow and the O'Connells of Kerry who managed to survive with some land, maintaining Gaelic cultural and social habits well into the eighteenth century. Hedge schools – illegal roadside schools (Penal Laws prohibited Catholic teachers and education) – grew up during the eighteenth century, with the successors to the ancient Gaelic brehons and poets teaching peasant children, keeping

87

alive their language, the history and stories of Gaelic Ireland, and even Latin and Greek. A strong communal spirit took root: *Meithaels*, a voluntary system whereby peasants assembled to farm each other's land, began to develop during the seventeenth century (and lasted until recently in the west of Ireland). Priests, often the only comforters of the people, came, together with Catholicism, to have a new hold. Denied education at home, thousands of Irish priests were educated at Irish colleges founded abroad, notably in the Spanish Netherlands, France, Portugal and Spain at Salamanca, Valladolid, Lisbon, Douai and Paris. Ordained, they returned to Ireland and a life of persecution and poverty in the cause of their faith. John Mitchel, a Protestant Irish nationalist transported as a convict in 1848, described their perseverance:

Imagine a priest ordained at Seville or Salamanca, a gentleman of high old name, a man of eloquence and genius, who has sustained disputations in the college halls on questions of literature or theology, and carried off prizes and crowns – see him on the quays of Brest, bargaining with some skipper to work his passage. He throws himself on board, does his full part of the hardest work, neither feeling the cold spray nor the fiercest tempest. And he knows, too, that at the end of it all for him may be a row of sugar canes to hoe under the blazing sun of Barbados. . .See him, at last, springing ashore, and hurrying on to seek his bishop in some cave, or under some hedge – but going with caution by reason of the priest catcher and the blood hounds.

Their consolation was flocks of devoted worshippers who often congregated in the open to celebrate Mass. The French philosopher, Alexis de Tocqueville, travelling in Ireland in the 1830s, was told by a priest in Connaught, 'The people give the fruit of their labours liberally to me, and I give them my time, my care, and my entire soul . . .Between us there is a ceaseless exchange of feelings of affection.'

By the close of the eighteenth century, economic differences had begun to accentuate those of religion and culture in Ireland. In northern Ireland where Dissenters (mostly Presbyterian) were a majority, these differences were clearly apparent. Compared to the rest of the country, the province of Ulster was more prosperous. John Wesley, visiting Ireland in 1778, remarked upon this, writing 'No sooner did we enter Ulster than we observed the difference; the ground was cultivated just as in England and the cottages not only neat, but with doors and windows.' The linen industry, which grew and flourished after the collapse of the Irish woollen trade, was the hub of this prosperity accounting for over 70 per cent of Irish exports by 1800. It had been encouraged and subsidized by the Irish government – the Irish parliament during the eighteenth century granted bounties on exports of canvas and sail-cloth – and since it did not compete with an English industry, Irish linen was allowed to enter Britain duty-free. In 1711 a Linen Board was established in Dublin to encourage the linen trade, but despite its attempts to spread linen manufacture throughout the country, the industry was concentrated in northern Ireland. By 1782, when a Linen Hall was built in Belfast, exports of linen – amounting to nearly £2 million a year by the 1770s – were no longer routed through Dublin, but were going directly from Ulster. The financial security enjoyed by people of all sorts involved in the industry meant that there was a discernibly higher standard of living in the north by the end of the eighteenth century, helping to generate the growth of a middle class which, as was shown with the United Irishmen, did not identify with the Ascendancy and had much in common with the Catholic Committee, whose members had also prospered during the century.

Between 1700 and 1800, Anglo-Irish trade alone expanded tenfold, from £800,000 to £8,300,000 a year. While the major proportion was made up of revenue from the linen trade, exports of beef (and illegally of wool) also contributed to commercial prosperity. An average of a hundred thousand head of cattle were slaughtered every year, and Irish salted beef was shipped to the Americas and elsewhere at considerable profit. Cork came to be known as the slaughterhouse of Ireland, and by 1800 had a population of 80,000. The Industrial Revolution had a strong effect in the eighteenth century, not only with the introduction of steam power in mills and foundries, but also on the growth of credit and banking. The Bank of Ireland was founded in 1783 by royal charter, and soon came to govern credit. The supply of cash reflected the growth of trade which had a three to fourfold increase between the 1720s and 1770s, and then trebled by 1797. The population of the country as a whole grew enormously during the eighteenth century (though by no means as fast as the money supply) from an estimated 1.1 million in 1672 to 2 million in 1732, 4 million by 1788, and in 1821 at the time of the first census in Ireland, 6.8 million. Roads and stagecoaches spread, easily connecting Dublin and the major towns and cities of the country for the first time. Improved sailing techniques and ship design made Irish ports accessible to European and transatlantic traders, facilitating trade. Agriculture, the greatest Irish industry, despite the Penal Laws (which had proved unenforceable), was dominated by farmers holding leases on the one hand, and labourers/cottiers on the other. There was not a straightforward Protestant landlord/Catholic tenant labourer division on the land: it was far more complex. Agricultural prices throughout the century rose sharply relatively to industrial prices, resulting in improved rural conditions (reflected in the population explosion): the Whiteboys and the Oakboys were men who had something to lose and something to gain, and not men who resorted to violence as a last desperate throw for survival. The yeomanry and militia forces which both sparked and subdued the 1798 rising were composed of Irish Catholics of a landholding or commercial group, as were many of the leaders of the United Irishmen. Tone's threat to unleash the 'men of no property' – the peasant labourers – was directed as much against the Ascendancy as against his own supporters anxious to improve their social and financial standing.

Ireland's increased prosperity, and its strategic geographical position, made it a valuable British possession particularly during the last three decades of the eighteenth century as Britain grappled first with the American Revolution and then with Republican and Napoleonic France. William Pitt the younger recognized this early in his career. He also realized that war, with its barriers to trade, could adversely affect the prosperity of large sections of the economy and thus foment discontent. For him, the 1798 rising was proof of this danger, and he determined to press for union between Ireland and Britain as the way to end discriminatory economic policies and counteract the economic nationalism of the Ascendancy. 'Ireland is like a ship on fire', said Pitt, 'it must be extinguished or cut adrift.' Aware too of Catholic alienation, Pitt planned Catholic emancipation as part of the union. In 1792 he had written to the viceroy, the earl of Westmorland, that 'the idea of the present fermentation, gradually bringing both parties to think of a union with this country, had long been in my mind. The admission of the Catholics to a share of suffrage would not then be dangerous.' Within weeks of the 1798 rising beginning, Pitt was at work winning Irish support for union.

Opposition to Pitt's idea for Anglo–Irish union was largely concentrated amongst the Ascendancy, reluctant to surrender the profitable levers of power and position their own parliament and

administration afforded them, and fearful of the political consequences of Catholic emancipation. In January 1799 the Irish house
of commons rejected Pitt's first Union Bill by 111 votes to 106, even
though Pitt had reluctantly agreed to drop Catholic emancipation
from the Bill and to pursue it only once union was agreed.

The issue of Catholic emancipation, combined with union, faced
Pitt with opposition from another source. In the north, contemporaries and successors of the Oakboys and Steelboys had come to
regard their Protestant religion almost as a trade union, and they
competed fiercely with Catholics for jobs. The 'Peep O'Day Boys'
protected the interests of Protestants, and the 'Defenders' those of
Catholics from the 1770s on. The United Irishmen's appeal to
northern Irish Protestants though marked, was limited, and the Peep
O'Day Boys gathered the bulk of Protestant and ex-Irish Volunteer
support in the north. On 21 September 1795, a clash at a crossroads
near the town of Armagh between the Defenders and the Peep O'Day
Boys, called the 'Battle of the Diamond', saw the Defenders routed.
To consolidate their victory, the Loyal Orange Association – the
Orange Order – was founded, oathbound to 'support and defend the
King and his heirs as long as he or they support the Protestant
ascendancy'. Not only were sectarian divisions again being felt, but
also the fundamentally conditional loyalty of Ulster Protestants to
the British government was spelt out. They would only be loyal and
obedient as long as the government maintained what they saw as
their interests. Pitt's Anglo-Irish union they perceived as a Trojan
Horse for Catholic emancipation which, since it would give
Catholics political power, could result in a growth of Catholics'
economic power at Protestant expense, and so they opposed it. The
crudely sectarian 1798 rising in Wexford re-awakened Protestant
fears of a Catholic backlash like that of 1641, and the Orange
Order's membership swelled.

In order to overcome opposition to union, during 1799 and 1800
Lord Cornwallis, the viceroy, and Lord Castlereagh, the chief
secretary, were entrusted by Pitt with the job of 'managing' the Irish
parliament. Places, pensions and peerages were offered as induce-
ments to members of the Irish parliament to secure their votes for
union. Irish peers were offered promotions in the peerage: over fifty
parliamentarians were ennobled or promoted. One and a quarter
million pounds were spent in bribes and 'compensation for disturb-

ance' by the government. By the time the second Union Bill was debated in the Irish house of commons early in 1800, Cornwallis' and Castlereagh's management had worked, and the Bill passed by 158 votes to 115. Henry Grattan, who had returned to politics to fight against union, reckoned that only seven MPs who voted for the Bill were unbribed. In the house of lords the Bill passed by 75 votes to 26. On 1 August 1800, King George III signed the Act of Union between Great Britain and Ireland, establishing the United Kingdom. On 1 January 1801 the Act came into force.

The Act was corruptly secured. Lord Cornwallis complained to a friend 'My occupation is of the most unpleasant nature, bargaining and jobbing with the most corrupt people under Heaven. I despise and hate myself for ever engaging in such dirty work, and am supported only by the reflection that without a Union the British Empire must be dissolved.' Bribery has been associated with the Act by historians ever since, but it should also be remembered that at the time political power was regarded as a possession with a market value. In England, MPs bought and landlords sold parliamentary constituencies; bribery of voters was commonplace. For the Ascendancy, their political power was worth a price and Pitt showed that he was prepared to have it paid. In addition, there was a very strong argument for union. The Ascendancy's position and power ultimately depended upon British power and authority, and though they never realized this clearly, the consequence was that the Ascendancy had to satisfy the British government with their stewardship. When Irish Ascendancy and commercial interests began to compete with British interests, when the Irish parliament began to demand separate power and gave force to Ascendancy economic nationalism, and when the Ascendancy-dominated Irish government failed to prevent an Irish rising in 1798, it was not very surprising that Pitt should decide upon union, if only to regain control of Britain's oldest colony. This point was made during the debates on the Union Bill. Lord Clare, lord chancellor of Ireland and a leading advocate of union, explained:

The whole power and property has been conferred by successive monarchs of England upon an English colony composed of three sorts of English adventurers who poured into this country at the termination of three successive rebellions. Confiscation is their common title and from their first settlement they have been hemmed in on every side by the old inhabitants of this island, brooding over their discontents in sullen indignation. What was the security of the English settlers for their physical existence? And what is the security of their descendants at this day? The powerful and commanding position of Great Britain. If, by any fatality, it fails, you are at the mercy of the old inhabitants of this island, and I should have hoped that the examples of mercy exhibited by them in the progress of the late rebellion would have taught the gentlemen who call themselves the Irish nation to reflect with sober attention on the dangers which surround them.

The immediate consequence of the Act of Union was the ending of the five-hundred-year-old Irish parliament. Grattan and the 'Patriot Party', who had succeeded in 1782 in securing greater power for the parliament than it had known since Poynings' Law came into effect in 1495, having opposed union regarded the Act as if it had ended Ireland's national identity. In fact, the Act translated Ascendancy parliamentarians from Dublin to Westminster, and the majority of people were not affected. As Lord Cornwallis accurately observed, 'The mass of the people of Ireland do not care one farthing about union.' Twenty-eight Irish peers, four bishops and one hundred Irish MPs were given seats in the new United Kingdom parliament in London. The position of the king's representative, the viceroy, became the lord lieutenant. Lord lieutenants had real power (including charge of defence and later police) and patronage. Under the lord lieutenant was the chief secretary who was a member of the cabinet in London and who had charge of the government of Ireland. The head of the Irish civil service (which, despite union, remained separate from the rest of the United Kingdom) was the under-secretary. He was a permanent civil servant, and some under-secretaries held office for over twenty years. The established Churches of both countries were united as the Church of England and Ireland, and Ireland's financial contribution to United Kingdom expenditure was fixed at two-seventeenths of the total.

As the nineteenth century progressed, it became clear that the Act of Union had far-reaching repercussions. While at first its effects seemed slight, the moving of Irish affairs to London meant that some more Irish landlords tended to remain absent from their estates. With the removal of the political excuses to which the two parliaments lent themselves, Irish discontents could be squarely placed at Westminster's door, thus encouraging Irish separatism. The union could be blamed for all Ireland's problems. Interestingly, however, during the nineteenth century, Irish politics came to concentrate on a demand for home rule and the return of an Irish parliament, rather than on the older revolutionary demand for complete independence. Irish Anglicans and Dissenters came to be the chief supporters of union as the political system became more democratic, seeing in it a safeguard that they would not be swamped by a Catholic, nationalist majority. Irish emigrants as full-fledged British subjects labouring in British industrial cities brought with them their anti-establishment nationalist politics, leaving a permanent mark upon the British political scene.

The first violent resistance to the new order came on 23 July 1803 when a fifty to sixty strong Dublin slum mob, led by a self-appointed general, Robert Emmet (1778–1803), attacked Dublin Castle (the seat of Irish administration), on its way dragging the lord chief justice of Ireland and his nephew from their coach and murdering them. Emmet was captured, eloquently defended by the government spy, Leonard McNally, and refusing a clergyman, publicly hanged, drawn, quartered and beheaded in Dublin. His 'Rising' was really an epilogue to 1798. He had spent some time in France where he had travelled after leaving Trinity College, Dublin, in protest at being disciplined for his membership of the United Irishmen. He was the youngest of seventeen children of the leading physician in Ireland, and according to subsequent government reports he used a £3,000 inheritance from his father to finance his rebellion.

Emmet's oratory and romantic nature, however, captured the imagination of the Irish people. His housekeeper, Anne Devlin (whose uncle, Michael Dwyer, was involved in Emmet's plans) bravely hid him. When he was arrested it emerged that he had refused the chance of escaping, insisting upon seeing his fiancée, Sarah Curran, whose father disapproved of the match, and was caught on his way to an assignation with her. His speech from the dock has become a classic expression of Irish nationalism:

Let no man write my epitaph; for as no man who knows my motives dare now vindicate them, let not prejudice or ignorance asperse them. Let them and me rest in obscurity and peace, and my tomb remain uninscribed and my memory in oblivion until other times and other men can do justice to my character. When my country takes her place among the nations of the earth, then and not till then, let my epitaph be written.

The steadfast, irrevocable determination which Emmet expressed has always been part of the pulse of Irish nationalism. Its romantic, idealized attraction has been expressed in countless ballads and songs sung everywhere there are Irishmen. The futility of his enterprise and its complete failure is usually ignored, and instead the sole fact that he stood against the government – against Britain – has become all-important and a moral victory. Time and again this phenomenon is to be seen in Irish nationalism, with defeat after defeat nevertheless inspiring further resistance, and always being presented in romantic terms to great propaganda effect. Abraham Lincoln remembered as a boy reading Emmet's speech from the dock by the firelight of his Kentucky cabin, and the text adorned many an Irish-American home, as it did Irish cottages. James Connolly, the Irish labour leader, a century later placed great significance on Emmet's slum support, convinced that in 1803 the Irish proletariat first came of age. If it did, its maturity was reflected by a rejection of violence and a preference for constitutional politics for the next sixty years.

The Catholic Church (with the possible exception of one bishop) had supported Pitt and the Act of Union because of his promise of emancipation and because the government undertook to subsidize various Catholic institutions and to endow the clergy throughout the country. Pitt also realized that emancipation would remove most Catholic grievances and thus encourage both the mass of people and the more wealthy and respectable Catholic class to support the union and bend their efforts to the general prosperity of the new kingdom. It is debatable whether emancipation would actually have had this effect if it had come with union. As it was, George III was implacably opposed to the measure, refusing to compromise his coronation oath to defend the Protestant faith in Great Britain and Ireland. 'I would rather give up my throne', said the king, 'and beg my bread from door to door throughout Europe than consent to such a measure'. Pitt, having given his word to press for emancipation, resigned, and by the time emancipation was granted, Irish politics and Anglo-Irish relations had been transformed by a brilliant Irish Catholic barrister, Daniel O'Connell (1775–1847).

O'Connell was a member of an old Gaelic Co. Kerry family which, protected by mountainous terrain, had managed to hold onto much of its ancestral land. O'Connell's father had circumvented the problems of being a Catholic Irish landowner in penal times by leaving his property in the legal possession of a Protestant friend.

Many of the Gaelic ways also survived in Kerry, and O'Connell was fostered at his uncle's home at Derrynane where he learnt Irish and became versed in the songs and legends of the people. Like many better-off Catholics, O'Connell was sent to France to finish his education. In France soon after the start of the Revolution, where another uncle, Count Daniel O'Connell, was a royalist colonel of the Irish Brigade and had been inspector-general of infantry, young O'Connell was horrified by French revolutionary terror and violence and became convinced of the wisdom of constitutional over revolutionary action. Subsequent generations of Irish nationalists, remembering the failure of O'Connell's peaceful attempt to achieve home rule for Ireland and the horror of the famine which seemed to cap his career, blamed O'Connell for his respect for law and for his constitutionalism. They neglected to remember the bloody failure of violence in 1798, or the hope that Pitt's espousal of emancipation gave for constitutional progress and reform. O'Connell was right to try another approach: 'that no political change whatsoever', as he put it, 'is worth the shedding of a single drop of human blood'.

Returning from France in 1793, O'Connell was one of the first to take advantage of the 1793 Catholic Relief Act which allowed Irish Catholics to enter the professions, and he began reading for the Bar at Lincoln's Inn in London. On the same day that Lord Edward FitzGerald was arrested – 19 May 1798 – O'Connell entered the Irish Bar. By then he had become a radical utilitarian in politics and, while in sympathy with the ideals of the United Irishmen, he was as horrified by their violence in 1798 as he had been by what he had seen in France five years earlier. In 1803 he joined a yeomanry corps of Dublin lawyers in the aftermath of Emmet's attempted rebellion. At the same time, he was making a mark for himself as an Irish nationalist. He had spoken out publicly against the Act of Union, and soon after the Act was passed he threw himself into reviving the Catholic Committee, now pressing for emancipation. The Committee at first was controlled by the remaining Catholic aristocracy who showed themselves willing to accept emancipation with safeguards – or 'wings' as contemporaries phrased it – so that the government should have some control over the appointment of Catholic bishops and priests. By 1808 O'Connell dominated the Committee, having taken the initiative away from the Catholic nobility and placed it in the hands of his middle-class supporters, resolutely arguing the case for emancipation without wings and, significantly, enjoying the support of the Catholic Church for his stand. In 1812 when the Catholic Committee dissolved, split over O'Connell's refusal to accept emancipation with wings, he had become the acknowledged leader of the emancipation movement. When he killed a member of the Dublin Corporation in a duel in 1815, his position was so strong that he remained unchallenged. However, the divisions within the Irish and English Catholic communities caused by O'Connell's approach meant that the traditional advocates of emancipation could not count on united Catholic support. Henry Grattan, who after the Act of Union spent the rest of his life as an Irish MP at Westminster championing the cause of emancipation with wings, on two occasions found O'Connell – supported by the Irish Catholic Church – lined up against him. In 1821, a year after Grattan's death, a Catholic Relief Bill with wings was passed by the house of commons, but thrown out by the lords. That same year, the scenes of almost hysterical Catholic loyalty which greeted George IV during his visit to Ireland showed that for the cause of emancipation to win through, the government would need practical demonstrations of its necessity. This O'Connell realized, and he turned his energy to harnessing emancipation and the Church to the great motive force of Irish nationalism. Under his leadership, emancipation became a quasi-national purpose, and within a few years, in the words of Gustave de Beaumont, he made Ireland 'a nation constitutionally in revolt'. Under his tutelage, Irish people came to believe that Catholic emancipation meant their emancipation.

The strength and organization of the Catholic Church was the key to O'Connell's campaign for emancipation in the 1820s. With the ending of most of the Penal Laws during the 1780s, the Church had been able to organize itself properly. In 1802 the teaching order of the Christian Brothers opened its first school, signifying a revived expansionist element in the Church as a whole and a determination to provide formal Catholic education for the mass of the people. Irish seminaries were opened, thus making the priest's vocation more easily accessible to Irishmen from humble backgrounds who had not been able to afford the enforced costs of education abroad during Penal times. In turn, this meant that an Irish priesthood developed in touch with and representative of the broad mass of Irish people. It was to this revived and reorganized Church that O'Connell turned to mobilize support for emancipation. He was convinced that if he could impress the government with the unanimity of Catholic Ireland on the question of emancipation, then success would follow. And the Church, commanding the loyalty and support of over 80 per cent of the country's population, was ideally placed to mobilize the support O'Connell wanted.

In 1823 O'Connell and Richard Lalor Shiel, a barrister and playwright, formed the Catholic Association of Ireland. It was a firmly professional and middle-class grouping. The following year it took off by breaking with tradition and allowing the enrolment of Catholic peasants as associate members at one penny a month. The 'Catholic Rent' as it was called raised an enormous amount of money for the Association. Over £1,000 a month was collected on average, and by March 1825, £19,000 had been raised. With the active involvement of the Catholic clergy, subscriptions were collected at church gates on Sundays, and branches of the Association – often with priests playing prominent parts – were formed in nearly every parish in Ireland. By 1828, although prohibited as a Catholic from taking his seat, O'Connell won one of the two Co. Clare constituencies in the general election that year. The following year, fearing insurrection, the prime minister, the duke of Wellington, forced an Emancipation Act through Parliament. On 13 April 1829 the Catholic Relief Act received the royal assent from a reluctant king whose opposition was only overcome by Wellington threatening to resign. The duke even had to fight a duel with a fellow Tory peer, Lord Winchilsea, who opposed him (Wellington fired wide; Winchilsea fired in the air). The act allowed Roman Catholics for the first time since 1691 to stand for and sit in parliament, and to hold all public offices except those of regent, lord chancellor of England and Ireland, and lord lieutenant of Ireland. Ancillary legislation brought wings, removing the forty shilling freeholder – the class of voters which supported O'Connell overwhelmingly – from the electoral register, with the consequence that the number of voters in Irish counties fell from about 100,000 to 16,000. This was designed to re-assure those who feared that Catholic democracy would mean Protestant disability. In this it was unsuccessful, and from the 1820s sectarian rioting in northern Ireland became increasingly commonplace. Ironically, the very group who benefited from emancipation – the Catholic commercial and professional class – had broadly the same economic and social interests as the Protestants who opposed them, while the group whose public demonstrations had brought emancipation about – the Catholic peasantry – did not benefit from the measure. Planter/native, Protestant/Catholic divisions were stronger than class interests. As Alexis de Tocqueville learned from a peasant during his travels in Ireland in the mid 1830s, 'The law does nothing for us ... To whom should we address ourselves? Emancipation has done nothing for us. Mr O'Connell and the rich Catholics go to Parliament. We die of starvation just the same.'

The major consequence of O'Connell's emancipation campaign was that mobilized peasantry became a coherent political force. The fact that they were first used to redress a Catholic grievance (although the emancipation campaign was presented by O'Connell in national terms), and were often led by priests at parish level, re-inforced sectarian divisions and firmly linked Catholicism to nationalism. At the same time, the campaign's constitutional nature and success was immensely important: for the rest of the century revolutionary Irish politics was largely rejected in favour of the parliamentary procedures adopted by O'Connell. That the campaign was successful, and was almost the first Irish political campaign that was, had a profound psychological effect: O'Connell was hailed as 'The Liberator' and venerated as the uncrowned king of Ireland; after 1829 any cause he advocated was guaranteed mass support. His rabble-rousing political style encouraged the grandest hopes amongst people of the humblest sort while firmly alienating opponents.

The people of Ireland thirty years after the union were experiencing a host of fundamental social and economic changes. From 1793 to 1815, Britain had been at war with France. The effect on the Irish economy was sharp, with an overall increase in prosperity, reflected by a vast increase in population. In turn, this had a marked effect on the use and ownership of land. Not only was there increased concern about the possession of land, but because the supply of European agricultural produce was largely denied to the British Isles during the Napoleonic Wars, the value of Irish land and its produce increased dramatically, and Irish landlords and farmers fared well.

Of the estimated 5.5 million people in Ireland in 1815, 90 per cent lived and worked in the countryside's fourteen million then profitable acres, 90 per cent of which was owned by about 5,000 men – the

Ascendancy. Ascendancy landlords usually sub-let to independent tenant farmers, many of whom also owned land outright themselves. Between 5 and 10 per cent of tenants were 'strong farmers' who owned or rented more than thirty acres. During the Napoleonic Wars they began to grow wheat to meet demand for flour, changing from dairy farming in the process, and thus giving more employment and prosperity to poorer sections of the agricultural community. Smaller tenant farmers – those with between five and thirty acres – were the most numerous tenant group. They concentrated on dairy farming, wheat and flax growing and shared with the cottiers the potato as their staple diet. Cottiers, the majority of people on the land, were mainly farm labourers enjoying the use of small plots in return for their labour. Many were itinerant, and they often formed the bulk of the population of the rapidly growing towns and cities of the country, huddled into atrocious housing, or emigrating to work in Scotland and England.

Irish industry was much less successful than Irish agriculture. After the union, protective duties were removed on both sides of the Irish Sea, with the result that Irish industries such as cotton and wool which competed with English equivalents, faced the full weight of technically advanced English competition. By the 1820s the woollen and cotton industries were collapsing, and only linen survived. This collapse coincided with a general recession following the end of the Napoleonic Wars in 1815. Agricultural prices and land values fell, and the 1820s were a decade of severe commercial and agricultural contraction, with dire consequences on the lives of millions of cottiers and small farmers. Agrarian unrest coincided with the periods of worst conditions, and secret peasant societies re-appeared: 'Carders', 'Threshers', 'Whitefeet' and most commonly 'Ribbonmen'. As with the Whiteboys and Oakboys before them, these societies acted to protect peasant interests, terrorizing their opponents – often murdering them. When the Catholic Relief Act was passed in 1829, it was against this background of violence and depression that the duke of Wellington became convinced that acquiescence to O'Connell's demands was the only alternative to civil war.

O'Connell exploited his position fully after 1829. Like many Irish nationalists after him, he began publicly to blame the union for Ireland's ills. In fact, the union was not responsible for the post-1815 recession, and during the 1820s Ireland enjoyed a net surplus in its financial transactions with the United Kingdom exchequer as well as in the value of its export trade. A report organized by Thomas Drummond, under-secretary for Ireland, in 1838 noted:

Signs of growing prosperity are, unhappily, not so discernible in the condition of the labouring people, as in the amount of the produce of their labour. The proportion of the latter reserved for their use is too small to be consistent with a healthy state of society. The pressure of a superabundant and excessive population. . . is perpetually and powerfully acting to depress them.

In these circumstances, however, it was easy instead to blame the union, and calls for its repeal certainly satisfied the labouring people who had supported O'Connell's emancipation campaign and whose hopes had been raised by him. In 1829 O'Connell retired from the Bar and became a full-time politician, supported for the rest of his career by public subscription amounting in some years to over £16,000 – 'The O'Connell Tribute' – a mark of the esteem he held amongst the ordinary people of Ireland.

Soon after O'Connell took his seat in the house of commons on 4 February 1830, together with about thirty other Irish Catholic MPs known as 'O'Connell's Tail' (the first Roman Catholic MPs in modern history), he began to campaign for the repeal of the Act of Union. But while in his campaign for emancipation he had found allies in British Catholics who had faced as much discrimination as their Irish co-religionists in the previous forty years, and in the Whig politicians who supported reform in principle, when it came to repeal of the union O'Connell was very much on his own. British politicians, with the memory of Napoleon still fresh and the strategic importance of Ireland for trade and defence in mind, would not support repeal. In addition, sectarian rioting in northern Ireland was becoming a frequent occurrence during the 1820s, providing a focus of opposition to Irish nationalism. Even some of those who might have been expected to support the Liberator were hostile to him, seeing him as a 'West Briton' – someone prepared to make Ireland English in all but name in return for the spoils of office. They remembered that in 1825 O'Connell had actually accepted a proposal for emancipation with wings attached – conditions which for the previous twenty years he had loudly rejected (the resultant legislation passed the commons but was thrown out by the lords) –

and they were convinced that his purpose was self, not national aggrandisement. They were also alarmed by the identification O'Connell had fostered in people's minds between Catholicism and nationalism, realizing (correctly) that sectarian divisions in Ireland would only be deepened and would lend themselves to political exploitation by O'Connell's and Irish nationalism's opponents. Thomas Francis Meagher, a later revolutionary nationalist, dismissively scorned the Liberator's triumph of Catholic emancipation as only enabling 'a few Catholic gentlemen to sit in Parliament and there concur in the degradation of their country'.

Despite the fact that he did not obtain support in parliament for repeal of the union, O'Connell soon found that there were distinct benefits to be had in exchange for his support of others' measures, particularly Whig and Radical measures. Indeed during the 1830s O'Connell developed what was, in effect, a parliamentary alliance with the Whigs, and his periods of severe repeal agitation after 1830 coincided with Tory periods of government. When the Whigs were in power, O'Connell preferred to concentrate on lesser, more immediate reforms. His method of seeking reform and change – constitutionally, backed up by mass support – and the way in which he used his parliamentary followers to support other Parties in return for reforms, acted as a model for the Irish Home Rule Party of Parnell and Redmond in the last decades of the nineteenth and the first years of the twentieth century. Emigration and famine, however, combined to halve Ireland's population between 1841 and 1901, destroying the peasantry upon whom O'Connell had depended. Nevertheless, under Redmond, constitutional methods almost succeeded and only the First World War prevented Ireland achieving home rule peacefully. Revolutionary methods became the preferred method only of a distinct minority, but one which was nevertheless able to appeal to the memory of 1798 and to the trans-sectarian idealism and nationalism of the United Irishmen and Wolfe Tone. As a result, two strains of Irish nationalism developed: popular constitutional nationalism and secret physical force nationalism, both in competition and both increasingly hostile to each other.

In 1840 O'Connell founded a Repeal Association on the lines of the old Catholic Association, including a church-collected subscription. The following year, with the Whigs out of office, O'Connell began a loud campaign for repeal. As in the 1820s, Protestants were again stirred into opposition by the fear that Protestant interests would be subsumed by Catholic ones in a self-governing Ireland. O'Connell launched a campaign against the tithe paid by Catholics and Dissenters alike for the support of the Church of Ireland, and when in 1838 the government agreed a 25 per cent reduction in the tithe, many Protestants saw this as an attack on their Protestant religion. They feared for their religious freedom and their land, and for their jobs which were concentrated in the linen, shipbuilding and engineering industries which depended upon British markets and British ports for survival. The Repeal Association was also seen as a threat by the government, not only because of its implicit threat to the unity and integrity of the United Kingdom, but also because of the volatile nature of the 'Monster Meetings' (as *The Times* called them) that O'Connell organized at historic and emotive sites. In 1843, the 'Year of Repeal' O'Connell declared, a Monster Meeting at Tara involved between an estimated 750,000 and one million people. As thousands of people made their way to another Monster Meeting at Clontarf in October that year, the government banned the meeting and (to the dismay of his followers) O'Connell obeyed the ban. He preferred a constitutional approach rather than outright opposition, and called for a 'Council of Three Hundred' to form a national representative body, forcing the government to act against him personally on the grounds of conspiracy and 'intimidation and demonstration of great physical force'. At the age of sixty-eight, O'Connell was found guilty and imprisoned for three months before the house of lords set aside the sentence. When he emerged from prison, he recognized the hopelessness of his campaign. The Young Irelanders, a group of bright young organizers and journalists who had played a vital part in the creation of the Repeal Association, were moving to break away convinced that O'Connell's constitutional policy might secure reforms, but would never secure Irish freedom. In addition, the peasantry were becoming increasingly concerned with the failure of their potato crops in the early 1840s, a sinister prelude to the great famine. In failing health, O'Connell left Ireland for the last time in January 1847 to make a scarcely audible appeal in the house of commons on behalf of his starving countrymen: 'Ireland is in your hands, in your power. If you do not save her she cannot save herself. I solemnly call on you to recollect that I predict with the sincerest conviction that a quarter of her population will perish unless you come to her relief.' His prediction was completely accurate. From Westminster he embarked upon a pilgrimage to Rome, dying in Genoa on the way. His heart was sent to Rome where it now lies in an urn in the Church of St Agatha. His body was brought back to Dublin, and after the biggest funeral that Ireland had ever witnessed, was buried in Glasnevin cemetery on 5 August 1847.

Dead, O'Connell was as controversial as he had been alive. John Mitchel, a Young Irelander who in later years became a constitutionalist, named O'Connell 'next to the British Government the greatest enemy Ireland ever had'. He blamed O'Connell for the failure of the Young Irelanders' insurrectionary plans in 1848 – the year after the Liberator's death – writing in his *Jail journal*:

Poor old Dan! Wonderful, mighty, jovial and mean old man! With silver tongue and smile of witchery and heart of unfathomable fraud! What a royal yet vulgar soul, with keen eye and potent sweep of a generous eagle of Cairn Tuathal – and the base servility of a hound, and the cold cruelty of a spider!... Think of the 'gorgeous and gossamer' theory of moral and peaceful agitation, the most astounding organon of public swindling since first man bethought him of obtaining money under false pretence. And after one has thought of all this and more, what then can a man say? What but pray that Irish earth may lie light on O'Connell's breast, and that the good God who knew how to create so wondrous a creature may have mercy upon his soul?

A harsh, bitter-sweet tribute for the man who had obtained for the mass of Irishmen greater liberty and greater coherence than any other Irish leader since the Norman invasion. His success was resented by physical force nationalists who never accepted that Irish freedom could be obtained peacefully. O'Connell was never able completely to exorcise the republican and revolutionary ideas of Wolfe Tone, and thus, ultimately, his constitutional politics were always vulnerable to the appeal of violent action. The Young Irelanders and the Fenians who followed him were to ensure that the threat of republican revolt was maintained.

The Young Ireland movement was essentially grouped around *The Nation* weekly newspaper, founded in October 1842 by Thomas Osborne Davis (1814–45), a Protestant barrister, poet and graduate of Trinity College, Dublin; Charles Gavan Duffy (1816–1903), an Ulster Catholic journalist; and John Blake Dillon (1816–66), like Davis a barrister and graduate of Trinity, and a member of a prosperous Co. Mayo Catholic commercial family. The movement's aim was to 'establish internal union and external independence', and it was largely influenced by the doctrines of the Italian republican nationalist, Giuseppe Mazzini. It was modelled on Mazzini's revolutionary society, 'Young Italy', and earnestly adopted his vision of a republican brotherhood of nations based upon non-sectarian principles of Christian charity. *The Nation* enjoyed a great deal of influence, regularly selling over 10,000 copies, and becoming the first weekly paper to circulate throughout Ireland. It proselytized for the ideals of the United Irishmen. It drew no distinction between Gaelic, Norman, Stuart, Cromwellian, and Williamite traditions, regarding them all as Irish. It printed the ancient Gaelic tales, told Irish history, praised Irish culture, art and craftsmanship, and publicized Thomas Davis' poems, one of which – 'A Nation Once Again' – became in the twentieth century Ireland's unofficial national anthem:

> When boyhood's fire was in my blood,
> I read of ancient freemen,
> For Greece and Rome who bravely stood,
> Three hundred men and three men.
> And then I prayed I yet might see
> Our fetters rent in twain,
> And Ireland, long a province, be
> A nation once again.

The Nation also carried a statement by Davis that was to become the definitive explanation of modern Irish nationalism:

We repeat, again and again, no hatred of the English. For much that England did in literature, politics and war, we are, as men, grateful. Her oppression we would not even avenge. We would, were she eternally dethroned from us, rejoice in her prosperity; but we cannot and will not try to forget her long, cursing, merciless tyranny to Ireland; and we do not desire to share her gains, her responsibility or her glory.

Arthur Griffith, the founder of Sinn Fein – the early twentieth-century nationalist Part – was to describe Davis as 'the prophet I followed throughout my life, the man whose words and teachings I tried to translate into practice in politics'. Davis throughout lent broad support to O'Connell's Repeal Association, but after his death (of fever) his successor as editor of *The Nation*, John Mitchel (1815–75), brought Young Ireland firmly to advocate rebellion.

John Mitchel was born in Dungiven, Co. Londonderry, the son of a Presbyterian minister. Like Davis and Dillon, he qualified as a barrister and was a graduate of Trinity College. After 1845 he rapidly became convinced by the famine of the futility of anything but revolution if conditions in Ireland were to change, and used *The Nation* as his platform. He was the first nationalist since 1798 to demand an Irish republic. A breach with O'Connell was inevitable, and in 1846 it occurred over a combination of O'Connell's willingness to make another political alliance with the Whigs in return for governmental positions for some of his supporters and relations, and his opposition (in line with that of the Church) to the setting up of the non-denominational Queen's Colleges. Mitchel led the attack on O'Connell on both issues, accusing him of compromising the principle of repeal by his actions. O'Connell replied that 'It is, no doubt, a very fine thing to die for one's country, but believe me, one living patriot is worth a whole churchyard full of dead ones', and insisted that members of the Repeal Association should pledge rejection of physical force. The Young Irelanders left the Repeal Association, propelled towards revolution by the suffering and destitution wrought by the famine (1846 was one of the worst years). Early in 1847 Mitchel began to publish in *The Nation* a series of letters from James Fintan Lalor (1807–49), the son of an O'Connellite MP and gentleman farmer from Queen's County (Co. Leix), who advanced the radical argument that the nature of land-ownership in Ireland lay at the heart of the famine and acted to circumvent Irish independence: 'A secure and independent agricultural peasantry is the only base on which a people rises or ever can be raised; or on which a nation can safely rest.' While recognizing the validity of private property rights, Lalor held that 'the entire soil of a country belongs as of right to the entire people of that country'. Prodded by Lalor, Mitchel translated this argument into a campaign for security of tenure for tenants. The campaign was unsuccessful. Irish peasants struggling for survival in the midst of terrible famine did not have time or energy for political campaigns, and the majority of Young Irelanders also found Mitchel and Lalor dangerously extreme.

Early in 1848, Mitchel and Lalor left Young Ireland, rejecting Duffy's and Dillon's arguments that a strong and independent Irish Party at Westminster offered the best hope of achieving their national aspirations, and founded a new paper, the *United Irishman*.

In it, Mitchel openly advocated rebellion, a 'holy war to sweep this island clear of the English name and nation'. Not surprisingly he was arrested in May 1848 on a charge of treason–felony, a new crime established by the Treason–Felony Act which received the royal assent in April that year and which was specifically designed to circumscribe men like Mitchel – 'any person who, by open and advised speaking, compassed the intimidation of the Crown or Parliament'. Mitchel was the first person arrested, tried, found guilty and sentenced to fourteen years' transportation under the Act. He served the first part of his sentence in Bermuda and then in Tasmania before escaping to the United States in 1853. Lalor, who suffered from a congenital spinal disease and was always in poor health, was also arrested in 1848. He was soon released on health grounds and died the following year. Without Lalor's radical intellectual leadership, contemporary revolutionary nationalists remained fixated upon their political purpose of Irish freedom, refusing to accept that economic and social reform might be the locomotive of national independence. As Lalor put it, they 'desired not a democratic, but merely a national revolution'. This was made quickly apparent by the abortive rising organized by another Young Irelander, William Smith O'Brien (1803–64).

O'Brien was an unlikely rebel. He was born into a wealthy Co. Clare family, and sent to Harrow School and Trinity College, Cambridge. He was elected the Tory MP for Ennis in 1828. In 1843 he joined the Repeal Association, proving himself a radical and critical member and winning the respect of *The Nation* in the process. He jocularly referred to himself as 'Middle Aged' Ireland, bridging the gap between O'Connell's 'Old' Ireland and Young Ireland, but in 1846 he sided with Mitchel against O'Connell over the Queen's Colleges, the Tory prime minister (and O'Connell's old political enemy) Sir Robert Peel's solution to end the demand for a Catholic university. O'Brien became the unofficial spokesman of Young Ireland in the house of commons, and as the famine progressed, became more extreme himself. In 1848 after Mitchel's arrest and transportation, O'Brien came to advocate insurrection on the grounds that there was no alternative method of alleviating famine distress and securing Irish freedom. He was also fired by the demagogic and popular Chartist campaign in Britain for parliamentary and social reform, and by the popular rebellions against autocratic government taking place across Europe in 1848. His determination to rebel was aided by public calls for revolution in the columns of the *Irish Felon* (the successor to the *United Irishman* which was suppressed when Mitchel was arrested), edited by Lalor and John Martin (1812–75), the son of an Ulster Presbyterian clergyman. In the closing days of July 1848, O'Brien and a motley assembly of half-starved peasants clashed with forty-six Irish Constabulary (the national police force formed in 1836) in what has become known as the 'Battle of the Widow McCormack's cabbage patch' at Ballingarry, Co. Tipperary. O'Brien was arrested soon afterwards and sentenced to death. The sentence was commuted to penal servitude for life, and he joined John Mitchel in Tasmania. He was released in 1854, but played no further part in Irish politics. 'The people', he explained, 'preferred to die of starvation at home, or to flee as voluntary exiles to other lands, rather than to fight for their lands and their liberties'.

The 'revolt' of O'Brien and the Young Irelanders in 1848 was a small and faintly ludicrous affair. However, their movement was important to the future pattern of Irish republican nationalism. They revived the principle of a non-sectarian independent Irish republic put forward first by Wolfe Tone and the United Irishmen. They produced the ideal of an Irish nationhood based upon the mix of Irish cultural heritage. They found – as did their successors – that the weight of the Catholic Church was firmly on the side of politicians prepared to work within the constitutional arrangements of Westminster. 'It is my sincere belief', wrote O'Brien shortly after his arrest, 'that it was through the instrumentality of the superior order of the Catholic clergy that the insurrection was suppressed.' *The Times* on 2 August 1848 reported that 'altogether there is no doubt that the Roman Catholic clergy here, as a body, have used their influence and most creditably for the preservation of the public peace by discountenancing rebellion'. Yet, while facing up to the fact of the Catholic Church's opposition to revolutionary Irish nationalism, Young Ireland ignored the growing Protestant opposition to their ideal Irish republic – the Orange Order had been reconstituted in 1845 – paradoxically calling for reconciliation without seeing that their goal made this impossible. In this, too, every one of their successors followed suit. Even when the Irish civil war was fought in 1922–3 over the Anglo-Irish Treaty which partitioned Ireland as a result of Orange and Unionist opposition to home rule, the actual cause of the fighting was not partition but the question of whether men, who during the previous six years had fought for a republic, could in all conscience take an oath of allegiance to the British king.

By the end of the century, there was some recognition of the significance of Young Ireland and the nature of the difficulties they faced in attempting revolt in the midst of famine, and at the moment when the mass of the Irish people seemed to have perceived that their survival was somehow related to their cultural traditions yet had determined to throw off the remnants of Gaelicism in an attempt to identify with their successful British conquerors. Douglas Hyde, later to become the first president of Eire, put this point in a lecture he delivered in Dublin in 1892, 'The necessity for de-Anglicizing Ireland':

Thomas Davis and his brilliant band of Young Irelanders came just at the dividing line, and tried to give to Ireland a new literature in English to replace the literature which was just being discarded. It succeeded and it did not succeed. It was a most brilliant effort, but the old bark had been too recently stripped off the Irish tree, and the trunk could not take as it might have done to a fresh one. It was a new departure, and at first produced a violent effect. Yet in the long run it failed properly to leaven our peasantry who might, perhaps, have been reached upon other lines.

Yeats, however, though he had absorbed Davis' teachings in his youth, came to disagree with him profoundly over his willingness to subordinate art to politics. To recommend this method of literature, he wrote, 'was to be deceived or to practise deception'.

In 1848 such arguments would have been academic. The Irish peasantry had been reached by one other devastating line, the great famine of 1845–9, the worst catastrophe of Irish history.

6

Famine and Fenians

The 1841 census divided the 8,175,124 people of Ireland into four categories according to their relative wealth: property owners and farmers of more than fifty acres; artisans and farmers with between five and fifty acres; labourers and smallholders with up to five acres, and the numerically insignificant fourth category, 'means unspecified'. Seventy per cent of the rural population were in the category of labourers and smallholders with five acres or less. They were spread throughout the country in three distinct patterns: a prosperous farming class and poor labouring class in the midlands and the south; a prosperous east and north, and an extremely poor and numerous class of impoverished smallholders in the west and south-western seaboard counties. The effects of the great famine reflected this pattern, with the west and south-west of the country hardest hit, and the labouring and impoverished smallholding groups bearing the brunt of starvation, sickness and death. Fever followed famine, and people all over the country died from its effects, but as far as death from starvation was concerned, the labouring population suffered almost to the exclusion of other groups. Thus in the midlands and the south, the prosperous farming class of people did not starve during the years of the 'Great Hunger'. The famine was never general in the rural community.

Between 1841 and 1851 the population fell by nearly 20 per cent to 6,552, 385. Total deaths were estimated by the census commissioners in the same period at 1,383,350 – certainly an underestimate since where whole families died, no returns were made, and not until 1864 was registration of births, marriages and deaths made compulsory. The census commissioners estimated that another 1,445,587 Irish people emigrated, mostly to America, in the same period.

The direct cause of the famine and its attendant demographic repercussions was the persistent failure of the potato crop in the years 1845 and 1846, and in the partial failure of the crop in each of the succeeding five years. By tradition, Sir Walter Raleigh is credited with the introduction of the potato to Ireland from America in 1586. Within two centuries it had become the principal vegetable food of the peasantry. It needed little labour to plant and harvest. It yielded a large amount on a small acreage, and so was ideally suited to the small tenant farmer. Together with buttermilk, it provided sufficient nutrition to sustain life and a reasonable state of health. By 1845 it had become the sole food of about one-third of the people, and bread, meat, grain or corn meal graced only the tables of the better off. Thus the effect of a potato crop failure could be devastating, and the effect of consecutive failures could be fatally destructive famine on a very large scale.

Famine had already struck in Ireland many times during the nineteenth century: in 1807, 1817, 1821–2, 1830–4, 1836, and 1839. However, while always accompanied by death and emigration, potato crop failure and famine had also always been localized. In 1845 the first signs of potato crop failure came in September when discolouration on the leaves of potato plants was noticed. When the crop was dug in October, hopes that failure would be small-scale and localized as in previous years were dashed, as over most of the country reports came in that there was no crop at all. The actual cause of the failure was *phytophthora infestans* – potato blight. The spores of the blight were carried by wind, rain and insects and came to Ireland from Britain and the European continent. A fungus growth affected the potato plants, producing black spots and a white mould on the leaves, soon rotting the potato into a pulp. The following year, the blight was general, and by the beginning of 1847 it was clear that a disaster of unprecedented magnitude was under way. Despite the fact that there was no blight in 1847, because of the small supply of seed potatoes the healthy crop that year merely reduced the extent of famine, it did not end mass starvation. Typhus, dysentery, scurvy, hunger oedema and relapsing fever ('Yellow Fever') brought death to areas of the country which had escaped the worst in the previous years. In 1848 there was widespread, though partial, crop failure again. In December, an outbreak of Asiatic cholera began which lasted until July 1849. Hundreds of thousands of people in various stages of starvation died from this and other fevers during the height of the famine, nearly all of them from the poorest section of the community, the small tenants and landless labourers. By the summer of 1847, three million people, nearly half the population of Ireland, were being fed by private charities – often organized by the Quakers – or at public expense. So many people died in so short a period of time, that mass graves were provided, often in ground specially consecrated for the purpose. Emigration soared from 75,000 in 1845 to 250,000 in 1851. Thousands of emigrants died during the Atlantic crossing (in 1847 there were 17,465 documented deaths) in 'coffin ships' plying a speculative trade, often little more than rotting hulks. Thousands more died of sickness at disembarkation centres.

The famine lasted in one part of the country or another from 1845 to 1849, with its effects lasting much longer still. The 1851 census revealed greatly enlarged urban populations, numerous workhouse inmates, and large numbers of people in receipt of outdoor relief, especially in the west and the poorer parts of the country. In the west, the famine had struck hardest. There, since the time of Cromwell the bulk of the population had been concentrated. In Co. Mayo in 1841, for example, there were 475 people for every acre of arable land, and in the province of Connaught as a whole, 64 per cent of the farms were smaller than five acres. Through these congested districts, famine diseases spread like wildfire.

The danger of famine inherent in dependence upon one particular source of food had not escaped the awareness of the government in London. A century earlier, in 1740–1, a previous famine had resulted in the deaths of an estimated 400,000 Irishmen. In 1832 famine had been accompanied by cholera. At the same time, the political philosophy of the day was *laissez-faire*, the belief in the efficacy of the unrestrained forces of the market in all circumstances, and in common with nineteenth-century European political practice, British political parties were all wedded to it. Nevertheless, the response of the Tory government under Sir Robert Peel in 1845–6 was prompt, efficient and interventionist.

Sir Robert Peel (1788–1850) was a politician noted for his dedication to administrative efficiency. Born in Lancashire, the son of a textile mill-owner, Peel entered politics in 1809 as an Irish Tory MP for Cashel, Co. Tipperary. In 1812 he was appointed chief secretary of Ireland, serving for six years – the longest of any chief secretary of the century. His tenure of office in Ireland was marked by the animosity Peel and Daniel O'Connell had for each other (O'Connell dubbed him 'Orange Peel', referred to him as 'a raw youth, squeezed out of I know not what factory in England', and was challenged to a duel by Peel in 1815), and by the imaginative – almost experimental – nature of his policies. He created in 1814 a police force, the Peace Preservation Police, quickly known as 'Peelers'; the following year he created a precedent by establishing a state grant for primary education, and during the famine of 1817 he demonstrated his flexibility and willingness to flout the common wisdom of the day by providing £250,000 for relief works. In 1829 he led in the debate on Catholic emancipation, supporting it in the house of commons while the prime minister, the duke of Wellington, supported it in the lords. Prime minister himself from 1834 to 35 and again from 1841 to 46, Peel showed himself willing to concede reform, but unwilling to consider constitutional changes, and he steadfastly opposed O'Connell's Repeal Association. In 1845 he granted an annual endowment of £26,000 to the Catholic seminary, Maynooth College, and introduced the non-denominational Queen's Colleges – the first state-created university colleges in British history – in an attempt to open higher education to Catholics. By the end of the year, growing famine distress in Ireland had convinced him of the need immediately to abolish the Corn Laws (tariffs on grain imported into the United Kingdom which in effect subsidized UK farmers) so as to lower the price of corn and therefore bread. The strong farming and landowning interests in the Tory Party opposed their leader on this issue. Peel persevered, splitting his Party and losing office the following year when, with Opposition Whig support, he forced the repeal of the Corn Laws through parliament: Benjamin Disraeli, the young Tory MP for Maidstone, leapt to prominence and ultimately the leadership of the Conservative Party by spearheading the revolt against Peel on this issue.

Repeal of the Corn Laws was only one of several measures Peel applied to relieve the effects of famine. In November 1845 he appointed a scientific commission to decide what should be done: they incorrectly diagnosed the nature of the potato blight, and so were ineffective, but this was not Peel's fault. He himself recognized that the first priority had to be the provision of food, and he personally authorized (without cabinet approval) the purchase of £100,000 of maize from the United States for distribution in Ireland by a Relief Commission he set up to coordinate relief work. To provide employment and thus money for starving Irishmen to buy food, early in 1846 he secured the passage of Acts which authorized improvements for Irish harbours and roads. He encouraged voluntary relief committees (about 650 were formed by August 1846) and established special food depots which released food supplies on to the open market so as to ensure that local traders would not be able to raise prices and capitalize on misery. Altogether, his policies worked: no one died from starvation alone while Peel was in office.

Having split his Party over the repeal of the Corn Laws, Peel was voted out of office at the end of June 1846. His successor as prime minister, the Whig Lord John Russell, came into office just as it was becoming clear that, for the first time, the whole potato crop of Ireland was blighted. Part of Peel's success in dealing with the famine lay in the fact that the 1845 crop failure was only partial. In 1846, Ireland was faced with famine of an altogether greater magnitude. This was compounded by Russell. Unlike Peel, who had pragmatically concentrated upon ensuring that there was enough food to feed those in desperate need, Russell was a doctrinaire exponent of *laissez-faire*. He also headed a minority government, dependent upon the votes of Tories who had found Peel too liberal. So, while the Whigs had supported Peel over the repeal of the Corn Laws, and while Russell himself had a liberal record, in order to stay in office he found it necessary to stick to political principles generally acceptable to Tories. In October 1846 he set out his approach to the famine: 'It must be thoroughly understood that we cannot feed the people...We can at best keep down prices where there is no regular market and prevent established dealers from raising prices much beyond the fair price with ordinary profits.' His policies emphasized employment rather than food for famine victims in the belief that private enterprise, not government, should be responsible for food provision, and that the cost of Irish relief work should be paid for by Irishmen. Peel's Relief Commission was abolished, and all public relief work was put in the hands of the 12,000 civil servants in the Board of Works who manfully tried to find work for nearly 750,000 starving people on top of all their normal responsibilities. Workhouses were built where, in return for hard (and often pointless) work, starving peasants were paid starvation wages. Tens of thousands of people died during the winter of 1846, forcing the government to accept that its policies were not working and that Peel's policy of state intervention in food supply and distribution was the only alternative. In March 1847, Russell authorized the general distribution of food to the destitute. No one who held as much as a quarter of an acre could qualify, however, with the result that hundreds of thousands gave up their holdings in order not to starve.

Private enterprise also contributed significantly to the alleviation of distress. Many individual landlords did the best they could for their tenants. Soup kitchens, freely feeding starving peasants, were established by landlords and notably by the Society of Friends and the British Relief Association. Unfortunately, some evangelical Anglican clergymen, particularly in the west of Ireland, brought distrust to the notion of soup kitchens with 'Souperism': offering nourishment to people in return for their conversion. Early in 1847, government-sponsored soup kitchens were established, and by August that year 3,000,000 people a day were being fed by them. But Russell and his colleagues never conceived of interfering with the structure of the Irish economy in the ways that would have been necessary to prevent the worst effects of the famine. There was no attempt to reform tenancies or agricultural practices. Instead, landlords (who were responsible for the rates of their tenants on holdings valued at £4 or less, even if rents were not paid) in some cases evicted tenants as a way of reducing rate bills (in 1850, 104,000 people were evicted), and farmers and merchants were able to export grain and cattle without government hindrance. One of the most remarkable facts about the famine period is that an average £100,000 of food was exported from Ireland every month: almost throughout, Ireland remained a net exporter of food.

In addition to private and government intervention, the Poor Law unions administered the bulk of relief work. The 130 unions in Ireland had been introduced in 1838 with the Irish Poor Law Act, extending the British Poor Law system to Ireland. Under this system each union was supervised by a Board of Guardians consisting of local ratepayers, responsible for workhouses where the destitute could work in exchange for subsistence wages. The unions were supported by local rates, and as a result whole districts were bankrupted through the unions' expenditure during the famine. In an attempt both to contain such bankruptcy and to extend work-house relief, in 1847 the government increased the number of unions to 162. The extent of their work can be judged by the numbers employed in relief works: 114,600 in October 1846; 570,000 in January 1847 and 734,000 in March. Over £7 million was spent by the government in grants and loans during the famine, much of this through the Poor Law unions.

It must be said that the government in London never properly appreciated the sheer magnitude of the famine. Official insensitivity was also something which other subjects in the United Kingdom faced: between June and October 1848, for example, 72,000 people died of cholera in England and Wales without the government intervening. It must also be pointed out that in the midst of the most awful suffering, starving Irishmen did little to help themselves. There were food riots, but no real uprising (1848 was a fiasco), and despite government encouragement, sea and river fishing was not taken up: it was as if famine victims simply accepted death passively as their inevitable fate. 'The forbearance of the Irish peasantry', the 1851 Census Commission declared, 'and the calm submission with which they bore the deadliest ills that can fall on man can scarcely be paralleled in the annals of any nation.'

Charles Edward Trevelyan (1807–86), in 1848 knighted for his services to Ireland, assistant secretary to the Treasury, was the civil servant most involved in Irish famine relief. Like Russell and Sir Charles Wood, chancellor of the exchequer (1846–52), Trevelyan firmly believed in the principles of *laissez-faire*, opposed new expenditure and raising taxes, and supported self-sufficiency. He was convinced of Malthus' theory that any attempt to raise the standard of living of the poorest section of the population above subsistence level would only result in increased population which would restore the previous situation, aggravated and enlarged. Thus in October 1846 he wrote that the overpopulation of Ireland 'being altogether beyond the power of man, the cure has been applied by the direct stroke of an all-wise Providence in a manner as unexpected and as unthought of as it is likely to be effectual'. Two years later after perhaps a million people had died, he wrote, 'The matter is awfully serious, but we are in the hands of Providence, without a possibility of averting the catastrophe if it is to happen. We can only await the result.' Sir Charles Wood replied in the same vein to an Irish landlord who in 1848 had written to him describing what was actually happening, 'I am not at all appalled by your tenantry going. That seems to me a necessary part of the process...We must not complain of what we really want to obtain.' Imprisoned by their attitudes, these men could stand by, convinced that they should not interfere in the divine retribution of the famine on the unruly, rebellious, treacherous Irish. As the *Times* leader of 30 August 1847 put it, 'In no other country have men talked treason until they are hoarse, and then gone about begging for sympathy from their oppressors. In no other country have the people been so liberally and unthriftily helped by the nation they denounced and defied.' 'The great evil with which we have to contend', Trevelyan himself declared in 1846, 'is not the physical evil of the famine, but the moral evil of the selfish, perverse and turbulent character of the people.'

The long-term consequences of the famine were varied and tremendous. The most notable was the tradition it firmly established of emigration, principally to the United States of America. Between 1845 and 1855, nearly two million people had emigrated from Ireland to America and Australia, and another 750,000 to Britain. By 1900 over four million Irishmen had crossed the Atlantic, and as many lived abroad as in Ireland. In the century up to 1930, it is estimated that one out of every two people born in Ireland emigrated. Between 1951 and 1961, net emigration from the country as a whole amounted to 437,682. Since then, emigration has fallen substantially, but it is still an element in Irish life.

There were other drastic consequences too. Potatoes declined rapidly in importance as the remaining farmers and tenants in Ireland after the famine changed over from tillage to grazing sheep and cattle. This in turn ended the practice of farm subdivision, and one son came generally to inherit farms intact. Emigration or a threadbare existence were the choices facing younger children, and practically every census between 1851 and 1961 showed a decline in Ireland's population (a 0.46 per cent population increase was reported in 1936–7, and an increase of 1.96 per cent shown in 1951). Part of the population loss reflected the increasing age at which Irish people in the main began to marry: in 1900 in rural Ireland the average age at marriage for men was thirty-nine and for women thirty-one. Late marriage was a characteristic of the Irish farming community before the famine, with only the labouring/cottier class enjoying early marriage. After the famine, the labouring/cottier class (which was hit hardest) was much reduced, and farmers became the largest single class on the land, a phenomenon reflected not only in the characteristic of late marriage, but also in a change in the nature of land-ownership. Indeed, the famine affected the farming community only slightly, and it emerged strengthened as a consequence. As labourers and cottiers died or emigrated, leaving their small-holdings, so small farmers extended their plots. In 1845 there had been nearly 630,000 holdings of up to fifteen acres (with each holding basically supporting a family); by 1851 there were only 318,000. In the same period, the number of holdings of fifteen acres or more increased from 277,000 to 290,000.

The famine also ended the widespread use of the Irish language. Gaelic, the natural language of 4 million Irish people in 1841, by 1851 was spoken only by 1.7 million; in 1911 by only 527,000. 'The Famine', wrote Douglas Hyde in 1891, 'knocked the heart out of the Irish language.' Speaking Irish had become firmly identified with poverty and peasanthood, with famine and death. In the later decades of the nineteenth century, Irish-speaking parents joined wholeheartedly with priests and teachers to force their children to speak only English. English was identified with success and well-being. It was the language of commerce, and the language of emigrant relatives too. The 1831 National Education Act established English as the language of Ireland's first national primary-school system. Hedge-school teachers before the National Schools were introduced had used tally-sticks, the *bata scoir* which Irish-speaking children wore around their necks, as a crude disciplinary measure. National School teachers adopted the *bata scoir* to help them end the use of Irish: every time a child was heard speaking in Irish, a notch was cut in the stick; at the end of the day the notches were counted and the child punished for each offence.

There is a depressing fatalism about the *bata scoir*, used by Irish people themselves and not forced upon them by any official edict. The great native Irish cultural force embodied in the language was consciously thrust aside by the very people whose national identity and pride it had sustained for centuries. No doubt this was a symptom of their wretched, conquered state when they perceived survival as depending upon their ability to conform to the image of their conquerors and governors. It is when people lose confidence in themselves that extremism flourishes. In many ways, Patrick Pearse and his colleagues in 1916 represented the last generation which had a coherent sense of Irish language and culture. Even then, while admiring a legendary past and attempting to emulate the legendary Gael, English was their language: their rebel proclamation of an Irish public in 1916 was printed and published only in English; the orders they gave their Irish Republican Army were in English; the letters and poems they wrote just before their executions were in English. Despite their rejection of the thought, their country had been Anglicized by a combination of education, social pressure and the famine.

Irish emigrants carried one other significant effect of the famine abroad: their hatred of Britain. Britain was blamed for the famine, and was the target of all their resentment. Irish emigrants to the United States came to form a body of political opinion consistently hostile to British interests. In both world wars, American isolationism was strongly supported by Irish–Americans. Substantial financial and propaganda support has come from America for every Irish national movement from the nineteenth-century Home Rule Party to the IRA today. American politicians and presidents have found it prudent, for domestic political reasons, to use their influence on Britain in Irish interests. In 1919–20, Eamon de Valera, Ireland's nationalist political leader at the time, considered himself better employed in America where he raised over five million dollars in less than two years and tried to influence the 1920 American presidential election in the Irish interest. Presidents Woodrow Wilson and Warren Harding both exerted diplomatic pressure for an Irish settlement upon Lloyd George's government. It was from America, too, that the Irish Republican Brotherhood, the most effective of all Ireland's revolutionary national movements, was financed and sustained from the time of its foundation in 1858.

Some of those who emigrated from Ireland during the famine, and some of the Young Irelanders who had contemplated rebellion, like Thomas Francis Meagher (1823–67) who in 1853 escaped from transportation and reached America, determined to organize further rebellion in Ireland. John Mitchel, another Young Irelander, instead adopted an O'Connellite approach after escaping with Meagher to America. He became a farmer in Tennessee and vociferously espoused the Confederate cause in the American Civil War, refusing to accept that Negroes or Jews had the same rights as Irishmen. He returned to Ireland in 1874 and was elected MP for North Tipperary the following year, only to lose his seat on the grounds that he was an escaped convict. A second election again returned him, but he died shortly afterwards in Newry where he is buried. Meagher settled in New York where he entered politics and was admitted to the Bar. When the Civil War started, he raised an Irish Brigade for the Union – the New York Irish Brigade (the 69th, 88th and 63rd New York Volunteers) – and was commissioned with the rank of brigadier general. He planned to battle-train Irish soldiers who would return to Ireland at the end of the war and liberate their own country. But his Brigade was decimated at the battles of Antietam (September 1862), Fredericksburg (December 1862) and Chancellorsville (May 1863), thus thwarting his hopes. After the surrender of the Confederate States, Meagher left the army with the rank of major general and was appointed acting governor of the Montana Territory. During a Missouri River flood in 1867, he fell from his ship and was drowned.

Another Young Irelander, James Stephens (1824–1901), quite independently shared Meagher's hopes for an Irish–American supported Irish rebellion. Unlike Meagher and Mitchel, Stephens had avoided arrest in 1848 and fled to France where he learnt about the Carbonari, a Franco-Italian secret society dedicated to revolutionary activity. He returned to Ireland in 1856 resolved to form an Irish secret society on the same lines, to work for Irish national freedom by revolution. For a year he journeyed all over Ireland covering three thousand miles, mainly on foot, assessing opinion and gathering supporters. Then, on St Patrick's Day, 17 March 1858, in Dublin, he formally established the Irish Revolutionary Brotherhood, later named the Irish Republican Brotherhood – the IRB. In rural areas the new society benefited from the tradition of agrarian secret societies, and hundreds of men took Stephens' membership oath:

I. . .do solemnly swear in the presence of Almighty God that I will do my utmost at every risk while life lasts, to make Ireland an independent democratic republic; that I will yield implicit obedience in all things not contrary to the law of God to the commands of my superior officers, and that I shall preserve inviolable secrecy regarding all the transactions of this secret society that may be confided in me. So help me God. Amen.

Six months after founding the IRB, Stephens sailed to New York where he raised money and support for the society with the help of two other Young Irelanders, John O'Mahony (1815–77), and Michael Doheny (1805–63). O'Mahony had escaped to France with Stephens in 1848, and had stayed with him until 1852 when he went to live in New York. He remained closely in touch with Stephens, sending him $400 early in 1858 which Stephens used to start the IRB. In New York, on the same day Stephens founded the IRB, O'Mahony founded an auxiliary Irish–American secret society which he named the Fenian Brotherhood after Finn MacCool's legendary band of warriors, the Fianna. Michael Doheny was a founder member of the Fenian Brotherhood, having escaped directly to New York after 1848. There he practised as a lawyer and as a propagandist of Irish nationalism. Under their leadership, the 'Fenians' (as both the Fenian Brotherhood and the IRB rapidly became known) prepared for another rising. However, while a capable organizer and the acknowledged Fenian leader or 'head centre', Stephens' efforts towards an Irish rebellion were marked by procrastination. Seven years after founding the IRB, Stephens (who had returned to Ireland in 1860) promised his American supporters that there would be a rising in 1865. With typical optimism he claimed that there were 85,000 Fenians in Ireland armed with 50,000 guns, and that there were a further 15,000 Fenians in the British army waiting for his word to rebel. A Fenian organizer in Britain, Michael Davitt (1846–1906), sent Stephens reports which buoyed his claims, while another organizer in Ireland, John Devoy (1842–1928), estimated that out of a British garrison of 25,000, 7,000 were members of the IRB. As events were to prove, these estimates were wildly exaggerated.

On 11 November 1865, seven weeks before the end of the year Stephens had promised would be known for a Fenian rising, Stephens was arrested and imprisoned in Richmond gaol, Dublin. A fortnight later, with the help of John Devoy and some Fenian warders in the gaol, he escaped and made his way to Paris and then New York. Using the title 'chief organizer of the Irish republic', with this escape Stephens caught the popular imagination, becoming a national hero literally overnight. However, his constant attempts to delay a rising for one reason or another (he had called off one planned rising in December 1865, and he tried to postpone another twelve months later), and his autocratic ways, alienated much of the IRB and the Fenian Brotherhood, and early in 1867 he left New York and returned to France in fear for his life. For the next twenty years he lived as an impoverished journalist in Paris until 1886 when, through the intercession on his behalf of Charles Stewart Parnell, and with the help of a public subscription, he returned to live quietly and in comparative comfort in Dublin.

Stephens had been betrayed by an informer who worked in the offices of the *Irish People*, a newspaper Stephens had established in 1863. The men involved in this newspaper – like those involved twenty years earlier with the Young Ireland newspapers – came to dominate revolutionary Irish nationalism. John O'Leary (1830–1907) an agnostic, Thomas Clarke Luby (1821–1901) a Protestant and Charles Joseph Kickham (1828–82) a devout Catholic, were the joint editors of the paper; Jeremiah O'Donovan Rossa (1831–1915) was the business manager. They were also the leaders, under Stephens, of the IRB. Under their control, the *Irish People* was stridently republican, and in September 1865 it was suppressed by the authorities and O'Leary, Luby, Kickham and Rossa were arrested and sentenced to long terms of imprisonment under the Treason–Felony Act. John Devoy, who briefly succeeded Stephens as acting head centre after Stephens' arrest in November, was also arrested in February 1866. Together with O'Donovan Rossa and Luby, he spent five years in English prisons before all three were released in 1871 on condition they did not return to Ireland until the period of their sentences had expired. They all went to New York where Luby and Rossa became journalists and Devoy became one of the most influential leaders of the Clan-na-Gael, the successor organization to the Fenian Brotherhood. Devoy, in fact, came to personify exiled Ireland. He played a crucial part in the IRB's attempt to secure German support for the 1916 rising, and despite a stormy relationship with Eamon de Valera in 1919–20, acted as the chief Irish–American organizer and fund-raiser for the IRA. Kickham was released from prison in poor health in 1869 and O'Leary in 1874, both becoming active supporters of the revival of Gaelic literature towards the end of the nineteenth century. Kickham's patriotic novel, *Knocknagow*, became the most popular book in Ireland. In 1915, Rossa's body was brought back to Dublin from New York and given a massive funeral on 1 August. At the graveside in Glasnevin cemetery, Patrick Pearse gave the funeral oration, ending with a cry: 'The fools, the fools, the fools! They have left us our Fenian dead, and while Ireland holds these graves, Ireland unfree shall never be at peace.'

Thomas J. Kelly (1833–1908) succeeded Stephens as IRB head centre after Stephens was deposed in December 1866. He had emigrated from Galway to the United States, and had fought with the 10th Ohio Regiment during the American Civil War. In 1865 he returned to Ireland as an emissary from the Fenian Brotherhood, charged to urge a rising on Stephens. He took part in Stephens' rescue from Richmond gaol and accompanied him on his escape to America. In January 1867 he travelled to London where, with the title 'acting chief executive of the Irish republic', he planned an Irish rising for 11 February to be preceded by a raid on the British army's arms depot at Chester Castle. The raid was abortive; leading Fenians were arrested, and the rising had to be postponed. A new date was set – Easter Sunday – but internal dissension, government spies and blizzard weather ruined Kelly's plans. On Easter Sunday, only a handful of Fenians turned out, and most of the leaders were arrested. If 1848 was tragi-comedy, 1867 was farce. Kelly was apprehended in Manchester with a colleague, Timothy Deasy. A week later, they were freed from a police van by a Fenian rescue party, and one of the police guards, Sergeant Brett, was shot dead. Kelly and Deasy were never recaptured. Kelly made his way back to America and relative obscurity; Deasy also went to America where he entered Massachusetts politics. Three of their rescue party were less fortunate – William Allen, Michael Larkin and Michael O'Brien. All three were captured and charged with Brett's murder, found guilty, and hanged on the morning of 23 November. Three weeks later, on 13 December, another Fenian rescue attempt was made to release some prisoners from Clerkenwell gaol in London by blowing a hole in the prison wall. The explosion killed twelve people at once (over the following weeks, a further eighteen died of injuries received from the blast; another 120 were wounded), and did not succeed in enabling the prisoners to escape. Public opinion was horrified, and the Fenians became firmly established in British minds as odious murderers and terrorists. A Fenian named Michael Barrett was eventually executed for the Clerkenwell explosion in the last public hanging in England.

A different perception of the Fenians existed in Ireland, however, and Allen, Larkin and O'Brien soon became the 'Manchester

Martyrs' and annual commemorations of their execution still take place. It was never proved that any of the 'Martyrs' had actually shot Brett, although in law all those found to be involved in an act in which murder is committed are equally *participes criminus* and they were convicted in the popular press before their trial had commenced. Two others charged with them avoided the death penalty – one was given a free pardon following representations from journalists covering the case; the other, Edward O'Meagher Condon, had his sentence commuted, but not before he said from the dock 'I have nothing to regret, or to retract, or take back. I can only say "God Save Ireland."' 'God Save Ireland' was immediately taken up as a catch phrase, becoming the title of a ballad which in turn became the marching song of the IRB and during the nineteenth century the unofficial national anthem. The trial and execution of the 'Martyrs' on flimsy evidence also reduced Irish faith in British justice and helped encourage a romanticization of Fenianism and the continuation after 1867 of the IRB.

In America even before the failure of 1867, the Fenian Brotherhood had broken into factions. One group under the command of an emigrant from Co. Monaghan and a former Union army general and Indian fighters, John O'Neill (1834–73), launched an 'invasion' of Canada in the summer of 1866. Between 600 and 800 Fenians crossed the Niagara river in flat boats near Buffalo, New York, and occupied the town of Fort Erie. Some days later another Fenian force crossed into Canada from Vermont. Both groups were easily routed, but not before they had operated under the name 'Irish Republican Army', the Fenian army of the Irish republic which they regarded as existing in theory, if not in fact. O'Neill was arrested by the American authorities and imprisoned for a while. On his release he abandoned Irish nationalist activities, and worked the last years of his life for a firm of land speculators.

The Fenians' theoretical republic was necessary to the Fenians to counteract the opposition they faced from the Roman Catholic Church. Religious loyalty was almost as powerful a force as nationalism on Irishmen. For centuries they were not in conflict, and O'Connell had welded them together in a powerful combination to achieve Catholic emancipation. However, after emancipation, Ireland as part of the United Kingdom provided the Church with the support of up to about eighty Irish Catholic MPs in the 1880s in the parliament of the greatest empire in the world. By the 1850s, the

Church was identifying more and more with the British government, using its influence to secure Irish nationalist political conformity with British constitutional practices. Irish Church leaders would campaign for social reforms, but would not campaign for Irish independence, and certainly not for physical force nationalism. The Fenians, the 1916 rising, the IRA in 1920 and the IRA again in 1922 were all condemned by the Church. Of course, the arguments for constitutionalism and against violence weighed heavily, but they were seen as dictating uniformity with British laws and British practices. As Dr Paul Cullen (1803–78), archbishop of Dublin, put it in 1865 (the following year he became the first Irish cardinal), if the Irish people were fairly treated 'revolutions and conspiracies, Whiteboys and Fenians, would no longer be heard of, and people would be happy and peaceable, and a source of strength to the empire at large'. Successive administrations acknowledged the special position of the Church in Ireland, starting with that of William Pitt the younger which from 1795 endowed the Catholic seminary, the Royal College of St Patrick at Maynooth, Co. Kildare with an annual government grant, fixed at £9,250 in 1808. In exchange, the College's staff and students took an oath of loyalty to the British monarch:

I. . .do take Almighty God and his only Son Jesus Christ my Redeemer to witness, that I will be faithful and bear true allegiance to our most gracious sovereign lord King George the third, and him will defend to the utmost of my power against all conspiracies and attempts whatever, that shall be made against his person, crown and dignity; and I will do my utmost endeavour to disclose and make known to his Majesty, and his heirs, all treasons and traitorous conspiracies which may be formed against him or them; and I do faithfully promise to maintain, support and defend, to the utmost of my power, the succession of the crown in his Majesty's family against any person or persons whatsoever.

When the president of Maynooth led the condemnation of the 1798 rising, and when the Church – which came to consist of Maynooth-trained priests – increasingly opposed rebel Irish nationalists, people in Ireland were not surprised. In 1845, Peel increased the grant to the Royal College to £26,360 per annum. In 1871 the grant was discontinued, replaced by a capital endowment of £369,000.

Peel's support of Maynooth was part of his attempt to introduce a system of higher education to Ireland acceptable to the Catholic Church. Under the 1845 Provincial Colleges Act, the government established three university Queen's Colleges at Galway, Cork and

Belfast with an annual grant of £30,000. In 1850 they were linked to form Ireland's second university, the Queen's University, open to Catholics and Protestants alike. At first the new Colleges were accepted by the Church, but as it became clear that the government would not allow any change in their non-denominational character, denying any Church the right to control the curriculum or academic appointments, and would not itself fund Chairs of Theology (although private endowments for this purpose were allowed), the Catholic hierarchy soon opposed the Colleges. They were denounced as the 'godless colleges', as 'a grave danger to the faith of Catholics'. Papal rescripts were issued condemning the Colleges. The bishop of Clonfert refused the sacraments to parents of students at the Colleges. In 1854 the Church founded its own Catholic University in Dublin in opposition to Queen's University, and in 1871 extended this opposition to Trinity College, Dublin, by banning Catholics from attendance there – a ban which Trinity itself never imposed. In 1908 the Queen's Colleges in Cork and Galway were amalgamated with the Catholic University to form the National University of Ireland. Queen's College in Belfast became the Queen's University of Belfast; Trinity and the private Magee College in Londonderry remained separate institutions in a denominationally divided higher education system. The ban on Catholics attending Trinity College was renewed as late as in 1956 by the Catholic archbishop of Dublin, and remained in force until 1970. Altogether, the Church's influence in education, let alone on politics in Ireland from the nineteenth century onwards, was an impressive testimony to its power not lost on Protestants in northern Ireland and elsewhere. In the 1860s, however, the Fenians were the first to feel the full strength of the Church.

As a secret oath-bound society, the IRB was anathema to the Church. Four papal bulls, 'In Eminenti' (1738), 'Providas' (1751), 'Ecclesiam' (1821) and 'Quo Graviora' (1825) had all condemned secret societies. Physical force Irish nationalism in the nineteenth century was also distinguished by the large number of Protestants involved, and this no doubt contributed to the Church's antipathy to it. Finally, the IRB was actually pledged to rebellion. Four conditions for rebellion to be justified were required by the Church, and it was rare for them to be met. They were a recipe designed to maintain the *status quo*. First, the government had to be habitually and intolerably oppressive. Secondly, rebellion must be a last resort after other means of opposition had been tried and failed. Thirdly, there must be a reasonable chance of success and of not making matters worse. Fourthly, the resistance to established authority must enjoy approval by a popular majority. It was no wonder that in 1861, three years after its formation, Archbishop Cullen excommunicated the members of the IRB *ipso facto*.

The IRB early on had foreseen the Church's hostility. John O'Mahony in 1859 had declared that Fenianism 'is neither anti-Catholic nor irreligious. We are an Irish army, not a secret society.' James Stephens in 1859 changed the IRB's original oath in an attempt to bring the society into conformity with O'Mahony's line of argument, dropping reference to a secret society. Throughout its life the IRB argued that it was the army and the government of the Irish republic, and therefore constituted a valid and *de jure* authority which circumvented the Church's objections to it and enabled it for over sixty years to recruit successfully among Catholic Irishmen. In 1864 the *Irish People* carried the argument further in a clear call for the separation of Church and state in a future independent Ireland: 'We saw from the first that ecclesiastical authority in temporal affairs should be shivered to atoms before we could advance a single step towards the liberation of our suffering country.' This call, together with their dedication to physical force, was Fenianism's most important legacy. Still, the church's opposition was unremitting. Immediately before the attempted Fenian rebellion in 1867, Bishop Moriarty of Kerry cursed the Fenians in resounding terms:

Oh, God's heaviest curse, his withering, blighting blasting curse on them . . .When we look down into the fathomless depth of this infamy of the leaders of the Fenian conspiracy, we must acknowledge that eternity is not long enough, nor hell hot enough to punish such miscreants.

In 1870, under the influence of Cardinal Cullen, the Sacred Congregation of the Holy See, otherwise known as the Roman Inquisition, with the authority of Pope Pius IX, banned the society and declared its members excommunicated. In the 1920s the IRA faced the same opposition. Bishop Cohalan of Cork on 12 December 1920 issued a decree excommunicating members of the IRA. On 10 October 1922 during the civil war, the Catholic Hierarchy in Ireland declared in a joint pastoral that the Irish Free State government was the legitimate government (as opposed to the government of the Irish republic which the IRA had recognized since 1916), and that the IRA, 'the Irregulars', were guilty of 'murder', 'robbery', 'criminal destruction' and 'molestation'. Just over ten years later in Spain, in complete contrast, the Catholic hierarchy there recognized and endorsed the rebellion of General Franco against the established and legitimate government of the Spanish Republic.

Ecclesiastical opposition to extreme Irish nationalism, while official and pronounced, was not, however, uniform. There were always 'patriot' priests and bishops who were prepared to give comfort to those whom their superiors opposed. When the Manchester Martyrs were executed, prayers and Masses for them were said in churches all over Ireland. This ambivalence within the Church enabled the IRB to argue that the opposition it faced from the Church was based in ignorance. Charles Kickham, the head of the IRB from its re-organization in 1873 until his death, had masterminded the Fenian reply to the Church. In the IRB constitution he drew up, the president of the IRB was declared the president of the Irish republic. The constitution also established a government of the republic with military and judicial powers. For members of the IRB after 1873, this was the only legitimate government in Ireland, and the only one they recognized. It gave them all the moral authority which, as practising Catholics, they needed. In 1920, the chaplain of the 3rd Cork Brigade, IRA, Fr Dominic, OFM, Cap., used the IRB argument to explain away Bishop Cohalan's excommunication of IRA men:

Now kidnapping, ambushing and killing ordinarily would be grave sins or violations of Law. And if these acts were being performed by the [IRA] as private persons (whether physical or moral) would fall under the excommunication [*sic*]. But they are doing them by and with the authority of the State and the Republic of Ireland. And the State has the right and duty to defend the lives and property of its citizens and to punish even with death those who are aiming at the destruction of the lives or property of its citizens or itself.

To the present day, this is the argument advanced by the IRA. In 1938 the IRA felt it necessary to seek the endorsement of their rump government of the Irish republic for a bombing campaign in England, and in 1971 the Provisional IRA called a press conference to announce that they enjoyed the endorsement of the same rump government for their campaign of violence in Northern Ireland.

7

Home rule?

The Fenian attempt at rebellion and their subsequent atrocities in 1867 forced Westminster's attention upon Ireland. 'Fenianism', wrote the philosopher and MP John Stuart Mill, burst 'like a clap of thunder in a clear sky, unlooked for and unintelligible'. It had confounded the assumption which had grown since the meek acceptance of the famine by the Irish people, that social reform was an adequate substitute for political independence, and that coercive measures could be enforced when necessary if social reform was also pursued. Thus *habeas corpus* had been suspended at nearly all times of political and agrarian unrest (1798; 1848); the Treason–Felony Act (1848) had been used against nationalist agitators, and at the same time Acts were passed granting emancipation (1828), establishing state-supported primary (1831) and higher education (1845) services, and reducing the effect of the tithe (1838). Mill was one of the first to realize that a better description of England's Irish problem might be Ireland's English problem. In 1868 he published an essay, *England and Ireland*, pointing out that Fenianism involved the ideal of freedom and was not simply wanton criminality. 'The difficulty of governing Ireland', he wrote, 'lies entirely in our own minds; it is an incapability of understanding.' Englishmen liked to explain Irish rebelliousness as the result of 'a special taint or infirmity in the Irish character', but this was wrong. Instead, he said,

There is probably no other nation of the civilized world, which, if the task of governing Ireland had happened to devolve on it, would not have shown itself more capable of that work than England has hitherto done. The reasons are these: first, there is no other nation that is so conceited of its institutions and of all its modes of public action, as England is; and secondly, there is no other civilized nation which is so far apart from Ireland in the character of its history, or so unlike it in the whole constitution of its social economy; and none, therefore, which if it applies to Ireland the modes of thinking and maxims of government which have grown up within itself, is so certain to go wrong.

Mill was attacked by the *Saturday Review* as 'the most recent and most thoroughgoing apostle of Communism'. The Irish landlord, Lord Bessborough, bluntly declared 'Mill ought to be sent to penal servitude as a Fenian.' One man, however, who was influenced by Mill was William Ewart Gladstone (1809–98).

In 1868 Gladstone had come to lead the Liberal Party which had been formed by the old Whigs and Tory supporters of Sir Robert Peel. He termed Mill 'the saint of rationalism'. Unlike Mill, Gladstone had always paid attention to Ireland, just before the famine predicting:

Ireland! Ireland! that cloud in the west, that coming storm, that minister of God's retribution upon cruel and inveterate and but half-atoned injustice! Ireland forces upon us these great social and great religious questions – God grant that we may have courage to look them in the face and to work through them.

Fenianism and the Clerkenwell explosion concentrated his thoughts on Ireland, and in 1868 he successfully fought a general election with the slogan 'Justice for Ireland', becoming prime minister for the first time and declaring 'My mission is to pacify Ireland.' One of his first acts was to disestablish the Church of Ireland in 1869, a logical supplement to Catholic emancipation. (It is worth noting that the Disestablishment Act also provided for land purchase by tenants of Church land – one of the first steps taken by government towards encouraging peasant ownership.) The 1861 census had revealed that there were only 690,000 Anglicans in Ireland's 5.7 million population, which meant that the five-sixths of the people who were not Anglicans were supporting in tithes the churches and the clergy of the Church of Ireland. He followed disestablishment with a Landlord and Tenant Act in 1870 which, for the first time, involved government in protecting tenants in relations with landlords. Landlords were required to pay up to £250 to tenants unjustly evicted, and tenants were helped to purchase their holdings by being able to borrow from the government up to two-thirds of the purchase price. The Act was not particularly successful – only 877 tenants took advantage of it to buy their land – but it was important because, as with the disestablishment of the Church of Ireland, it was conceived and introduced by a government without any violent political or social agitation for its purpose preceding it in Ireland. Both Acts strengthened the appeal of constitutional political action in Ireland at a time when violent action was again threatening.

Land-ownership in Ireland had changed significantly since the famine. Small farmers had generally expanded their holdings at the expense both of the smallest farmers and of cottiers and labourers – the people who died during the famine and who formed the bulk of emigrants during it and afterwards. Many landlords had also suffered financially as the result of the famine's demands on their rates through the Poor Law system: two Encumbered Estates Acts had been passed in 1848 and 1849 by which landlords who failed to meet their financial obligations could sell their estates to effect repayment. Within ten years, 3,000 estates totalling five million acres – one quarter of the land of Ireland – changed hands under the Acts, sometimes to speculators but more often, it seems, to other landed families. In all these cases, however, the tenants on the estates simply found themselves with new landlords, many of whom were convinced that congested smallholdings had been chiefly responsible for the famine disaster. As a result, and in order to make estates more efficient, at the end of the famine the rate of evictions soared and between 1849 and 1852, over 300,000 tenants were evicted. These were the people who emigrated or became itinerant labourers, finding work in different parts of the United Kingdom according to the season. Some must have starved. However, throughout the 1850s and 1860s, rural prosperity increased, and not only did farmers and landlords enjoy an improved standard of living, but folk of the poorest sort did too. By 1870, per capita tobacco consumption (a useful guide to the living standard of the lower classes) had risen to the English level.

Rural prosperity, however, did not mean an end to agrarian disturbance, and in some cases actually encouraged conflict. The replacement of impoverished smallholders and cottiers by larger tenant farmers in the interests of estate efficiency often resulted in trouble. In 1850 a Tenant Right League was founded by Charles Gavan Duffy and an influential journalist and English Quaker who converted to Catholicism, Frederick Lucas (1812–55). The aim of the League was to secure the 'Ulster Custom' of fair rent; fixity of tenure while rent was paid, and the right of free sale of one tenant's holding to another. The 'Three Fs' as they were known existed in practice principally in Ulster, and the Tenant Right League's campaign to extend them to the rest of the country attracted the initial support of the Ulster Tenant Right Association which had been founded three years earlier by William Sharman Crawford (1781–1861), a Protestant Co. Down landlord and Liberal MP for Dundalk. Together, Crawford, Duffy and Lucas campaigned for the legalisation of the Ulster Custom with financial compensation for tenants for eviction and for improvements they made to their properties. Gavan Duffy's and Lucas' idealistic concern for evicted tenants was not reflected by the League's members, who were, in the main, prosperous tenant farmers frightened by the prospect of eviction in a period (1847–53) or agricultural depression. In Ulster, the Tenant League initially enjoyed the support of solid (Presbyterian) tenants who were made aware of their precarious legal position if landlords (Anglican) wished to evict them. However, in 1851, as the result of a papal announcement of territorial titles to Catholic bishops in England, anti-Catholicism swept England and in Ulster support for the League (which in the south was closely associated with Catholic priests) rapidly withered away. After the July 1852 general election, about forty Irish MPs formed themselves into the 'Independent Irish Party' to secure the Tenant League's objectives and the repeal of the Ecclesiastical Titles Act (passed in 1851 forbidding Catholic bishops the use of British territorial titles). The Party's religious concern alienated Crawford (defeated in the general election) and any residual Ulster support. Over the next year, as agricultural prices improved, support for the League declined and the Party began to split between those willing to take office without securing the Party's programme; those who saw themselves as champions of Catholic interests (known as 'The Pope's Brass Band' because of their ostentatious piety and clericalism), and those who placed land reform as their principal objective. Lucas died in Rome in 1855 while seeking the pope's support against the alleged hostility of the Irish bishops to the League. Gavan Duffy emigrated to Australia in 1856, disgusted with the Independent Irish Party and despairing of the League's hopes. Within four years both the League and the Party had collapsed. In Australia, Duffy entered politics becoming prime minister of Victoria in 1871. He was knighted for his services there two years later, and retired in 1880 to Nice in the south of France where he died. His son, George, was one of the signatories to the 1921 Anglo-Irish Treaty which established the Irish Free State.

In the 1860s, Fenianism frequently attracted the attention of the mass of the Irish people. As Bishop Moriarty pointed out: 'Fenianism, with all its fraud and falsehood, with all its braggart cowardice, and with that hatred of religion which marked its every utterance, found sympathy and raised strange hopes in the Irish poor. And unfortunately, the Irish poor means the Irish people.' After the abortive 1867 rising, Gladstone's reforming legislation produced a reaction in favour of peaceful politics. Irish wrongs were increasingly seen as stemming from the union, and though it was by no means clear that the union had an overall adverse effect on the Irish economy, Isaac Butt (1813–79), the son of a Church of Ireland rector in Co. Donegal, was able to exploit the issue of the union to revive Daniel O'Connell's call for its repeal. Part of Butt's purpose was to wrest the initiative in Irish politics away from the Fenians, and in 1870 he founded the Irish Home Government Association, replaced in 1873 by his Irish Home Rule League.

Butt had succeeded O'Connell as Ireland's foremost barrister. In 1848 he had defended William Smith O'Brien and other Young Irelanders. In the 1860s he defended many leading Fenians, including John O'Leary. A Tory as a young man, he came to favour Irish independence, but rejected it in politics on the pragmatic grounds that no British government would accept outright repeal of the union. Accordingly, he developed the home rule proposal, whereby an Irish parliament, subservient to Westminster, would have control of Ireland's domestic affairs, leaving Westminster responsible for foreign and defence matters. With the introduction of the secret ballot in 1872 for United Kingdom parliamentary elections, home rule was given a fair test: Butt and his supporters won 59 of the 103 Irish seats in the house of commons in the 1874 general election. Within three years, however, Butt who was generally described as 'an old fashioned gentleman' had fallen out with most of the other Irish Home Rule MPs who had adopted the filibuster as a means of drawing attention to themselves and who in any case were politically more extreme than their leader. In 1877 he lost the leadership of the Home Rule Confederation of Great Britain, which he had founded in 1873 to gather the support of Irishmen in Britain, to a young and energetic MP, Charles Stewart Parnell (1846–91). In 1880, a year after Butt's death, Parnell also became leader of those Irish MPs who had formed themselves into the Irish Parliamentary Party.

Parnell was a Protestant landlord and High Sheriff of Wicklow, having inherited the family estate at the age of thirteen when his father died. He was brought up under the influence of his strong-minded American mother who proclaimed (rather than practised) anti-British opinions and whose father, Admiral Stewart, had achieved fame in the US navy fighting Britain during the war of 1812. Aged twenty-nine, he won a Co. Meath seat as a Home Ruler in a by-election in 1875, rapidly gaining notoriety in the house of commons. He was hated by British parliamentarians and political journalists whose cry, within a year of his entry to the house, was 'Something really must be done about Mr Parnell.' His extremism also attracted the attention of the IRB. In 1877 and again in 1878, Parnell met leading members of the IRB and Clan-na-Gael, the organization in the United States founded in 1867 as the successor to the Fenian Brotherhood. He impressed them as favouring 'the absolute independence of Ireland', and John Devoy – now one of the Clan-na-Gael leaders – proposed a 'New Departure' to Parnell and the IRB whereby the physical force separatists would cooperate with the constitutionalists for specific objectives on the basis of a 'general declaration in favour of self-government instead of simple federal home rule' and the pursuit of 'a vigorous agitation of the land question on the basis of a peasant proprietary, while accepting concessions tending to abolish arbitrary eviction'. In 1879, Charles Kickham, president of the IRB, decided that the society could not formally cooperate with constitutionalists, but that individual members might. Shortly afterwards Michael Davitt (1846–1906), a Fenian imprisoned in 1870 and released in 1877 following a campaign led by Parnell for the amnesty of Fenian prisoners, approached Parnell to lead a new campaign for land reform. On 21 October 1879 Davitt founded the Irish National Land League in Dublin with Parnell as its president: the New Departure had produced its first fruits. Davitt threw the prestige and the support the IRB enjoyed amongst the peasantry behind Parnell, while Devoy galvanized Irish America behind him too. During a visit to America in the winter of 1879–80, Parnell seemed to affirm his part of the bargain by stating in a speech at Cincinnati that he wanted to cut 'the last link which keeps Ireland bound to England'.

Michael Davitt was born in the west of Ireland in Co. Mayo where, when he was four, his family had been evicted from their farm. They moved to Lancashire where Davitt worked as a child-labourer in a cotton-mill until 1856 when in a mill accident his right arm was torn off by machinery. He joined the IRB and was involved in the attempted raid on Chester Castle in 1867, and until his arrest three years later, acted as a weapons buyer for the Fenians. He was always interested in Irish land reform, and he joined the New Departure because he became convinced that methods short of rebellion offered more hope of achieving it. He was also attracted by Parnell's radicalism and by a statement to peasants the MP made at Westport, Co. Mayo, in the summer of 1879: 'You must show the landlords that you intend to hold a firm grip on your homesteads and lands. You must not allow yourself to be dispossessed as you were dispossessed in 1847. You must not allow your small holdings to be turned into large ones.' Davitt's Land League rapidly became a mass political and social movement, guaranteeing Parnell's Irish Party faithful support while Parnell campaigned for land reform.

In 1879, agriculture was in the throes of severe recession. Three bad harvests after 1876 had brought to an end the prosperity of the 1850s and 1860s. Evictions, reflecting both a renewed drive for efficiency and an inability to pay rent, rose from 463 in 1877 to 1,238 in 1879 and 2,110 in 1880. Foreign competition, facilitated by the advent of transoceanic steamships, brought lower agricultural prices, so farmers faced not only a fall in output, but also a fall in income. Smallholders also suffered severely from the loss of output, and the combination of their distress with the fear and worry of decline amongst farmers of even the larger sort found expression in the Land League, giving the League a powerful force. Echoing the arguments of Lalor and the Young Irelanders, the League's Declaration of Principles spelled out its radical nature:

The land of Ireland belongs to the people of Ireland, to be held and cultivated for the sustenance of those whom God decreed to be the inhabitants thereof. Land being created to supply mankind with the necessaries of existence, those who cultivate it to that end have a higher claim to its absolute possession than those who make it an article of barter to be used or disposed of for purposes of profit or pleasure.

This assessment of the relationship between land and nationality was shared by Parnell and Fenians like Davitt and Devoy. It was at the heart of the New Departure, and it had the important effect of reducing – if only for a time – the antagonism between revolutionary and constitutional nationalists, moderating the one and making more extreme the other. By 1887 a Royal Irish Constabulary report ('Royal' was added to the title in 1867 for the Constabulary's efforts in subduing the Fenians), marked 'very secret', stated that of the eighty-three Parnellite MPs, twenty-one were probably members of the IRB; two were probably ex-IRB men, and four more were fellow-travellers.

For nationalists of all sorts, the Land League marked an important development because it tested for the first time the willingness of the government to support the Ascendancy class as landlords and not as governors. In 1876 an official analysis of the rents of Irish landlords was used by Michael Davitt to show that of the 19,288 men who owned Ireland, 110 owned over four million acres (20 per cent of the country) and 1,878 others owned over nine and a half million acres. Altogether, nearly 70 per cent of the land of Ireland was owned by fewer than 2,000 people, while some 3 million tenants and labourers did not own any significant property at all. Accordingly, the League demanded the redistribution of land-ownership to tenants, with compensation for landlords. It also maintained a simultaneous demand for the Three Fs. The aggressive nature of the League was denoted by its slogan, 'Rent at the point of the bayonet', and its campaign was soon called the 'Land war'. Rents were withheld until the last possible moment, and in some areas a policy of ostracizing land-grabbers (tenants who took an evicted tenant's holding), landlords and their agents was followed, with the public endorsement of Parnell. At Ennis, Co. Clare, in September 1880, the newly elected leader of the Irish Parliamentary Party said:

When a man takes a farm from which another has been evicted, you must show him on the roadside when you meet him, you must show him in the streets of the town, you must show him at the shop-counter, you must show him at the fair and at the market-place and even in the house of worship, by leaving him severely alone, by putting him into a sort of moral Coventry, by isolating him from the rest of his kind, as if he were a leper of old, you must show him your detestation of the crime he has committed.

One of the first to suffer this moral Coventry was the Co. Mayo land agent for Lord Erne, Captain Charles Boycott, whose name has since become a synonym for ostracism. Fifty Orangemen and over 1,000 troops helped harvest the crops on the Erne estate, at an estimated cost to the government of £10,000 or, as Parnell put it, 'one shilling for every turnip dug from Boycott's land'. Despite its novelty and the attention it gathered, the boycott played only a small part in the Land League's campaign. The rent strike and sheer violence were the most frequently employed weapons in the Land war. Throughout the country, League members resorted to lawlessness in the old Whiteboy and Ribbonmen traditions. Hayricks were burned, land-lords' cattle maimed, and some landlords were even murdered. Agrarian outrages recorded by the Royal Irish Constabulary (RIC) soared from 2,500 in 1880 to over 4,400 in 1881. The prime minister, Gladstone, was obliged to crack down. He warned 'If there is still to be fought in Ireland a final conflict between law on one side and sheer lawlessness on the other, then I say, gentlemen, without hesitation, the resources of civilisation are not yet exhausted.' In March 1881 he secured a Coercion Act suspending *habeas corpus* in Ireland. The next month he introduced a Land Law bill designed to defuse the Land war. It guaranteed the Three Fs to all tenants (except leaseholders and those in arrears with their rent) and established Land Courts to fix fair rents. Parnell and the Land League, however, refused to endorse the Bill, and after it became law the immediate reduction in agitation Gladstone had expected did not materialize. Gladstone accused Parnell of 'marching through rapine to the dismemberment of the Empire' and blamed him directly for the continuing violence of the Land war. On 12 October 1881, Parnell was arrested under the Coercion Act and imprisoned without trial in Kilmainham gaol in Dublin. 'The Chief', as he was called by his followers, became a hero overnight by being imprisoned. All the country's leading patriots, throughout history, had at some time in their careers been incarcerated by the government, and now Parnell joined them in this distinction.

Within a week of entering Kilmainham, on 18 October, Parnell joined other leading Irish Party MPs in the 'No Rent Manifesto' calling upon supporters of the Land League to withhold rent pay-ments. This was intended to increase the pressure on the govern-ment to include leaseholders and tenants in rent arrears within the benefits of the Land Law Act. It resulted in the government instead declaring the Land League illegal. It did not obtain the support of the mass of tenants largely because the Land Law Act was already working in favour of the two-thirds of tenants throughout the country who were not leaseholders or in arrears with their rents. The one-third excluded from the Act, however, resorted to violence. Over the next seven months, 3,498 agrarian outrages were recorded compared to 2,633 outrages in the equivalent period twelve months earlier. Both Gladstone and Parnell were convinced by this that some arrangement had to be found to end the violence. In an informal understanding known as the 'Kilmainham Treaty' they came to an agreement that in return for the Irish leader's support for the Land Law Act and his promise to try to end agrarian outrages, the government would end coercion, release other Land League leaders from prison and would pass legislation waiving tenants' rent arrears and bring them within the framework of the Act. Parnell was released on 2 May 1882, from his point of view having secured an excellent bargain. He was always willing to use the threat of violence to secure political objectives, and he was personally ambivalent about violent action. However, he was also very aware of the danger to his leadership posed by men of violence who could always depict him as being too cautious, or insufficiently enthusiastic about a course of action. Thus his release enabled him to reassert his authority in Ireland in exchange for general promises of support for Gladstone and the Land Law Act, and in return for specific guarantees from the government. Parnell's interest in defusing violence gave the Act the chance Gladstone wanted. Agrarian outrages soon diminished. The Land Courts reduced rents by an average of between 15 and 20 per cent. The legislative security of the Three Fs met the principal demands of the Land League's supporters (though only a few, 731, tenants made use of the land purchase provisions of the Act by which a Land Commission advanced three-quarters of the purchase price to be repaid over thirty-five years at 5 per cent). Above all, the Act in practice demonstrated that the democratic age was unfolding at the expense of the Ascendancy landowning class who could no longer assume their interests would be held paramount at Westminster.

Four days after Parnell's release from Kilmainham, on 6 May 1882 an act of violence threatened not only the Kilmainham Treaty but also Parnell's career. The chief and under-secretaries for Ireland, Lord Frederick Cavendish and Mr Thomas Henry Burke, were both horribly murdered with surgical knives in Dublin's Phoenix Park as they were walking together on Lord Frederick's first evening in Ireland as chief secretary. The atrocity was the work of a breakaway group from the IRB, the 'Irish National Invincibles'. Parnell immediately wrote to Gladstone offering to resign as an MP and retire completely from politics if the prime minister thought it would serve any purpose. His offer was refused. In January 1883, twenty-six men were arrested for the murders; one of them, James Carey, turned Queen's evidence resulting in five executions and two sentences of penal servitude. Carey, who had taken a leading part in the murders, was set free and with government help sailed secretly for South Africa. He was followed by an Invincible, Patrick O'Donnell, who murdered him on the *Melrose Castle* sailing from Capetown to Natal. O'Donnell himself was immediately arrested and was hanged for the murder at London's Newgate prison in December 1883. As a consequence of the renewed fears of Fenian violence conjured up in Britain by the Invincibles, Gladstone's government created the Special Irish Branch of the police force at Scotland Yard. There had been an earlier Special Irish Branch in 1869–70, but this new one was given permanent status and was the precursor of today's British Special Branch.

There was another dramatic sequel to the Phoenix Park murders. In 1886 in a series of vindictive articles entitled 'Parnellism and Crime' complete with pages of facsimiles of letters, *The Times* accused the Irish leader of condoning the killings and of being directly implicated in Land war crimes, including murder. For three years Parnell fought these charges until he was completely cleared in February 1890 by a Special Parliamentary Commission. The letters *The Times* had used were proven forgeries. Richard Pigott, a sometime pornographer, journalist and Irish home ruler, confessed to having forged them, fled to Spain and committed suicide. Vindicated, Parnell was universally acclaimed. He was also able fully to exploit the position his Party had gained in the 1885 general election as it became clear that Gladstone had been converted to the principle of home rule for Ireland.

There were three significant changes in the Irish Party MPs returned at the 1885 general election. First, the eighty-six Irish MPs elected (one was for an English seat) were the largest number the Party had obtained until then. The Party eclipsed the Liberal Party in Ireland and saw the elimination of the Conservative Party in southern Ireland, thus marking the pattern of future Irish politics. Secondly, all eighty-six were pledged to vote together, and Party funds provided salaries and expenses for those deemed in need (the first time this had happened in British politics), thus reducing the attractions of office, reinforcing Party loyalty and developing a coherent voting power in the house of commons. Thirdly, the massive enfranchisement of new voters carried out by the 1884 Reform Act had increased the Irish electorate from about 230,000 to over 700,000. This in turn had influenced and made more representative the composition of the Irish Party: the number of Catholic Irish Party MPs went up from fifty-five in 1880 to seventy-five; the number of MPs who were farmers and shopkeepers went up from two in 1880 to twenty-two; the number of MPs who were landlords like Parnell went down from twenty-three in 1874 to give in 1885. In addition, since October 1884 the Irish Party enjoyed the full and public support of the Irish Roman Catholic bishops who looked to it to secure legislation favouring Catholic teaching, especially in education, in Ireland. Priests rapidly came often to play leading roles in constituency party selection committees. The combination of these changes reinforced Gladstone's conversion to Irish home rule.

The Liberal leader by 1885 had become convinced of the justice of the home rule case, but had remained silent in public on the issue while he tried privately to secure its agreement by the Conservatives. On 17 December, at the end of the general election some newspapers published a strong indication by Gladstone's son, Herbert, that his father favoured home rule. This, the 'Hawarden Kite', came too late to influence the election results which gave the Liberals with 335 seats to the Conservatives' 249 a majority of 86: the same number of seats as Parnell's Irish Party. In January 1886, Gladstone at the age of seventy-six formed his third administration and announced his intention of pressing ahead with home rule for Ireland. On 8 April he introduced the first Irish Home Rule Bill, in his opening speech indicating the reasons that had converted him:

I cannot conceal the conviction that the voice of Ireland as a whole is constitutionally spoken. I cannot say it is otherwise when five-sixths of its lawfully-chosen representatives are of one mind on this matter. . .I cannot allow it to be said that a Protestant minority in Ulster, or elsewhere, is to rule the question at large for Ireland.

In his reply, his opponents – including Liberals on this issue – argued that home rule would be only a first step to complete independence. One fiery Orangeman, William Johnston MP, declared that if the Bill passed and an Irish parliament were set up, 'the dictates of that Irish parliament would be resisted by the people of Ulster at the point of a bayonet', while a leading Liberal, Lord Hartington, MP for Rossendale, speaking in the house of commons, put another point echoed by Orangemen: 'The Parliament which would be restored would not be a Protestant, but would be a Roman Catholic Parliament. The Established Church has been swept away; and instead of a Roman Catholic priesthood, which at the time of the Union was without political influence at all, we have a Roman Catholic clergy wielding a large political influence.' Gladstone was also accused of simply trying to stay in power by 'buying' Parnell's support, but in fact as a result of his conversion he lost the support of nearly one-third of his Liberal MPs, and not even the Irish Party's votes were enough to secure the passage of the Bill. It was defeated on 8 June 1886 by 343 votes to 313, with 93 Liberals voting against their government. Six weeks later, Gladstone resigned. In 1893 during Gladstone's fourth administration his second Home Rule Bill was passed by the house of commons but rejected by the house of lords, and the 'Grand Old Man' of British politics retired at the age of eighty-four the following year, warning that 'ruder and more dangerous agencies' would flourish again in Ireland if home rule was not passed.

Gladstone's personal commitment to home rule was the most important factor in the Liberal Party's adoption of it as policy. Parnell, in 1890 at the height of his power and fame having been completely exonerated of any involvement in the Phoenix Park murders or Land war crimes, was brought down by one of the most sensational divorce cases of the century, splitting the Irish Party in the process and so leaving Gladstone alone capable of instituting home rule.

Mrs Katherine O'Shea, the wife of the Independent Irish MP for Co. Clare, Captain William O'Shea, began an affair with Parnell in 1880. Between 1882 and 1884 Mrs O'Shea bore Parnell three children. The Captain, despite later claims to the contrary, it seems was well aware of the relationship between his leader and his wife and used it to secure political advantage for himself: it was strongly suspected that he was blackmailing Parnell as well. Nevertheless,

Parnell went to great lengths to keep the affair secret, adopting extraordinary disguises, as William O'Brien, MP for Mallow, recalled forty years after meeting Parnell one day in December 1886 in dense fog at Greenwich:

I suddenly came upon Parnell's figure emerging from the gloom in a guise so strange and with a face so ghastly that the effect could scarcely have been more startling if it was his ghost I met wandering in the eternal shades. He wore a gigantic fur cap, a shooting-jacket of rough tweed, a knitted woollen vest of bright scarlet and a pair of shooting or wading boots reaching to the thighs – a costume that could not well have looked more bizarre in a dreary London park if the object had been to attract attention.

In fact, the affair was widely known, even in government circles. The Liberal home secretary, Sir William Harcourt, had Parnell followed by detectives for political purposes, and received regular reports of the Irish leader's visits to Mrs O'Shea.

In 1889 Captain O'Shea filed for divorce on the grounds of his wife's adultery, and in February 1890 named Parnell as co-respondent. The effect was shattering. The moral case for Irish home rule as recognition of a separate Irish nationality had helped secure the vital support of the numerous and politically well-organized British non-conformists for the Liberal Party. The O'Shea divorce case presented Parnell as being immoral, and organized non-conformism made it clear to Gladstone that it would not support the Liberal Party if it cooperated with an adulterer. The case sullied the cause of home rule. It resulted in the Conservative Party, non-conformists and the Catholic Church all denouncing Parnell as unfit to lead anything, let alone to be in public life, and it meant that Gladstone and the Liberal Party could no longer cooperate with the Irish Party while it was led by him. Parnell refused to step down. His Party, which at first supported him, at a famous meeting on 6 December 1890 in Committee Room 15 of the house of commons, rejected his leadership: forty-five of the seventy-two MPs present at the meeting opted to continue the alliance with the Liberals that Parnell and Gladstone had forged in 1886. Three days before the Committee Room 15 meeting, the standing committee of the Irish hierarchy had condemned him too. 'Parnellism', proclaimed Bishop Nulty of Meath, 'springs from the root of sensualism and crime.' In the Irish Parliamentary Party as a whole, Parnell had the support of a minority – thirty-two MPs. To keep his position, Parnell argued that the majority of his colleagues, by deserting him in favour of the Liberal alliance, had compromised the independence of the Irish Party. He was theoretically correct in this assertion, but the anti-Parnellite Irish MPs demonstrated more sober political judgement. Unlike Parnell, who was prepared to rend the Irish Party and set aside the cause of home rule in favour of the cause of his own continued leadership, the anti-Parnellites sought to maintain the home rule cause and the Liberal alliance upon which, in practical political terms, that cause depended. Nevertheless, Parnell had brought nationalist Ireland closer to realizing its dreams than any other man. Despite the O'Shea divorce case and the opposition to him from the Church and within his own Party, he could still inspire Irish people. He fought back, proving his courage and leaving a legacy of unflinching determination which was to act in W. B. Yeats' phrase as a 'tall pillar, burning in the gloom' for future Irish leaders. Suffering from illness, Parnell in 1891 launched himself on a speech-making tour of Ireland to regain his support, but in three successive by-elections between December 1890 and July 1891, his candidates were defeated by anti-Parnellites. In May he married Katherine O'Shea in a civil ceremony. Five months later on 6 October, aged forty-five, he died in Brighton.

James Joyce in his autobiographical *A portrait of the artist* depicted dramatically the respect and the hatred which Parnell had generated in the last year of his life and which lasted after his death:

Dante turned round violently and shouted down the room, her cheeks flushed and quivering with rage:
Devil out of hell! We won! We crushed him to death!
Fiend!
The door slammed behind her.
Mr Casey, freeing his arms from his holders, suddenly bowed his head on his hands with a sob of pain.
Poor Parnell! he cried loudly. My dead King!

The Irish Party for the next nine years mouldered in mutual recriminations and in-fighting, losing its parliamentary effectiveness and coming to the point of collapse. After Gladstone retired in 1894 having tried and failed to achieve home rule with his second Bill, the Conservatives held power from 1895 to 1905, and the cause seemed hopeless. In addition, a powerful Irish unionist opposition to home rule was developing parallel to the growth of an Irish cultural and literary nationalism which had nothing to do with constitutional politics. Together, these developments began to tighten the springs of extremism from which violence was to uncoil.

The 1885 general election, followed by another the following year after Gladstone's third ministry collapsed over the first Home Rule Bill, marked a vital political shift in the United Kingdom. The almost complete elimination of the British Parties from southern and parts of northern Ireland, and their replacement by the Irish Party, demonstrated the overwhelming popularity of home rule in Ireland. Gladstone's and the Liberal Party's espousal of home rule in 1886 seemed to make it only a matter of time before the Irish Party's cause was successful: despite the moral and idealistic arguments advanced by Gladstone, practical arguments that a home-ruled Ireland (with Britain responsible for foreign and defence matters) would provide an independent financial base to pay for Irish tenants' land purchases (thus removing a burden from the British taxpayer) weighed more heavily. The defection over home rule of a wing of the Liberal Party under Lord Hartington, representing the old Whig landowning interests in the Party, had been expected. What had not been foreseen was the simultaneous defection of another wing under Joseph Chamberlain who contradicted the argument that home rule would benefit British taxpayers and instead argued that British taxpayers would face a heavier burden if the flow of taxation from Ireland to the exchequer ended. Unlike his erstwhile colleagues in the Liberal Party who believed that Irish tenants' desire to own their land would best be met by selling it to them through an Irish parliament to which they would pay their debt rather than to the alien British one, Chamberlain agreed with the Conservatives that land reform could be encouraged without granting home rule too. He also was convinced that home rule would herald the break-up of the Empire. 'Where in all this is the integrity of the Empire?' he asked, stating that home rule was 'tantamount to a proposal for separation. . .I would prefer that Ireland would go free altogether from any claim on the part of this country, provided also that we might be free from the enormous responsibility a sham Union would certainly entail.' Chamberlain and Hartington together led ninety-three Liberal Unionists into the lobby with the Conservatives, defeating the first Home Rule Bill in the house of commons and the second Home Rule Bill seven years later in the house of lords. Parnell's death and the subsequent ineffectiveness of the Irish Party did nothing to change their minds, and in 1892 the Liberal Unionists became officially part of the Conservative and Unionist Party.

For the Conservatives, the events of 1886 provided a political base which was to make them the dominant British Party for the next eighty years. The addition of the Liberal Unionists gave them a built-in electoral majority. The debate over home rule gave them the opportunity to rally behind the union and the empire; it also gave them the opportunity of securing between fifteen and twenty-five Irish Unionist seats in the house of commons – a noteworthy proportion of the 336 seats needed there for an absolute majority. In January 1886 the National Union of the Conservative Party (the policy coordinating body of the Party) decided to seize both opportunities and launched a campaign to maintain the Anglo-Irish union. Lord Randolph Churchill (1849–95), Conservative chancellor of the exchequer and leader of the house of commons from July to December 1886, travelled to Belfast in February where, using the slogan 'Ulster will fight; Ulster will be right', he played in his own words 'the Orange card' – stirring up the Orange Order to anti-home rule sectarian riots. 'I decided some time ago', he explained, 'that if the Grand Old Man went for home rule the Orange card would be the one to play. Please God it may turn out the ace of trumps and not the two.'

Lord Randolph was an ambitious and brilliant politician. He had made a name for himself and a small band of followers as 'The Fourth Party' in the house of commons by wittily and intelligently criticizing Gladstone while at the same time scoring points over his own Party leaders amongst whom he thus expected to be propelled by parliamentary if not public acclamation. His February 1886 speech in Belfast had made an indelible mark on Irish politics. Before he spoke on behalf of the Conservative Party, the Orange Order had declined in strength. It had suffered a major defeat when Gladstone's Disestablishment of the Church of Ireland was passed in 1869, and by 1886 many Irish unionists had come to accept that home rule was inevitable. Sectarian animosities in northern Ireland, however, prevailed throughout the century and could always be stirred up. When the Conservative Party publicly declared itself firmly in support of the union, not only were Irish unionists' hopes revived, but their political allegiance went to Churchill and his Party. And since Churchill had chosen the Orange Order as the most readily available, effective means of mobilizing Irish unionism, not only were religious differences again emphasized, but also the membership and influence of the Order increased. Within a year, 73,000 Orangemen volunteered to resist home rule by force if necessary, and as the debates on the first home rule bill proceeded at Westminster, they were marked by rioting and disturbance in northern Ireland where Irish unionism was concentrated.

Industrialization in Ireland during the nineteenth century had taken place principally within a thirty-mile radius of Belfast and consisted of the relatively highly-paid textile, shipbuilding and engineering industries. The 1911 census showed that 22 per cent of the population of Ulster, compared to 14 per cent in the other three provinces, were engaged in industry and commerce. The rest of Ireland not only was agricultural and less prosperous than the north-east, but also did not provide a market for the north-east's products. This in turn made Belfast's factory production export-orientated towards Britain, its largest market and the staging post for re-exports, giving people of all classes in the industrialized north-east a vested interest in the union. In Ulster as a whole, the 'Ulster Custom' had a similar effect in rural areas where increasingly prosperous tenants slowly diminished the power of the landlords, coming to share similar interests with them, and with both tenants and landlords making profits from the sale of foodstuffs to the industrialized towns and cities of Ulster which in turn depended upon the British market. Thus people in northern Ireland possessed a homogeneity made peculiar by the additional factor of religion. Not only were the majority of people in north-east Ulster Protestants (landlords tended to be Anglican; workers and others were often non-conformists – frequently Presbyterian – though of course areas within the north-east had Catholic majorities), but the majority of industrial and commercial concerns were owned by and employed mostly Protestants. In 1911, Protestants comprised 76 per cent of the population of Belfast and held 92 per cent of the city's jobs in shipbuilding and 88 per cent of the jobs in engineering industries. Protestant workers were prepared to accept the political leadership of their Protestant employers in return for employment. Northern Protestant unionist politicians speedily realized that religious discrimination as the basis of political allegiances had the added benefit of stifling strong labour movements. As Ramsay MacDonald, the British Labour Party leader, declared in 1912 in the house of commons, 'Whenever there is an attempt to root out sweating in Belfast, the Orange big drum is beaten.'

The Liberals' support for home rule, and the increased and determined support Conservative opposition to it found among Irish unionists, forced the Conservatives to come up with an Irish policy of their own. They perceived Irish peasants' land hunger as irrational, but nevertheless as being the basis of their opposition to the union. This was translated into a policy which maintained that there was no real demand for home rule in Ireland, but that there was real demand for land reform, and so by attending to this real demand (by selling tenants land with a series of beneficial reforms) they could kill home rule with kindness. The policy had the advantage of fighting nationalists (who, since Lalor, had used land-reform arguments for home rule) on their own terms. It also was able to meet renewed land-reform agitation in 1886 after the defeat of the first Home Rule Bill.

The mid 1880s saw another bout of economic recession which had the effect of falling prices, profits and opportunities in agriculture. Once again, tenants fell into arrears with their rents on a large scale and the Land League became active in their support, launching a 'Plan of Campaign' under which tenants on estates where rents were considered excessive lodged a 'fair' rent with trustees who offered the total collected to the landlord. If the landlord refused to accept, he would receive no rent at all, and the money collected was to be used to fight evictions and to support those evicted instead. The Plan was conceived by Timothy Michael Healy (1855–1931), an Irish Party MP who was to become first governor general of the Irish Free State. He split with Parnell in 1886 over the Galway by-election when Parnell forced Captain O'Shea upon the constituency despite local objections and the fact that O'Shea refused to take the Irish Party whip. Healy remained a firm opponent of Parnell, taking a lead in deposing him from the Irish Party's leadership in 1890–1. His Plan was never endorsed by Parnell, but three other members of the Irish Party took up Healy's idea: Timothy Charles Harrington (1851–1910); William O'Brien (1852–1928) and John Dillon (1851–1927). Harrington, MP for the Harbour Division, Dublin, and secretary of the Irish Party, outlined the Plan in an article published in *United Ireland* (the organ of the Land League and the Irish Party, founded in 1881 by Parnell). O'Brien, MP for Mallow, was the editor of the paper. Dillon, MP for east Mayo, had been imprisoned with Parnell in Kilmainham in 1881–2, and from there had been one of the signatories with Parnell of the 'No Rent Manifesto' calling upon tenant farmers to 'pay no rent under any pretext'. With the Plan, all three hoped to revive the agitation and disturbances which had characterized the earlier Land war and thus not only force concessions which they believed the house of commons would not otherwise make, but also demonstrate that home rule and land were inextricably connected no matter what Conservatives and unionists might think. Within months, some 20,000 tenants were involved on 116 estates. In December the government declared the Plan 'an unlawful and criminal conspiracy', and Parnell exerted his influence to limit its operation. Nevertheless, for five years the Plan continued. Just as in the Land war, landlords were attacked and sometimes murdered; animals were killed and injured. In Britain, where people were traditionally kind to animals, the commonplace maiming of them during the Land war and Plan of Campaign helped generate a growing racist dislike of the Irish, increasingly exhibited in cartoon depictions of the Irish as simian monsters.

The Plan had some success in reducing rents (the average rent reductions imposed by the Land Courts in the later 1880s rose to nearly 30 per cent), but the violence of the campaign (although never as extensive as Land war violence) in the long run was self-defeating. The Conservative chief secretary from 1887 to 1891, Arthur James Balfour (1848–1930), saw the Plan as a crucial test of his Party's policy. He resolved to combat it with a mixture of strict law enforcement and coercion, while steadfastly pursuing the policy of land reform. He was determined to make the union succeed, and clearly stated his approach upon taking office: 'I shall be as relentless as Cromwell in enforcing the obedience to the law, but at the same time I shall be as radical as any reformer in redressing grievances... Hitherto English governments...have been all for repression or all for reform. I am for both.' Accordingly, he lent full support to landlords carrying out evictions. He used the RIC to protect those embroiled in conflict with the Plan and selectively to arrest Plan ringleaders. Sometimes he sanctioned wholesale estate clearances. In September 1887 he won the title 'Bloody Balfour' for defending the

RIC who at Mitchelstown, Co. Cork, had fired into a crowd of Land Leaguers killing three people and wounding others (the 'Mitchelstown Massacre'). In 1889 he sanctioned the use of battering rams to effect evictions. By May 1891 the Plan, denied popular support in Britain because of its violent methods, came to an end (though on 101 of the 116 estates originally involved, the tenants in fact won) with tenants holding out on only eighteen estates. As instrumental as Balfour's coercion in ending the Plan was the expense the Plan was put to in Tipperary where, following a wholesale estate eviction, it financed a new town – 'New Tipperary' – and tried to support the inhabitants. Finally, Parnell and the Church had also publicly opposed the Plan with Pope Leo XIII in 1888 issuing a rescript condemning both the Plan and boycotting as contrary to the teaching of the Church. Of the Plan's leaders, Harrington sided with Parnell in the O'Shea divorce case. He became lord mayor of Dublin (1901–2), and remained an Irish Party MP until his death. Dillon and O'Brien became anti-Parnellites. O'Brien maintained his land-reform activities, forming the United Irish League in 1898 in an attempt to renew agitation. Together with Dillon, he played a leading part in re-uniting the Irish Party in 1900 under the leadership of the Parnellite, John Redmond. In 1918 Dillon became leader of the Party, but was defeated in the general election that year and retired from politics, dying nine years later in London. O'Brien did not contest the 1918 general election and ten years later, like Dillon, he also died in London.

The 'kind' part of Conservative policy was implemented by Balfour with the same determination as the coercive part. One of his first decisions as chief secretary was in 1887 to introduce a Land Act extending the 1881 Land Act to leaseholders (approximately 100,000 people). The following year he brought in another Land Act doubling to £10 million the amount set aside by the 1885 Act (the 'Ashbourne' Act, named after Lord Ashbourne, the Conservative lord chancellor of Ireland who drafted it) which enabled tenants to borrow from the government the full purchase price of their land, to be repaid over forty-nine years at 4 per cent interest. Between 1885 and 1888 over 25,000 tenants took advantage of these Acts to purchase between them 942,600 acres. In 1891 Balfour's third and most important Land Act came into effect, advancing £33 million at preferential interest rates to tenants who wanted to buy their farms:

it was an enormous leap in the scale of government participation, amounting in one stroke to three times as much as had been provided by all previous Acts. In addition, he established in 1891 the Congested Districts Board to purchase land in the 'congested' parts of the south and west of Ireland, redistribute it to tenants, and to make improvements to farm buildings and organization. By the time the Board was wound up in 1923, it had spent £11 million, redistributed two and a half million acres to 59,510 tenants, and encouraged the fishing and some home industries in the poorest parts of the country.

Balfour's younger brother Gerald, chief secretary from 1895 to 1900, amended the 1891 Act with a Land Act of his own in 1896 which did away with many of the earlier Act's restrictive clauses and increased still further the funding made available for land purchase. In 1898 he carried through an Irish Local Government Act which gave Ireland the British system of local government. This was one of the most important conciliatory measures implemented by the Conservatives. It was instrumental in shifting decisively political power in the country away from the old Ascendancy landowning interests to the democratic nationalist majority of farmers and shopkeepers. It also provided through local authorities the administrative and fiscal experience which was a training ground for self-government.

In 1903 George Wyndham, a Conservative and Gerald Balfour's successor as chief secretary (1900–5), sponsored the greatest Land Act of all. It advanced the then revolutionary notion that landlords should be encouraged to sell estates entire rather than piecemeal, and that sales should proceed if three-quarters of the tenants on an estate agreed. Wyndham personally became increasingly upset by social conditions in Ireland, and his representations to London on the subject finally cost him the secretaryship. In 1909 a Liberal Land Purchase Act introduced an element of compulsion to such estate sales. By 1921, as a result of the Wyndham Act, the government since 1903 had advanced nearly £100 million; over eleven million acres had changed hands, and over 250,000 tenants had bought their land. The Act was praised by John Dillon as having 'the effect of changing the whole character of the peasantry. Instead of being careless, idle and improvident, they have become like the French peasantry, industrious and economical, even penurious.' It effected possibly the most far-reaching piece of social reform in Ireland since the union, irreparably weakening the economic and political base of the landlord class while consolidating an agrarian-based conservative society with Catholic values centring on the family, land inheritance and the Church. The vast majority of Irish people after the famine, conscious of the ever-likely recurrence of disaster, instinctively calculated precisely the number of people each individual farm and holding could sustain while supporting a social order which maintained the economic security granted by the Land Acts. Thus the post-famine phenomena of emigration and late marriage were secured by a combination of legislation and a popular instinct for survival. Demoralization was also present in this combination, but the emigration of those most frustrated meant that those who stayed benefited from continuity and the social, political and technical improvements that characterized the age of industry and reform which began two hundred years ago. That this age was an 'English' one, secured in Ireland by legislation passed by English politicians in the seventy years after the famine, hastened (together with the collapse of the Irish language) the Anglicization of Ireland. With justifiable pride, politicians at Westminster looked upon their reforming legislation as solving the Irish problem. Together with Karl Marx, they made the mistake of thinking that economic problems were more significant than political ones. Kindness had beneficial results; it had valuable social and political consequences, but it could never hope to extinguish the flame of independence or the Irish perception of centuries of unkindness and injustice.

8

Dissent

The seventy years after the famine witnessed not only the profound social, economic and political changes encapsulated in land reform legislation, but also a resurgence of Gaelic and Orange sensibilities. But while Orangeism was directly politically and economically motivated, Gaelicism – at least to begin with – was not. Indeed, a cultural idealism encompassing Protestantism and unionism, Catholicism and nationalism, was the basis of the Gaelic renaissance of the later nineteenth century. It did have an important political element which harked back to the idealism of Grattan and Wolfe Tone, but it was far more concerned with re-awakening interest in every element of the Irish past so as to restore pride and self-confidence in all Irishmen. In 1841 the Archaeological Society of Ireland was formed. In 1884 the Gaelic Athletic Association (GAA) was founded 'for the preservation and cultivation of our national pastimes, and for providing amusements for the Irish people during their leisure hours'.

Michael Cusack (1847–1907), a teacher, and Maurice Davin (1864–1927), a noted athlete, were the co-founders of the GAA at a meeting in the billiard room at Hayes' Commercial Hotel in Thurles, Co. Tipperary. Cusack (who liked to be called 'Citizen Cusack' and was the model for the Citizen in James Joyce's *Ulysses*) was acting in connivance with the IRB which in 1883 had resolved to initiate an athletic organization as another way of propagating nationalism and attracting young men who might be recruited to its cause of national independence. The IRB preferred to remain in the background so that the GAA would not be obviously 'Fenian' and therefore suspect in the eyes of the Church and the authorities. Within three years, under IRB influence the GAA had become ostentatiously political, introducing a rule banning members of crown forces and prohibiting its own members from participating in non-Gaelic games. Cricket was especially frowned upon: hurling (today Ireland's national game), Irish football (the ball can be handled) and handball were the three sports most actively encouraged.

From 1887 onwards, the GAA was regarded by the Special Branch of the RIC as an adjunct of the physical force national movement, and its activities and members were regularly reported. In 1891, two thousand Fenian-minded GAA men marched with their hurley sticks draped in black in Parnell's funeral cortege. From 1913 to 1916, the GAA provided excellent cover for IRB men practising military drill, using hurley sticks as substitutes for rifles. The (Catholic) archbishop of Cashel, Dr Thomas Croke, a notable 'patriot priest' who had supported the Land League and was the foundation patron of the GAA, summed up the spirit of the Association in a letter he wrote to the organizers in December 1884 (still quoted by them with approval). He decried the fact that Ireland was:

importing from England not only her manufactured goods, which we cannot help doing, since she has practically strangled our own manufacturing appliance, but together with her fashions, her accents, her vicious literature, her music, her dances and her manifold mannerisms, her games also and her pastimes, to the utter discredit of our own grand national sports and to the sore humiliation of every son and daughter of the old land...And what have we got in their stead? We have got such foreign and fantastic field sports as lawn tennis, polo, croquet, cricket and the like – very excellent I believe, and health-giving exercises in their way, still not racy of the soil but rather alien on the contrary to it, as are indeed, for the most part, the men and women who first imported and still continue to patronize them...If we continue travelling for the next score years in the same direction that we have been going in for some time past, condemning the sports that were practised by our forefathers, effacing our national features as though we were ashamed of them, and putting on, with England's stuffs and broadcloths her masher habits, and such other effeminate follies as she may recommend, we had better at once, and publicly, abjure our nationality, clap hands at the sight of the Union Jack, and place England's 'bloody red' exultantly above the 'green'.

The somewhat fanatical anti-English attitude voiced by Croke remained with the GAA. However, the GAA also really did help foster a new sense of Irish pride, catching the imagination of rural Ireland as well as that of intellectuals concerned about the apparent impoverishment of Irish culture. In 1893 the most important Gaelic revival organization, the Gaelic League, was founded by three academics: Douglas Hyde (1860–1949), Eoin MacNeill (1867–1945), and the Rev. Eugene O'Growney (1863–99).

The Gaelic League was dedicated to the 'de-Anglicization of Ireland', but unlike the GAA it was also determinedly non-political and non-sectarian. Hyde, a Protestant and later first president of Eire, was a unionist; MacNeill was a supporter of the Irish Party, and O'Growney was a Catholic priest–scholar. Hyde's 1892 lecture, 'The Necessity for de-Anglicizing Ireland', was the inspiration behind the League: 'In order to de-Anglicize ourselves', he said, 'we must at once arrest the decay of the language.' The League set out to save the language and extend its use. It published Irish language textbooks, encouraged the GAA and organized traditional dances – 'ceilidhs'. In 1901 Hyde's play *Casadh an tSugain* (*The twisting of the straw rope*) was the first Irish language play ever to be performed in a professional theatre (the author played the leading role). By 1904 there were 593 branches of the League with a membership of over 50,000. It successfully pressed to make Irish an essential subject for entry to the National University of Ireland, and in 1908 Hyde became the first professor of modern Irish at University College, Dublin. O'Growney's language textbook, *Simple lessons in Irish*, became part of the paraphernalia of nationalists, enjoying one of the largest and longest print-runs of any book in the British Isles. Membership of the League became almost a *sine qua non* of membership of the IRB, and IRB influence (as with the GAA) forced the politicization of the League and Hyde's resignation as president in 1915 in anger at it. After the failure of the 1916 rising, the League was unique amongst nationalist organizations in not being banned, so providing revolutionary nationalists with their only cover for reorganization.

Despite its success as a nationalist organization, however, the League failed in its specific objective of reviving the Irish language. The 1891 census established that there were 680,000 Gaelic speakers in Ireland compared to 1.7 million in 1851. The 1926 census revealed an 18 per cent fall – 120,000 – in the number of Gaelic speakers since 1891, despite over thirty years of Gaelic League activity. After the setting up of the Irish Free State in 1922, the League successfully campaigned to make Irish compulsory at primary-school level. In 1923 it succeeded in making Irish an essential qualification for entry to the civil service (a requirement dropped in 1975). As a result, the language became more of a job ticket than a national exercise, and while in theory 27 per cent of the Irish Republic's population of 3.2 million can speak Irish today, in fact only an estimated 3 to 4 per cent actually do.

The sheer vitality of ancient Irish literature had always attracted scholars, but as publicized by the League, Gaelic tales had an effect that crossed national boundaries. Standish James O'Grady (1846–1928), a man of letters, played a leading part in this development by publicizing in English the folktales, songs and myths of the Gaelic past. O'Grady was largely responsible for the 're-discovery' of Cuchulain, quickly turned by Yeats and others into a symbol of nationhood. Isabella Augusta, Lady Gregory (1852–1932), the wife of Sir William Gregory, an Irish landlord and one-time Whig under-secretary for Ireland, was one of those who became an ardent admirer of Gaelic legends and tales as a result of O'Grady's writings and Gaelic League publicity. Meeting Yeats in 1897, she became his patron and threw open her home at Coole Park, Co. Galway, to the brilliant generation of Irish writers inspired, like her, by the Gaelic past. In 1904, Lady Gregory and Yeats founded Dublin's Abbey Theatre for the performance of Irish plays by Irish playwrights. It opened with performances of Yeats' *On Baile's Strand* and Lady Gregory's *Spreading the news*.

The Irish writers who came to prominence in the years around the turn of the century read like a catalogue of literary giants. William Butler Yeats (1865–1939) and James Augustine Aloysius Joyce (1882–1941) were the two greatest Irish writers of the twentieth century. Yeats, born in Dublin, was brought up and educated in England. He was instrumental in translating Irish literature to a worldwide English-speaking audience, thus ensuring that it did not become a narrow, nationalistic and parochial affair. In 1923 he was awarded the Nobel Prize for literature. Joyce, also born in Dublin, was educated at Ireland's leading Jesuit private schools – Clongowes Wood and Belvedere College. Unlike Yeats, Joyce was more interested in Ireland's present than her past. From 1904 until his death he lived in Italy, Switzerland and France, not returning to Ireland for the last twenty-seven years of his life. He found Irish life, particularly the influence of the Catholic Church, constricting and oppressive although his major novel, *Ulysses*, while being banned in Britain and the United States was never prohibited in Ireland. George

Bernard Shaw (1856–1950), along with Yeats and Joyce, was one of the greatest writers in English of the twentieth century. He was born in Dublin too, but after his mother moved to London when he was eighteen, he made his career there, choosing his subjects from British rather than from Irish life. Only one major play, *John Bull's other island*, written in 1904 at the request of Yeats, concerns itself with Shaw's homeland. Nevertheless, throughout his life he maintained his interest in Ireland, defending the Easter Week rebels of 1916. In 1925 he received the Nobel Prize for literature. In his will he endowed the National Gallery of Ireland with the royalties from his play *Pygmalion*; the revenues from *My fair lady*, the film version of the play, have made the Gallery one of the wealthiest in the British Isles. Other notable men of letters springing from Ireland at this time included George Augustus Moore (1852–1933), Oscar Fingal O'Flahertie Wills Wilde (1854–1900), John Millington Synge (1871–1909), and Sean O'Casey (1880–1964). With the exception of Joyce and Moore who were both born Catholics, all were Protestant (although Wilde converted to Catholicism). Moore converted to Anglicanism and Joyce repudiated the Church.

The writings of the Irish literary renaissance helped restore an honest sense of dignity and pride in things Irish. In the process of achieving this honesty they often had to brave the prejudices and antagonism of some of their countrymen who, like Arthur Griffith, the founder of the nationalist Sinn Fein Party, sought to use every means including literature to further the cause of Irish nationalism. Synge's play, *In the shadow of the glen* (1903), in which the heroine runs off with a traveller, was denounced by Griffith because 'all of us know that Irish women are the most virtuous in the world'. Synge's *The playboy of the western world* (1907) caused an outcry with a line 'It's Peegeen I'm seeking only and what'd I care if you brought me a drift of chosen females standing in their shifts itself', indicating that Irish chastity might not be perfect. O'Casey's play, *The plough and the stars* (1926), was met with riots because it presented IRA men as less than heroic. The fact that O'Casey had organized for the IRB and the Citizen Army before the 1916 rising was forgotten in the uproar. Yeats also faced a certain opposition from narrow nationalists. In 1894 he had joined a breakaway group from the IRB, the Irish National Brotherhood, entering police reports as 'a literary enthusiast, more or less of a revolutionary'. This, together with his literary eminence, gave him a special position with nationalists and when in 1925 as one of the first Senators of the Irish Free State he spoke against the legislation that made divorce illegal in the Free State, he was able publicly to condemn the catholic, conservative attitudes of the State's new rulers:

I think it is tragic that within three years of this country gaining its independence we should be discussing a measure which a minority of this nation considers to be grossly oppressive. I am proud to consider myself a typical man of that minority. We against whom you have done this thing are no petty people. We are the people of Burke; we are the people of Grattan; we are the people of Swift, the people of Emmet, the people of Parnell. We have created the most of the modern literature of this country. We have created the best of its political intelligence.

His plea was ignored. The social and cultural oppression of the new State, like the political and economic oppression of the old, maintained the pressure to emigrate on all those who would not conform. Joyce, Shaw, Wilde and O'Casey all left Ireland to practise their art. To the present day, despite tax benefits and family ties, it is noteworthy that many Irish writers still prefer to live abroad. The catholic social and cultural attitudes responsible for this diaspora of Irish talent have also lent weight to Protestant unionist opposition to Irish nationalism.

From the 1880s onward, Protestant unionists argued for the maintenance of the Act of Union on the grounds of economic and social advantage. Lord Randolph Churchill's cementing of the virulently anti-Catholic working-class Orange Order to the foundation of what became the Irish Unionist Party ensured a mindless component of religious bigotry to the politics of unionism. Very rapidly, the cry of 'Defend our Protestant religion' became, like the 'Orange Card', a shorthand for the political mobilization of northern Irish Protestants in defence of what they perceived as their economic and social freedoms which would somehow be destroyed in an Ireland independent of Britain. Despite the fact that this attitude persists to the present day, and that various actions (like the 1925 repeal of divorce legislation) by Dublin governments since 1922 have helped justify northern Protestant fears, upon examination religious distinctions emerge as convenient tags and not as central to political divisions. Northern Protestants provided much of the leadership of Irish nationalism throughout the nineteenth century. Northern Protestants in the early twentieth century were instrumental in reviving the IRB which launched the 1916 rising. Southern Catholics, in the majority in Southern Ireland, have never entrenched discrimination against Protestants in jobs or housing. And while northern Protestants have entrenched discrimination against Catholics in jobs in Northern Ireland where they are a majority, this is because of the convenience of the religious tag which means to a Protestant that a Catholic is a nationalist, disloyal to the union, and a member of a feckless, inferior nation prepared to undercut hard-working Protestants. If Irish Catholics were black, it would be seen that the parallels with Rhodesia in the 1960s and 70s would explain many of the illogical and logical reasons for Protestant Irish unionism and for Irish nationalism. This awareness has given rise to an academic and political debate as to whether or not there are two nations in Ireland.

The concept of nationalism is predicated upon the idea of nation which depends in turn upon there being a more or less defined national territory and government carrying the natural allegiance of the community. This is, of course, an artificial concept and in the absolute sense nationalism is a myth. However, in the real world people both accept the national concept (it is, after all, a salutary concept helping to counteract self-interest and to provide cohesion to the state), and actively provide their allegiance to it. In Ireland, northern Protestant determination to maintain the Anglo-Irish union, and the countervailing pressure of (mostly Catholic) Irish nationalists, has called into question the proposition that there is one nation in the country with a sense of common nationality, geography, history and culture. Those who argue that there is only one nation ignore Protestant protests that they do not share a common culture or history and attribute the political and social divisions between unionists and nationalists to British manipulations. In particular, Churchill's playing of the Orange Card in 1886 is seen as a conspiratorial move to divide the Irish working class in the interests of British capitalism and imperialism. They do not accept that Churchill – however cynically – exploited attitudes and feelings that were natural to Protestants concentrated in predominantly working-class northern Ireland. Taking account of this, in 1973 the Socialist Workers Association for a Democratic Settlement of the National Conflict in Ireland published a pamphlet, *One island, two nations,* arguing that northern Irish Protestants are 'a distinct nation, or at least part of one', and that Catholic imperialism, not British, has been responsible for working-class divisions on religious lines in Northern Ireland. Northern Protestants proved their separate nationality, the Workers' Association claims, when in 1912 'the ability of its ruling class to rally all its members into a common alliance ready if necessary to fight for a national objective' was successfully demonstrated. The proponents of the two nations theory assume social class to be the natural bond of nationhood. Thus working-class Protestants in Northern Ireland naturally fall into the category of nation. The logic of this argument fails, however, when pressed: on the one hand, it is patently absurd that every class (even if only those that are numerically large are considered) has claims to separate nationhood, and on the other hand northern Protestants are not distinct from other British or Irish communities, themselves part of a British or Irish nation encompassing differences seen as distinctive in Northern Ireland. The conditional loyalty to Britain exhibited by northern Irish Protestants, and their own part in Irish history, has made them different in their attitudes but not distinct in national terms (despite the fact that they themselves often reject an Irish identity) from either Britain or the rest of Ireland. They do have some of the characteristics of a nation (principally a keen self-awareness) but to be a separate nation they would have to be prepared to maintain themselves against all comers. It is possible that this might happen but it is not yet the case. A more accurate awareness of Irish nationality is that there is an Irish (Catholic) nation and a distinctive social and economic (Protestant) community which is emphasized by its own geographical place in Ireland. This community straddles both the Irish and the British nations exactly as was intended by the original plantation policy. Its members are true victims of geography and history.

Opposition to the cause of home rule for Ireland in 1886 had mobilized northern Irish Protestants for the first time in a coherent political form. In 1885 a political association of unionists, the Irish Loyal and Patriotic Union (ILPU), was founded in Dublin to contest parliamentary elections against home rulers. In 1891 it became the Irish Unionist Alliance reflecting southern Irish unionist interests, always more patrician than northern unionism. With Gladstone's public conversion to home rule, in January 1886 the Ulster

Loyalist Anti-Repeal Union was formed in Belfast in competition with the ILPU, reflecting Ulster rather than Irish unionism with direct (though unofficial) ties to the Orange Order. Also in January, an Irish Unionist Party was formed by Irish Unionist MPs in the house of commons. By 1912, Irish unionism was controlled by the Joint Committee of Unionist Associations (established in 1907), the largest and dominant part of which was the Ulster Unionist Council which had been formed in 1904 as the central and coordinating executive for Ulster opposition to home rule. The galvanizing of Irish unionism was given new impetus in 1906 when the Liberals won a landslide general election victory with a majority of 106 seats over all other parties combined, ending twenty years of almost uninterrupted Conservative and Unionist government.

The Liberals had made no mention of home rule in their election campaign, and most liberals were glad to be rid of the proposal which had divided their party and helped spell electoral defeat for so long. However, in 1907 the MP for North Bristol, Augustine Birrell (1850–1933), already in the Liberal cabinet for the Board of Education, was switched to become chief secretary for Ireland.His influence began to re-kindle Liberal interest in Irish home rule. His very first act was to present an Irish Council Bill to parliament which – had it been accepted – would have provided a small measure of home rule. The Bill was furiously criticized by unionists as too much and nationalists as too little, and was withdrawn by the government. Birrell then turned to land reform, securing the 1909 Land Purchase Act which helped force landlords to sell land to tenants. Until the 1969 rising ended his career, Birrell was popular and respected and became the longest-serving chief secretary in Irish history. He became friendly with the leaders of the Irish Party, particularly John Dillon and John Edward Redmond (1856–1918), personally encouraging home rule.

The Irish Party's Parnellite and anti-Parnellite wings had reunited in 1900 under the leadership of John Redmond, an able and experienced politician who proved his qualities as far as his Party was concerned by playing a major part in securing with Wyndham the 1903 Land Act. Through the influence of his father, an MP, Redmond was appointed a clerk of the house of commons, one of the main positions of the institution affording an intimate knowledge of the parliamentary process and of parliamentarians. He entered politics himself in 1881 as MP for New Ross. From

1885 he was MP for North Wexford, and from 1891 until his death, he sat as MP for Waterford. He refused to regard the Liberals as betrayers of home rule after their 1906 election victory, preferring instead to maintain the Irish Party's unofficial alliance with them that had existed since 1886, and supporting the tremendous programme of social reform undertaken by the Liberal government, from April 1908 led by Herbert Henry Asquith (1852–1928).

The determination of Asquith and his colleague the chancellor of the exchequer, David Lloyd George (1863–1945), to press ahead with expensive and radical reforming legislation despite strident Conservative opposition, brought Ireland once again to the forefront of politics. Coupled with the ever-increasing expense of Britain's arms race with Germany, measure such as the introduction of old-age pensions, labour exchanges and unemployment benefits required large increases in taxation. In 1909, in order to raise the necessary funding, Lloyd George introduced his 'People's Budget' which, though passed by the house of commons, was defeated in the house of lords where the Conservatives enjoyed an hereditary majority. In December 1909, Asquith called a general election on the issue of whether a commons-based government or the house of lords ruled the country. He won with a greatly reduced majority which gave Redmond's seventy-five Irish Party MPs the balance of power for the first time since 1885 (eight more Irish MPs were members of the land reform All for Ireland League, and they tended to vote with the Irish Party at Westminster). In return for the Party's continued support of the Liberals, Asquith agreed to introduce a Home Rule Bill.

In many ways, this deal was a lifeline for the Irish Party which for over thirty years had campaigned unsuccessfully for home rule. By 1910 in Ireland there were several incipient competitors (both constitutional and revolutionary) for the Party's dominance of nationalist politics. One in particular, the Sinn Fein Party (meaning 'We Ourselves'), consciously set out to force the pace of constitutional agitation for home rule. Sinn Fein was founded on 28 November 1905 by a disparate group of nationalists some of whom, like Arthur Griffith (1871–1922), were opposed to any idea of combating the Irish Party in elections, and some, like Bulmer Hobson (1883–1969), were revolutionary nationalists anxious to defeat the irish Party so as to swing public opinion towards violent, rather than towards non-violent agitation. Griffith is generally credited as the father of Sinn Fein because of his leading part in organizing the new Party (despite the fact that from the start it took a form he had opposed) and because of his role in developing a Party philosophy through his book, *The resurrection of Hungary: a parallel for Ireland* (1904). In this he argued for a dual Anglo-Irish monarchy on the Austro-Hungarian model of the *Ausgleich* of 1867, with the re-introduction of Grattan's Irish parliament – 'the King, Lords and Commons of Ireland' – which would govern an independent Ireland made self-sufficient by import and export controls. Griffith had enjoyed an early flirtation with the IRB, and although there is evidence that he remained a member of the society until 1916, after 1905 he devoted himself to constitutional politics. By 1907 Griffith and Sinn Fein were divided about contesting parliamentary elections and by-elections. In 1907 a Sinn Fein candidate had an impact in the North Leitrim by-election fighting on an abstentionist platform (if successful, Sinn Fein candidates would not take their seats at Westminster). This was the only parliamentary contest Sinn Fein took part in until 1917. Under Griffith's influence, it instead concentrated on organizing the Irish county councils to coordinate their support for home rule and thus pressurize the Irish Party further. By 1911 Sinn Fein was almost moribund. Many of its members had left with Hobson in 1910 angry with Griffith's moderate constitutionalism. The remaining members figured more prominently in police reports than in politics as Redmond's success at Westminster made Sinn Fein's objectives seem unnecessary.

In 1912 Asquith introduced the Liberal Party's third Home Rule Bill, having the previous year secured with the Parliament Act the reduction of the house of lords' veto power to two years. At this point, seeing that the last constitutional obstacle to home rule had been overcome, Irish unionists became desperate. The Home Rule Bill was passed three times by the commons in 1912, 1913 and 1914, and each time it was rejected by the lords. nevertheless, as required by the Parliament Act, the Bill automatically became law in 1914, receiving King George V's royal assent on 15 September. The legislation set up an all-Ireland parliament in Dublin, with control over all matters except defence and foreign policy. It seemed that at last the hopes of Grattan, O'Connell, Parnell and Redmond would come true. But, six weeks before the King signed the Bill into law, at 11 p.m. on 4 August, the United Kingdom had declared war on Germany. All Parties agreed that the Act would not be implemented until the war was over.

Other events in the years since 1910 had threatened civil war in the United Kingdom over Irish home rule, and made the advisability of major constitutional change at the outbreak of the First World War dubious in the extreme. Under the leadership since 1910 of the Dublin-born barrister and an MP for Dublin University (Trinity College's formal name), Sir Edward Henry Carson (1854–1935), Irish unionists in northern Ireland in 1912 had sworn an oath to fight against home rule. Carson was both a brilliant tactician and an orator. In 18956 he had devastated his classmate Oscar Wilde in cross-examination during the writer's libel action against the Marquis of Queensberry, resulting in Wilde's imprisonment for 'gross indecency'. On 28 September 1912 he led 471,413 unionists in signing 'Ulster's Solemn League and Covenant':

Being convinced in our conscience that home rule would be disastrous to the material well-being of Ulster as well as to the whole of Ireland, subversive of our civil and religious freedom, destructive of our citizenship and perilous to the unity of the Empire, we whose names are underwritten, men of Ulster, loyal subjects of His Gracious Majesty King George V, humbly relying on the God whom our fathers in days of stress and trial confidently trusted, do hereby pledge ourselves in solemn covenant throughout this our time of threatened calamity to stand by one another in defending for ourselves and our children our cherished position of equal citizenship in the United Kingdom and in using all means which may be found necessary to defeat the present conspiracy to set up a Home Rule Parliament in Ireland. And in the event of such a Parliament being forced upon us, we further solemnly and mutually pledge ourselves to refuse to recognize its authority.

Once again, the conditional loyalty of northern Irish Protestants was being clearly expressed. They would deny parliament's authority unless parliament did what they wanted. Stressing this even further, Carson went so far as to set up a 'Provisional Government' for Ulster that would commence the day home rule came into effect, and (through the Orange Order) established a quasi-army, the 'Ulster Volunteer Force' (UVF) in January 1913 with the help of Lord Roberts, VC, Britain's most distinguished military commander. The UVF was under the command of another leading military man, General Sir George Richardson, a retired veteran of the Indian army, who had over 100,000 men drilling and training regularly within weeks of the formation of the Force. A defence fund was collected in subscriptions and donations amounting to over £1 million which was used to buy arms in Germany. Fourteen weeks before the First World War started, on the night of 24 April 1914, 24,000 rifles and three million rounds of ammunition were landed illegally by the UVF at the port of Larne, Co. Antrim, after telephone wires had been cut, the local police locked up and the town taken over by detachments of the UVF.

The actions of Carson and the UVF were clearly criminal, if not treasonable, in the same way at the actions of the Young Irelanders and the Fenians. Carson revelled in the danger he courted and in the challenge his activities represented to the government. He told a London audience in 1912 before travelling to Belfast that 'he intended when he went over there to break every law that was possible'. 'I do not care twopence whether it is treason or not', he declared. 'I do not even shrink from the horrors of civil commotion. I am a rebel, a Sussex–Irish rebel, and all my Ulster friends are all rebels.' Asquith's government preferred officially to ignore Carson and the UVF, unwilling to lend them further notoriety by arresting him or openly confronting the UVF. The government's problems were increased by the full-blooded support given to Carson by the Conservative Party led by Andrew Bonar Law (1858–1923), the Canadian-born son of a Presbyterian minister who had emigrated from Ulster. Bonar Law, at a Conservative rally at Blenheim Palace, Oxford, on 27 July 1912, proclaimed 'I can imagine no lengths of resistance to which Ulster will go which I shall not be ready to support, and in which they will not be supported by the overwhelming majority of the British people.' As a result, Asquith could not count upon the usual political understandings between British governments and oppositions, or on broad political support.

The extraordinary activity of Irish unionists, and the equally extraordinary statements on the part of the Conservative Party which prided itself upon its respect for law, were the results of deep-rooted fears. The unionists were convinced that a united home ruled Ireland would undermine their economic base and directly threaten their social values. And along with the Conservatives, they were also frightened that Irish home rule would lead to the break-up of the Empire by which they put so much emotional and political store. There were states in India and colonies in Africa and the Far East which had just as good a claim – sometimes better – as Ireland to self-government. In addition, they were conscious of the war clouds building up over Europe and saw home rule as a danger to British morale. At the time, these were strong arguments, and only one man was prepared to act against Carson, the Conservatives and the UVF: the youngest member of Asquith's cabinet, the first lord of the Admiralty, Winston Leonard Spencer Churchill (1874–1965).

Winston Churchill was the eldest son of Lord Randolph Churchill but, unlike his father, he enthusiastically supported home rule. In 1915 he was demoted within the cabinet as part of the Unionist price for their cooperation in the wartime coalition; six months later he left the cabinet of his own accord. In February 1912 he travelled to Belfast to campaign against Carson, and was forced to speak in a field outside the city as he was denied the use of Ulster Hall (where his father had played the Orange Card in 1886), threatened by a mob, and burnt in effigy on the Shankill Road. At Bradford on 14 March 1914 he clearly warned unionists and Conservatives that if they really were involved in a 'treasonable conspiracy' and not just in 'loose, wanton and reckless chatter', then, he said, 'Let us go forward together and put these grave matters to the proof.' Three days earlier he himself had gone forward and ordered the Royal Navy's 3rd Battle Squadron to hold exercises sixty miles from Belfast in the Firth of Clyde in a show of strength to impress the government's opponents. Under his prompting, the government also ordered Lieutenant General Sir Arthur Paget, commander-in-chief in Ireland, to prepare to defend weapons depots in Ulster and to send troop reinforcements to the province. Paget, who had a reputation for excitability, resisted these instructions on the grounds that they might increase tensions in Ulster and that the railwaymen of the Great Northern Railway, Orange to a man, would refuse to move his troops. On 19 March at a final conference on these orders in London, Paget had to be told not to be 'a blood fool' after he had aggressively admitted his unionist sympathies, but he secured the verbal agreement of Sir John French, chief of the Imperial General Staff, that officers domiciled in Ulster would be allowed to 'disappear'; all other officers would have to obey orders.

In Dublin the following day, Paget called his officers together. He gave them a colourful account of his instructions, referring to the government as 'those swine' and painting a picture of inevitable bloodshed in Ulster as a consequence of their decisions. That evening at the Curragh military camp, twenty-five miles from Dublin, Brigadier General Sir Hubert de la Poer Gough, his three colonels and fifty-five officers of the 3rd Cavalry Brigade notified Paget that they would resign rather than move against Ulster unionists. Three days later, Gough and his three colonels were assured in London by Sir John French and Major General (later Field Marshal) Sir Henry Wilson, director of military operations at the War Office, that the troops under their command 'will not be called upon to enforce the present Home Rule Bill in Ulster, and that we can so assure our officers'. Wilson, who was a fanatical unionist, quite improperly kept Carson and Bonar Law informed of the government's plans, and when Sir John French told him in confidence that the government proposed 'to spray troops all over Ulster as if it were a Pontypool coal strike', Wilson reported every word. The prime minister, Asquith, disavowed the pledge Gough and his officers had been given. French and the minister for war, Colonel J. E. B. Seely, resigned, accepting responsibility for the pledge. But the damage had been done: an impression had been created that the British army could not be relied upon to do its duty if that meant opposing unionists in Ireland.

The 'Curragh Mutiny', as these events were called, reduced the force of Churchill and the government's determination to implement home rule by blunting the possibility of military action against the UVF. In the United States, President Woodrow Wilson declared that Carson 'ought to be hanged for treason', but all Asquith could say was 'I have rarely felt more hopeless in any practical affair.' Similarly, John Redmond and the Irish Party preferred to let Asquith's Liberal government deal with Irish unionists directly, placing their confidence in the legislative rather than the political process, refusing to compromise on the principle of all-Ireland home rule enshrined in the 1912–14 Government of Ireland Bill. While Carson and his followers were in practice prepared reluctantly to accept home rule for most of the country in return for 'county option' (whereby the counties with unionist majority populations – the four north-eastern counties of Down, Antrim, Armagh and Londonderry – could opt out of a home ruled Ireland and remain governed directly by Westminster), the Irish Party maintained that the unionists were bluffing and that they would accept all-Ireland home rule once it was implemented. Having successfully withstood a threat from extreme nationalists in Sinn Fein, the Irish Party after 1912 was more concerned to secure home rule, in the process largely ignoring the implications of social unrest made evident by the activities of James Larkin (1876–1947) and the Dublin lock-out of 1913.

'I have got a divine mission', Larkin would proclaim, 'to make men and women discontented', and he found personal contentment in doing so. He also found abundant cause for his cry in the slums of Dublin: one third of the capital's population of about 350,000 typically lived in one-room tenements, without light, water or sanitation. Unemployment was chronically high, averaging 15 per cent, and even for those with jobs average pay was £1 per week – 12.5 per cent below the poverty line – while unskilled labourers (the largest single grouping of employment) could expect only about twelve shillings a week. Sickness, especially tuberculosis, was rife, and the death rate between 1901 and 1911 was the highest of any city in Europe, averaging 24.7 per 1,000 people compared to 17.3 per 1,000 in the country as a whole. It was not surprising that given these conditions 'Big Jim' Larkin should soon gather a mass following for his socialist and trade union projects. He was a practical syndicalist regarding class struggle in the form of industrial action as more effective than conventional politics in securing for the trade union movement the control of the means of production. 'I am a rebel and the son of a rebel', he would declare, 'I recognize no law but the people's law.' In 1909 he founded the Irish Transport and General Workers Union (ITGWU) with headquarters at Liberty Hall, Dublin. From 1910 he was aided by James Connolly (1868–1916), his second-in-command. Both men had been born in Britain of Irish parents – Larkin in Liverpool and Connolly in Edinburgh – and both spoke with the accents of their birthplaces, often causing amusement amongst their Irish followers. However, within four years of the founding of the ITGWU, Larkin and Connolly had succeeded in securing improved wages and conditions for many of their supporters. In 1911 they founded a weekly newspaper, *The Irish Worker*, which enjoyed an average circulation of 20,000 and was sued for libel seven times in its first year of publication. It also attracted the attention of the G Division of the Dublin Metropolitan Police both for its socialism and for its nationalism.

The combination of socialism and nationalism specially distinguished Larkin and Connolly from other British and European socialists of the time. It also markedly influenced the subsequent development of Irish socialism which has not been able to dissociate itself from Irish nationalism and identify with a greater socialist internationalism. 'Nationalism without socialism', wrote Connolly, 'without a reorganization of society on the basis of a broader and more developed form of that common property which underlay the social structure of Ancient Erin, is only national recreancy.' Fundamentally, both Larkin and Connolly were nationalists first and socialists second. In an article by Connolly published in *The Workers' Republic* (a successor to *The Irish Worker* which had been suppressed by the government in 1915) on 8 April 1916, this prior nationalist loyalty was made clear:

The cause of labour is the cause of Ireland; the cause of Ireland is the cause of labour. They cannot be dissevered. Ireland seeks freedom. Labour seeks that an Ireland free should be the sole mistress of her own destiny, supreme owner of all material things within and upon her soil.

This view was regarded by other nationalists with great suspicion, and by unionist workers in the north as risible. The ITGWU remained essentially Dublin-based, disaffiliated from 1909 to 1911 from the Irish Trades Union Congress, and madly unpopular with the leaders of the Irish Parliamentary Party (many of whom were Dublin employers) as well as with Arthur Griffith and his Sinn Fein. Griffith criticized ITGWU strikes and policies as attacks on the growth of Irish capitalism which he regarded as the bedrock of national independence. In particular, the Dublin employers' lock-out of ITGWU members in 1913 spurred Griffith to outright attack.

The Dublin lock-out of ITGWU members was organized by a supporter of the more conservative elements of the Irish Party, William Martin Murphy (1844–1919), a rail and tramway tycoon, to force the collapse of the union. In August 1913, under Murphy's direction, the Employers' Federation which he had founded demanded written undertakings from their workers that they would not join the ITGWU or any other union. Those who refused were dismissed. The lock-out lasted six months, with 25,000 workers and a further 25,000 of their dependants being affected. Larkin and Connolly were condemned on nearly all sides with only some of the more extreme nationalists like Pearse and socialites like Countess Markievicz and the artist William Orpen lending them support. An official inquiry criticized the employers for imposing anti-union restrictions and criticized Larkin's favourite tactic of the sympathetic strike. The Catholic Church condemned the locked out workers and 'Larkinism'. The British Trades Union Congress, while helping to support the families of ITGWU members, refused to take sympathetic strike action. Griffith encouraged dissension amongst workers by accusing Larkin and Connolly of playing England's game. Their 'new unionism' was an English import, as far as Griffith was concerned, and the lock-out confirmed his view that they were 'doctrinaires whose ultimate message to man is to give up his God, his country, his family and his property and be happy'. In February 1914 the ITGWU collapsed and men returned to work on the employers' terms. Eight months later Larkin went to the United States to raise funds. He was there for nine years, throwing himself into trade union activities and sabotaging cargoes to Britain during the First World War, and in turn being thrown into Sing Sing prison for these activities. He was released in 1923, returned to a triumphant welcome in Dublin, and spent the rest of his life in Irish trade union and Irish Labour Party politics.

During the lock-out, Connolly had formed the 'Irish Citizen Army' (ICA) to protect pickets in clashes with the police. After Larkin left for America, both the remnants of the ITGWU and the ICA came under Connolly's direct control. With the help of dedicated organizers (one of whom was the playwright, Sean O'Casey) Connolly concentrated on forging a new, strongly nationalistic trade union movement, and became increasingly strident in his calls for armed rebellion against British rule. His ICA flag depicted a silver plough and stars on a green background: the plough symbolizing the dignity of labour; the stars the hopes of man, and the green the nation, Ireland. Part of Connolly's hope was to provide a nationalist and socialist counterpart to the Ulster Volunteer Force through the ICA: in this he failed and the ICA remained a miniscule, though tightly knit force of only just over 200 men. Another, non-socialist organization, the Irish Volunteers, instead became the nationalist counterpart to the UVF.

In October 1913, in reaction to the development of the UVF, a Midland Volunteer Force was formed by nationalists in Athlone. Denis Patrick Moran (1872–1936), the owner–editor of *The Leader*, an influential nationalist journal (it had led the vitriolic criticism of

Synge in 1907 for his *Playboy of the western world*), was one of the first to see the significance of the Midland Volunteers, and used his columns to urge the formation of 'Irish Volunteer Companies' on the Midland model throughout the country. This idea was taken up by Bulmer Hobson within the IRB, and the society's leaders decided to try to create just such a force in the same manner as they had created the Gaelic Athletic Association: by themselves remaining in the background but controlling the organization through pliable front-men. Almost immediately, a front-man innocently presented himself: Eoin MacNeill (along with Douglas Hyde, a founder of the Gaelic League). MacNeill, quite independently of any IRB influence, had published an article entitled 'The north begun' in the Gaelic League journal, *An Claidheamh Soluis* (*The sword of light* or *The flaming sword*) on 1 November. In this article, MacNeill praised the founding of the UVF as giving a lead which nationalists should follow in order that Irish home rule should not be set aside by unionist militancy. Within days he was approached by IRB representatives, and he accepted their proposal that he form and front an Irish Volunteer organization with their secret help. On 25 November the Irish Volunteers were founded in the Rotunda Rink in Dublin, with Eoin MacNeill as their leader. From the start, MacNeill made plain that the object of his Volunteers was 'to secure and maintain the rights and liberties common to the whole people of Ireland'. He was a supporter of the Irish Party, and pledged himself against any use of the Irish Volunteers against the Party's interests. The Volunteer motto, 'Defence not Defiance' the same motto as the 1779 Volunteers), accurately summed up MacNeill's constitutional and anti-revolutionary approach. This was to result in the most severe consequences for the IRB and their directly revolutionary plans.

With the formation of the Irish Volunteers, the revolutionary hopes of the IRB were given a major boost. For forty years the society had vainly tried to mobilize opinion and attract more than a few members. By the turn of the century, it had lost much of its sense of purpose and its members seemed more concerned with the details of Dublin municipal politics than with the cause of Irish independence. In December 1907, Thomas James Clark (1858–1916) was sent from the United States by the old Fenian John Devoy to revive the IRB. Clark's father was a member of the Church of Ireland and a soldier (he rose to the rank of sergeant) in the Royal Artillery. His mother was a Catholic, and although his parents' marriage was Anglican, Clarke was baptized a Catholic at Parkhurst, Isle of Wight, where his father was serving when he was born. In 1880 he emigrated to the United States and joined Clan-na-Gael. Three years later he returned to England to take part in an unsuccessful Fenian dynamite campaign against military and police installations. He was caught and sentenced to fifteen years' imprisonment. Upon his release he was made a Freeman of the city of Limerick before returning to America in 1899. When he came back to Ireland in 1907, he was fanatical in his determination to launch another Irish rebellion using the IRB in conjunction with financial support from Clan-na-Gael.

Clarke soon gathered around him an equally dedicated group of young IRB men, mostly (like Bulmer Hobson) from the north. One of them, Sean MacDermott (1884–1916), a barman in Belfast, became business manager of an IRB-financed newspaper, *Irish Freedom*, established in 1910 by Clarke to act as a vehicle for extreme nationalist opinion. By 1912, Clarke was treasurer and MacDermott secretary of the IRB which could boast 1,500 members, all dedicated to rebellion. The following year with the formation of the Irish Volunteers, the IRB's membership formed the activist core of Volunteer companies all over the country. IRB members – unknown to MacNeill – secured most of the leading appointments in the organization and effectively controlled it. However, this control was short-lived. Within ten months over 180,000 men had enrolled in the Volunteers, forcing Redmond and the Irish Party to participate. Redmond was frightened that the Volunteers might forget their motto and revolt or take some challenging action which would upset the home rule arrangements, and he was also frightened that they might become a political force appealing to Irish people over the head of the Irish Party. Accordingly, he demanded control of the organization. The provisional committee of the Volunteers (the governing body) on 15 June 1914 decided by eighteen votes to nine to accept Redmond's demand on the grounds that otherwise there would be a split and factional in-fighting would only weaken their purpose of ensuring that home rule was implemented. The IRB's control was over. Clarke and MacDermott were furious, particularly because Hobson and five other members of the IRB on the provisional committee had voted to accept Redmond's demand. Hobson argued that since Redmond's enormous popularity would ensure that he controlled the mass of Volunteers whatever happened, it was better to roll with the punch and to maintain whatever revolutionary impetus possible from within. Clarke and Mac-Dermott accused Hobson of having betrayed the IRB: 'When they demanded to know how much I had been paid by Redmond for selling the Volunteers, I realized I could not discuss policy on that level or work with people who thought like that. I was shocked to find that men so sincere and devoted had such paltry minds.' From this point on, the IRB became even more secretive, with Clarke and MacDermott only trusting an inner circle, developing a secret society within a secret society.

Shortly after the outbreak of the First World War, Clarke arranged a meeting with a number of the more extreme nationalist leaders (including Connolly and Griffith but excluding MacNeill) in Dublin on 9 September. They all agreed that England's difficulty was Ireland's opportunity, and that advantage should be taken of the war to launch another Irish rising. The Irish Volunteers were the most obvious sizeable potential rebel grouping, particularly since their dramatic arming in the last days of July 1914, with rifles and ammunition smuggled from Germany by Robert Erskine Childers (1870–1922) in his yacht, the *Asgard*.

Erskine Childers was one of the brightest and most glittering of his generation. He had been a clerk of the house of commons after passing the civil service examinations in 1894 with the third best results. He was a skilled yachtsman and the author of an enormously popular and influential book, *The riddle of the sands* (1903), based upon his own nautical experience in the North Sea. The book gave a fictional account of German plans to invade England and was cited in the run-up to the First World War by those who were convinced of Britain's military unpreparedness for war. He himself became convinced of the justice of home rule for Ireland, and in the summer of 1914 collected £1,500 with his friend, Sir Roger Casement (1864–1916), which they used to buy 1,500 rifles and 45,000 cartridges in Germany and Belgium. On 26 July 1914, Childers sailed the *Asgard* into Howth harbour outside Dublin with 900 rifles and 26,000 cartridges. In a carefully planned operation, 800 Dublin Volunteers landed Childers' cargo. (A week later another yachting friend of Childers brought the remaining rifles and bullets to Kilcoole, Co. Wicklow.)

As the Dublin Volunteers marched back into the city with their new rifles, they were stopped by a mixed force of the Dublin Metropolitan Police (DMP) and the King's Own Scottish Borderers, who managed to confiscate only nineteen rifles from the Volunteers who rapidly dispersed. The soldiers and police were jeered and booed by slum crowds as they returned to Dublin. In Bachelor's Walk, the Borderers panicked and fired into the crowd around them, killing three and wounding thirty-two people. The victims were given large funerals and memorial services were held for them in churches throughout the country. An inquiry into the incident censured officials and led to the dismissal of the Assistant Commissioner of Police. Different lessons were learned by the different groups involved in these events. The police and civil service judged that firm action against the Volunteers was likely to be penalized by the government, and this contributed to the ease with which Volunteers drilled and paraded even after the start of the World War. The Volunteers were confirmed in their view that while the authorities were prepared to arrest (and shoot) Irish nationalists, they were not prepared similarly to act against Irish unionists engaged upon similar gun-running and militarist enterprises.

Carson and Redmond both set aside their differences with the outbreak of war and supported the fight for 'the freedom of small nations' against Germany. Special arrangements were made for the Ulster Volunteer Force to enroll *en mass* in the British army in a new Division, the 36th, the Ulster Division. Similar arrangements were refused the Irish Volunteers. The Division elected its own officers which was a smack across the face for Redmond: the government was saying that there would be one set of Irish citizen troops, but not another. In an important sense, the descendants of the planters were being armed with privilege by the government, while the 'native' Irish were being treated as second-class. Despite being naturally resentful at this second-class treatment, Redmond made a speech to an Irish Volunteer parade at Woodenbridge, Co. Wicklow, on 20 September, saying 'Go on drilling and make yourselves efficient for the work, and then account yourselves as men, not only in Ireland itself, but wherever the firing line extends, in defence of right, of freedom, and of religion'. Faced with this clear call to enlist, tens of thousands of Irish Volunteers did so. The IRB minority in the Volunteers decided that since in practice the organization had been split by Redmond's call between those who would fight for the United Kingdom (the majority) and those who would not, they might as well make the split formal. Eoin MacNeill, who had willingly fronted for the IRB at the formation of the Volunteers, agreed to lead the anti-Redmondite faction and on 21 September 12,000 of them split away, keeping to themselves the name 'Irish Volunteers' and leaving over 100,000 Redmondites to the new name of 'Irish National Volunteers'. For days later a small group of IRB volunteers and Citizen Army men under the leadership of Tom Clarke and James Connolly prepared to break up a recruiting meeting at Dublin's Mansion House to be addressed by the prime minister, Asquith, and John Redmond. They had to drop their plan when troops turned out to protect the meeting, but there could be no doubt about their rebellious, revolutionary intentions. MacNeill was fully aware of the IRB's purpose, but he thought that he had sufficient influence amongst Volunteers generally to moderate IRB extremism. In this mistaken belief he was encouraged by some of his closest henchmen in the Volunteers who, unknown to him, were also members of the IRB.

The director of organization and Press Secretary of the Irish Volunteers was Patrick Henry Pearse (1879–1916), the son of a Protestant non-conformist English stone-carver and a Catholic Irish mother. His father had successfully established a business in Dublin, and Pearse grew up in a relatively comfortable home. He joined the Gaelic League in his teens, and developed a passionate interest in the Irish language and Gaelic culture and lore. In 1908 he founded a bi-lingual private school, St Enda's, in Dublin, and five years later was a founder-member of the Irish Volunteers. He was, like Eoin MacNeill, a supporter of the Irish Party, but in December 1913 he joined the IRB having been converted by the arguments for physical force. An excellent orator, he gained national notice on 1 August 1915 with his 'the fools, the fools, the fools!' graveside speech for an old Fenian, Jeremiah O'Donovan Rossa, in which he also declared:

Life springs from death, and from the graves of patriot men and women spring living nations. The defenders of this Realm have worked well in secret and in the open. They think that they have pacified Ireland. They think they have purchased half of us and intimidated the other half. They think they have foreseen everything.

Four months earlier, in May, he had joined a top secret IRB military committee (from which MacNeill was excluded) formed by Tom Clarke to plot a rebellion.

Clarke's military committee was a sub-committee of the IRB's Supreme Council. Under Clarke's chairmanship, Sean MacDermott, Eamonn Ceannt (1881–1916) and Patrick Pearse were its founder-members in May 1915. Ceannt was a senior IRB man and a leading member of the Gaelic League. He was also Commandant of the 4th Battalion, Dublin Brigade, Irish Volunteers. They were charged with the responsibility of organizing and launching a rebellion before the end of the first World War. Their first plan was for a rising in September 1915, but they had to cancel their arrangements after MacDermott was arrested and imprisoned for four months just after the committee's formation, and after their plans to obtain arms from Germany that year failed.

In July 1914, Sir Roger Casement had travelled privately to New York where he met John Devoy and other leaders of Clan-na-Gael. Devoy, kept fully informed by Clarke, had already been in touch with the German ambassador to the United States, and had asked for German military support for an Irish rebellion. A month later, just after the outbreak of war, Casement sailed to Germany with Devoy's blessing, hoping to secure support for Clarke and Devoy's plans and to form an Irish Brigade from prisoners of war. In November 1914 he succeeded in bringing the German government to announce, in a document he himself had drafted, that as far as Ireland was concerned, 'Germany desires only a national prosperity and a national freedom.' In forming an Irish Brigade he was much less successful, obtaining only fifty-five recruits from among Irish prisoners by 1916.

Before 1916, the truth was that revolutionary Irish nationalism was the province of a small minority: the IRB and its fellow-travellers. The overwhelming majority of Irish people between them either wanted home rule under Britain or union with Britain. Full Irish independence was not regarded as practical in economic and political terms. Britain may have been the age-old enemy, but the new age of the twentieth century had brought with it a pragmatism which made old idealisms look unnecessary and out of place. Unionist and home rule Irishmen volunteered in great numbers for the British army, happy to bury their differences and to fight for the maintenance of the British Empire and the freedom of small nations on the European mainland. Over 200,000 Irishmen had joined up by the end of the war, and 60,000 never returned. Sean O'Casey described the scene in Dublin as thousands marched to the troop-ships: 'The stoutest men from hill, valley and town came pressing into the British army. Long columns of Irishmen went swinging past Liberty Hall down to the quays, to the ships waiting to take them to a poppy-mobbed grave in Flanders.' As they marched they sang 'It's a long way to Tipperary', giving the war its song. By voluntarily joining up (conscription was not introduced in Ireland), Irishmen were voting with their feet (and their lives) in favour of the constitutional cooperation with Britain epitomized by John Redmond, and against the complete separation of the two countries desired by the IRB.

Popular rejection of their objectives did not dismay the IRB. Clarke's military committee pressed ahead with its plans, increasing nation-wide rising. James Connolly had been taken as a member because of its persistent threats to launch a rebellion with his minuscule Citizen Army. He taunted that the Volunteers might march well, but would they ever fight? And Clarke and his colleagues worried that unless Connolly was made privy to their plans, he would jeopardize them by forcing the government to tighten security. Joseph Mary Plunkett (1887–1916), a poet, joined the committee after he travelled secretly to Germany in 1915 on IRB instructions to help Casement secure military support for their planned rising. He was co-treasurer and a member of the executive of the Irish Volunteers (the organization's day to day controlling body). In April 1916, the last person to join was Thomas MacDonagh (1878–1916), another poet who had been Pearse's first member of staff at St Enda's. He was also director of training on the headquarters' staff of the Irish Volunteers, and he had organized the Volunteers' collection of the rifles and ammunition from Erskine Childers at Howth in 1914. These seven men were responsible for the Easter 1916 rising.

Working through the normal channels of command, most of which they controlled, the members of the IRB military committee prepared the Irish Volunteers and the Irish Citizen Army for rebellion. Drills, route marches and mock attacks on strongpoints were practised in Dublin and in the countryside. Through John Devoy who was in close touch with the German ambassador in Washington, the Committee maintained contact with Sir Roger

Casement in Germany. Together, they arranged early in April with the German government for a ship, the *Aud*, disguised as a neutral Norwegian trawler, to land 20,000 rifles in Tralee Bay between Friday 21 and Monday 24 April. Easter Sunday, 23 April, was the actual day set for the rebellion. They also seem to have expected much more help than the Germans were in fact prepared to give. Casement, aware of the committee's misapprehensions, sailed to Ireland in a German U-boat, intending when he arrived to warn Clarke and to do his best to stop the rising which he was convinced would otherwise fail dismally.

The governmental authorities in Ireland were aware that trouble was brewing. The lord lieutenant, Lord Wimborne, the chief secretary, Augustine Birrell, and the under-secretary for Ireland, Sir Matthew Nathan, had been alerted by RIC and DMP reports to the fact that rebellion was being considered by some Irish Volunteers who might be in touch with Germany and a 'German landing at an early date' was rumoured. Birrell, noting Irish recruiting figures, the popularity of Redmond and the handful of Irish as opposed to National Volunteers, refused to take the reports seriously, saying 'I laugh at the whole thing'. Nathan agreed, insisting that the Volunteer leaders did not intend insurrection. Wimborne alone pressed for the arrest of Volunteer and Citizen Army leaders and the suppression of both organizations. However, Birrell and Nathan argued that such action would probably spark the revolt Wimborne feared, and the government decided not to take repressive action. A month before the rising, Birrell had written to Lord Midleton, the leader of the southern Irish Unionists who, like Wimborne, was worried by Volunteers parades and posturings, 'to proclaim the Irish Volunteers as an illegal body would be in my opinion a reckless and foolish act and would promote disloyalty to a prodigious extent'. The plans of Clarke and the military committee for a rising remained a well-kept secret, ensuring that for the first time in modern history an Irish uprising would have the advantage of a large measure of surprise.

The surprise was by no means total, and largely reflected the misjudgements of Birrell and Nathan. In the weed preceding Easter Sunday 1916, all the rising plans went wrong. Within two weeks of the start of the World War, the Russian navy, unknown to the Germans, captured the German naval code and offered it to the British Admiralty. Winston Churchill, first lord of the Admiralty, immediately sent a destroyer to Murmansk to collect the code, and for the rest of the war British intelligence was able to read German naval messages. As a result, Birrell and Nathan had foreknowledge of the arrival of the *Aud* and of the intended rising. They put the RIC and DMP on alert and prepared to arrest Volunteer leaders on Easter Saturday. The conspirators also encountered serious opposition to their schemes from Eoin MacNeill who, as president of the Volunteers, could command the obedience of most of its members. He all along maintained that the Volunteers' purpose was to defend the 1914 home rule settlement, and that defiance of the government could only be sanctioned in defence of Volunteer arms. Accordingly, the military committee planned to circumvent MacNeill's authority by pretending that mobilization of the Volunteers for the rising was simply another routine drill. In this way they calculated that the majority of Volunteers, whether approving or not, would find themselves taking part in a rebellion and be faced with a *fait accompli*. At the same time, in order to ensure that their plans for rebellion were implemented (and not simply the ostensible man-oeuvres), the military committee saw to it that most Volunteer officers were sworn into the IRB: it was thus presumed that the military committee's orders would be loyally followed despite anything MacNeill might command. However, in the days before Easter Sunday, the committee attempted to persuade MacNeill to rebellion. On the Tuesday before Easter he was shown a document proclaiming the confiscation of Volunteer arms and the arrest of Volunteer leaders. This 'Castle Document' which purported to be drawn up by the authorities in Dublin Castle, the seat of government in Ireland, was probably forged by Joseph Plunkett and Sean MacDermott (though possibly on the basis of a genuine draft document). The important points were that it accurately reflected Castle plans and that MacNeill believed it and so adopted a more belligerent stand himself. The following day – Wednesday 19 April – he ordered the Volunteers to prepare to defend their arms. On Thursday, Bulmer Hobson discovered that the planned rising was only forty-eight hours away, and told MacNeill who immediately realized that he had been duped all along and wrote out orders cancelling the Easter Sunday nationwide manoeuvres. However, instead of issuing these orders at once, MacNeill sought out members of the IRB military committee and argued with them to stop the rising. He wavered himself and reluctantly agreed not to stand in their way after they had revealed to him the full extent of their preparations, including their contacts with Germany. Then, when he heard the news on Easter Saturday that the *Aud* had been intercepted by the Royal Navy, and that Sir Roger Casement had been arrested near Tralee, Co. Kerry, within hours of landing from his submarine, MacNeill decided that the rising was doomed to failure and finally issued his orders cancelling the Easter Sunday manoeuvres which he knew to be a cover for insurrection. He sent couriers all over the country to deliver these orders and to tell local Volunteer commanders to do nothing on Sunday, and he published a cancellation notice in the *Sunday Independent* for all to see. In Dublin Castle, the authorities monitored developments and, seeing MacNeill's notice, decided that they could relax and that there would be no trouble. Wimborne alone still pressed for the arrest of between sixty and one hundred leading Volunteer and Citizen Army men, receiving the necessary authorization from London on Easter Monday when it was too late.

Despite the almost complete collapse of their plans, the military committee decided to press ahead. Patrick Pearse, using his position as director of organization of the Volunteers, presented MacNeill's cancellation order only as a delay, and himself ordered the Volunteers to mobilize on Easter Monday instead. James Connolly did the same with the Citizen Army. Monday was a sunny bank holiday, and thousands of Dubliners had left the city for the day, many going to the Fairyhouse races. Passers by paid little attention to Volunteers and Citizen Army men gathering in front of Liberty Hall. Altogether, perhaps only 700 men and boys turned out because of confusion over MacNeill's Sunday cancellation (though afterwards, allegations of cowardice were made against many who knew what was planned but did not turn out). At mid-day Connolly and Pearse marched with one group into Sackville Street (re-named O'Connell Street in 1924), wheeled left half-way up and rushed into the General Post Office. They arrested a British officer who had been buying stamps, and turned everyone else out of the building which they made their headquarters for the next five days. There James Connolly addressed his men and told them that they were no longer members of the Irish Citizen Army or of the Irish Volunteers, but of 'the Army of the Irish Republic'. The IRA was back in the field for the first time since the Fenian 'invasion' of Canada in 1867.

Other groups occupied strategically placed buildings and positions in the city. Boland's Bakery Mills, which commanded the main road into Dublin from Kingstown (now Dun Laoghaire), was occupied by members of the 3rd Battalion, Dublin Brigade, Irish Volunteers under their commandant Eamon de Valera (1882–1975). De Valera, born in New York of an Irish mother and Spanish father, was to become the dominant personality in Irish politics after 1922, and the political leader of Irish nationalism after 1918. Under his command, 3rd Battalion outposts on Northumberland Road and Lower Mount Street (Clanwilliam House) put up some of the most determined resistance during the rising, killing and wounding 234 British soldiers, over half the total British casualties of the whole rebellion. Another (Citizen Army) group tried to capture Dublin Castle, but after killing the policeman on duty, they were repulsed by the guard. Dublin's Four Courts, the College of Surgeons on St Stephen's Green, the South Dublin Union, Mendicity Institution and Jacob's biscuit factory – all buildings covering access roads to the city centre – were occupied and held in the name of the Irish Republic proclaimed in posters put up by the rebels all over the capital. Patrick Pearse read the proclamation on two occasions to curious crowds in Sackville Street during Easter Monday afternoon:

Irishmen and Irishwomen: In the name of God and the dead generations from which she receives her old tradition of nationhood, Ireland, through us, summons her children to her flag and strikes for her freedom. Having organized and trained her manhood through her secret revolutionary organization, the Irish Republican Brotherhood, and through her open military organizations, the Irish Volunteers and the Irish Citizen Army, having patiently perfected her discipline, having resolutely waited for the right moment to reveal itself, she now seizes that moment, and, supported by her exiled children in America and by gallant allies in Europe, but relying in the first on her own strength, she strikes in full confidence of victory.

Seven signatories – the seven members of the IRB's Military Committee – with Thomas J. Clarke heading the list, followed the text of the proclamation. It was their rebellion, and it was to be the most successful, though one of the most short-lived in Irish history.

Hardly any fighting took place in Dublin in the two days that followed the seizure of the GPO. Looters ransacked the shops in and around Sackville Street. An unsuspecting party of Lancers were fired on as they rode past the GPO on Easter Monday afternoon. On Tuesday night, troops from Britain and the Curragh military camp began to arrive and on Wednesday afternoon they started to close in on rebel positions. Many of the soldiers who had come directly from Britain thought at first that they were in Belgium, only realizing their mistake when ordinary Dubliners started to cheer, encourage and welcome them. Food and drink was pressed upon them by local people, appalled by the rising. By Thursday, British units had penetrated the side streets around the GPO and had started to shell the building. On Friday evening, the centre of Dublin was a mass of flames. On Saturday afternoon, 29 April at 3.45 p.m. Pearse, now entitled president of the provisional government of the Irish Republic and commander-in-chief of the IRA, surrendered.

Outside Dublin, hardly any fighting (or rebellion) had taken place. MacNeill's countermanding order and couriers had succeeded in arresting revolt. At Ashbourne, Co. Meath, members of the 5th Battalion, Dublin Brigade, Irish Volunteers, clashed with the RIC killing eight and wounding fifteen. In Galway, a group of Volunteers attacked the RIC station at Oranmore, killing one constable and wounding two others. Five Volunteer brothers, the Kents, at their farmhouse in Castlelyons, Co. Cork, fought a gun-battle with the RIC on 2 May, three days after Pearse's surrender, killing an RIC head constable. In Dundalk, Enniscorthy and in parts of Ulster and Munster, Volunteers mobilized and there were some skirmishes, but no other real fighting took place. The rebellion was confined almost completely to Dublin where £2.5 million damage was caused. Its success lay not in itself, but in the effect of the government's reaction.

9

The fight for freedom

During and immediately after the rising, Irish people were confused and dismayed by what had happened. Twenty-nine Irishmen in British regiments; fourteen Irishmen in the RIC; five Irishmen in the Training Corps (known as 'Gorgeous Wrecks' because of their age and from the initials 'GR' on their buttons and buckles); three Irishmen in the DMP, and six members of the Redmondite Irish National Volunteers had been killed fighting the rebels. Total casualties were over 3,000, including 132 soldiers, RIC and DMP killed and a further 397 wounded, and sixty rebels killed. Tens of thousands of families with husbands, fathers, sons and brothers in the British army naturally reacted violently against those they saw as stabbing in the back soldiers fighting in France and Flanders. Everybody realized that the rebels had been more than foolhardy, and there was almost unanimous initial support of the government's attitude to them as traitors. The rebel proclamation referring to their 'gallant allies in Europe' was cited as evidence of their collusion with Germany, embroiled in total war with the United Kingdom. General Sir John Maxwell had arrived as commander-in-chief in Ireland on Easter Friday 1916, and for him the operation of martial law provided a clear course of action. He had fought in the Boer War and had served in the Sudan and Egypt. To him, the rising in Ireland was an act of supreme treachery for which he was going to teach 'these infernal fellows a lesson they would not soon forget'. He told Lord Wimborne 'I am going to ensure that there will be no treason whispered for a hundred years.' Probably fewer than a total of 900 men and women had taken part in the rising. During the week, a steady trickle of new recruits had joined in: about 1,000 rebels were recorded as surrendering on Easter Saturday. Within four days Maxwell had convened courts martial for them while arresting

2,500 more people, including Arthur Griffith and Eoin MacNeill, and charging them with complicity in the rising.

One woman and 120 men were tried by the courts martial: ninety were sentenced to death. Patrick Pearse was the first to be condemned. At his trial his courage impressed his judges, and the president of the court was reported to be 'terribly affected by the work he had to do'. Early on Wednesday morning, 3 May, he was shot by firing squad in Kilmainham gaol. Tom Clarke and Thomas MacDonagh followed Pearse to death that same morning. The next day Patrick Pearse's younger brother, William, and three other men were executed. On Friday John MacBride, husband of the suffragette and Irish nationalist agitator Maud Gonne (with whom Yeats declared himself hopelessly in love), was also shot in Kilmainham. He had not known about the rising plans and had been as surprised as the rest of Dublin on Easter Monday, but like his friend Michael O'Rahilly ('The O'Rahilly') who was killed charging from the GPO during the fighting, MacBride had felt impelled to join the rebels. He had been second-in-command of a small Irish Brigade that had fought for the Boers during the Boer War, and many believed that his execution was British revenge for this, rather than for anything he had done during Easter week.

By the end of the first week in May, opinions were already changing. Redmondite National Volunteers patrolled Sackville Street after the rising, helping troops and police keep order. Rebel prisoners were jeered and booed as they were marched to prison, but Redmond himself was worried by Maxwell's handling of the situation. He realized that public opinion was slowly swaying towards the rebels as a result of the executions as people like the socialite Lady Fingall began to report that they were 'watching a stream of blood coming from beneath a closed door'. George Bernard Shaw warned the government that they were 'canonising their prisoners'. The prime minister, Asquith, heeded these warnings and sent two telegrams to Maxwell saying that he hoped there would be no more executions except in special cases. Maxwell obviously considered that there were several more special cases: four more executions took place on 8 May and another the following day. The drawn out pace of executions was now clearly changing men's minds just as Redmond had feared. John Dillon, deputy leader of the Irish Party, himself demonstrated the extent to which this had happened

when on 11 May in the house of commons he lost his self-control
and shouted 'I am proud of their courage and if you were not so
dense and stupid, as some of you English people are, you could have
had these men fighting for you. . .it is not murderers who are being
executed; it is insurgents who have fought a clean fight, however
misguided.' The following day the last two military executions took
place: Sean MacDermott and James Connolly. Connolly, whose
ankle had been shattered by a bullet in the TOP, was shot strapped
to a chair. MacDermott who, with Clarke, had masterminded the
rising, in his letter to his family captured the romantic feeling and
expressed the theory of blood sacrifice that had inspired them all.
'You ought to envy me', he wrote. 'The cause for which I die has
been rebaptized during the past week by the blood of as good men
as ever trod God's earth. . .It is not alone for myself I feel happy, but
for the fact that Ireland has produced such men.' The rebel leaders
had believed that rebellion was necessary if only to keep alive the
flame of Irish freedom, and they calculated – correctly as it turned
out – that their deaths in that romantic cause would inspire another
generation of rebels.

The fifteen executions which took place between 3 and 12 May
were not considered harsh by Maxwell and many in authority. On
21 February the battle for Verdun had begun with tremendous loss
of life. In April and May preparations were underway for the crucial
battle of the Somme which began on 1 July and which was to cost
600,000 Allied dead and wounded – 400,000 of them British. Pearse,
in a poem he had written only hours before his death, had noted Irish
people's scorn for the rising. The poet and storyteller, James Stephens,
an eyewitness of events in Dublin, described how women in particular were 'viciously hostile' to the rebel prisoners as they were paraded
through the streets of Dublin. Seven Roman Catholic bishops
denounced the rising, and the *Irish Catholic* described Pearse as 'a
crazy and insolent schoolmaster', ridiculing the rebels as 'rogues
and fools'. Local councils passed resolutions calling for 'the severest
punishment' and deploring 'the outbreak which brings the blush of
shame to every honest Irishman'. Yet, by 10 June Tim Healy, one
of the leading anti-Parnellites who was soon to become the first
governor general of an Irish Free State, was writing to his brother:

I never knew such a transformation of opinion as that caused by the
executions. . .They have lost the hearts of the people beyond all hope of
retrieving their mistakes. Clerics have discovered that 'the probable hope

of success' needed to justify rebellion does not necessarily mean military success, and that Pearse achieved his object and 'builded better than he knew'. His executioners would now give a good deal to have him and his brother back in jail alive.

The fourteen men executed in Dublin were buried in quicklime in Arbour Hill barracks. Thomas Kent, condemned for his part in the affray at his home in Castlelyons, Co. Cork, was executed and buried in Cork gaol. Sir Roger Casement, captured before the rising started, was sent to the Tower of London charged with high treason. From a purely legal standpoint he had no defence to the charge. To discredit him perhaps with an eye to his being found guilty but insane, however, his diaries revealing his homosexuality were photographed by officials at the Home and Foreign Offices and circulated with the tacit approval of government ministers to journalists and people of influence, it should be stressed, however, that the judge in the case did not see them. John Redmond was so shocked by them that he refused to campaign on Casement's behalf, and so it was with many others too. Early on the morning of 3 August 1916, Casement was hanged in Pentonville gaol, becoming the sixteenth Irish martyr of that year. His speech from the dock on the fourth day of his trial is a classic statement of Irish nationalism:

If true religion rests on love, it is equally true that loyalty rests on love. The law I am charged under has no parentage in love, and claims the allegiance of today on the ignorance and blindness of the past. . .Loyalty is a sentiment, not a law. It rests on love, not restraint. The government of Ireland by England rests on restraint, and not on law; and since it demands no love, it can evoke no loyalty. . .For if English authority be omnipotent – a power, as Mr Gladstone phrased it, that reaches to the very ends of the earth – Irish hope exceeds the dimensions of that power, excels its authority, and renews with each generation the claims of the last. The cause that begets this indominatable persistency, the faculty of preserving through centuries of misery the remembrance of lost liberty – this surely is the noblest cause ever man strove for, ever lived for, ever died for.

No one else was executed for involvement in the rising, but 1,867 men and women out of the 3,500 originally arrested by Maxwell were interned and gaoled in Britain – the rest were released after questioning in May and June. Most of those interned were held at Frongoch camp in Wales where a young and energetic Corkman, Michael Collins (1890–1922), was quickly recognized as a natural leader. Collins had left Ireland in 1906 to work in London as a clerk. There he became an active member of the GAA, the Gaelic League and the IRB, returning to Dublin towards the end of 1915 to take part in the rebellion he and other IRB men realized was coming. He fought as aide-de-camp to Joseph Plunkett in the GPO during the rising, and was arrested with the rebel leaders. In Frongoch, he gathered around him a group of men from west Cork, often referred to as 'The Mafia' by other prisoners, and with their help organized the IRB in the camp and listed those who would be willing to continue the fight for the Irish Republic proclaimed during the rising.

On 23 December 1916, Collins and 600 others were released from internment. Hundreds more had been given their freedom in previous months. The chief secretary for Ireland admitted that the political consequences of keeping so many men interned without trial for so long were more dangerous than letting them go. In January 1916, conscription had been introduced in Britain leaving Ireland excluded because informed opinion, including Carson, considered that more troops would be needed to enforce it there than would be raised by it. By December, over 90,000 southern Irishmen had already volunteered for the British army since the start of the war, and on the battlefields of Belgium and France they might start to wonder for precisely which small country's freedom they were fighting. There was also the ever-pressing need for more troops as casualties mounted in the trenches and shell holes of the Western Front (a serious attempt was even made at one stage to conscript those prisoners in Frongoch who – like Collins – lived in Britain), and Irish government officials advised that Irish opinion, pacified by the release of prisoners, would be more likely to veer back towards support of the war effort and thus produce more volunteers. Perhaps most important, however, was the need the government felt to take American opinion into account. As the First World War ground on, the prospect of prying the United States from its policy of neutrality to hasten an Allied victory over Germany and Austria–Hungary was too precious for Britain to jeopardize. Within a week of James Connolly's execution, the British ambassador in Washington had reported an anti-British shift in American opinion. This may have played a part in securing the setting aside of the death sentence passed on Eamon de Valera who, because of his American birth, could claim United States citizenship. De Valera, who had commanded the Boland's Bakery Mills outpost during the rising, after Connolly's execution was the senior surviving rebel leader.

Made anxious by the change in Irish opinion and by its effect in America, Asquith and his cabinet decided to try and implement the 1914 Government of Ireland Act before the end of the war. An Amending Bill enabling the six most unionist and Protestant counties of northern Ireland to vote themselves temporarily out of the operation of the Act had been passed by both houses of parliament in 1914 but had not received the royal assent. This provision now became the nub of negotiations with Redmond's Irish Party and Carson's Unionists conducted by David Lloyd George (1863–1945), minister of munitions in the war cabinet. Lloyd George had a difficult task. In May 1915 Asquith's Liberal government gave way to a coalition government to pursue the war. Liberals, Conservatives, Irish Unionists and Labour, with Asquith remaining as prime minister, formed the new government in which Redmond and the Irish Party were not included (Redmond refused Asquith's invitation to join). Sir Edward Carson was appointed attorney-general, becoming for a time a senior member of the cabinet. He resigned from the government in October 1916 in protest at the failure to aid Serbia and the way that Asquith was running the war. Thus in late 1916, Lloyd George was faced with the task in his negotiations of reconciling the aspirations of the vast majority of Irishmen for home rule with the domestic political requirements of Asquith's coalition partners. With inspiration and guile, he held separate discussions with Unionists and Irish Party leaders, persuading the former – despite their long-standing opposition to the principle of home rule – to accept it for all but their six north-eastern counties, and persuading the latter that this arrangement was only temporary. When Redmond found out that Carson had been privately assured 'We must make it clear that at the end of the provisional period Ulster does not, whether she wills it or not, merge in the rest of Ireland', he demanded that Lloyd George publicly deny this and make clear instead that a united, home ruled Ireland was the prospect. On 22 July 1916, Redmond was officially informed that the proposed settlement of a divided Ireland was to be permanent in the terms of the assurance Lloyd George had given to Carson, and the negotiations ended with Redmond refusing to accept the proposals. Nevertheless, as Tim Healy pertinently said, 'Redmond has left the Irish cause in a worse position than it ever was placed in by his concession of the six counties, as it can't be obliterated'. It was also significant that the

Unionists had at last accepted the validity of the principle of home rule. But most of all, the breakdown in negotiations for home rule coupled with the apparent acceptance of partition by the Irish Party indicated to many Irishmen that if they wanted self-determination they would have to find another Party and, quite possibly, given Redmond's constitutional failure, would have been prepared to revert to revolutionary methods too.

In December 1916, Lloyd George succeeded Asquith as prime minister having secured the support of the coalition partners for an aggressive war policy. Carson joined Lloyd George's government as first lord of the Admiralty, a position he held until July 1917 when he was moved without departmental responsibility to the war cabinet itself before resigning six months later in protest at the government's overruling of his proposals for Ireland and its war strategy. One of the most important tasks facing Lloyd George remained the problem of Ireland with its continuing effect on American (and dominion) opinion. Within three weeks of becoming prime minister, he had ordered the release of the remaining Frongoch prisoners as a gesture of goodwill towards Irish nationalists. In May 1917 he took up Redmond's idea of an Irish Convention involving unionists and nationalists in another attempt to reach a settlement, and the following month as the Convention met at Trinity College, Dublin, he ordered the release of the remaining 1916 rebels who were met by thronging, cheering crowds in Dublin. De Valera was immediately adopted as the Sinn Fein candidate for a by-election in East Clare which he won with more than twice the number of votes cast for his Irish Party opponent. A revitalized Sinn Fein was now coming forward to give voice to the ideals of the rising. Of the nine parliamentary by-elections Sinn Fein contested between February 1917 and June 1918, it won six. The Party boycotted the Convention which ended in April 1918 without any agreement being reached. Redmond, having been fooled once, was unwilling to accept partition and in any event was forced to take an intransigent stance in order to combat Sinn Fein's growing popularity. Sir Edward Carson and the Unionists, once again re-assured privately by Lloyd George that nothing would be agreed without their consent, would not be budged from their refusal to accept a united, home ruled Ireland. Redmond died in March 1918 knowing that the Irish Party, which for over forty years had dominated Irish politics, was broken.

Immediately upon his release in December 1916, Michael Collins had thrown himself into the work of organizing for another rebellion. His energy and determination gained his rapid advancement in the IRB. Using the secret society's members, and contacts he himself developed, he was soon practically running Sinn Fein which had been catapulted to prominence by the 1916 rising which had been popularly (and quite incorrectly) presented as 'The Sinn Fein Rebellion'. In October 1917 a Sinn Fein Ard Fheis – Party Conference – was held in Dublin and Party policy agreed. Griffith's monarchist home rule bias was dropped in favour of 'securing the international recognition of Ireland as an independent Irish republic. Having achieved that status the Irish people may be referendum freely choose their own form of government.' Successful Sinn Fein parliamentary candidates would not take their seats at Westminster and would instead form an Irish national 'Constituent Assembly. . . to speak and act in the name of the Irish people'. Eamon de Valera was elected president of the Party in place of Griffith. By the time of the first post-war general election in December 1918, Sinn Fein's popularity was such that of the 105 Irish MPs returned, seventy-three were Sinn Feiners. John Dillon, Redmond's successor as leader of the Irish Party, was defeated in East Mayo which had elected him in every election since 1885. Only six Irish Party MPs were elected, and twenty-six Unionists. Among the successful Sinn Fein candidates were Michael Collins (South Co. Cork); Eamon de Valera (East Co. Clare); Arthur Griffith (West Co. Cavan) and the Countess Markievicz (St Patrick's, Dublin), a participant in the 1916 rising and the daughter of a wealthy Anglo-Irish landlord. She had been sentenced to death in 1916, reprieved, imprisoned and then released in June 1917. In December 1918 she became the first woman to be elected to the house of commons. Refusing to take her seat, she enabled Lady Astor to become the first woman actually to sit in the house twelve months later.

Sinn Fein's electoral success was dramatic. It forced the issue of Irish independence since the Party's demand for an Irish republic implied the break-up of the United Kingdom which was something that the government, maintained after the war as a Liberal–Conservative coalition under Lloyd George's premiership, was not prepared to contemplate. Pressing its point, Sinn Fein proceeded non-violently, setting up its Constituent Assembly named 'Dail Eireann' (parliament of Ireland) in Dublin's Manion House on

21 January 1919. Forty-two of the Sinn Fein members, including de Valera, were in gaol, exiled or avoiding arrest, on suspicion of involvement in what the government called a 'German Plot' in 1918 to launch another Irish rising before the end of the war, or in some cases because they had opposed with too much fervour the government's proposals during the war's final year to extend conscription to Ireland. The twenty-seven members who attended the dail's first session quickly agreed a Declaration of Independence re-affirming the 1916 Republic and established a government of their own for it. A hero of the 1916 rising, Cathal Brugha (Charles Burgess, like Patrick Pearse, the son of an Englishman), was elected first president of the dail on the understanding that he would step down in favour of de Valera when he was free. Michael Collins became dail minister for home affairs. A 'Democratic Programme' was also approved which, echoing the arguments of Lalor and the Young Ireland movement, declared 'the right of the people of Ireland to the ownership of Ireland. . .all rights to private property must be subordinated to the public right and welfare'. Two months later, Collins became minister for finance and Brugha minister for defence in a reshuffle carried out by de Valera upon his appointment as dail president.

Michael Collins was the mainspring of post-1916 Irish nationalist activity. He rapidly came to dominate the IRB, becoming its secretary early in 1917. Within Sinn Fein, he was recognized as the principal organizer, and within the Irish Volunteers, more properly known as the Irish Republican Army after 1916, he was the leading tactician and strategist. He was determined to avoid a repeat of 1916 which he described as 'bungled terribly costing many a good life. It seemed at first to be well-organized, but afterwards became subjected to panic decisions and a great lack of very essential organization and co-operation'. Using the IRB and money and connections supplied to him by Mrs Tom Clarke, he organized IRB circles throughout the country to provide the nucleus of Sinn Fein and IRA groups. In November 1917, a month after the Sinn Fein Ard Fheis, he arranged a secret IRA convention at which de Valera was elected president of the army. In March 1918 he masterminded the formation of an IRA General Headquarters' Staff, securing the appointment of a close and trusted colleague, Richard Mulcahy (1886–1971), as chief-of-staff while himself preferring the key position of adjutant-general from which he could concentrate on training and preparing the secret army for rebellion. On the IRA's governing executive (elected at the 1917 Convention), he held the post of director of organization. He devised the stunning escape of de Valera and two others from Lincoln gaol on 3 February 1919 by using IRB contacts to smuggle them a key to the prison's locks. Throughout the national movement his ability and efficiency became legendary.

Collins' organizing genius was vital to all sections of the national movement which, after 1918, became an uneasy alliance between constitutional and revolutionary nationalists. Divisions constantly flared up, and the device of having de Valera as president of all the important constitutional and revolutionary organizations (except the IRB whose hidden hand, often in the form of Collins himself, was in every organization) was made ineffective by his long absences in prison or, after 1919, in the USA. Despite its wide influence, the IRB was regarded with suspicion by many and with animosity by some leading nationalists. De Valera was vehemently opposed to the continuation of the IRB, leaving the society after the rising. He argued that the time for secret societies was over and that given the enormous renewed popularity of the cause of Irish independence, the machinations of the IRB were positively dangerous. Brugha was opposed to the IRB for a different reason. He was convinced that the 1916 rising had failed because IRB men had not turned out as planned, and ever afterwards he opposed the society. After 1918, Brugha also became increasingly hostile to Collins, accusing him of using the IRB to extend his influence. These tensions were super-imposed upon the traditional hostility between constitutionalists and revolutionaries, and the result was a fragility at the heart of the independence movement. Sinn Fein members of the dail had won the 1918 election with the promise that they would take the case for Ireland's independence to the Peace Conference which had followed Germany's surrender ending the First World War. But as the Conference proved reluctant to take up the Irish cause and to interfere in what Britain held was a domestic political matter, so revolutionaries like Collins began to make the pace of Irish revolt.

The essentially constitutionally minded dail was always hesitant about acknowledging the IRA or assuming responsibility for IRA activity. To begin with, the IRA's GHQ Staff, who were nearly all members of the dail as well, were also reluctant (with the exception of Collins) to authorize attacks on British soldiers and the RIC. As a result, IRA activity was at first carried out by local units on their own initiative (often prompted by IRB men) in defiance of their superiors in Dublin. In 1918 a Tipperary IRA leader, Sean Treacy, disturbed by the constitutional approach of Sinn Fein, had declared 'If this is the state of affairs, we'll have to kill someone and make the bloody enemy organize us!' On 21 January 1919, the same day the dail first met, Sean Treacy and his IRA group, acting on their own, shot dead two RIC men at Soloheadbeg, Co. Tipperary, inaugurating the 'Troubles'. By 1920, the dail tacitly accepted the IRA's violent activity. Still, not until March 1921 did the dail formally recognize the army that had been fighting on its behalf, and de Valera was able to declare 'From the Irish Volunteers we fashioned the Irish Republican Army to be the military arm of the Government. The army is, therefore, a regular State force, under the civil control of the elected representatives.' In fact, this was not actually the case since the IRA never completely accepted the dail's authority. The political value of keeping the dail distanced from the IRA was perceived by the dail's and the IRA's leaders as being outweighed by the danger of having two sources of authority competing for the loyalty of nationalists. Therefore, in August 1919, members of the dail and of the IRA both took an oath of allegiance to 'defend the Irish republic and the government of the Irish republic which is Dail Eireann against all enemies, foreign and domestic'. In order to accommodate this new oath, the IRA, which had a constitution of its own requiring its members on oath to recognize the authority only of its own governing body, the executive, now drafted a new constitution. The lingering suspicion of constitutionalists in the dail was reflected in its clauses, with the IRA executive insisting upon the right to approve the appointment of the dail minister for defence. Together with the oath of loyalty to the Irish republic, this was to have a profound effect upon Irish history within two years.

Eamon de Valera was the man under whose leadership the disparate elements of Irish nationalism grouped. His was the public face; Collins' the clandestine one. While Collins secretly planned and prepared for violent confrontation with the police and military forces of the United Kingdom, de Valera constantly emphasized Sinn Fein constitutionalism and the popular endorsement by Irish voters of Sinn Fein objectives in the 1918 election. After de Valera's escape from Lincoln gaol, Cathal Brugha stepped down as president of the dail as agreed. De Valera was unanimously elected in Brugha's stead, making him president of the three main nationalist bodies – the dail, Sinn Fein and the IRA – and head of the dail government of their Irish republic. Collins was appointed minister for finance in the new cabinet and was charged with raising a public loan to finance the dail in 'propagating the Irish cause all over the world' and in establishing a dail administration in Ireland. De Valera himself went to America in June 1919, four months after his escape from gaol, convinced that the key to Irish independence lay in bringing American opinion to bear on Britain. Arthur Griffith was left as acting president of Sinn Fein and the dail, and Cathal Brugha (who, as minister for defence was responsible anyhow) as acting president of the IRA. For the next eighteen months, de Valera campaigned in America raising $5 million and mobilizing Irish–American politicians in an unsuccessful attempt to secure pro-Irish independence platforms in both the Republican and Democratic Parties' presidential election conventions in 1920. While de Valera was away, undeclared war began in earnest between the IRA and British forces in Ireland.

By September 1919, Collins had succeeded in penetrating the Dublin Castle headquarters of the 'G' Division of the Dublin Metropolitan Police, the plain-clothes detectives who were the British government's principal intelligence group in Ireland. Several 'G' Division personnel sympathetic to the nationalist cause voluntarily acted as Collins' agents, and on one occasion Collins was even able to read the file on himself, so extensive were his contacts. In September, he also formed his 'Squad' of hand-picked gunmen entrusted with the killing of police agents, informers and detectives. The previous month, IRA groups all over Ireland had attacked RIC barracks, as a result of which the Castle authorities banned most nationalist organizations including the dail, Sinn Fein and the IRA. The dail continued to meet in secret, but its suppression showed that Lloyd George's British Liberal–Conservative coalition government was prepared to meet force with force if necessary. By the end of the year, it was clear that the struggle for Irish independence was going to be violent and bloody.

With the connivance of Collins, local IRA leaders carried out more and more attacks on British forces despite frequent orders to the contrary from IRA GHQ and the refusal by politicians in the dail to recognize the IRA or support IRA activities. In December 1919 the

IRA's chief-of-staff, Richard Mulcahy, made it clear to a party composed of members of Collins' Squad and Dublin IRA men who ambushed Lord French, the lord lieutenant of Ireland, that the dail and IRA leadership might have to repudiate the ambush as part of the effort to present a constitutional and responsible front. During 1920, as growing numbers of IRA men went 'on the run' in the countryside, they were formed into flying columns (the most famous being that led by Tom Barry in Co. Cork) carrying out guerrilla attacks on British military formations and on the RIC. Outside Dublin, Cork carried most of the burden of the war. Two lord mayors of Cork, who were also the local IRA leaders, died during the fight. Thomas MacCurtain was shot dead in his own bed on the night of 19 March 1920: the coroner's jury investigating his murder found that it 'was organized and carried out by the Royal Constabulary'. His successor in the IRA and as lord mayor, Terence MacSwiney, was arrested at an IRA meeting in the City Hall five months later and immediately went on hunger-strike in protest. He starved for seventy-four days, dying in Brixton gaol on 25 October. In northern Ireland, in contrast, there was little IRA activity as local leaders and IRA GHQ quietly accepted that majority opinion was against them.

The main thrust of the IRA campaign was against RIC men and their barracks. Collins recognized that the RIC, drawn from the Irish people themselves, was the IRA's single most dangerous opponent, and so he set about intimidating RIC men with violence and by implementing a policy of ostracizing RIC families. By the end of June 1920, fifty-five RIC and DMP men had been killed and seventy-four wounded, and by the end of July 1921, 2,000 of the 10,000 regular RIC had resigned from the force. In order to protect the widely flung RIC, in the spring of 1920 hundreds of RIC barracks were evacuated. In April that year, 315 of the evacuated buildings were burned down in one night in the IRA's largest operation of the war. Four weeks later, the *Irish Times* stated 'The King's government has virtually ceased to exist south of the Boyne and west of the Shannon.' To meet the IRA campaign, Lloyd George and the cabinet determined to strengthen the RIC with ex-servicemen and officers recruited in Britain. In March 1920 the first reinforcements arrived in Ireland dressed in a mixture of RIC green-black and Army khaki 'pending the arrival of RIC uniform'. On 28 April a group of them rampaged through Limerick breaking shop windows and assaulting civilians, so earning the title 'Black and Tans' after a local pack of hounds. In July 1920 the Auxiliary Division of the RIC was formed. They wore the RIC uniform with distinctive glengarry caps and golden harp badges. Together, these two adjuncts of the RIC earned the fear and hatred of nearly everyone in Ireland. Their purpose was never clearly spelled out, but their actions proved them to be as terroristic in concept as they perceived the IRA to be. On 20 September, Black and Tans sacked and burned part of the town of Balbriggan, Co. Dublin, as a reprisal for the shooting of an RIC head constable, killing two townspeople. Three days later, Field Marshal Sir Henry Wilson, the dedicated unionist who as director of military operations in 1914 had plotted with those involved in the Curragh mutiny, recorded in his diary that 'the police and the Black and Tans and the 100 Intell. officers are all carrying out reprisal murders'. On 28 September, Wilson protested to the prime minister against reprisals on the grounds of military principle:

I had 1½ hours this evening with Lloyd George and Bonar Law. I told them what I thought of reprisals by the Black and Tans and how this must lead to chaos and ruin. Lloyd George danced about and was angry, but I never budged. I pointed out that these reprisals were carried out without anyone being responsible; men were murdered, houses burned, villages wrecked . . . I said this was due to want to discipline and this must be stopped. If these men ought to be murdered then the Government ought to murder them.

As the *Westminster Gazette* pointed out, 'Unless the Government take very stern and convincing steps to stop reckless reprisals on Irish towns, these reprisals will begin to horrify the world even more than the crimes which provoked them.' The government decided to make their reprisal policy official by sanctioning retaliation against the IRA by destroying property. The first official reprisal occurred on 29 December 1920 at Midleton, Co. Cork, where six houses were destroyed following an ambush nearby in which three RIC were killed. In the period between the unofficial reprisal at Balbriggan and the official one at Midleton, the scale of fighting in Ireland had increased dramatically.

On 14 October 1920, Sean Treacy, who had started the shooting at Soloheadbeg, was killed in Talbot Street, Dublin, after a running gunfight with soldiers and detectives. Ten days later Terence MacSwiney died. On 1 November, an eighteen-year-old IRA man and medical student at University College, Dublin, Kevin Barry, was hanged in Mountjoy gaol for his part in an ambush attempt. His death, following so soon after MacSwiney's, made a profound impression on public opinion everywhere. On 9 November, in a speech at London's Guildhall, Lloyd George misjudged opinion and his government's effectiveness and stated 'We have taken the steps by which we have murder by the throat.' Within two weeks, on Sunday 21 November, murder at the hands of Collins' Squad caught twelve British officers by the throat. Most of the twelve were involved in undercover intelligence work. Their deaths began 'Bloody Sunday'. That afternoon at Croke Park, Dublin, where the all-Ireland Gaelic football final was being played between Tipperary and Dublin, Auxiliaries and Black and Tans, incensed by the shootings that morning and thinking that an IRA meeting was taking place at the grounds, fired upon spectators and the teams. Twelve people were killed including a child, a woman and a Tipperary player. In the evening three men being held on suspicion of being members of the IRA were riddled with bullets by Auxiliaries in the guard-room of Dublin Castle. Despite the danger, Collins attended their funeral. A week after Bloody Sunday, Tom Barry's flying column successfully ambushed eighteen Auxiliaries at Kilmichael, near Macroom in Co. Cork, killing seventeen of them. Two weeks later, Auxiliaries and Black and Tans went on another rampage, burning parts of the centre of Cork city to the ground, causing damage estimated at £3 million.

Just as the IRA executive had feared in 1919 when they agreed the oath of allegiance to the dail as the 'Government of the Irish Republic', the level of violence so frightened constitutionally minded dail members that peace moves began which demonstrated that there were Sinn Feiners prepared to accept less than an Irish republic – a point Lloyd George was quick to grasp. On 30 November Roger Sweetman, the dail member for North Co. Wexford, wrote to the Press suggesting a conference 'to put a stop to bloodshed in this country'. Three days later the Sinn Fein Galway County Council passed a resolution: 'As adherents of Dail Eireann request that body to appoint three delegates to negotiate a truce.' Two days after this, Father Michael O'Flanagan, acting president of Sinn Fein (Arthur Griffith had been arrested in the clamp-down that followed Bloody Sunday), sent a telegram to Lloyd George: 'You state you are willing to make peace at once without waiting for Christmas. Ireland also is willing. What steps do you propose?' Michael Collins, acting president of dail eireann after Griffith's arrest, saw the danger of an open split between the dail and the IRA on the issue of peace, and warned 'There is a very grave danger that the country may be stampeded on false promises and foolish, ill-timed actions.' Still, conversations between Sinn Feiners and emissaries from Lloyd George continued. In a note from Arthur Griffith smuggled out of Mountjoy gaol, Collins found that Griffith had gone so far as to submit a formula for a truce to Lloyd George. Learning of all this in messages from Collins, de Valera not surprisingly decided that it was time he left America and returned to Ireland. On Christmas Eve 1920, he arrived in Dublin. Knowing of his return, the British cabinet decided that he should not be arrested unless some definite criminal charge could be laid against him: Lloyd George had recognized the value of keeping a line open to those behind the IRA.

The day before de Valera's arrival in Dublin, a new Government of Ireland Act replacing the 1914 Act came into force. The product of a year's debate and discussion at Westminster, this Act legislated for the partition of Ireland along the lines set out by Lloyd George in 1916, and for two home rule governments in Ireland, one in Dublin for twenty-six counties and one in Belfast for the six north-eastern counties (thus guaranteeing Carson and his northern Irish unionists a built-in electoral majority there). Provisions were made for the eventual unification of Ireland, but only when and if the northern unionists wanted it. Incorporated in the Act was Carson's proposal for a Council of Ireland which he described as 'the biggest advance towards unity in Ireland'. It was conceived as a forum for the discussion of matters of mutual interest between North and South and as a possible means of regaining unity. Disappointed by his failure to maintain the Union, and by the measure of self-determination forced upon Northern Ireland, Carson in 1921 left the House of Commons, taking a seat as Baron Carson of Duncairn in the Lords as a Lord of Appeal. There, although a judge, he continued to make political speeches. Ironically, the unionists were now the ones who accepted home rule. Despite the fact that the Act implemented partition, the IRA and the dail still maintained their public determination to fight on for their all-Ireland republic, completely independent of Britain. They refused to accept the Act. However,

under the Act a general election was held in the twenty-six counties
on 19 May 1921 to return members for the parliament of Southern
Ireland. The dail decided to adopt these elections as its own and
Sinn Fein, unopposed in 124 of the 128 new constituencies, swept
the board. The four Dublin University seats of Trinity College were
won by Unionists. Six days later another general election was held
in the six counties for the parliament of Northern Ireland; forty
Unionists and twelve Nationalists (the old Irish Party now in
alliance with Sinn Fein in the North) were returned.

Sinn Feiners elected in both elections (130 in all) now formed the
second dail which maintained itself as the parliament of an all-
Ireland republic. The four southern Unionists from Trinity College
formally met as the parliament of Southern Ireland and immediately
adjourned. De Valera, aware of the differences between the dail and
the IRA and realizing that a constitutional rather than a revolutionary solution to the Irish troubles had been made probable by
partition, determined to demonstrate his own authority as nationalist leader. He also needed to test the IRA's willingness to take orders
from the dail government. Accordingly, at his direction, the dail
ordered the IRA to destroy the Dublin Customs House, the beautiful
eighteenth-century masterpiece of the architect James Gandon. The
Customs House was the centre of nine civil service departments,
including the Revenue and the Local Government Board. Despite
Collins' opposition to the scheme on the grounds that the attackers
would probably all be captured along with their weapons, and that
this would be a loss the IRA could ill afford, on the afternoon of 25
May 1921 the 120 (or thereabouts) members of the Dublin Brigade
of the IRA who had arms, systematically burned the building to the
ground. Five of the attackers were killed by troops and police who
quickly arrived on the scene. Eighty were captured.

These losses effectively crippled the Dublin IRA. Collins at one
time reckoned that in all Ireland he could field perhaps a maximum
of 3,000 men. He was constantly badgered for arms and ammunition
by IRA commanders, and by June 1921, owing to lack of guns and
bullets, the IRA had resorted to burning unionists' houses and
property. A new British military policy of saturating areas of IRA
activity with troops and RIC had successfully placed the IRA on the
defensive. When George V opened the new parliament of Northern
Ireland in Belfast on 22 and June and appealed 'to all Irishmen to
pause, to stretch out the hand of forbearance and conciliation, to

forgive and forget', the moment was opportune. Lloyd George responded, glad of the chance to convince his Conservative coalition partners and the country that he was doing all he could to reach a satisfactory settlement and end violence in Ireland. He wrote a letter to de Valera 'as the chosen leader of the great majority in Southern Ireland', inviting him to attend a peace conference with Sir James Craig, the newly elected prime minister of Northern Ireland, Carson's successor as Unionist leader. De Valera, after consulting his own supporters and northern and southern Unionists, and with the approval of Collins and the IRA leadership, finally agreed. A truce was signed and at mid-day on Monday 11 July 1921, fighting between the IRA and British forces stopped. Collins is reported to have said afterwards to the chief secretary for Ireland, Sir Hamar Greenwood, 'When we were told of the offer of a truce we were astounded. We thought you must have gone mad', because in his judgement the IRA could not have lasted more than another three weeks. He was also under no illusions as to what the truce meant: 'Once a truce is agreed and we come out into the open', he wrote to a friend, 'it is extermination for us if the truce should fail . . . we shall be, in the event of a truce, like rabbits coming out from their holes.' Since Soloheadbeg in January 1919, over 1,500 people on both sides had been killed during the Troubles.

On 12 July, de Valera arrived in London and for ten days negotiated with Lloyd George about a settlement. He also saw Sir James Craig who asked 'Are you going to see Lloyd George alone?' 'Yes', replied de Valera. 'Are you mad?' said Craig. 'Take a witness. Lloyd George will give any account of the interview that comes into his mind or that suits him.' By 1921, the 'Welsh Wizard's' cleverness and duplicity were legendary. After several months of jockeying for position, a conference was agreed without any preconditions as to the unity or independent republican status of Ireland. Nevertheless, Lloyd George privately assured Craig and the Unionists that their six counties would remain under their control. On 11 October a delegation of five plenipotentiaries led by Arthur Griffith and Michael Collins and appointed by de Valera and the dail to negotiate a settlement, met Lloyd George and other members of the British cabinet at 10 Downing Street. De Valera stayed behind in Dublin not (as his enemies said) because he was frightened of being tainted by the compromise he saw as inevitable, but because he perceived the inherent weakness in the republican movement: that dogmatic republicans might split away from the first indication that the Irish republic for which they had fought might not be obtained. By staying back, he believed he could monitor and control dissent, and by requiring the plenipotentiaries to report back to him and his cabinet before they agreed any settlement, he thought his absence from the negotiations would buy the Irish delegates time for reflection at the crucial moment. In the event, de Valera was disappointed on both counts and, as William Cosgrave, later to become the first prime minister of the Irish Free State, argued in the dail, it was a pity to have 'their best player among the reserves'. Just before 3 o'clock in the morning of 6 December the Irish delegation signed their acceptance of an Irish Free State, 'faithful to H.M. King George V, his heirs and successors by law', and a partitioned Ireland, in the 'Articles of agreement for a Treaty between Great Britain and Ireland' – commonly called the Treaty. Over the following seventeen years, Irish Free State governments negotiated with the British government the details of each Article, and the resulting agreements technically constitute the Treaty.

During the negotiations, Lloyd George had insisted upon the partition established by the 1920 Government of Ireland Act, and that Southern Ireland would give allegiance to the British crown (the focal point of unity in the United Kingdom and for the British Empire and Commonwealth). De Valera and his cabinet had instructed Griffith and Collins that they should agree to such allegiance or to partition. However, early on in the negotiations, Griffith had personally and privately agreed to Lloyd George's suggestion of a Boundary Commission which would adjust the border between North and South, on the grounds that a fair-minded Commission was bound to reduce the area of Northern Ireland such that, he thought, it would become economically unworkable. As someone who did not object to monarchy in principle, Griffith was more interested in a united Ireland than in an Irish republic. Only hours before the Treaty was signed, Lloyd George revealed Griffith's agreement on partition to the startled delegation, and Griffith announced that he, personally, would sign the Treaty even if none of the others did. Then, as Sir Austen Chamberlain, a member of Lloyd George's cabinet, later recounted, the prime minister declared that the agreement of each delegate was required and held up two envelopes, saying:

I have to communicate with Sir James Craig tonight. Here are the alternative letters I have prepared, one enclosing the Articles of Agreement reached by His Majesty's government and yourselves, the other saying that Sinn Fein representatives refuse the oath of allegiance and refuse to come within the Empire. If I send this letter it is war – and war in three days! Which letter am I to send?

Believing Lloyd George's threat, and thus denied time to consult de Valera and their colleagues in Dublin, Collins and the other delegates followed Griffith and signed. They rationalized their acceptance of the Treaty on the grounds that the dail's acceptance of it was also necessary, so that by signing they were simply enabling a debate on the Treaty to take place and were not presenting the dail with a *fait accompli*. Yet before going to bed that night, Collins wrote to a confidant: 'Think, what have I got for Ireland? Something she has wanted these past seven hundred years. Will anyone be satisfied at the bargain? will anyone? I tell you this: early this morning I signed my death warrant.'

The Treaty was welcomed by most people, weary of bloodshed and violence. However, the oath they had taken to their republic weighed heavily with those who had fought for it, and one by one each nationalist organization split, the majority in each case opposing the Treaty except in the dail where a majority of members supported it. The IRB, pledged to an Irish republic since its formation sixty-four years earlier, how, headed by Collins, advised its members to make up their own minds. In the dail, the debates were emotional and bitter. Collins argued for the Treaty on pragmatic grounds: that it gave freedom and security in the form of the Irish Free State as well as being a major step towards the republican ideal. He also emphasized that the history of Ireland was not, as so many people maintained, one of constant armed resistance to British rule; it was a history of 'peaceful penetration. . .It has not been a struggle for the ideal of freedom for 750 years symbolized in the name Republic. It has been a story of slow, steady economic encroach by England. . .Nobody notices, but that is the thing that has destroyed our Gaelic civilization.' He was convinced that the Treaty gave Ireland a unique opportunity to halt this penetration. De Valera opposed the Treaty, countering it with an alternative of his own, 'Document No. 2', in which he proposed 'External Association' with the British Commonwealth whereby the king would be recognized

only as head of the Commonwealth and there would be no oath of
allegiance. Partition and the other substantive points of the Treaty
were incorporated in the document, but it was defeated in the dail
debates. De Valera then argued that to accept the Treaty would be
to deny the republic, and then Ireland would only have the freedom
Britain would allow. He told an anecdote of his days in prison to
make this point: 'Our warders told us that we could go from our
cells into the hall, which was bout fifty feet by forty. We did go out
from the cells to the hall, but we did not give our word to the British
jailer that he had the right to detain us in prison because we got that
privilege.' Hardly a word was said on either side about partition,
and the arguments centred on the issue of the oath, the crown and
the republic.

The dail voted to accept the Treaty on 7 January 1922, dividing
sixty-four to fifty-seven. De Valera broke down in tears and resigned
as president of the Irish republic and head of the dail government.
He was succeeded as president of the republic by Arthur Griffith.
On 14 January, under the terms of the Treaty, a new government –
the provisional government of Ireland – was formed – self-appointed
– by supporters of the Treaty, with Collins as its chairman. Its
function was to take over the administration of Southern Ireland
until the Irish Free State was formally established, and until then it
was answerable only to the British government and not to the dail
or to the parliament of Southern Ireland. This resulted in a tangled
conceptual and technical situation. The dail and its government,
now led by Arthur Griffith, had decided to accept the Treaty. But
the Treaty established the bi-cameral parliament of Southern Ireland
set up by the 1920 Government of Ireland Act as the sole legitimate
parliament, and so the dail was no longer a valid assembly as far as
supporters of the Treaty were concerned. There was a natural reluctance to admit this fact, pro-Treatyites blurred these distinctions by
arranging that the provisional government and the dail cabinet
consisted of the same people. The two governments ran in harness,
sharing meetings and responsibilities and rarely clarifying the difference between them. Griffith remained head of the dail government
of the Irish republic; Collins was a member of Griffith's dail cabinet
as dail minister for finance. For de Valera and opponents of the Treaty,
the dail government was the only authority they recognized. As de
Valera said immediately after the vote in the dail to accept the Treaty:

The Irish people established a Republic...Therefore, until such time as the Irish people in regular manner disestablish it, this Republic goes on. Whatever arrangements are made [the dail] is the supreme sovereign body in the nation; this is the body to which the nation looks for its supreme Government, and it must remain that – no matter who is the Executive – it must remain that until the Irish people had disestablished it.

Together with his supporters, he refused to attend meetings of the parliament of Southern Ireland, to obey decisions promulgated in the name of the provisional government, or to take the oath of allegiance to the king.

Few Irishmen regarded the Treaty as a victory. Michael Collins saw it as a 'stepping stone', as a means of 'going forward to our ideal of a free independent Ireland'. Arthur Griffith viewed it similarly: 'The principle I have stood on all my life is the principle of Ireland for the Irish people. If I can get that with a Republic, I will have a Republic; if I can get that with a monarchy, I will have a monarchy.' Opponents of the Treaty, however, concentrated in the IRA, were absolutely determined to resist all compromise on the complete separation of Ireland from Britain for which they had fought. The spectre of civil war began to loom large, and Collins began to wonder if the Treaty was worth it. Ever since 1920 there had been murderous attacks by Orangemen on Catholics in Belfast, culminating in over 250 deaths in the first six months of 1922. Collins became more and more angry about his inability to do anything about these killings, on one occasion declaring to a group of northern IRA officers that 'Lloyd George can have his bloody Treaty' unless the attacks stopped. He went even further, and in June 1922 began to send arms which his provisional government obtained from the British to the IRA in Dublin to replace their weapons which were being used by the IRA in the North: not the action of a committed supporter of the Treaty. However, at the same time the provisional government began to recruit a new army, the National Army, of its own, often from ex-British army men, to replace – and if necessary to oppose – the IRA.

For the overwhelming majority of the IRA, the Treaty was a betrayal of the republic they had fought for. As 1922 progressed, the significance of their 1919 oath of loyalty to the dail as the government of the republic became clear. Arguing that by accepting the Treaty the dail had betrayed the republic, they withdrew their allegiance re-investing their own executive with all powers and declaring loyalty to the Irish republic proclaimed in 1916 (now, in their view, without a government even if – as de Valera said – Arthur Griffith was technically head of the republic's government although he was disloyal to it). They also cited their own constitution and refused to accept the authority of the dail (and provisional government) minister for defence, Richard Mulcahy, who tried to assert control over them. The fact that Mulcahy was also IRA chief-of-staff was held to be secondary to his ministerial office. At an IRA convention in March 1922 banned (ineffectively) by the provisional and dail governments, the IRA elected Liam Lynch (1890–1923), officer commanding their 1st Southern Division, to succeed Mulcahy as chief-of-staff. Based in Cork, one of the areas where anti-Treaty feeling was strongest, Lynch was a tall, studious, shy man with a strong religious bent. He now became the focus of attention as the IRA repudiated their allegiance to the dail on the grounds that it had ignored the oath to the republic, and declared once again that their own executive was the only body whose authority they would recognize. A minority IRA group for whom Lynch was too cautious broke away and occupied the Four Courts in Dublin, hoping that the National Army would attack them and thus force Lynch and the rest of the IRA to attack the National Army in turn, thus providing in themselves the anvil upon which to break the embryonic Free State. Finally, events came to a head, but not in the way Collins or the IRA expected. On Thursday 22 June, Field Marshal Sir Henry Wilson was murdered on the steps of his home in Eaton Square, London, by two IRA gunmen probably acting at Collins' behest, implementing an order he may have given only days beforehand. At the time, however, the British government held the Four Courts IRA responsible and pressured the provisional government to act against them. The following Monday one of the Four Courts men was arrested by soldiers of the National Army, and in retaliation the Four Courts IRA captured the National Army's deputy chief-of-staff. Two days later, at 4.07 a.m. on the morning of 28 June, Collins' men opened fire on the Four Courts with 18-pounder guns borrowed from the British army earlier that night, and the Irish civil war began in earnest.

Fighting and skirmishes between the IRA and the National Army had occurred in many parts of the country with increasing frequency in the weeks before the Four Courts was attacked. Various unsuccessful attempts had been made to resolve differences between pro- and anti-Treatyites, and Collins and de Valera even agreed to an electoral pact for the Southern Irish general elections held on 16 June. Under this pact, an official panel of Sinn Fein candidates was divided between the two sides in such a way as to preserve the pre-election balance between them. In Cork, four days before the poll, Collins in the eyes of de Valera broke the pact by asking electors 'to vote for the candidate you think best of'. In subsequent speeches, Collins spoke strongly in favour of the pact, but when the results came in there was a clear majority for his pro-Treaty candidates – fifty-eight seats to thirty-six – and the anti-Treaty share of votes and seats was nearly halved. Collins and his supporters came to see themselves as defending democracy: but then, as the IRA pointed out, no one had voted for the 1916 rising or for the troubles which had produced the Treaty and the step towards full independence which Collins was now defending. It was never made clear which assembly – the dail or the parliament – the elected candidates would actually sit in, and before this was resolved the civil war had begun.

Part of the explanation for the civil war lay in the youthfulness of those involved. Even in 1916, Tom Clarke had been regarded as old, aged only fifty-eight; Connolly was forty-eight, while Pearse, MacDermott, Plunkett, Ceannt, and MacDonagh were all in their late twenties to mid-thirties. After their executions, the leadership fell to even younger men. Six years later in 1922, de Valera was forty; Griffith fifty; Collins thirty-two and Liam Lynch thirty-three. They all shared a patriotic idealism, but many of their followers (often younger still) found themselves unable to reconcile the pragmatic political approach of the pro-Treaty side with the pure idealism of a free and independent Irish Ireland which had attracted them in the first place to fight and to campaign against Anglo-Irish union.

De Valera had consistently argued with the IRA against resorting to violence again. However, after the attack on the Four Courts, events swept him aside. He had been in the United States or in prison for most of the time between 1916 and 1921, and so was not really known by or in touch with rank-and-file anti-Treatyites. By June 1922, because of his political defeat in the dail, he was no longer president of the dail's Irish republic or head of the dail government. His conviction that the differences between the pro- and anti-

Treatyites should be settled peacefully (and therefore constitutionally) struck the IRA as defeatist, and his influence waned dramatically. He admitted his own helplessness and, forced to choose, opted
to re-enlist as a private in the 3rd Battalion, Dublin Brigade, IRA,
relinquishing the leadership of the republican side in the civil war to
the chief-of-staff of the IRA, Liam Lynch in Cork.

Six weeks after the attack on the Four Courts, Arthur Griffith died
of a brain haemorrhage, leaving both the presidency and headship of
the dail's by now completely nominal Irish republic vacant. After
attending the funeral Collins journeyed to Cork where, on 22 August
during an ambush at a place called Beal na mBlath, on a misty
evening at twilight, he was killed by a bullet in his head. He had
apparently been trying to make contact with Lynch to try to put a
stop to the war, but his death ended hope of an early peace. Within
the next twelve months, seventy-seven IRA men were executed by
National Army firing squads, and many more 'shot while trying to
escape'. In comparison, the British had executed twenty-four men
between 1919 and 1921 (though several hundred more were killed in
other circumstances).

Erskine Childers, who after 1918 had become the principal
propagandist of the Irish republican cause, was one of the first to be
executed. After his capture by the National Army, Childers had
applied for an order of *habeas corpus* and appealed for his liberty to
the Dublin High Court. No judgement had been delivered when, at
dawn on 24 November 1922, he was shot by firing squad at Beggars
Bush Barracks in Dublin, solely on the authority of the provisional
government. Three days later the IRA retaliated by announcing that
the members of the parliament of Southern Ireland who had voted to
support the government's policy of executions might themselves be
shot by the IRA. On 6 December, the anniversary of the Treaty, the
Irish Free State formally came into existence, with the members of
the provisional government (now replaced) forming the State's first
government answerable to the Southern parliament. The following
day the government of Northern Ireland exercised its Treaty option
of contracting out of the Free State and remaining separate. Also that
day, Brigadier Sean Hales, a member of the Southern parliament
who had supported the execution policy, was shot dead in a Dublin
street by IRA gunmen. The next morning, 'as a reprisal for the
assassination of Brigadier Hales', four leading Four Courts IRA

men who had been imprisoned since June were shot by the National Army in Mountjoy gaol. More than any other event of the war, these executions shocked people to the core and seared the bitterness of fraternal strife upon the republican mind, providing future generations with a hatred of the Free State and of those who participated in it.

With the formal establishment of the Free State, the constitutional positions of the two sides in the civil war had become clarified. William Cosgrave (1880–1965), a founder-member of Sinn Fein and of the Irish Volunteers, had succeeded Collins as chairman of the provisional government in August 1922, subsequently becoming the first president of the executive council of the Irish Free State. He made it clear that as far as he and his supporters were concerned, 'the functions of the second Dail came to an end on June 30th...The sovereign assembly of Ireland is now the Parliament elected in June last.' However, the second dail had never been suspended or superseded by a third dail (although the Southern parliament, for political purposes, confusingly referred to itself as the third dail and subsequent parliaments continued this practice in sequence). This meant that the IRA was able to 'reclaim' the dail, reform its government, and so present a political and constitutional front to match that of the Free State. Thus it was that the IRA's executive at the end of October 1922 called upon 'the former President, Eamon de Valera, and the faithful members of Dail Eireann, to form a Government, which they have done'. At the same time, de Valera continued to urge the IRA to stop fighting, declaring that the IRA and not himself or republican politicians had to accept responsibility for the civil war: 'The Army Executive must publicly accept responsibility. There must be no doubt in the mind of anybody in this matter. This pretence from the pro-Treaty Party that we are inciting the Army must be ended by a declaration from the Army itself that this is not so.' The IRA did not make such a statement, instead indicating its distrust even of republican politicians by reserving to itself the right to make final decisions in the matter of peace and war, and by giving only conditional allegiance to de Valera's new government 'in all its legitimate efforts to maintain and defend the Republic'. Reluctantly, de Valera accepted this compromise. However, as the weeks went by the hopelessness of the republican cause became more and more apparent. The Free State enjoyed popular support; its ruthlessness demoralized the IRA and made it hard for IRA men to find refuge, and the rapidly growing National Army with its British equipment and ex-IRA leadership soon controlled most of the twenty-six counties. De Valera, his government, and most of the IRA had to stay in hiding. Nevertheless, Liam Lynch was determined to fight to the bitter end, refusing de Valera permission to attend IRA executive meetings on the grounds that he was preaching defeatism. On 10 April 1923, Lynch was killed in the hills near Clonmel, Co. Tipperary; on 27 April de Valera and Frank Aiken, Lynch's successor as IRA chief-of-staff, jointly published an order to the IRA to stop fighting: they were beaten

The Free State government ignored the IRA's unilateral cease-fire. On 2 May 2 IRA men were executed by National Army firing squad. Three weeks later, de Valera issued another message: 'Soldiers of the Republic, Legion of the Rearguard: the Republic can no longer be defended successfully by your arms. Further sacrifice of life would now be in vain.' What was left of the IRA hid their guns and went home or emigrated. There was no formal end to the civil war, just as there had been no formal start. The Free State government stopped their executions, but continued to arrest and imprison those suspected of IRA membership, In October 1923, over 11,000 prisoners were in gaols or camps. They started a mass hunger-strike in protest at their continuing detention. Forty-one days later, after several men had died, and after fierce hatreds had divided those on strike from those who had given up or refused to strike, the fast was called off. Then, in dribs and drabs, the men were released.

There was a small sequel to the civil war in 1924. Because fighting was over, the national Army – 60,000 strong and costing £18 million per annum – was reduced in size and many of its officers reduced in rank as an economy measure (or because many officers held rank above their ability). In February, these changes were published in 'GHQ Staff Memorandum No. 12'. Many of those affected were members of a semi-secret 'IRA Organization' within the National Army. They were principally men who had been close associates of Michael Collins (most of the Squad were involved) in pre-civil war days, and after Collins' death had found themselves increasingly out of sympathy with the new leadership of the Free State. They did not like the number of ex-British army personnel at all levels of the National Army; they were worried by the prospect of finding that the Free State was the end for which they had fought, not the stepping stone to that end, and they felt passed-over and insecure. The GHQ Memorandum about Army jobs sparked off a 'mutiny' by the IRA Organization which culminated in the arrest of most of its members and in the resignations of the minister for defence; the minister for industry and commerce, and the chief-of-staff, quartermaster-general and adjutant-general of the National Army. The Free State government emerged stronger than before as it soon became clear that the IRA Organization spoke only for itself and had little support outside its own ranks.

10

Southern Ireland

Right into the 1970s the events of the seven years after 1916 dominated political and cultural life in Southern Ireland. Political Parties won and lost elections as much for their policies as for their echoing of civil war divisions. Between the two principal Parties there was no doctrinal difference, and they attracted support largely on the basis of which civil-war side they represented. This was compounded by the initial youthfulness of Free State politicians on both sides which, as time went on, was translated into an extraordinary longevity amongst the political elite. Thus in 1959 Sean Lemass (1900–71) became taoiseach (prime minister) having fought in the GPO in 1916; in the IRA during the Troubles, and in the Four Courts IRA in 1922: he retired from politics, as taoiseach, in 1966. Eamon de Valera, Lemass' immediate predecessor as taoiseach, served as president of Ireland from 1959 to 1973. Time and again, the hopes and the myths of the Troubles were held up by politicians as justification for votes and for policies, and the same hopes and myths were held up by the IRA as justification for the continuation of their violent struggle for a completely free and independent Ireland.

The polarization of attitudes and the energies consumed by the civil war prevented any immediate radical social or political changes in the Free State. At the end of the war, the Free State government and its supporters (largely culled from amongst the strong farmers and businessmen who had backed the old Irish Party) clearly opted for conservatism. They welcomed the home rule the Treaty had obtained and were content to govern Ireland in the British manner, with only the addition of Irish language requirements in education and the civil service. Repressive social legislation catering to Roman Catholic sensibilities (although it should be said that this was a time of conservative reaction worldwide) was early on the agenda of the

Southern parliament. A Censorship of Films Act was passed in 1923; a Censorship of Publications Act followed three years later together with an Act prohibiting divorce. The social and economic reforms which had been advocated by some members of Sinn Fein and the IRA during the Troubles were set aside by the rulers of the new State, partly because most of the reformers had opposed the Treaty, and partly because the challenges and the rewards of government proved attractive enough to them.

The greatest single achievement of the new rulers was to establish their new State with popular, democratic support, and in forcing its acceptance on republican politicians who had opposed the Treaty and who came to speak for defeated anti-Treatyites. In March 1926, de Valera split Sinn Fein and the IRA for a second time (the first split having occurred over the Treaty) by proposing that attendance at the parliament of Southern Ireland should become 'a question not of principle, but of policy'. Again, the IRA (Sinn Fein was – and still is – its political arm and voice) could not bring itself to accept this compromise on principle. The civil war had been fought largely over principles, and this was one of the more important. De Valera personally admitted that he was swapping republican idealism for political expediency, and seriously urged Sinn Fein to expel him so that its purity would not be tarnished by his action. He resigned his leadership and membership of Sinn Fein and in May formed a new Party, Fianna Fail (Soldiers of Destiny – the Irish legend on the insignia of the 1913 Irish Volunteers), sub-titled 'The Republican Party' and described by Sean Lemass as 'a slightly constitutional Party'. He had taken the name from the same band of heroes the Fenians had chosen. Its objects were to secure 'the political independence of a united Ireland as a Republic'; to restore the Irish language; land reform and to make Ireland economically self-sufficient.

The formation of Fianna Fail marked the general return to constitutional procedures to resolve differences and disagreements. Only a very weak IRA (Frank Aiken, chief-of-staff of the IRA, and many other IRA men joined Fianna Fail) and a much reduced, electorally insignificant Sinn Fein continued the tradition of revolutionary action (the IRB had disintegrated during the civil war, rent by conflict over the Treaty). The Constitution of the Free State had originally provided one of the best hopes of averting the civil war

since many believed that it would be 'republican' in concept. Michael
Collins had been chairman of the drafting committee and had
privately assured anti-Treatyites that many of their anxieties would
be removed by the Constitution. Collins actually did try to produce a
Constitution which would have made the Irish Free State a republic
in all but name, but found the complete intransigence of Lloyd
George and his government on the matter impossible to overcome
since their opposition was firmly grounded in the text of the Treaty.
When the Constitution was finally published on 16 June 1922 (the
day of Southern Ireland's general election), it was seen to be anything
but republican and it heated up the simmering civil war. The oath of
allegiance to the crown, as agreed in the Treaty, was incorporated.
The parliament of Southern Ireland was to be called the 'Oireachtas'
and was to consist of the king, an upper house, the senate appointed
by the government and a lower proportionally elected house, dail
eireann. The king was head of state and his representative in Ireland
was the governor-general (the first was Timothy Healy, Parnell's old
opponent from Irish Party days) who took up residence in the
Vice-regal Lodge in Phoenix Park, Dublin. The Westminster parliament passed the Irish Free State (Constitution) Act, 1922, giving the
Constitution legal force and demonstrating that the Free State owed
its existence to Westminster, not Dublin, exactly as republicans had
claimed.

At the end of the civil war in 1923, Southern Ireland was in dire
straits. Unemployment throughout the 1920s (and the 1930s)
remained at chronically high levels, ameliorated not by effective
government policies, but by the great sore of emigration. By 1926,
43 per cent of Irish-born men and women were living abroad, constantly reinforcing the tradition of departure dating from the famine
years of the 1840s. Of Southern Ireland's 2.9 million population in
1926, over 800,000 were living in 'overcrowded conditions' (more
than two persons to a room), mainly in the slums of Dublin where
the scale of infant mortality was horrendous: the average death rate
of children in the slums aged between one and five years was 25.6
per 1,000. For the new State, it should have been a clear priority to
clear the slums and improve the conditions of life of their inhabitants, particularly since so much political capital had been made from
them during the years of British rule. Instead of tackling these
economic and social disasters head on, the Cumann na nGaedheal

government (the pro-Treaty Party founded in March 1923 by William Cosgrave, chairman of the executive council (prime minister) of the Irish Free State) ignored its own radical Sinn Fein heritage and that of its parliamentary ally the Irish Labour Party, and pursued a policy of balancing the budget with anchorite zeal. Virtually every governmental act was seen in terms of the budget rather than in terms of the electorate. The result was politically disastrous in the long run for pro-Treatyites, while also helping to sustain the habit of violence in Ireland. Republican, anti-Treaty politicians immediately benefited as people reasoned – and were encouraged to do so – that reform was more likely to come from them. In turn, in the crucial first years of the new State, this also tended to justify the violent opposition of the IRA which, like the politicians, rapidly seized the politics of social and economic injustice as its own, presenting itself as the harbinger of a national idealism betrayed by the Free State.

In fairness to Cumann na nGaedheal, however, the civil war had inevitably dampened any reforming ardour there was in the government as it was naturally forced to look to Britain for military and economic support. With the end of fighting in 1923, the government had to deal with rebuilding the infrastructure of local government and services. Railways, roads, bridges had all been destroyed on a large scale since 1919. Many local authorities had ceased to function along with the services they provided. A police force, the Garda Siochana, had to be established as successors to the RIC and DMP. The creation of Northern Ireland had left the Free State with very little industry, and so new industry as well as agricultural prosperity were vital.

It was not surprising, therefore, that the government opted for conventional economic policies, concentrating on administrative efficiency. The Ministers and Secretaries Act, 1924, instituted a major piece of administrative reform by reorganizing the civil service into eleven departments including a new department of lands and agriculture (agriculture was made a separate department in 1928) – a recognition of the fact that the Free State was an agricultural country with 61 per cent of the population in 1926 living outside towns or villages. Continuity of personnel and system was maintained with the pre-Treaty British civil service. In 1935 a Commission of Inquiry reported that there had been no disturbance 'of any fundamental kind' in the civil service and that 'the same main tasks of administration continued to be performed by the same staffs on the same general basis of organization and procedure' as had been the case under British administration. This was an exceptional achievement in any circumstances, and Cosgrave's government deserved full praise for it, especially since upon this civil service (which numbered only about 20,000 in the 1920s, and around 35,000 in the 1960s) fell the entire burden of administering the country.

At the same time, this civil service reform made no attempt to change the way in which government was conducted, nor did it seek to change the attitudes, assumptions and practices of the civil service itself. It demonstrated that the Free State could be seen as a rational extension of the British system (and thus, by inference, of Britain) and that revolutionary experiments such as the dail courts which had been advocated by Sinn Fein during the Troubles were not going to be indulged. Indeed, a second element of major importance was the abolition of the dail courts (the last sat in 1922) and the passing of the Courts of Justice Act, 1924, which together with the Garda Siochana Act, 1924, re-established the rule of law in the twenty-six counties with an unarmed police force and court system which quickly gained the acceptance and the respect of most sections of the community. The 1925 Local Government Act rationalized local authorities and the services they provided, notably by setting up boards of health in county council districts to administer poor relief. No longer was public assistance linked directly to the British workhouse system. Instead, the able-bodied were relieved as far as possible in their own homes, while the old, the sick and the infirm were looked after in hospitals or county homes. The conditions of life for those on public assistance were still harsh, but poverty was not treated by the State as if the poor themselves were responsible for it.

The government also completed the tremendous land reform legislation introduced by previous United Kingdom governments by passing a Land Act and a Land Law Act in 1923 which together reconstituted the Land Commission (established by the 1881 Land Act) as the government's own agency for transferring land to tenants, made compulsory the sale of land designated for transfer to tenants under previous Land Acts, and removed and reduced rent and purchase payment arrears. Nevertheless, the hopes and the enthusiasm that had characterized the nationalism of Patrick Pearse and James Connolly was lost. A special, distinctively Irish society – the sort of society which nineteenth-century nationalists had dreamed about – was set aside in favour of one imitating Britain, economically backward and dependent upon Britain, but since no longer part of the disparate United Kingdom vulnerable to Catholic pressure. In many respects, the Ireland envisaged by Pearse and most of the men of 1916 and 1919–21 was not the Free State. In Pearse's words:

A free Ireland would not, and could not, have hunger in her fertile vales and squalor in her cities. Ireland has resources to feed five times her population; a free Ireland would make those resources available. A free Ireland would drain the bogs, would harness the rivers, would plant the wastes, would nationalize the railways and waterways, would improve agriculture, would protect fisheries, would foster industries, would promote commerce, would diminish extravagant expenditure (as on needless judges and policemen), would beautify the cities, would educate the workers (and also the non-workers, who stand in direr need of it).

Some measures did accord with this recipe. The Shannon scheme, begun in 1925, was completed in 1929. It involved the government in massive state intervention to provide a national electricity supply by means of water-powered generators in a weir system on the river Shannon near Limerick city. The electricity supply board was created to regulate the service and was given £10 million to fund the system. One of the greatest achievements of the government was the successful reassertion of law. But it was essentially British law, not Irish. The Brehon Laws, which the dail courts had tried to establish, may have been impractical in the twentieth century, but at least they were Ireland's own. The point was that the young ministers and parliamentarians of the Free State surrendered the high ground of idealism for the harsh practicalities of administration, leaving that ground to their political opponents and to the IRA. Within four years of the end of the civil war, the political consequences of this surrender became clear.

In June 1927, just over a year from its formation, Fianna Fail won forty-four seats in the Free State's second general election (the first was in August 1923) while Cumann na nGaedheal's representation slumped from sixty-three to forty-six seats out of the 153 in the Southern Irish parliament (dail). However, de Valera and his followers could not bring themselves to take the oath of allegiance to the king required by the Treaty and so were turned away when they tried to take their seats. A fortnight later, on Sunday 10 July, Kevin O'Higgins, the thirty-five-year-old deputy leader of Cumann na nGaedheal, minister for justice and acting minister for external affairs, was assassinated on his way to Mass. O'Higgins was the strong man of the government in that his hard work and intellectual energy underpinned much of the government's activity and policy. He was (incorrectly) blamed by republicans for masterminding the execution policy pursued by the government during the civil war, and his death was at the hands of three ex-IRA men acting on their own initiative. They were never caught or officially identified. In reaction to his death, the government passed its fourth Public Safety Act imposing severe penalties, including death, for membership of the IRA, and an Electoral Amendment Act which changed election law with the effect of forcing Fianna Fail either to take their seats and the oath of allegiance to the king, or to pursue their principles to the point of probable political oblivion. De Valera and Fianna Fail, having in practice recognized everything about the Free State except the oath, now chose to accept the oath rather than forfeit their seats in the dail. On 11 August 1927, the Fianna Fail Party's elected representatives swore allegiance to King George V and his heirs and successors, and took their seats as *Teachta Dala* (TDs – dail deputies). Ever afterwards, de Valera and his supporters insisted that they had not, in fact, taken the oath, and went to extraordinary lengths to prove their case. De Valera later explained in the dail:

I said 'I am not prepared to take an oath. I am not going to take an oath. I am prepared to put my name down in this book in order to get permission to go into the Dail, but it has no other significance.' There was a Testament on the table and in order that it could be no misunderstanding I went and I took the Testament and put it over and said, 'You must remember I am taking no oath.'

These manifestly absurd antics impressed few. They did, however, reveal the passionate intensity behind de Valera's struggle against the Treaty and the depth of feeling in the anti-Treaty side. Whether or not the Treaty was a step towards freedom was irrelevant at this stage: what mattered was which side had been taken in 1922. It also mattered that in law Fianna Fail TDs had taken the oath and entered fully into Free State constitutional politics. The Cumann na nGaedheal government must be presumed to have realized that by forcing Fianna Fail into parliament, the consequence would be that sooner or later Fianna Fail would form a government. It was entirely logical that this should have been both the government's awareness and intention since its members had fought the civil war for the rule of law and for the Free State Constitution. Ensuring Fianna Fail's participation in the constitutional process was perhaps the most important action of Cosgrave's government (although it must be remembered that Fianna Fail no doubt privately welcomed being 'forced' into the Free State: there was no other point in their formation than their preparedness and wish to enter Free State politics). What was also important was that members of Fianna Fail, representing much of the post-1916 Irish republican idealism, brought with them into the Free State most of the anti-Free State side with, as de Valera was to demonstrate, Collins' stepping-stone approach to the Treaty as their policy. In this they had little competition since, after Collins' death, Cumann na nGaedheal had shown itself content to make the Treaty work as an end in itself.

The deeply divisive debates over the Treaty and what it had really obtained for Ireland underpinned Free State politics. On this level, as well as on the economic level, Cumann na nGaedheal steadily lost ground to Fianna Fail. The Army Mutiny in 1924, while helping the government demonstrate its commitment to the rule of law, nevertheless tokened its loss of idealism and a disillusionment at its core. Within months of the Mutiny, a major political crisis confirmed to everyone that the government was not seeking to develop the Treaty, but was – as republicans claimed – treating it as a final agreement.

Article 12 of the Treaty had provided that if Northern Ireland decided not to join with the South in a united Ireland, then a Boundary Commission consisting of three persons would be set up to 'determine, in accordance with the wishes of the inhabitants, so far as may be compatible with economic and geographic conditions, the boundaries between Northern Ireland and the rest of Ireland'. It was never clear whether this meant that major or only minor boundary changes were contemplated. Nationalists assumed that there would be major changes; Northern unionists were adamant that only minor changes in the existing six-county boundary would be considered. On 7 December 1922, the day after the Irish Free State formally came into being, the government of Northern Ireland officially notified both the Westminster and Dublin governments of the North's determination to remain separate from the South. In 1924, despite attempts by the Northern government to avoid boundary negotiations, a Boundary Commission was appointed consisting of Joseph R. Fisher, a leading Northern Irish Unionist; Eoin MacNeill, the Free State minister for education, and Mr Justice Richard Feetham of the South African Supreme Court who was a neutral chairman. Throughout 1925 the Commission deliberated. MacNeill (and the Free State government) were under the impression that the British government, as had been indicated to Collins during the Treaty negotiations in 1921, would support the Free State in securing that the Boundary Commission would recommend the reduction of Northern Ireland from six to four counties, thus making it too small, they thought, to be viable economically or politically, and making unification with the South inevitable. Such a deal was given further credence by the fact that (based on the 1911 census) in the counties of Fermanagh and Tyrone there was a Catholic (and therefore presumed nationalist) majority, and that in parts of the counties of Londonderry, Armagh and Down this was also the case. By the end of 1925, however, it was clear that Justice Feetham interpreted Article 12 quite differently, agreeing with Fisher that the Article dictated that the concern of the Commission was not the size of Northern Ireland, but the detailed arrangement of the existing boundary between North and South. On 7 November the *Morning Post* newspaper broke this story from which Irish nationalists accused Feetham of bowing to Unionist political influence. He resigned. MacNeill having failed to secure significant boundary changes also resigned both from the Commission and from the Free State government, forcing a political crisis.

By prior agreement between the Dublin, Belfast and Westminster governments, the findings of the Boundary Commission were to be legally binding. MacNeill's resignation meant that in order to prevent official presentation and publication of the findings, which, in view of the popular expectations in the South that the Commission would substantially reduce the North, would be politically very damaging, the Free State government had to act swiftly to save face and to come up with an alternative acceptable to Belfast. Accordingly, on 3 December 1925, a tripartite agreement was signed in London between all three governments, revoking the powers of the

Boundary Commission. In exchange, the boundary between North and South remained unchanged and the Treaty's provisions for a Council of Ireland were effectively annulled, thus satisfying Northern unionist demands. In order for the Free State government to emerge with some credit, Britain agreed to release the Free State (and Northern Ireland) from its Treaty obligations to meet part of the United Kingdom's national debt and certain British military and police service pensions. North and South, it was agreed, would in future meet together to resolve differences and to discuss matters of mutual interest 'in a spirit of neighbourly comradeship'.

Nothing could hide the fact that this was a major setback for the Free State and for Irish nationalism. De Valera and his supporters leapt to attack the government for selling out 'our fairest province' by accepting the permanence of the North–South border in practical terms. De Valera's criticism was firmly based in the romantic idealism he shared with the IRA of a free, undivided, independent Irish republic. While this view doubtlessly encouraged de Valera to enter constitutional politics in the Free State as the best means of controlling and influencing political developments in Ireland, the IRA took a different course. For them, the Boundary Commission debacle reinforced the conviction that the only way to secure concessions from governments, let alone unification of Ireland, was by force. In Southern Ireland, no one apart from the unfortunate government seemed to recognize the harsh realities of religious and political divisions in Northern Ireland. De Valera was never able to accept his responsibility for undermining the government, denying it political support at home when it was most needed in the national interest. For its part, the IRA was never able to accept that politics – not force – had secured whatever lasting advantages Ireland enjoyed in relation to Britain. It may have been politics backed by force or the threat of force, but it was constitutional activity that had secured the 1921 Treaty, and it was the supporters of constitutionalism who had defeated the IRA in the 1922–3 civil war. The IRA, while consistently regarding the Treaty as a defeat, were not able to see that it had been a defeat of force and that force had not, in the IRA's own terms, actually secured a lasting advantage from Britain. This contradictory view (that force had won concessions; that force was defeated in 1919–21) persists to the present day in IRA mythology and is reflected in their cry for 'arms, not argument'. Nevertheless, by maintaining the romance of an indivisible 'republic', both de Valera and the IRA in different ways were to hand on to succeeding generations the simplistic notion that force, particularly when applied at times of Britain's difficulty, offered the best hope of ending partition and securing a completely independent Irish republic.

The Cumann na nGaedheal government was also determined to prove its nationalist zeal, and strove to prevent de Valera and his supporters from painting it as 'West British'. It had some success in this propaganda war, and its cultural policies recognizably survived successive administrations into the 1970s. Gaelic League idealism was met in education: the Irish language became a compulsory subject in all schools, a natural corollary to the Free State Constitution's declaration that Irish was 'the national language'. Knowledge of the language was made a requirement for entry to the civil service, the legal profession, the Garda Siochana and the armed forces. In sport, Cumann na nGaedheal catered to Gaelic Athletic Association ambitions by holding a national sporting festival in 1924, the Taillteann Games, in an effort to re-create the legendary Gaelic games festival which had last occurred around 1100. Sadly, in both cases the effort was misconceived. Patrick Pearse had once castigated the English system of education in Ireland as the 'murder machine' because of its imposition of the English language upon Irish-speaking children. The fact was, however, that by 1922 the English language was commonplace, with children of all classes being encouraged at home to use it in preference to Irish. In addition, with the establishment of an Irish government in Dublin, people assumed that the work of cultural nationalism was properly a government concern, and their own enthusiasm could be directed elsewhere: while in 1922 there had been 819 active branches of the Gaelic League, by 1924 there were only 139. In 1965 a government White Paper reported that while most people favoured support for the Irish language in principle and equated it with 'national or ethnic identity, or as a symbol of cultural distinctiveness', only about 4 per cent of the population outside the Gaeltachti (those few and sparsely populated areas where Irish was generally spoken) used the native language 'very frequently and intensively'. It would seem that once the obvious British presence was removed, and with it some of the social pressure to conform to a British ideal, then the cause of the

Irish language weakened because it was no longer so clearly necessary for an Irish nationalist to resist the steady encroachment of English. In many ways, the official sponsorship of the language by the government, by removing anti-language pressure, helped to speed its further demise. In 1926, 543,511 people (18.3 per cent of the population) lived in Gaeltachti; in 1971 the figure was 70,568 (2.4 per cent) and today it is estimated that perhaps only 32,000 people are native speakers.

In sport, cultural nationalism was more successful. The Tailltcann Games of 1924 failed to establish a national sporting festival, as much because sports (at least in democracies) are a voluntary leisure activity for most people, attracting audiences and participation depending upon the excitement they generate, as because in the wake of the civil war government schemes were rejected by many. As a result, Gaelic games remained the province of the GAA, developing in competition with soccer and cricket, so that by the 1970s Gaelic football and hurling were attracting mass followings not because of state compulsion but because the games are first and foremost fast-moving and exciting. The GAA has always maintained itself as an avowedly nationalist organization, until 1971 banning its members from playing or attending 'foreign' games and still echoing its original antipathy to the RIC by refusing membership to those in the police or armed forces in Northern Ireland.

In its foreign policy, the Cumann na nGaedheal government quietly achieved a notable, lasting success. Faced by *de facto* dominion status in the Treaty, the Free State applied itself to making this status co-equal with that of the United Kingdom within the Commonwealth. Irish diplomatic missions were appointed to non-Commonwealth countries. The Free State became a member of the League of Nations. At the Imperial Conferences of the British Empire and Commonwealth, Irish ministers took the lead in insisting upon the right of dominions to exercise sovereignty equal to that of the United Kingdom. The term 'British Commonwealth of Nations' by the early 1930s had generally superseded the use of 'British Empire'. In December 1931, the United Kingdom parliament passed the Statute of Westminster, at last formally recognizing the co-equality of the dominions with the United Kingdom and the right of dominion parliaments to reject or change British legislation affecting them. Within the Commonwealth, it was generally conceded that this advance in the constitutional relationship with Britain was in large part due to the pressure exerted by the Irish Free State, South Africa and Canada. The Statute of Westminster effectively established the political independence of the Free State in relation to Britain (as Winston Churchill pointed out during the debates on the Statute, it meant, for example, that the Free State dail could legally repudiate the Treaty), justifying to many the original acceptance of the Treaty and the civil war fight for constitutional advance. However, less than three months after the Statute's enactment, the Cumann na nGaedheal government was decisively defeated at the polls in the March 1932 general election.

The last years of the government were marked by consistent domestic political failure to the point that even the success of the Statute of Westminster was perceived in Ireland as confirming Cumann na nGaedheal as the 'Commonwealth Party', as de Valera tauntingly called them during the election campaign. Defeat was largely the government's own fault. It had made no strong appeal to idealism throughout its tenure of office, preferring instead to argue its case on pragmatic grounds. It was not even the 'Commonwealth Party': it was Irish nationalist, but it allowed de Valera and Fianna Fail the nationalist flag with hardly any fight. With a kamikaze-like determination in the face of ever-deepening world recession, with unemployment soaring as factories closed and exports dropped, budgets were balanced by decreasing public expenditure and actually reducing the salaries of public employees. An austerity budget was even introduced on the eve of the 1932 general election. To the surprise of no one outside the government, Fianna Fail won seventy-two of the dail's 153 seats with 44.5 per cent of the poll, compared to Cumann na nGaedheal's fifty-seven seats and 35.3 per cent of the poll.

The 1932 general election was a watershed in the development of the Irish Free State. The government Party peacefully handed over power to Fianna Fail (in coalition with Labour and some Independents), the Party of those who had been ruthlessly and completely defeated in the civil war ten years earlier. There was some discussion amongst some generals about staging a military coup to prevent Fianna Fail's assumption of power, but this was speedily squashed by members of the outgoing government and other generals. Fianna

Fail TDs and ministers took office with revolvers in their pockets – one Fianna Fail TD was observed assembling a sub-machine gun in a telephone box in Leinster House – only to find that these precautions were unnecessary. The new State had come of age, and was able to demonstrate a political maturity which was to confirm the constitutional ethos.

That Fianna Fail had completely accepted constitutional procedures was not immediately apparent. In September 1931, de Valera founded a national newspaper, the *Irish Press*, to present Fianna Fail opinion which was frankly pro-IRA, still centring on the debates of 1922. In the dail, the Party had defended IRA members against prosecution by military tribunals under a Public Safety Act passed in October 1931. That same year Fianna Fail and the IRA had marched together in the annual commemoration of Wolfe Tone at Bodenstown. During the 1932 general election, IRA units had actively campaigned for Fianna Fail, employing a peculiarly forceful style of canvassing. De Valera in the dail just before the election described IRA men as 'animated with honest motives', and gave every indication that a Fianna Fail electoral victory would mean the vindication of the stand the IRA had made in 1922 against the Treaty. In the first years of Fianna Fail government (there was another general election in 1933 which Fianna Fail won with 49.7 per cent of the poll, obtaining an overall majority for the first time in the dail with seventy-seven seats), de Valera seemed to be justifying this expectation. One of his very first acts as chairman of the executive council of the Irish Free State was formally to write to the Rt Hon. J. H. Thomas, British secretary of state for the dominions, giving notice of his intention to remove the oath of allegiance from the Free State Constitution and to suspend land annuity payments (those sums payable by Irish tenants to the United Kingdom exchequer in repayment of loans advanced to them for the purchase of land under the various Land Acts from 1870 onwards). Both these issues were close to the IRA heart which had become increasingly socially conscious during the 1920s. Under the tutelage of Peadar O'Donnell, the leading theoretician of republican socialism in the IRA, by 1931 the IRA had gone so far as to found *Saor Eire*, 'an organization of workers and working farmers' as it described itself, with three objectives:

1. To achieve an independent revolutionary leadership for the working class and working farmers towards the overthrow in Ireland of British Imperialism and its ally, Irish Capitalism.
2. To organize and consolidate the Republic of Ireland on the basis of the possession and administration by the workers and working farmers of the land, instruments of production, distribution and exchange.
3. To restore and foster the Irish language, culture and games.

The IRA, faced by a conservative Cumann na nGaedheal government and a constitutionally minded but strongly nationalist Fianna Fail, had for the moment decided that the new politics of socialism offered the best means of obtaining the revived, re-Gaelicized Ireland of their dreams. As Cumann na nGaedheal government looked to Britain as a model, and as Fianna Fail committed itself to enter the procedures of the Free State, the IRA turned left. An IRA mission travelled to Moscow, asking for arms (unsuccessfully). Information the IRA received from a sympathizer in Scotland Yard was sold to Soviet agents. Some IRA officers even received military training in Russia. With de Valera in power, many in the IRA thought that his Free State government would couple socialist reforms with an aggressive nationalism, and accordingly lent Fianna Fail their support.

Fianna Fail's election manifesto in 1932 had concentrated on the issues of the oath, economic self-sufficiency and land annuities, and had stepped delicately around the issue of a thirty-two county Irish republic. In government, de Valera was quickly perceived to have meant no more and no less than he had said. His determination to abolish the oath and to suspend land annuity payments to Britain, and generally to establish a relationship with the United Kingdom akin to that he had advocated in his 'Document No. 2' ten years earlier where the king would be recognized by a united Ireland only as Head of the Commonwealth with which Ireland would be associated, soon resulted in serious conflict between the two countries and the need at home to establish confidence in his government while he pursued his policy. The IRA, increasingly irked by de Valera's fundamental conservatism in domestic matters, began to revert to violence, forcing de Valera to choose between its radical idealism and the constitutional opportunities of government. Before he had to make this choice, however, de Valera brought the Free State into an 'Economic war' with the United Kingdom.

By the end of 1932, in response to de Valera's demands for the abolition of the oath and land annuities which he then proceeded to implement unilaterally, Britain imposed a tariff on Irish agricultural produce entering the United Kingdom. De Valera retaliated by imposing duties on British exports to Ireland. It was a ridiculous 'war' on de Valera's part. Since 96 per cent of Irish exports went to Britain, British tariffs had a far greater impact upon Ireland than Irish tariffs had upon Britain. In addition, the notion that Ireland could be self-sufficient and enjoy a reasonable standard of living was a misconception. Imported fuel, machinery and raw materials were essential to Irish economic survival. But in the cause of self-sufficiency and ending the oath and land annuities, de Valera was prepared to cut off a lot more than his nose to spite his face. For him, it seems clear, the conflict was a re-enactment of that over the Treaty. He was mesmerized by the issues involved. Irish agricultural exports dropped from £35.8 million in 1929 to £13.5 million in 1935, with cattle exports being specially affected, dropping from 775,000 head to just over 500,000 by 1933; in 1934 Britain imposed a quota of 50 per cent of the 1933 figure. Total United Kingdom exports to Ireland fell from £43.5 million in 1929 to less than £18 million in 1935. There were some benefits to the Free State, but they cost dear. By 1936 acreage under wheat had risen from 21,000 in 1931 to 255,000 in response to government calls for self-sufficiency in food, but agricultural prices slumped with the drastic fall in exports, so Irish farmers fared badly all the same. By 1935 the traditional release of emigration had stopped functioning as a consequence of the world recession. Protectionism – for that was the nature of the tariff conflict with Britain – did result in a major increase (40 per cent between 1931 and 1936) in Irish industrialization, particularly in footwear and leather goods (benefiting from cattle surpluses and low prices) and in areas where domestic output had been low: glass, paper, metals, bricks. A £1 million road-building programme was instituted to mop up unemployment, and for the first time Dublin slum families were re-housed and slum clearances begun. National income, on the other hand, fell by about 3 per cent between 1931 and 1938, while the United Kingdom in contrast experienced an increase of about 27 per cent in the same period. In 1931, Irish incomes had averaged 61 per cent of those in Britain; by 1939 they averaged 49 per cent. Between 1932 and 1938, Irish industrial exports fell by one third and agricultural exports were more than halved. The decline in people's standards of living, while abroad there was a general recovery from the recession which had followed the great stockmarket crash of October 1929, meant that emigration rapidly rose again in the later 1930s, further contributing to a decline in potential home demand for Irish goods and services. Between 1936 and 1946, emigration averaged 18,711 people a year, compared to an annual average of 16,675 between 1926 and 1936. In fairness to de Valera and his policy it should be remembered that the recession began in 1929 (three years before Fianna Fail came to power) and it is impossible to be certain if the 'Economic war' accentuated the recession or not.

By 1935, faced by the economic consequences of his relations with Britain and of the world recession, de Valera agreed to compromise. A coal–cattle pact was reached between both governments that year by which Britain agreed to allow her Irish cattle imports to increase by one third, and de Valera agreed that the Free State would only import coal from Britain. Three years later, on 25 April 1938, a settlement took place which ended the Economic war. Against British claims of £104 million for land annuities and other payments, £10 million was accepted. Both countries also dropped most tariff restrictions, although developing Irish industries were allowed continued protection. Britain also handed over the naval bases (the 'Treaty Ports') retained by the Royal Navy under the 1921 Treaty and gave up her rights to their use agreed in the Treaty. In many ways this was an act of appeasement by Britain. By relinquishing her rights and generously surrendering her claims, Britain took an important step to ensure Southern Ireland's friendship. Perhaps the really significant element in the settlement, however, was that it represented a coming-of-age in de Valera and Fianna Fail. At last they had recognized and accepted that Ireland was, in fact, economically dependent upon Britain and therefore could not be self-sufficiently independent. The handing back of the Treaty ports confirmed the reality of dominion status and Dublin's independence of action (as was to be demonstrated by Southern

Ireland's neutrality during the Second World War). Altogether, the settlement established the conditions of modern Irish development: political freedom at home and in foreign policy combined with economic cooperation with Britain.

At home during the 1930s, Fianna Fail also came of age. Growing traditional IRA disenchantment with de Valera's policy of using the Treaty as a stepping-stone to greater independence (the IRA traditionalists really wanted another Fight for Freedom with Britain), and growing radical/socialist IRA disenchantment with tariff protection (which was seen as supporting Irish capitalism), meant that the IRA as a whole began to oppose Fianna Fail. De Valera's refusal to purge pro-Treatyites from the military and civil forces of the state, while wise in the interests of democracy, was another source of IRA anger. However, a great deal of this opposition was defused by de Valera who granted those who had fought against the Treaty the same military pension rights as those who had fought for it. The IRA was further weakened in 1934 when the minority socialist element broke away to concentrate on proselytizing for republican socialism, with many ending up in an Irish Brigade fighting against Fascists in the Spanish civil war. Those that remained in the secret army were increasingly involved in street violence, fighting the 'Blueshirts', an organization of pro-Treaty supporters, many with 1919–21 IRA experience.

The Army Comrades Association had been formed in 1932 from ex-Free State National Army members. Its purpose was to promote the welfare of its members, but it soon became a quasi-military volunteer force supporting Cumann na nGaedheal and pro-Treatyites generally who feared Fianna Fail would deny them free speech and other democratic rights. In July 1933 Eoin O'Duffy, who had been dismissed by de Valera as commissioner of the Garda Siochana immediately after the February 1933 general election, took over the leadership of the Association which was re-named the National Guard. At about the same time, its members began to wear a uniform of dark trousers and a blue shirt (thus the popular name 'Blueshirts'), ostentatiously modelling themselves on the fascist movements of Europe, including a Nazi style salute, and began to pick fights with IRA men and the IRA with them. If they had ever come to power, the Blueshirts might have shown themselves to be Fascist, but they always voiced democratic principles even if their actions did not match. In September 1933 following a ban against the Blueshirts as the 'National Guard', they combined with Cumann na nGaedheal and the small National Centre Party (representing farmers and ratepayers) to form a new political Party, Fine Gael or the United Ireland Party, under O'Duffy's leadership. After the first flush of enthusiasm, the new Party found that Fianna Fail's grip on power was strong. In 1934 the Fianna Fail government introduced legislation to prevent uniforms being worn, and banned the Blueshirts in their new names of the 'Young Ireland Association' and then the 'League of Youth'. By the end of the year, Fine Gael was in disarray and O'Duffy had resigned as leader after the parliamentary Party made clear it would have no truck with violence and illegality. He was succeeded as leader by W. T. Cosgrave. In January 1935 the Party's strongest plank – an appeal to farmers against the consequences to agriculture of the Economic war – was significantly weakened by the coal–cattle pact. In 1936 the senate, where opposition to Fianna Fail in parliament was concentrated, was abolished. O'Duffy's final exploit was to lead a group of 600 Blueshirts to Spain in 1936 to fight for the fascist side there. He died in Dublin in 1944 and was given a state funeral.

Following the thuggery and fighting between the IRA and the Blueshirts, opinion turned against both groups. When in 1935 and 1936 IRA execution squads began to murder opponents, culminating with the murder of the seventy-two-year-old retired Admiral Somerville at his home in Co. Cork (he was acccused of being a spy because he gave local youths references for the Royal Navy), de Valera with widespread public support cracked down, proclaiming the IRA an illegal body in June 1936. In the process, Fianna Fail demonstrated at last that it might be ardently nationalistic, but it was also constitutional. From this point on, Party politics were able to develop without either of the major Parties ever considering an appeal to extra-parliamentary forces for support.

In 1937 de Valera introduced a new Constitution which, with amendments, has remained in force ever since. The position of governor-general – the king's representative in Ireland – was abolished. In its place a popularly elected president was designated as head of state (Douglas Hyde, the founder of the Gaelic League in

1893, was the first president). The name of the twenty-six counties was changed from the Irish Free State to Eire or Ireland (no mention was made of 'Republic': de Valera was always conscious that the 1916–21 struggle had been for an independent united Ireland, and he never claimed that the twenty-six counties represented this ideal). The head of government was changed from president of the executive council to 'taoiseach'. The national territory was declared to be 'the whole island of Ireland, its islands and the territorial seas' (much to Northern Irish unionist resentment, this clause has never been repealed), but 'pending the re-integration of the national territory', the laws of Eire would only apply to the twenty-six counties. A two-chamber parliament was restored with a lower, proportionally elected house, the dail, with full legislative power, and an upper, partly appointed house, the seanad, with powers only of delay (it rapidly became a house for failed dail TDs and the exercise of government patronage). Article 44, which was to become the subject of controversy, recognized the 'special position' of the Roman Catholic Church as representing the religion of 'the great majority of the citizens', but at the same time guaranteed 'freedom of conscience and the free profession and practice of religion'. In a 1972 referendum, Eire voters overwhelmingly supported the removal of the section of Article 44 giving the Church its 'special position'. One of the conditions that recurred in the Constitution and still remains, however, was that various rights (freedom of expression, assembly, religion) would be 'subject to public order and morality'. In turn, this was interpreted in a distinctly Catholic manner, an indication of which was Article 41 under which the State was required to try to ensure 'that mothers shall not be obliged by economic necessity to engage in labour to the neglect of their duties in the home...no law shall be enacted providing for the grant of a dissolution of marriage'.

The Constitution was criticized at the time only by a minority. Most people welcomed it as an enlightened combination of the liberal values of parliamentary democracy and Catholic moral teaching. At the time there was a common wisdom in the Catholic world that Catholic social principles could be applied to secular life to create an overtly Christian state. This was what de Valera had set out to do, establishing on the one hand the separation of Church and State and on the other the primacy of Catholic moral teaching and the State's obligation to abide by it. Women complained about the

Constitution's patriarchal assumptions. Southern Irish Protestants accepted Article 44, experience already having proved to them that their welfare was not threatened by Catholic Ireland. Political opponents principally criticized the office of president because, some thought, it would be used by de Valera to extend his personal power. Douglas Hyde's unopposed election to the office soon demonstrated that such fears were groundless. The president, elected in his own right, would always be guaranteed authority as co-guardian with the dail of people's rights.

The homogenous nature of Southern Irish society, massively Catholic (the 1926 census revealed that 92.6 per cent of the Free State population professed Catholicism), helped the rapid acceptance of the Constitution, itself reflecting the nature of the State. Between 1850 and 1875, under the organizational genius and direction of Ireland's first Cardinal, Paul Cullen, the modern Roman Catholic Church secured its hold on Irish people. Its great strength was that it always drew its priesthood and bishops from the people in Ireland, and so was nationally regarded as a national church, even if at times possessed of ultramontane leanings. The Mass was regularized in churches (as a result of the Penal Laws, poverty and the establishment of the Church of Ireland, there were few Catholic churches in the country before the famine, and Catholic services were frequently held outdoors or in private homes); the rosary, novenas, benediction, vespers, devotion to the Sacred Heart and to the Immaculate Conception, pilgrimages, shrines and a host of devotional manners were introduced. All were adopted with vast enthusiasm in Ireland, and right into the 1960s Catholic Irish congregations were full (a feature of the Irish Church revived by Pope John Paul II's visit to the country in 1979) and genuine attention was paid to ecclesiastical pronouncements. In 1970 the Irish Church maintained 6,000 missionaries all over the world. Crucial to this strength was the easy identification made between the Church and Irish nationalism. Both had suffered persecution; both harked back to pre-Reformation times. Despite the fact that the Church, particularly under Cullen, consistently sided with the authority of the State against radicals and revolutionaries, it was also perceived in Ireland as sustaining Irish interests. Nowhere was this more clear than in Northern Ireland where being a Catholic was (and is) taken as being synonymous with being an Irish nationalist. The respect for authority which the Irish Church proclaimed (and which was integral to the Church's own functioning) was further sustained by the natural conservatism of a predominantly agricultural society and the fact that the majority of the Irish Church's priests and bishops were drawn from the sons of farmers. For such a Church, the sanctity of marriage and the rights of property were taken as absolutes. In a 1927 joint pastoral of the Irish Hierarchy, this conservatism was once again expressed:

These latter days have witnessed, among many other unpleasant sights, a loosening of the bonds of parental authority, a disregard for the discipline of the home, and a general impatience under restraint that drives youth to neglect the sacred claims of authority...The evil one is ever setting his snares for unwary feet. At the moment, his traps for the innocent are chiefly the dance hall, the bad book, the indecent paper, the motion picture, the immodest fashion in female dress – all of which tend to destroy the virtues characteristic of our race.

Against this background, it was not surprising that Northern Irish Protestants after 1921 consistently resisted integration with the South. Irish unity within the United Kingdom had meant that Irish Catholics were a part of the (Protestant) whole; Irish unity in an independent Ireland was perceived as meaning that Northern Protestants would become part of a Catholic whole where Catholic sensibilities and restrictions would dominate.

The IRA from 1922 onwards faced the full force of Church disapproval. Excommunicated for their opposition to the Free State in 1922–3, the IRA's political initiatives were also condemned. *Saor Eire* was described as 'communistic' by the Church, and this contributed to its rapid collapse (a month after its formation it was banned by the government with Church support). After 1932, Fianna Fail policies and demeaning skirmishing with Blueshirts further reduced IRA appeal. The 1937 Constitution even persuaded some of its members of the legitimacy of the re-named Free State – Sean MacBride, IRA chief-of-staff, resigned from the organization because he was satisfied by de Valera's Constitution. However, as a result of the government's failure to re-unite the country in its 1938 settlement with Britain, the IRA gained new life. Border posts and customs houses were attacked during November and December that year. In December, the rump of the second dail – those anti-Treatyites elected to the dail in 1921 who had also stayed away from

Fianna Fail – handed over its theoretical powers as the government of the Irish republic proclaimed in 1916 to the IRA's Army Council. For the IRA, this was an important constitutional move. Once again it gave them a theoretical legitimacy to defend the republic they had been fighting to establish ever since 1916. With the loss of men like O'Donnell and MacBride, the traditionalists who saw violence as the only answer to partition were firmly in control. On 12 January 1939 an IRA ultimatum was sent to the British foreign secretary, Lord Halifax, demanding British withdrawal from Northern Ireland within four days or else face the consequences of 'appropriate action' by the IRA. Not unexpectedly, neither Halifax nor the British government replied to or complied with this ultimatum, and so the IRA launched its 'S-Plan': a bombing campaign in England reminiscent of the Fenians in the 1860s and 1880s, aimed at disrupting services. On 16 January, seven explosions severely damaged some power stations and cables in London, Birmingham, Manchester and Alnwick. More explosions occurred the following day. On 4 February, large time-bombs were detonated in London in the Tottenham Court Road and Leicester Square underground stations, and there were other explosions in the city and in Coventry. Two days later, a large bomb was set off against the wall of Walton gaol in Liverpool. Bombings continued throughout February and March. On 29 March two large bombs damaged Hammersmith Bridge in London. The next day more bombs went off in Birmingham, Liverpool and Coventry. On 31 March, seven bombs exploded in London. During April, Sean Russell (who had succeeded Sean MacBride as IRA chief-of-staff) travelled to the United States to raise money from Irish–American groups to continue the campaign. On 5 May, two tear-gas bombs went off in Liverpool cinemas and four bombs exploded in Coventry and two in London. Later in the month, cinemas were set on fire in London and Birmingham. On 9 June a letter-bomb campaign disrupted post offices and postal services. On the evening of Saturday 24 June, as crowds came out of cinemas and theatres, a series of explosions around Piccadilly Circus in London brought down the front of the local Midland Bank and caused chaos as people panicked. On 26 July bombs went off at London's Victoria and King's Cross stations; the following night three massive explosions in Liverpool destroyed a bridge and wrecked the post office in the city centre. On 25 August a bicycle-bomb exploded in Coventry killing five people instantly and injuring another sixty. Some of those involved were arrested, but it was the advent of draconian security measures with the Second World War which actually brought the IRA's campaign to an end. Over the next eight months eleven people were killed and over 120 injured.

The effect of the IRA bombings was in Britain to alienate public opinion completely and encourage Hibernophobia, and in Ireland first to shock and then to horrify people, and to bring to bear the full wrath of Fianna Fail and the government against the IRA. Throughout 1938 and 1939, de Valera conducted an anti-partition campaign, and at first could not believe that the IRA (which he knew to be very weak) was behind the bombings. There was even a suggestion that it was an Orange plot to discredit his attempts peacefully to settle the border question. Soon realizing that the IRA was, after all, responsible, de Valera cracked down as harshly as Cumann na nGaedheal before him. IRA and republican marches and demonstrations were banned. In June an Offences Against the State Act was passed providing for trial by military tribunal and for the arrest and detention of people without trial. Having declared Eire neutral at the outbreak of war, during the Emergency (as the period of the Second World War was called in Eire), de Valera's government executed six IRA men, allowed two more to die on hunger-strike in prison (another died in 1946, after the war), and shot three while they were attempting to escape or avoid arrest. Abortive Nazi German overtures to the IRA during the war helped justify de Valera's actions on the grounds that IRA activity against Britain might compromise Irish neutrality and possibly even force Britain to invade Eire. To the IRA, however, these executions and deaths were the final proof that de Valera was a 'Free Stater', a puppet of Britain, as willing to compromise the national ideal for the reins and patronage of power as W. T. Cosgrave and the Cumann na nGaedheal government of 1922–32 had been.

The public reason for de Valera's statement of neutrality in September 1939 was the continuation of partition. In truth, Irish public opinion was still often anti-British and de Valera would have faced serious opposition within Fianna Fail and the country as a whole if he had chosen to join Britain and the rest of the Commonwealth in the war. Fine Gael, although more seriously divided on the issue, broadly supported the policy (James Dillon, son of John Dillon and deputy leader of Fine Gael, courageously opposed neutrality on moral grounds, and was expelled from the Party as a result). Winston Churchill offered the possibility of a united Ireland after the war in return for Eire's participation, but de Valera adamantly refused, not convinced that Churchill could force unionists to agree to unity and seeing neutrality as the proof that he had secured effective independence for the twenty-six counties. In 1919 he had written that 'our whole struggle is to get Ireland out of the cage in which the selfish statecraft of England would confine her – to get Ireland back into the free world from which she was ravished – to get her recognized as an independent unit in a world league of nations'. While personally sympathetic to the Allies, neutrality was also de Valera's chance to give effect to his view of Anglo-Irish relations. During the war years, faced by harsh economic conditions as trade plummeted, about 93,000 Irishmen emigrated – nearly all to Britain because of the hazards of the Atlantic crossing – finding work in munitions factories, docks, the railways. Over 50,000 Irishmen served in the British Army during the war. Allied airmen who came down in Ireland were allowed home, while Germans were interned. But punctiliously observing the forms of neutrality, in 1945 de Valera even went so far as to pay his condolences officially to the Nazi German minister in Dublin upon the death of Hitler. 'So long as we retained our diplomatic relations with Germany', he explained, 'to have failed to call upon the German representative would have been an act of unpardonable discourtesy to the German nation.'

With the end of the war in Europe, Churchill in his victory speech broadcast to the world by the BBC on 15 May 1945 insisted upon condemning Ireland's neutrality:

Had it been necessary we should have been forced to come to close quarters with Mr de Valera. . .With a restraint and poise to which, I venture to say, history will find few parallels, His Majesty's Government never laid a violent hand upon them, though at times it would have been quite easy and quite natural, and we left the de Valera Government to frolic with the German and later with the Japanese representatives to their hearts' content.

Three days later de Valera replied on Radio Eireann, Eire's national broadcasting organization (it began transmissions on 1 January 1926 as 'Radio 2RN', a phonetic play upon 'to Eireann', changing its name in 1932), reaching perhaps a tenth of the audience Churchill had enjoyed. It was a brilliant reply, touching the nation's consciousness, rebuking Churchill:

Mr Churchill makes it clear that in certain circumstances he would have violated our neutrality and that he would justify his action by Britain's necessity. It seems strange to me that Mr Churchill does not see that this, if it be accepted, would mean that Britain's necessity would become a moral code...Could he not find in his heart the generosity to acknowledge that there is a small nation that stood alone not for one year or two, but for several hundred years against aggression; that endured spoliations, was clubbed many times into insensibility, but that each time on returning consciousness took up the fight anew; a small nation that could never be got to accept defeat and has never surrendered her soul?

In 1948, Fine Gael in coalition with the Labour Party and Clann na Poblachta, a new, ardently republican party formed in 1946 by Sean MacBride and other leading ex-IRA men, won the general election and ended sixteen years of uninterrupted power by Fianna Fail. The new government was led as taoiseach by John Aloysius Costello (1891–1976) of Fine Gael: W. T. Cosgrave, who had succeeded Eoin O'Duffy as Fine Gael leader in 1935, had retired from politics in 1944 with Richard Mulcahy (the 1919–21 IRA chief-of-staff and Collins' successor as commander-in-chief of the Free State National Army during the civil war) then becoming leader. Mulcahy, largely because of continuing civil war animosities, was not acceptable to Clann na Poblachta as head of the coalition, and so Costello, a barrister who had been attorney-general from 1926 to 1932, became a compromise leader. His government (prompted strongly by Clann na Poblachta) quickly turned its attention to the social issues which de Valera had left to one side during his attempts to prove the strength of Irish sovereignty and to deal with the economic hardship of the Emergency. The great achievement of the coalition was its successful effort to eradicate tuberculosis, masterminded by the young and idealistic Clann na Poblachta minister for health, Dr Noel Browne. He mortgaged part of the future health service revenue to raise the funds necessary to build, equip and staff the hospitals and clinics needed to fight the disease which regularly accounted for 3–4,000 deaths a year. Within a few years, deaths from tuberculosis became relatively infrequent: 1,600 in 1952; 694 in 1957.

The most startling piece of reform was the declaration that Eire was a Republic. On 7 September 1948, while on a visit to Canada, Costello at a press conference confirmed speculation that a Republic would be declared. This caught many cabinet ministers by surprise: while discussions had taken place between Costello and some cabinet members about it beforehand, it had not been discussed in full cabinet. Still, it was consistent with Clann na Poblachta's republicanism and so not opposed by that Party; it was immaterial to Labour, so accepted by them, and despite the traditional pro-Commonwealth leanings of Fine Gael, they too accepted it for the sake of Party and coalition unity and because it was thought (quite wrongly) that by calling the country a Republic, the IRA would no longer feel justified in resorting to violence. In fact, the change had no effect on the IRA, and merely served to make more permanent the partition of Ireland. Before 1949 there was always the hope that within the British Commonwealth, Northern Ireland and Eire might one day unite peacefully. After 1949, Northern Irish unionists were even more estranged from Eire.

Reforms were undertaken in other areas as well. In 1949 the Land Rehabilitation Project was introduced which over ten years used massive state aid (£40 million) to develop four million acres of profitable land which had not been used (or had fallen into disuse) because of lack of investment. An Anglo-Irish Trade Agreement was signed in 1948 which secured higher prices for Irish agricultural exports to Britain. The state-sponsored Industrial Development Authority was founded in 1949 to plan and encourage industrial investment and expansion. The Authority subsequently became a model sought out by many other countries because of its success in combining public and private enterprise: in 1979 it negotiated some 1,500 new industrial projects with a prospective 35,000 new jobs over the next five years. One attempt at major reform, however, resulted in one of the most significant political controversies in Ireland.

As part of his attempt to improve Irish health, Dr Browne determined to try and implement a scheme along the lines of the British welfare-state national health service. Being particularly concerned about the high level of infant mortality in Eire (in larger towns the rate was over 100 deaths per 1,000 births – ten times more than tuberculosis deaths), he decided to introduce free health care and education for all mothers and children up to the age of sixteen

– the Mother and Child Scheme. The Irish Medical Association opposed the Scheme (even going so far as employing a private detective to report on Dr Browne), arguing that it was socialist and that by introducing a state interest in patients it would interfere with the doctor–patient relationship. As in Britain, where the medical profession employed the same arguments in opposing the national health service, these arguments could have been overcome. But Browne also faced the opposition of the Catholic Hierarchy who wrote to the taoiseach, Costello, declaring that in their opinion the Scheme threatened the sanctity of the family. In the view of the bishops, the effects of the Scheme would be

in direct opposition to the rights of the family and of the individual and are liable to very great abuse...If adopted in law they would constitute a ready-made instrument for future totalitarian aggression. The right to provide for the health of children belongs to parents, not the State. The State has the right to intervene only in a subsidiary capacity, to supplement, not to supplant.

Browne strove to allay the bishops' fears, telling Costello, 'I should have thought it unnecessary to point out that from the beginning it has been my concern to see that the Mother and Child Scheme contained nothing contrary to Catholic moral teaching', but to no avail. He refused to compromise on the free nature of the Scheme and, denied the support of the cabinet and his own party (Costello told Browne the government could not support a scheme the Church found objectionable on moral grounds, and Sean MacBride, leader of Clann na Poblachta, asked Browne to resign), Browne left the government in April 1951, releasing the correspondence on the affair to the press. A month later, as a result of defections from Clann na Poblachta over government proposals to increase the price of milk, the coalition lost its majority in the dail, and after the ensuing general election de Valera formed a government.

The affair demonstrated the power of the Church and the conservative nature of the State, convincing Northern Irish Protestants, for example, that a united Ireland would be a clericalist Ireland. In an editorial on Browne's resignation, the *Irish Times* pointed out that not only had the free Mother and Child Scheme as well as a promising political career been lost, but 'the most serious revelation, however, is that the Roman Catholic Church would seem to be the effective government of this country'. The British ambassador in Dublin, Sir Gilbert Laithwaite, reported to London that the affair had 'brought out the dominating position and authority claimed by and conceded to the Roman Catholic hierarchy' and that 'above all, the effect of the incident has been to set back decisively any prospects that there might have been (and these were never more than the slightest) of an understanding between North and South over partition'. The collapse of the Scheme, the fall of the government and Browne's resignation cannot be attributed solely to the influence of the Church. There were tensions about policy generally within the coalition, and there were tensions within Clann na Poblachta and between Browne and MacBride which also contributed. The influence of the Irish Medical Association was also considerable. Nevertheless, the point was that the relationship between Church and State was crucial to the whole affair. The Church certainly did not seek the conflict, nor did it do anything except make its opposition to the Scheme clear. It had a genuine, if fuddy-duddy concern that a free Scheme might encourage extra-marital sex, and it also considered that while the Church had a proper interest in the moral life of people, the State did not. Its opposition was sufficient to decide the government, and this the bishops knew. However, it was a pyrrhic victory. Most people resented the Church's influence against the Scheme, and anti-clericalism, always a strong element in Fianna Fail, was strengthened. Over the next twenty-five years episcopal influence rapidly declined and the Church itself became far more liberal in its attitudes. In 1973 the church actually welcomed the introduction of a free health service. In 1979 the government was able to withstand Church opinion and legalize the sale of contraceptives to married persons in chemists' shops on production of a doctor's prescription.

In 1951 de Valera's government was in a minority in the dail, only surviving with the support of some Independent TDs. Nevertheless, it passed some of the most important legislation of the post-war years. A Health Act in 1953 introduced a means-tested medical service for those 'unable to provide by their own industry or other lawful means the medical or surgical appliances necessary for themselves and their dependents'. Every person applying for the service was scrutinised individually on their ability to pay (in 1958, 28.5 per cent of the population was recorded as being eligible for free attention: a striking comment on the country's standard of living). In 1952 an Adoption Act permitted adoption (as long as the adopting parents were of the same religion as the child and its parents – the Church's influence again), and a Social Welfare Act coordinated state benefits and pensions for widows and orphans, as well as instituting a compulsory national insurance system involving contributions from employers and employees. These measures, together with Browne's successful health legislation, established an embryonic welfare state (clearly modelled on Britain) in Eire. However, of more immediate concern to the electorate was the country's dismal economic situation. Years of high inflation and the continuation of rationing into 1954 (it had begun in 1939 as an Emergency measure) lost Fianna Fail support. In an attempt to reduce inflation, the government increased the tax burden from £98 million to £103 million in 1953–4. In May 1954, hoping for popular endorsement, de Valera called a general election, only to return instead to opposition with fewer seats (sixty-five) than at any time since 1932. Costello became taoiseach for the second time of a coalition government of Fine Gael and Labour with Clann na Poblachta and Independent support in the dail.

The 1954 general election revealed a political development of significance: a two-party system was growing with Labour always a consistent third. In the 1951 election, Fine Gael's strength in the dail had increased from thirty-one seats to forty; in 1954 it went up again to fifty. Fianna Fail maintained its dail strength throughout (sixty-eight seats in 1948; sixty-nine in 1951; sixty-five in 1954). Independents and newer parties were beginning to be squeezed out (Clann na Poblachta went from ten seats in 1948 to two in 1951 and three in 1954; Independents went from twelve to fourteen to five). Fianna Fail, in power for twenty-one of the State's thirty-four years, had become the natural party of government, and Fine Gael had staged a remarkable recovery again to become a serious alternative to Fianna Fail. The odd thing was that there were still no doctrinal differences between the two Parties, and while civil war divisions were always close to the surface, political debate and contest had become concerned principally with efficiency and competing electoral promises. This has remained the characteristic of Irish politics to the present. Electoral phenomena like the initial success of Clann na Poblachta or in the general election of 1981 the return of pro-IRA Sinn Fein candidates do not seem to have affected the two-Party domination. Labour, which might have been expected to make an appeal – at least occasionally – to a larger audience than has been the case, found that the reforming legislation of Fianna Fail and coalition governments satisfied the electorate. Another problem the Labour Party faced was that its origins – echoing those of the British Labour Party – were firmly rooted in industrial trade unions and the cities, and it did not have a natural appeal for the conservatively minded agricultural community which comprised half the population. Emigration, rather than socialism, was the impoverished Irishman's answer to social discontent.

Emigration was an intractable part of Irish life until the mid-1960s. From an average of 18,711 emigrants a year in the ten-year period ending in 1946, emigration rose to an average of 23,913 a year in the period 1946–51; 39,352 a year in the period 1951–6; 42,400 a year in 1956–61. In the 1960s, for the first time since the famine, emigration fell dramatically, averaging 16,121 a year between 1961 and 1966 and 10,781 a year in 1966–71. The relationship between emigration and living standards is a complex one, but without doubt the rapid decline of emigration can be correlated with the rapid economic development of the 1960s, as can the fact that in 1966, for the first time, Eire recorded an increase in population (2.33 per cent), confirmed in 1971 with another increase (3.27 per cent) bringing the population to 2.978 million. The improvement in standards of living and the buoyancy of Eire's economy was due, in large part, to economic planning.

The idea that bureaucrats can actually plan anything successfully is somewhat quaint, but in Ireland it happened. It should also be said that the 1960s worldwide was a time of increasing prosperity and world trade, and Ireland would have enjoyed some benefit in any case. But the coincidence of bureaucratic awareness, pragmatic governments and favourable economic circumstances made a tremendous difference. The 1922–32 Cumann na nGaedheal government was the first administration to indulge in a form of economic planning with the setting up of bodies like the Electricity Supply Board and the Agricultural Credit Corporation which by regulating power and credit were to become central features of the Irish economy. However, not until the 1950s was it accepted in Ireland, let alone in most countries outside the Soviet bloc, that the State had a legitimate and often guiding part to play in the economic life of the nation. While it was always accepted that the State was primarily responsible for creating suitable economic climates through taxation and monetary policies, the proposition that the State should also be involved in detailed matters such as job and industry creation was new, reflecting the influence of the English economist John Maynard Keynes. Of course, in Ireland as elsewhere, economic intervention by the State had occurred – the Land Rehabilitation Programme and the Shannon Scheme were massive examples – but it had been haphazard, not part of a coherent plan.

In January 1949, Costello's government published a White Paper, *Ireland's long term recovery programme*, setting out expectations on imports and on production (mainly agricultural and mainly for export). This was required by the United States in exchange for Marshall Aid, £47 million of which Ireland received in 1948–51. The programme was actually produced by the department of external affairs and not the department of finance which, at the time, did not approve of the idea of economic planning, preferring the conservative, classical economic notions of the free market. Seven years later the attitude of the department of finance changed with the appointment of T. K. Whitaker as its secretary during Costello's second coalition government. Whitaker had entered the civil service in 1934 and had joined the department of finance four years later. His appointment to the senior post in the department, like all such appointments, was made by the government of the day, but was not an exercise in political patronage: the tradition of an independent civil service established during the union in the nineteenth century survived the Troubles and subsequent political turmoils. One of Whitaker's first actions was to write a memorandum urging long-term planning aimed at expanding the economy, implicitly recognizing that an industry-based Irish economy could not be self-sufficient but would have to import and export to survive. That same year the coalition government passed a Finance Act which provided tax incentives for exporters. The coalition government was defeated in a general election in March 1957 (Clann na Poblachta withdrew its support citing lack of progress on ending partition as the reason, thus forcing an election; continuing economic difficulties resulted in the defeat), and de Valera became taoiseach once again at the age of seventy-four, leading a Fianna Fail government with seventy-eight seats in the dail – an overall majority of ten. This government was to be one of the most energetic post-war administrations, publishing Whitaker's memorandum as a White Paper, *Economic development*, in November 1958.

De Valera retired as taoiseach in June 1959 when he was elected

president. He was re-elected in 1966, serving altogether for fourteen
years as head of state. He died in 1975. As chairman of the executive
council and then taoiseach, he had run the affairs of Ireland for
twenty-two of the State's first thirty-seven years. The Party he
founded and dominated, Fianna Fail, was in power for thirty-seven
of the State's first fifty years. His interest in a revived rural, Gaelic
Ireland pronouncedly influenced Irish development, providing a
natural political corollary to the conservative nature of the country
as was demonstrated in his Constitution, which is still in force.
Without doubt, he was the father of modern Ireland.

De Valera's successor as taoiseach was Sean Lemass, an old IRA
man who had proved to be one of the ablest and most astute Fianna
Fail ministers. Between 1932 and 1942 he had masterminded a
major house-building and re-housing programme (132,000 houses
were built), and during the Emergency as minister for supplies he
managed rationing and the efficient direction of resources so that the
economy did not grind to a halt. As taoiseach from 1959 until 1966
(Fianna Fail lost eight seats in the 1961 general election before its
economic policies began to have real effect, and Lemass then headed
a minority government), he implemented Whitaker's recommenda-
tions. Foreign companies were offered tax-free periods while they
established themselves in Ireland and began production. Firm
administrative measures were taken to streamline state bodies and,
with tax benefits, to encourage export industries. The government
pressed banks to make credit available for economic expansion and
generally removed restrictions. Results came quickly. In 1960 the
volume of exports from the twenty-six counties exceeded the 1929
volume for the first time. By 1966, exports by volume were 59 per
cent above the 1929 level. Agricultural output rose by 9 per cent in
the 1960s, but the real growth came in the industrial sector where
output increased by 82 per cent between 1959 and 1968. Unemployment rapidly fell in consequence. Real incomes rose by 4 per cent a
year from 1959 to 1963. The move from economic nationalism to
economic internationalism inherent in this export-orientated policy
also involved recognition of Ireland's economic dependence upon
Britain, her traditional principal trading partner (47 per cent of Irish
exports went to the United Kingdom in 1979; 50 per cent of imports
came from the UK). Thus when Britain applied for membership of
the European Economic Community in 1961, Ireland followed suit

not only because membership was a logical step to take on behalf of Irish exports penetrating the European market, but also because British membership and Irish exclusion would have been disastrous for the Irish economy, forcing a repeat of the 'Economic war' of the 1930s with EEC tariff barriers being raised in Britain against Irish goods. Along with Britain, Ireland was finally admitted to membership of the EEC in 1973.

The new prosperity ushered in by Lemass and Whitaker was not created by them, but was allowed and encouraged to develop. The intelligent exercise of imaginative policies provided a framework within which economic development took place. The changes involved were dramatic, representing a sea-change in politics away from civil war memories and the narrow nationalism of Griffith's Sinn Fein Party which had coloured the major Southern Irish Parties after 1922. Instead, Eire today is an aspiring, modern, industrialized nation no longer trammelled by political and cultural romanticism, tuned into a wider world. The economy is small, and – like Britain's – dependent upon trade. Gross domestic product in 1990 was $33,900 million, giving a per capita earning rate of $9,690 and an impressive real growth rate of 4.1 per cent per annum. Agriculture, right into the 1960s the most important sector, is still significant, accounting in 1990 for 10 per cent of the economy and 5 per cent of the workforce of 1,293,000 people, providing 85 per cent of the Republic's food needs. Industry – principally food products, construction, brewing, textiles, clothing, chemicals, pharmaceuticals, machinery, transportation equipment, glass and crystal – accounts for 37 per cent of gross domestic product and about 80 per cent of exports, and employs about one-quarter of the workforce. Services, largely in public employment, account for about 57 per cent of employment.

The principal exports of the Republic are chemicals, data-processing equipment (an industry that grew up during the 1980s), industrial machinery, live animals and animal products. The main imports are food, animal feed, chemicals, petroleum and petroleum products, machinery, textiles and clothing. In 1987, after years of deficit, the balance of payments was brought into surplus, and in 1990 exports amounted to $24,600 million and imports to $20,700 million. About 34 per cent of exports and 41 per cent of imports were to and from the United Kingdom, demonstrating the far-reaching changes in dependencies that membership of the European Community has brought since 1979: 50 per cent of Ireland's exports and 25 per cent of imports in 1990 were to and from members of the Community other than the UK. The rate of inflation, which reached double-digits in the late 1970s, was down to 3.3 per cent in 1990.

An important backdrop to impressive economic performance in the 1970s was the proportion of the workforce employed by public bodies. Between 1967 and 1982, public sector employment increased from about 138,000 to about 226,000, representing a growth from 13.4 per cent to 19.6 per cent. An additional 70,000 people were employed by semi-state bodies (like Aer Lingus, the national airline), a number that remained fairly constant throughout the 1970s. In a period of growth such as the 1960s and 1970s, such a proportion of the labour market dependent upon the state could be – and was – justified in terms of the equitable distribution of national wealth. State-sponsored employment was seen in civil service and government circles as a way of creating jobs and reducing emigration – ministers praised public sector employers for increasing their staffing levels. To some extent it was a form of spreading the risks of modernization, with the state adjudicating taxpayers' payment of the bulk of the cost. But as growth declined and recession bit in the 1980s, this policy required higher taxes and thus reduced national competitiveness, especially since the public sector does not actually *make* items that could be sold or exported. Changing the balance of employment away from services and towards productive enterprises was a necessary and painful process for the country, resulting in severe political controversies during the 1980s. High unemployment – 16.6 per cent in 1990 (along with Spain, the worst rate in western Europe) – and increased rates of emigration (an estimated 280,000 people left Ireland in the 1980s), however, have been prices paid for change.

As we have seen, for more than twenty years after 1959 the population grew and emigration declined, with the result that by 1981 more than half the inhabitants were aged thirty years or less. In 1979, the population numbered 3.368 million; in 1991 it was 3.489 million, and continuing to grow. The birth rate in 1991 was almost twice the death rate – 15 births/1,000 population; 9 deaths/1,000 population. But emigration during the 1980s at an estimated average rate of 28,000 annually (it varied yearly between 5 and 13 emigrants per 1,000 population) meant that while the national population remained young, it did not contain many of the younger people who, in the previous decade, had stayed at home.

An important difference underlay renewed emigration compared to previous exoduses. In the 1980s, emigration was fundamentally a function of Irish achievement; emigrants were not driven by want or persecution. High levels of unemployment had an effect, but this was only one factor. Emigrants were well-educated (Ireland achieved one of the highest general levels of education in Europe in the 1970s and 1980s) and skilled workers, looking for opportunities that Ireland is too small to offer. And they now looked for opportunities in new lands in Europe and not simply in the traditional emigrant destinations of Britain, North America and Australia

The political effects of these social and economic changes has been enormous, not least upon the desires and ambitions of a young electorate, changing the traditional preponderance of Irish politics. Younger voters did not know what the quarrels conditioning the Party system were about. The influence of the Roman Catholic Church and Catholic morality has greatly diminished, and the traditional Fianna Fail–Fine Gael polarities broke down in the 1980s, but not to the degree that the youthfulness of the country in 1981 had suggested. Nevertheless, the 1980s were to be politically volatile as younger voters increasingly made themselves felt. There were five general elections and three referendums. Fine Gael changed leaders once, Labour three times, and Fianna Fail split with the creation of a new party, the Progressive Democrats

Charles Haughey led Fianna Fail throughout the 1980s. His family had come from the North, and his father had been a republican in the civil war. He was a career politician, aggressively nationalist about the North and still saw Britain as an imperial power; he took pride in subtle domestic political compromises. As taoiseach, his leadership was marked by openness to ideas and willingness to undertake economic and social reform – albeit at the prodding of coalition partners. His perceived anti-Britishness harked back to an earlier generation and also made it difficult for him convincingly to endorse Anglo-Irish agreements and cooperation in the war against terrorism in the North (see chapter

11). Garret FitzGerald, leader of Fine Gael, referred scathingly to this element of Haughey's politics, in an easily misconstrued phrase, as his 'flawed pedigree'. Margaret Thatcher, who as British prime minister throughout the 1980s dealt repeatedly with Haughey and FitzGerald, compared the two men:

Mr Haughey had throughout his career been associated with the most Republican strand in respectable Irish politics. How 'respectable' was a subject of some controversy . . . I found him easy to get on with, less talkative and more realistic than Garret FitzGerald . . . Charles Haughey was tough, able and politically astute with few illusions and, I am sure, not much affection for the British . . . Garret Fitzgerald prided himself on being a cosmopolitan intellectual. He had little time for the myths of Irish Republicanism and would have liked to secularize the Irish Constitution and state, not least – but not just – as a way of drawing the North into a united Ireland. Unfortunately, like many modern liberals, he overestimated his own powers of persuasion over his colleagues and countrymen. He was a man of as many words as Charles Haughey was few. (Margaret Thatcher, *The Downing Street Years* (Harper Collins, London, 1993), pp. 388, 393)

Such a description Haughey undoubtedly would have worn with pride. He was to be taoiseach four times in the 1980s, but he was the first Fianna Fail leader never to win an overall majority in the dail, and his tenure was marked by deepening rifts within the Party.

Economic and social (as is now the case in democracies) rather than nationalist issues were the heart of politics in the Republic, and Haughey's political efforts were dominated by the need – broadly agreed by Fine Gael and Labour – to cut the country's deficit and public spending. In June 1981, Fianna Fail, after a half-hearted effort at economic reform, entered a general election with a twenty-seat parliamentary majority. Despite winning more seats than any other party, it lost its majority. Garret FitzGerald's Fine Gael formed a government with the support of the Labour Party.

FitzGerald's mother was a Belfast Presbyterian and a republican sympathiser during the civil war; his father was a leading nationalist journalist and Free State politician (first foreign minister of the Free State) in the 1920s. Perhaps as a result of this lineage, he had a deep emotional commitment to peace in the North. He was an almost stereotypical member of what might be termed the Irish *nomenklatura*: that small group of metropolitan, well-educated men and women who did not emigrate, preferring to inhabit universities, the civil service, nationalized industries, newspapers and magazines at home, peppered with stints abroad. FitzGerald had a career typical of the Irish elite, enabled by being part of a small talent pool in a small country. He was a barrister, research and schedules manager for Aer Lingus for eleven years, a university lecturer in economics for fourteen years, a journalist, and a television commentator. He was variously Irish correspondent for the BBC, *The Economist*, and the *Financial Times*. He entered politics in 1965, and at the age of forty-six in 1973 became the Republic's foreign minister. Following Fine Gael's defeat in the 1977 general election, he became Party leader.

As taoiseach, FitzGerald inherited Haughey's problem: how to overturn the 1960s and 1970s political consensus on economic management without losing elections. With more than 20 per cent of the electorate dependent upon state jobs, the reductions in public expenditure necessary to contain deficits had very direct political consequences. In January 1982, the dail by a single vote rejected a cost-cutting Fine Gael budget that proposed to reduce subsidies on milk and butter, and to impose value added tax on children's clothes and shoes. On 18 February, thirty weeks after Fine Gael's taking office, there was another general election. Fine Gael lost two seats; Fianna Fail gained seven seats and, with the support of the three Sinn Fein The Workers' Party (the political wing of the Official IRA) TDs and two independents, Haughey became taoiseach for the second time on 9 March 1982.

Haughey's second term in office was marked by internal Party wrangling and public scandal. Desmond O'Malley, minister for industry and commerce in the 1977–81 Fianna Fail government, imperiled the creation of the Fianna Fail administration by challenging Haughey's leadership immediately after the February election. He was finally persuaded to withdraw in the name of Party unity. Another senior Fianna Fail TD, George Colley, refused a cabinet position when he was denied the position of tanaiste (deputy prime minister), and then in June made a thinly veiled public attack on Haughey in a speech whose theme was 'low standards in high places'. There followed a summer of scandals. Haughey's election agent was charged with personation; a double murderer was arrested in the attorney general's apartment; newspapers carried allegations (in due course shown to be true) of illegal phone-tapping by the government. In October, a Fianna Fail TD proposed a vote of no confidence in Haughey's leadership, and a month later the government lost such a vote prompted by its proposals to cut back the health service. On 24 November 1982 a general election gave Fianna Fail seventy-five seats (a loss of ten), Fine Gael seventy (a gain of seven), Labour sixteen (a gain of one), and five to others. Garret FitzGerald became taoiseach for the second time at the head of a Fine Gael–Labour coalition.

The troubles and terrorism in the North, reawakened in 1969, inevitably impinged upon politics, not least by fuelling an awareness that Ireland was out of step with Britain and much of Europe in areas of social policy. As the 1980s opened, it was impossible to divorce and illegal to purchase contraceptives without a doctor's prescription, or to have an abortion in the Republic. In 1981, anti-abortion campaigners – the Pro-Life Amendment Campaign (PLAC) – concerned that abortion might one day be legalized, secured a pledge from Haughey to hold a referendum to make clear that while not specifically prohibited in the Constitution, it would always be illegal. FitzGerald honoured the pledge in September 1983, and in a low poll (54.6 per cent), by a two-to-one majority voters rejected abortion in all cases except when a mother's life might be threatened by an unborn child. It was an interesting result on two grounds. First, the Church had campaigned vigorously for a big anti-abortion vote, but the turnout was disappointing, an index of its reduced authority. Second, there was a clear division between rural Ireland and Dublin on the issue, suggesting that as Dublin grew (as it had been steadily doing), the balance of opinion could well change towards a more cosmopolitan view. Within ten years such a change had taken place.

Contraception next generated division. In 1985 a bill allowing the sale to people aged eighteen or more of condoms without prescriptions, and the sale of other contraceptives, but only from chemists and health boards, was passed by the dail despite the opposition of Fianna Fail and the Church. Desmond O'Malley refused to toe the Fianna Fail line on the issue, and voted for the bill: in February he was expelled from the Party. Later in the year, another Fianna Fail TD, Mary Harney, was expelled for supporting the Anglo-Irish agreement whereby the Republic recognized the position of Northern Ireland within the United Kingdom and in return was recognized by the United Kingdom as having status in

Northern Irish affairs (see chapter 11). Together, O'Malley and Harney in December formed a new party, the Progressive Democrats. In January 1986 they were joined by two more TDs defecting from Fianna Fail.

On 26 June 1986 came a referendum on divorce. The Church waged a vigorous campaign to maintain the ban embedded in the constitution. Early opinion polls indicated a large majority of people in favour of legalising divorce, but as the campaign progressed, anti-divorce spokesmen placed telling emphasis on the provisions of Irish law that, unless simultaneously reformed, would see the erosion of divorced women's legal and financial rights. The result, in another relatively low turn-out – 59 per cent – was 63.5 per cent to keep the ban. As in the 1983 vote on abortion, there was a strong Dublin–rural split.

In January 1987, four Labour Ministers resigned from Fitz-Gerald's coalition when it was proposed to cut public expenditure by £300 million, thus forcing a general election, held on 17 February. Economic issues dominated the three main Party platforms, but there was broad agreement between them on the need for austerity in order to strengthen the country's economy and reduce emigration: 30,000 people were estimated to have left the country in 1986 alone. The Anglo-Irish agreement did not become an election issue: Fianna Fail, which had opposed the agreement, undertook to honour it. The Progressive Democrats argued for radical economic remedies, and gained substantial support in consequence, winning fourteen seats and displacing Labour, with twelve seats, as the third Party. Fianna Fail won eighty-one seats and Fine Gael fifty-one. When the dail met on 10 March, Charles Haughey was elected taoiseach (by the Speaker's casting vote) for the third time. He pledged to continue with economic reform, and Fine Gael and the Progressive Democrats supported him in this.

In May 1989, Haughey called yet another election, seeking to capitalize on the popularity that economic reform had apparently won for his government. He had more than halved the budget deficit, increased the annual rate of growth in the economy to over 4 per cent per annum, and for the first time in many years had secured and maintained a surplus in the balance of trade for over a year. These successes were due in large part to Ireland's membership of the European Community, especially the benefits accruing from

Community grants and easement of trade. Community membership had a transforming quality for the country, enabling and accelerating change and improvement. Levels of unemployment (17 per cent) and emigration (an estimated 40,000 in 1988; 43,000 in 1989), however, remained high, and public expenditure cuts had affected welfare and social services and thus poorer families who traditionally tended to support Fianna Fail. The election was held on 15 June, and the result brought disappointment to Haughey, who had been hoping to obtain an overall parliamentary majority. Fianna Fail won seventy-seven seats, Fine Gael fifty-five, Labour fifteen, the Workers' Party (having dropped its Sinn Fein association) seven, the Progressive Democrats six, and others six more. After two weeks of bargaining, a Fianna Fail–Progressive Democrat coalition was formed, and Haughey was elected taoiseach for the fourth time. It was the first time in its history that Fianna Fail was partner in a coalition. Garret FitzGerald resigned the leadership of Fine Gael soon afterwards, saying that it was time for younger men to take the lead. He was succeeded by Alan Dukes, who had been his minister for finance.

Haughey was to receive a further disappointment in the 7 November 1990 presidential election. His candidate, Brian Lenihan, a leading Fianna Fail stalwart and minister for foreign affairs, entered the campaign as favourite. Controversy arose about Lenihan's actions nearly nine years earlier in January 1982. It was alleged that he had tried to put political pressure on the president, Patrick Hillery, an old Fianna Fail colleague, over whether or not to call an election at that time. Lenihan denied making telephone calls to the president, but then a tape-recording was released in which he was heard to admit that he had made the calls. He was defeated by Mary Robinson, who had made a name for herself as a leading campaigner for divorce, contraception and women's rights. Robinson gained nearly 52 per cent of the vote, becoming the Republic's first woman president. Like FitzGerald, she came from the Irish elite. Both her parents were doctors. She was sent to finishing school in France, then attended Trinity College, Dublin, to study law, going on to obtain a master's degree at Harvard Law School in 1967. Coming back to Dublin, she married Nicholas Robinson, the son of a Protestant banker and a former political cartoonist of the *Irish Times*. She had three children and made a legal career as an advocate for women's rights, joining the Labour Party and serving in the senate for twenty years. In 1985 she left the party in protest at its refusal to support her view that unionists should have been involved in the negotiations leading to the Anglo-Irish agreement; five years later she accepted Labour's nomination for the presidency. In the presidential election she won the support of most women, particularly after Fianna Fail tried to smear her as a bad wife and mother.

One scandal too many finally tripped Haughey. Early in 1992, Sean Doherty, a former Fianna Fail minister for justice, revealed that Haughey had been fully informed of the illegal government phone-tapping in 1982. The Progressive Democrats threatened to withdraw from the coalition, forcing Haughey's resignation on 30 January. Albert Reynolds, who had unsuccessfully challenged Haughey for the Party leadership in November 1991, was elected taoiseach and Party leader in his place.

Reynolds faced a rapid succession of major political crises. Within days of his taking office, in the 'X' case (so called because the identity of the girl in question was protected by law), the High Court ruled that a pregnant fourteen-year-old girl, allegedly raped by her best friend's father, could not travel to England for an abortion and banned her from leaving the country for nine months. The girl was reported to have threatened suicide if she was forced to bear the child. On 26 February, the Supreme Court overturned this ruling. In its judgement the Court criticised ambiguity in the 1983 anti-abortion constitutional amendment, and held that European Community law guaranteeing freedom of movement overrode the High Court's ban. The girl travelled to London and had an abortion. The case aroused intense debate and interest, calling into question the basis of the Republic's legislation when set against its international undertakings and the experience of thousands of Irish women: an estimated 4,000 women go every year to Britain for abortions. Reynolds promised another abortion referendum.

The nature and future of the European Community became central issues in a further referendum held on 18 June 1992. The Maastricht Treaty, signed by the heads of government of the Community in December 1991, creating the European Union and devolving more authority to European bodies at the expense of national parliaments, required ratification by each member state.

Some weeks earlier, Denmark had rejected the Treaty in a referendum, and suddenly Irish voters were placed in the position of effectively determining the future of the Community. A second rejection of the Treaty would have forced its collapse generally, and thus set back the cause of the more integrated and centralised Union. In the event, in a 57.3 per cent turnout, nearly 68 per cent of voters endorsed the Treaty.

Four months later, the Fianna Fail–Progressive Democrat coalition government fell apart when Reynolds accused Desmond O'Malley of dishonest testimony to a judicial inquiry into fraud in beef exports. O'Malley and the Progressive Democrats resigned from the government. Reynolds had forced the issue in the hope of gaining an overall majority – his standing was high in opinion polls – and of calming unrest within Fianna Fail: the Party did not like the coalition with the Progressive Democrats and blamed O'Malley and his colleagues for the resignation of Haughey and the defeat of Lenihan. In the resulting November 1992 election, however, Fianna Fail obtained its lowest number of seats – sixty-seven – in nearly forty years; Fine Gael fared even worse with forty-five seats, and the Progressive Democrats won ten. Labour made sweeping gains, winning thirty-three seats. Three separate referendums on abortion issues raised by the 'X' case took place at the same time as the election: the right to receive information about abortion services, the right to travel for an abortion, and the mother's right to life in cases of a life-threatening illness or event to her. The wording of the mother's right to life referendum was regarded as unsatisfactory by all sides, who combined to urge its rejection. The other two referendums passed with large majorities. The Church, obviously aware of the strength of feeling and the change in attitudes in Ireland, issued a low-key statement reiterating its opposition to abortion.

Not until January 1993 was another coalition put together, this time between Fianna Fail and Labour. Reynolds, elected taoiseach for a second time by the dail, promised extensive social reforms. In May, the sale of contraceptives in the Republic was made legal without age limit. In June, homosexuality between consenting adults was legalized, and the age of consent was lowered to seventeen. Government and public opinion for decades had been winking at these practices, and there had been a negligible number of prosecutions. In contrast to Spanish habit into the 1970s, for example, people were not routinely stopped and questioned at ports of entry to see if they possessed contraceptives. It was, in fact, a rare prosecution – the Dublin management of the Virgin chain of stores in effect challenged the government to prosecute them by publicizing the selling of contraceptives – that triggered reform of the law. The two bills involved were passed by the dail without a vote, reflecting the changed attitudes the awakening of a young electorate in the 1980s and the 'X' case had generated. The coalition government also continued legal reforms that had been put in train by Haughey to secure the rights of women if they divorced, and announced that a referendum on divorce would be held in 1994 after the reform legislation was in place.

In the decades since 1960, economic revival, generally improved prosperity, population growth and the shedding of traditional Catholic influence has renewed overall confidence in the nation. Emigration, once a harbinger of hopes and energies denied, in the 1980s testified to renewed drive in the country as young people entrepreneurially sought wider opportunities abroad. Membership of the European Union (until 1 November 1993 the European Community) has also aided national confidence, not least by lessening dependency on Britain. It has expanded imagination and opportunity enormously. In foreign affairs generally, Ireland's confidence has steadily grown. Following entry into the United Nations in 1955, successive governments have pursued a policy of broad support for Western democracies tempered by a keen anti-colonialism and concern for the Third World. Irish military units have formed important elements in UN peace-keeping forces in the Congo, Cyprus, Kashmir and the Middle East. Within the European Union, Ireland has voted for expanded membership and federalism.

Modern Ireland is not the country Tom Clarke, Patrick Pearse, James Connolly, Eamon de Valera or the men of 1916–21 envisaged. None of them were modernisers: they were either intellectuals or rural fundamentalists. It is not a self-sufficient and self-preoccupied united Gaelic state. For the first time in centuries Irish people have a justified confidence that they can put world change to their own use. Ireland today is a country of entrepreneurs, farmers, bankers, industrialists, successful artists and writers (since 1969, at the instigation of Charles Haughey, royalties from artistic and creative work have been tax-free). Indeed, the 1916 Rising is no longer celebrated and, not least because of terrorism in Northern Ireland in the name of Irish nationalism, the revolutionary antecedents of the state are seen by many as an embarrassment. The trauma and horror of violence in the North has forced home the knowledge that the romantic vision of Irish nationhood that inspired men and women from Wolfe Tone onwards is probably impossible to achieve by violent means. 'To break the connection with England' – Tone's objective – is unlikely ever to happen completely in economic terms, and in political terms the connection has always existed, first as a colony, then in the union, followed by the 1921 Treaty relationship of 'the common citizenship of Ireland with Great Britain'. Tone's great hope of uniting 'the whole people of Ireland, to abolish the memory of all past dissensions, and to substitute the common name of Irishman in place of the denominations of Protestant, Catholic Dissenter', because of the polarizing force of terrorism, now looks as far away as ever before.

11

Northern Ireland

Unlike the Free State after 1921, Northern Ireland did not experience a civil war. The 1920 Government of Ireland Act had partitioned Ireland and established parliaments for both Southern and Northern Ireland (the six counties of Antrim, Armagh, Down, Fermanagh, Londonderry and Tyrone). Northern Ireland was a new and unique part of the United Kingdom, in area 5,452 square miles (smaller than Yorkshire and less than one fifth of the area of Ireland) with a population of 1.256 million (in 1926) composed of a two to one Protestant majority over Catholics which was translated politically into a permanent Unionist majority. To the present day, never fewer than nine of the twelve Northern Irish MPs at Westminster have been Unionists. In the parliament of Northern Ireland, between 1929 and 1968, Unionists held never fewer than thirty-four of the fifty-two seats. The first general election for the parliament held in May 1921 was also the first to use proportional representation in the United Kingdom (it was abandoned in 1929 in favour of the traditional first-past-the-post system): forty Ulster Unionist Party MPs were returned. Until direct rule of the province by Westminster was established in March 1972, the Ulster Unionist Party won every single general election and formed every single government. Its connections with the Orange Order were always close: every single Northern Ireland prime minister was a member of the Order. Irish and Ulster unionists had consistently argued for the continuation of the union between Ireland and Britain, and had not sought the creation of Northern Ireland, but had accepted it, in the words of Sir James Craig, its first prime minister, as 'a supreme sacrifice in the interests of peace'. The concept of the province had been to achieve unionist control: to have included the other three counties of Ulster – Cavan, Donegal and Monaghan – would have meant a much closer religious and hence political balance. It was also to meet the undoubted objections of unionists to being governed by men whom they perceived as Roman Catholic Irish nationalists, ex-Sinn Fein and ex-IRA almost to a man. But it was the entrenchment of unionist majority that came first. As Walter Long, Carson's predecessor as Irish Unionist leader, in 1920 reported to the British cabinet committee on Ireland, 'the new province should consist of the six counties, the idea being that the inclusion of Donegal, Cavan and Monaghan would provide such an access of strength to the Roman Catholic party, that the supremacy of the Unionists would be seriously threatened'.

Sir James Craig (1871–1940) succeeded Sir Edward Carson (1854–1935) as leader of the Ulster Unionists in 1921 upon Carson's appointment as a lord of appeal. Carson was an Irish, not an Ulster Unionist. He had fought for the Anglo-Irish union and once it was destroyed he retired from the fray. Craig's government established the police and administrative systems that were to dominate the province for fifty years. While in Southern Ireland the 1921 Treaty modified the provisions of the 1920 Government of Ireland Act, in Northern Ireland the Act went into force unchanged. The parliament of Northern Ireland consisted of a popularly elected fifty-two member house of commons and a twenty-six member senate, twenty-four of whose members were elected by the house of commons; the other two were the lord mayor of Belfast and the mayor of Londonderry. A governor performed royal functions. The parliament had complete powers except in matters relating to the crown, peace and war, foreign relations, defence, external trade, cables and wireless, citizenship, air and navigation, lighthouses, dignities and titles, coinage, weights and measures, copyright, patents, the Supreme Court, income tax and profits tax. The overriding sovereignty of the Westminster parliament was stated in section 75 of the Act as being 'over all persons, matters and things in Northern Ireland'. The Northern Ireland parliament was specifically entrusted with responsibility for 'the peace, order and good government' of the province.

Tumult surrounded the province's formation. Riots were taking place in the streets of Belfast while King George V opened the Northern parliament there in June 1921. Between 1920 and 1922 nearly 300 people were killed in riots and shooting incidents, mostly in Belfast. In 1922 alone, 232 people were killed including two of the new parliament's Unionist MPs; nearly 1,000 more were injured; 400 people (nearly all IRA men) were interned and more than £3 million worth of damage was done. To meet this disorder, the Northern Ireland parliament passed the Constabulary Act in June 1922, setting up the Royal Ulster Constabulary in succession to the Royal Irish Constabulary, under the control of the Northern Irish minister for home affairs. Like the RIC, the RUC was armed and combined a civilian and a military role which was strengthened by its close association with the 'A', 'B' and 'C' Ulster Special Constabulary, formed in 1920 to combat the IRA in the north. One third of all RUC places were intended for Catholics, but less than 20 per cent of the force were Catholics at any time. IRA intimidation at first prevented Catholics joining the Constabulary, but it was also perceived as a unionist and Orange force by Irish nationalists who, in any case, chose not to believe that Northern Ireland would last very long – that Irish unity was inevitable – and thus stayed apart from the creation and development of the institutions of the province. Since they did not want Northern Ireland to exist, they had no incentive to make it work. They were encouraged in this attitude by successive Southern Irish governments which consistently advocated the principle of Irish unity. In practical terms, the fact was that Northern Ireland governments were pronouncedly anti-Irish nationalist and the Constabulary forces saw the Catholic community in general as a threat to the province's security, so even if Northern nationalists had not abstained from the workings of the province, the likelihood was that they would have faced discrimination in any case.

Along with the Orange Order, the Special Constabulary was in the vanguard of anti-Catholicism. Special Constables were drawn nearly entirely from membership of the Ulster Volunteer Force which had been re-formed by Colonel Wilfrid Spender, a pre-1914 UVF veteran, and Sir Basil Brooke, a wealthy landowner and future prime minister of Northern Ireland. 'A' Specials were attached full-time to the RUC for six-month periods; 'B' Specials were part-time (and the most numerous) and 'C' Specials were a general reserve for emergencies. As a result, by the middle of 1922 there were over 50,000 full and part-time policemen in Northern Ireland: one to every six households in the province. The 'A' and 'C' Specials were disbanded in the 1930s; the 'B' Specials became a permanent adjunct of the RUC. On 1 August 1969 'B' Specials numbered 8,906 constables, not one of whom was a Roman Catholic. They were disbanded in 1970 and replaced by the volunteer Ulster Defence Regiment under military control.

To enable the RUC and the Special Constabulary to restore order in 1922, the Northern parliament following earlier British prece-dents enacted the Civil Authorities (Special Powers) Act by which the Northern Ireland minister for home affairs could 'take all such steps and issue all such orders as may be necessary for preserving the peace and order'. The minister could delegate his powers to any RUC officer he chose. In addition there was a blanket provision which effectively gave the minister or his delegate sweeping power: 'If any person does any act of such a nature as to be calculated to be prejudicial to the preservation of the peace or maintenance of order in Northern Ireland and not specifically provided for in the regulations, he shall be deemed guilty of an offence against the regulations.' The Act was renewed each year from 1922 to 1933 and then made permanent, remaining in force until 1972 when it was replaced by Westminster's Northern Ireland Act and direct rule. Similar legislation to counteract IRA activity and the threat of violence was enacted in the South (the 1939 Offences Against the State Act in the South is still in force): Northern Ireland was not alone in this respect.

To the unionist majority in Northern Ireland, these measures were necessary not only for the security of the province, but also to protect the lives of Protestants and unionists and to deal with the third of the province's population which refused to accept its legitimacy. To the nationalist minority in the North, these measures confirmed unionist domination. After the 1925 tripartite agreement which settled the boundaries of the six counties and dropped the 1920 Government of Ireland Act provision for a Council of Ireland, it became clear to some Northern nationalists that the best hope for their community was constitutional opposition within Northern Ireland (although the Nationalist Party itself did not become the loyal opposition until 1965). The old Irish – Nationalist – Party Northern leader, Joseph Devlin (1872–1934), having abstained in 1921, in 1925 took his seat in the Northern parliament (from 1932 housed at Stormont, outside Belfast, in an impressive and specially built parliament house), and at Westminster. One of his major points was that Northern Ireland was not economically viable: the same point that Michael Collins had believed in 1921. They both overlooked the fact that, over all, the North was more prosperous than the South and that 'the poor' were better off in the North too. Northern economic viability was simply geared more directly to Britain's and world trade. Nevertheless, despite the fact that the bulk of Irish industry was concentrated in the North, the Northern economy was exceptionally vulnerable to changes in world trade and prosperity, and nationalists were able to play upon this. In 1921, unemployment in the North averaged 18 per cent. In the fifteen years to 1939 it averaged 23 per cent, comparable with the levels in Wales and North-East England. Its industries, though large, were labour intensive and not diverse – linen, shipbuilding and agriculture– and all were vulnerable to British and world competition and changes in world trade. By 1933, as a result of the great depression, employment in the Belfast shipyards had dropped from 20,000 in 1924 to 2,000, and the Harland and Wolff yards did not launch a single ship. Private and corporate investment tended to be concentrated in British industries and government securities rather than in Northern Ireland, thus denying Northern industry capital for expansion, re-equipping, research and development. However, in 1938 Westminster agreed to meet Stormont's budget deficits, and this gave Northern Ireland stability for the first time, removing one of the nationalists' principal arguments. The arrangement did not change economic conditions, it merely subsidized them, and unemployment has proved a persistent problem in Northern Ireland for most of its existence.

In this state of decline, competition for jobs kept sectarian divisions alive. Riots, which had died down in the late 1920s and early 1930s (in 1932, unemployed Protestants in Belfast had even demonstrated in support of unemployed Catholics who had been attacked by 'B' Specials), began again. In 1935 sectarian riots during the summer marching season (the Orange Order every year traditionally celebrated on 12 July William of Orange's victory at the Battle of the Boyne and on 12 August the raising of the siege of Londonderry) ended with eleven people dead and 600 injured. Riots have featured prominently in the history of the province. Riots in the late 1960s heralded the violence and bloodshed unleashed by the IRA and various 'loyalist' groups since 1968.

Discrimination also fuelled divisions. In the Northern Ireland civil

service, separate political loyalties, social and educational disadvan-
tage and discrimination meant that Catholics never even applied for
jobs in proportion to their population numbers. As a result, as late as
1969, of the 209 people in the technical and professional grades of
the civil service, only 13 were Catholics. Of the 319 in higher
administrative grades, on 23 were Catholics. Of the 115 people
nominated by the government for service on nine public bodies,
only 16 were Catholics. This was the result of two generations of
abstentionism and discrimination in a province where the answer to
the question 'Which school did you go to?' told any Northern
Irishman any other's religion, probable political allegiance and
social condition. Unemployment, always high, also tended to be
concentrated amongst Catholics: in 1972 a survey indicated that
average male unemployment was twice as high in Catholic areas as
in Protestant. In local elections, gerrymandering took place, sometimes on a large scale. One of the clearest examples was in the city
of Londonderry. In 1966 the city's electorate consisted of 20,000
nationalists and 10,000 unionists, yet the city corporation was
Unionist controlled (and had been ever since the North's 1922 Local
Government Act had ended proportional representation for local
government elections). The reason for this was threefold. First, the
local election franchise (as opposed to the general election franchise)
was limited to ratepayers and their wives which meant that the
generally poorer nationalist population suffered (in Londonderry,
this had the effect in local elections of reducing the total nationalist
electorate by one quarter to 14,500, while the unionist electorate
was reduced by one eighth to 8,800). This restricted franchise system
remained in force until 1969 when James Chichester-Clark's Unionist government finally instituted an adult franchise of one man one
vote in local as in general elections. Secondly, a business vote gave
firms up to six votes depending upon the rateable value of their
property. This had been the case in the United Kingdom as a whole
until 1946, but with the Elections and Franchise Act passed by
Stormont in 1946, the system was retained in Northern Ireland until
1969. While various studies have shown that in general Northern
Ireland's peculiar franchise only had a small electoral effect, it is
also clear that in some areas like Londonderry the effect could be
significant. Thirdly, boundary revisions were conducted by local
authorities and Stormont governments. In areas with nationalist

majorities. Stormont governments generally saw to it that boundaries were drawn so that the nationalist vote was concentrated in one constituency.

In Unionist controlled Londonderry, 10,000 nationalist voters were in one ward and returned eight councillors; the unionist vote was split between two wards returning twelve councillors between them. In parliamentary elections for both Stormont and Westminster, similar boundary juggling ensured large Unionist parliamentary majorities and the largest parliamentary constituencies in the United Kingdom. With two-thirds of the province's population Protestant, Unionists were bound to dominate electorally in any case. if Westminster had taken action earlier to increase Northern Ireland's parliamentary representation (five new parliamentary constituencies were created in Northern Ireland by Westminster in 1981, after sixty years bringing the number from twelve to seventeen), then there would have been more scope for greater Catholic/nationalist representation.

Tied into electoral discrimination was housing. Housing, as in the rest of the United Kingdom, was a local government matter. Since the franchise in local elections was geared to rates, this meant that the siting of houses could affect the vote unless the occupants shared the political allegiance of the area. Sometimes in urban areas, authorities ran out of land to develop and, with the generally high fertility rate amongst Catholics (although it should also be noted that Catholic emigration from the province was higher than Protestant), this meant that in general Catholics faced more crowded housing conditions than Protestants, as Unionist local authorities opted at times simply to stop building houses rather than risk jeopardizing Unionist majorities by housing Catholics (and therefore nationalists) in Protestant areas. No secret was made of this. In 1936 Omagh Rural Council, Unionist controlled although the electorate was two-thirds nationalist, stated that despite the need for housing in their area they were reluctant to build houses because 'our political opponents are only waiting the opportunity to use this means to outvote us in divisions [i.e. electoral districts] where majorities are close'. A Unionist member of Enniskillen Borough Council in 1963 baldly declared 'We are not going to build houses in the south ward [unionist] and cut a rod to beat ourselves later on. We are going to see that the right people are put into these houses and we are not making any apology for it.' However, local concentrations of people on religious/political grounds did not mean that one section of the population was housed while the other was not.

Discrimination in housing by the late 1960s was not, in fact, significant and was actually conducted more by Catholics against Protestants in Catholic areas than vice versa. In the province as a whole there was no systematic discrimination in housing against Catholics. There was some discrimination against large Catholic families (local authorities could decide whether applicants for housing with large families had demonstrated need or social irresponsibility) with a 12 per cent difference against Catholics in the proportion of families with more than six children assigned public housing. But because large families were five times more numerous among Catholics than among Protestants, Catholics still constituted 78 per cent of all large families in public housing. With generally high levels of unemployment and poor housing (the 1961 census found that 51 per cent of all households lacked modern amenities such as a fixed bath or hot-water tap) there was great competition for public housing and public jobs (it was the same in the South), with individual cases of discrimination receiving publicity and colouring attitudes. In nearly all cases where discrimination did occur, religion was the deciding factor. A terrible effect was to emphasize religion as *the* difference between people, sustaining a sectarian (rather than an economic) division in the North as practically the only one. On both sides a spoils system operated in politics with the electoral winner taking all.

Until the 1960s, leaders of both communities did little to bridge the divisions between them. Sir James Craig, created Viscount Craigavon of Stormont in 1927, prime minister until his death in 1940, said in the Northern Ireland parliament in 1934, 'I am an Orangeman first and a politician and a member of this Parliament afterwards . . . All I boast is that we have a Protestant Parliament and a Protestant State.' Sir Basil Brooke, prime minister of the province from 1943 to 1963, upon his appointment as Northern Irish minister for agriculture in 1933 dismissed the 125 Catholic workers on his estate to set an example to other landowners. 'Catholics', he was reported as saying, 'were out to destroy Ulster with all their might and power. They wanted to nullify the Protestant vote and take all they could out of Ulster and then see it go to hell.'

John Miller Andrews, prime minister from 1940 to 1943, in 1933 investigated the employment of porters at the Stormont parliament and reported, 'I have found that there are thirty Protestants and only one Roman Catholic – there temporarily.'

This was matched to a certain extent by de Valera's 1937 Constitution in the South favouring the Roman Catholic Church; by Cardinal MacRory, primate of Ireland, stating in 1931 that 'the Protestant Church in Ireland is not even a part of the Church of Christ' (*Irish News*, 18 December 1931) and, more understandably but no less provocative to unionists, by nationalist politicians declaring that they refused to recognize the crown. There were some moments of mutual goodwill as, for example, in 1936 when two bishops, one Anglican and the other Catholic, together called upon their flocks to live together harmoniously, but bigotry, discrimination, fear and hatred on both sides were more general.

After the confirmation of Northern Ireland's boundaries in 1925, de Valera's 'Economic war' (1932–5) emphasized partition by the tariff barriers placed between the South and the North as part of the United Kingdom. The Second World War helped build the wall of partition, briefly reviving the North's economy and clearly separating the six counties from the neutral twenty-six in the South. By the end of the war, Belfast shipbuilders had launched more than 170 warships; Northern Irish farmers had doubled the area of land under cultivation, and the government had provided training ground for 120,000 American troops. 'Without Northern Ireland', said General Dwight D. Eisenhower, 'I do not see how the American forces could have been concentrated to begin the invasion of Europe.' London-derry and Belfast had provided important air and naval bases during the battle of the Atlantic, and in 1945 the German U-boat fleet was directed to surrender at Londonderry.

After the war, Eire's decision to leave the Commonwealth and to declare itself a Republic necessitated the passing of corresponding legislation, the Ireland Act, at Westminster to recognize that Eire 'ceased, as from the eighteenth day of April, nineteen hundred and forty-nine, to be part of His Majesty's Dominions'. It was another brick in the wall of partition, and the Act gave a clear guarantee to the North which has since been the basis of Unionist politics: 'Northern Ireland remains part of His Majesty's Dominions and of the United Kingdom and it is hereby affirmed that in no event will

Northern Ireland or any part thereof cease to be part of His Majesty's Dominions and of the United Kingdom without the consent of the Parliament of Northern Ireland'

The development of the British welfare state further strengthened the barriers between North and South. A national health service came into effect in Northern Ireland in 1948, providing free health care for the whole population in contrast to the South. That same year saw the introduction of national insurance in the North, providing greater social security benefits than existed in the South. The most important welfare measure, however, was the North's 1947 Education Act which extended grants for university and higher education, raised the school-leaving age to fifteen, and for the first time provided free secondary education on the British 1944 Education Act model. The effect of the Act was that poorer (and therefore predominantly Catholic) students as last benefited from (secular) higher education. The first generation to come through the new educational system reached maturity in the 1960s when students everywhere seemed to be demonstrating and protesting, and provided the impetus for the civil rights movement culminating in the strife that has torn the province apart.

Housing, constantly high unemployment and the electoral system were the targets of civil rights protests. Catholics were no longer able to accept the unionist rationale that the security of the province demanded discrimination. Terence O'Neill, who had succeeded Brookeborough (Sir Basil Brooke was created Viscount Brookeborough in 1952) as prime minister in 1963, courageously tried to accommodate the liberal spirit of the decade without splitting the Unionist Party. The post-war growth of mass communication had brought a questioning of authority, reflected in the USA by a wide disposition to protest forcefully which in turn was adopted by people in most other countries. The tactic of civil disobedience was seen to be particularly successful as distinguished protesters in Europe and the United States were manhandled by police as they sat and prayed and sang against nuclear weapons and the Vietnam War.

O'Neill sought to improve good relations with Eire, and thus reduce tensions and offer hopes. He was the first Northern Ireland prime minister to visit a Catholic school. He emphasized the importance of economic expansion to improve living standards and to reduce job competition and unemployment. In 1964 he created a ministry for development; the following year his New Towns Act established the new town of Craigavon and eight other growth areas. He granted recognition to the Dublin-based (and therefore 'alien') Irish Congress of Trade Unions. A new sense of growth and good feeling was generated amongst Catholics and Protestants. Without telling his cabinet colleagues, he invited Sean Lemass, the Eire taoiseach, to meet him at Stormont. On 14 January 1965, Lemass came. It was the first meeting between Northern and Southern prime ministers since December 1925. In November 1965, O'Neill called an election and won with an increased vote for the Unionist Party. The Nationalist Party, recognizing O'Neill's efforts to conciliate its supporters, agreed to become the official opposition for the first time in its history. The problem O'Neill faced, however, was that his actions were mainly symbolic, changing little while encouraging Catholic hopes and the fears of hard-line unionists. 'What do a bridge and a traitor have in common?' asked the Rev. Ian Paisley, one such hard-liner. 'Both cross to the other side.' Brian Faulkner, Unionist prime minister from 1971 to 1972, later considered that O'Neill's meetings with Lemass 'started the slide away of support for O'Neill within the Unionist community'. By 1969, defections and resignations (including some leading ministers and two future prime ministers) from O'Neill's government over the by then connected issues of conciliation and security, forced his resignation at the end of April 1969 in the interests of Party unity. Before this happened, however, civil disobedience and violence had come to plague the streets of Northern Ireland.

A new generation of Catholic nationalist and republican leaders had formed the Northern Irish Civil Rights Association (NICRA) in February 1967 to campaign against discrimination. A series of demonstrations and then riots followed during 1968. Protestant Unionist counter-demonstrators saw in NICRA a new, sophisticated attempt to undermine the North, playing on O'Neill's conciliatory style. Unionists did have a point: some ex-IRA men were in NICRA (although the IRA itself stayed apart), and the first NICRA mass meeting was followed by a song which the organizers had intended to be 'We shall overcome', but those gathered rendered instead 'A nation once again', the unofficial anthem of Irish nationalism. On 9 October 1968, People's Democracy was founded by students at Queen's University as a radical, socialist offshoot of NICRA. To many, People's Democracy (as distinct from NICRA) was seen to be the principal instigator of violence in the North, a view subsequently endorsed by the historian and political commentator Dr Conor Cruise O'Brien:

They emerged as the left-wing of the Civil Rights movement, but they weren't really interested in Civil Rights, they were interested in revolution which they saw or said they saw in terms of class, but which in Northern Ireland conditions could only be, as usual, Catholics versus Protestants. They denied that. They said that was a bourgeois deception and had much rhetoric to that effect. What they were after in the long term was revolution. In the short term it was confrontation, and in particular they sought to discredit the bourgeois government of Terence O'Neill. They played, I think, quite deliberately into the hands of his right-wing opponents because all this brought revolution, or at any rate turmoil into being. They therefore marched in Protestant areas, allegedly to spread their non-sectarian views, but in reality to provoke, and they did provoke. . .and both their activities and the reactions to them helped to undermine the government of Terence O'Neill and to destroy the moderate centre in Ulster, for which I think they bear a terrible responsibility before history. (BBC World Service, *Ulster – What went wrong?*, 8 June 1981)

Whether the few hundred members of People's Democracy were quite so central to the collapse of the moderate centre of opinion and the government of Terence O'Neill is probematical. What is certain is that People's Democracy in late 1968 and early 1969 was at the centre of nearly every violent confrontation between civil rights demonstrators and the RUC and unionists. A civil rights march from Belfast to Londonderry, organized by People's Democracy, on 4 January 1969 was attacked just outside Londonderry at Burntollet Bridge by a Protestant mob wielding cudgels with nails hammered through. The RUC gave the marchers no protection. Later that day, RUC and 'B' Specials ran amok in Londonderry's Catholic Bogside district. In retaliation, the residents there sealed off the Bogside and declared it 'Free Derry'. These events combined to break the alliance that had been developing under O'Neill's fosterage between moderates in both communities in the North. Faith in reform through democratic processes and the law had been bludgeoned away by the actions of protectors, the RUC and 'B' Specials, leaving the campaign for civil rights in the more radical hands of People's Democracy, and the defence of Catholics increasingly in the hands of the IRA.

O'Neill's successor in April 1969 was James Chichester-Clark, under whose premiership the first deaths in the streets occurred. The new prime minister tried to reduce tensions by establishing ombudsmen to deal with complaints against central and local government. Housing was taken away from local authorities and placed with a housing executive which allocated housing on the basis of need. Chichester-Clark secured the passage of an Incitement of Hatred Act which instituted methods to prevent discrimination in jobs. A ministry of community relations and an independent community relations commission were established. The ratepayers' franchise in local elections was abolished. Local government was reorganized, as a result of which in the local elections of May 1973, Londonderry passed out of Unionist control. But the reforms were too late.

During the summer of 1969, serious rioting began again in Londonderry. Gerry Fitt, a leading member of NICRA at the time, recalled:

It all began because of another one of those days that we have to celebrate and commemorate in Northern Ireland. The 12th August 1969 was the anniversary of closing the gates of Derry in 1689, and they are always occasions which spark off trouble. After the parade had passed there was the usual sporadic street rioting and the police did use very strong-arm tactics to intimidate those who were engaged in the riot, to such an extent that the whole situation escalated and got out of hand. Then I think for the first time in Northern Ireland we saw the use of the petrol bomb. . .They were able to keep off the police by burning them, by throwing them from the top of the flats, etc. They were able to keep them out of that area for two days. In the meantime it was getting massive publicity in all the media here in the United Kingdom and further afield. And it looked like a siege. Derry is a city of sieges, all throughout its history. And then one of the leaders of the civil rights movement in Northern Ireland. . .issued a statement and called upon the nationalist people in Belfast to come out on the streets to engage in activity against the police and so withdraw the police force from Derry where almost the total police force of Northern Ireland were in action over the previous two days. . .The sum total of that was that on 14th August there was fierce sectarian murdering and killing between the Falls Road and the Shankill, and factories were bombed, places were looted. It was the worst outbreak of violence that I can ever recall in Northern Ireland. (BBC World Service, *Ulster – What went wrong?*, 8 June 1981)

Four months earlier on 30 March and in April, just before O'Neill resigned, some bombs had gone off at power stations in the province. At first it was thought to be the work of the IRA, only later emerging that hard-line unionists had been responsible: they had hoped that the IRA would be blamed and that O'Neill would be forced to resign because he was providing insufficient security. O'Neill resigned for other reasons, but these April bombs had another, far more important effect: they led to the first influx of additional troops to Northern Ireland when on 20 April the ministry of defence in London announced that 550 soldiers would be despatched to aid the civil authority, but not to deal with demonstrations or public order. This was the first distinct Westminster involvement in Northern Ireland since 1922, and it was to bring into question the province's constitutional status.

Before 1966, Northern Irish affairs were seldom discussed in Westminster. The British home secretary answered for Northern Irish matters there, but whenever matters of substance were raised, the convention was to defer them to the Northern Ireland government. Between 1945 and 1969, the British home office had no civil servants working full-time on Northern Ireland. There were no formal channels of control or supervision of the Stormont government or parliament, beyond the financial and budgetary arrangements monitored by the Treasury. By August 1969, as a result of summer rioting, tension was high in the province. On 13 August the RUC, exhausted and frightened by the scale of violence in Londonderry (700 of the RUC's total force of 3,000 were involved in the Bogside riots which began on 12 August), allowed 'B' Specials to patrol Belfast in armoured cars with 9 mm Sterling sub-machine guns. By 15 August, eight people had been killed by the police forces; total casualties were ten dead and 145 civilians and four policemen wounded by gunfire. A subsequent commission of inquiry under Lord Hunt of Llanvair Waterdine led to the disbandment of the 'B' Specials in October and the disarming of the RUC (not for long: by 1971 the force was armed again to deal with violence). On 14 August at 5 p.m. in Londonderry, British troops took to the streets (welcomed by Catholics) for the first time in fifty years to uphold law and order.

For the Westminster government, the violence of 12–15 August 1969 – in the words of Gerry Fitt 'the worst outbreak of violence I can ever recall in Northern Ireland' – was the turning point, and direct intervention followed. For the first time in several years IRA men had fired at the RUC in Belfast and had retaliated against Orangemen who attacked Catholics. Civil rights ceased being the central issue, to be replaced by physical force republicanism versus unionism, Catholics against Protestants. The British Labour home secretary, James Callaghan, began to pressure Chichester-Clark to reform the RUC and to talk to Catholic leaders. 'Free Derry' and other Catholic 'No Go' areas were left alone. In June 1970 the United Kingdom general election changed the government and under the new Conservative prime minister, Edward Heath, Reginald Maudling became home secretary. Deciding that Callaghan's policy had not worked (attacks on troops and police with firearms and explosives were becoming common, and IRA activity within the Catholic community had dramatically increased), Maudling allowed the security forces to move into Catholic ghettos. One such operation in July in the Lower Falls area of Belfast uncovered 208 weapons, 250 lb (113 kg) of explosives and 21,000 rounds of ammunition. Five people were killed during the operation and seventy-five injured. The army, which in 1969 had been welcomed as protectors by Catholics, now became as hated by them as the RUC, confirming to many that the IRA was their best protection. Many moderate Catholics blamed Maudling for unleashing the army and thereby fuelling tensions and violence. In the Westminster house of commons, Maudling stated that the IRA had declared war on the British government. During 1970, twenty-five people died and there were 153 explosions.

After 1945, the IRA had begun to re-define its policy, coming to concentrate on forcing Northern Ireland into union with Eire. Its secondary purpose became the imposition of a socialist society in a united Ireland. The riots and demonstrations which began in the North in 1968 were not, however, inspired by the IRA who, like the Northern government, were taken by surprise. In 1956, the IRA had launched an abortive campaign against Northern Ireland. With men drawn almost completely from Eire, they tried to organize guerrilla columns in the six counties, but were driven out by the combination of a broadly hostile civilian population and an efficient RUC. In 1962, the IRA formally called off their campaign, and over the next six years its leaders decided that political rather than military activity offered the best hope of Irish unification. In 1968, Cathal Goulding, the IRA chief-of-staff, announced that the IRA was for socialism and against violence. When the violence flared in the North, the more traditionally minded (and more numerous) members of the secret army broke away from the official IRA leadership in December 1969, forming the Provisional IRA (and its political counterpart, Provisional Sinn Fein, calling itself 'Sinn Fein, Kevin Street' after its Dublin address to distinguish itself from the official Sinn Fein Party). The Provisionals believed that there would be large-scale killings of Catholics by Protestants in the North unless they intervened. The Official IRA argued that by intervening the Provisionals would ensure the sectarian nature of Northern conflict and throw away any hope of working-class, socialist solidarity between Protestants and Catholics. To what extent this hope was realistic is uncertain, but there is no doubt that the Provisionals confirmed religion rather than civil rights as the principal division in the North. The Officials, with some lapses and splits, have maintained a separate identity, opposed to violence in general, though resorting to the gun for specific purposes. The split in the IRA was crucial to the conflict in the North because the Provisionals, with the financial support of Irish–Americans and, by roundabout means, the supply of sophisticated Soviet weapons, rapidly became an effective guerrilla/terrorist force.

The effect of Northern violence on the South was considerable, forcing Fianna Fail and Fine Gael to re-assess their traditional approach to Irish unity. While remaining committed to the principle of unity, Fine Gael in the late 1960s and during the 1970s came to recognize that Northern unionists' desire to remain within the United Kingdom meant that the prospect of Irish unity had to be seen as long-term. Fianna Fail, on the other hand, found itself more consciously committed than ever before to the principle of unity in the short-term. Jack Lynch, Lemass' successor as Fianna Fail leader and taoiseach from 1966 to 1973, in reaction to violence in the North warned in August 1969 that Eire 'can no longer stand by' and mobilized the Irish army in border areas to provide refugee camps for fleeing Northern Catholics, sending shock waves through Northern Protestant communities who for a while thought that the South was about to invade the North. In 1971 his government in the European Court of Human Rights charged the British government with torturing fourteen terrorist suspects in Northern Ireland. In January 1978 the Court exonerated Britain of the charge of torture, but found against her for degrading and inhuman treatment. Lynch also consistently maintained that unity could only come about through consent and not through violence, and took steps to demonstrate the South's willingness to take account of Northern Protestant fears by securing the end to the Roman Catholic Church's 'special position' in the Eire constitution, and by passing a harsh Offences Against the State (Amendment) Act to crack down on the IRA. However, some of Lynch's cabinet colleagues were, it seems, less committed to the idea of unity by consent, and gave the Provisionals active support instead.

In April 1970, Liam Cosgrave (W. T. Cosgrave's son), the Fine Gael leader of the opposition in the dail, alleged that members of Lynch's government were providing arms for the Provisional IRA. In May, Lynch dismissed two senior ministers: Charles Haughey, minister for finance, and Neil Blaney, minister for agriculture and fisheries. Kevin Boland, minister for local government, and Michael O'Morain, minister for justice, resigned in sympathy with Haughey and Blaney. Haughey, who had been a strong candidate for the Fianna Fail leadership in 1966 after Lemass' retirement, Blaney, John Kelly, a Belfast Citizens' Defence Committee organizer (and brother of Billy Kelly, the Provisional IRA Belfast commander), and an Irish army officer, Captain James Kelly, were then charged with conspiracy to import arms and ammunition illegally. They were found not guilty, but during their trial it emerged that they had been involved in or had knowledge of discussions with the IRA; that in August and September 1969 it seemed that they had similarly been involved in persuading IRA traditionalists to break away and form the Provisional IRA on the understanding that the Provisionals would not indulge in Southern politics or operations; that something in the region of £30,000 of Irish government money which had been designated for relief work in the North had instead been used to import 500 pistols and ammunition – the direct cause of the 'Arms Trial', as it became known, because the arms consignment was discovered by the customs authorities at Dublin airport. It also emerged that some IRA men from Londonderry had been trained in the autumn of 1969 at an Irish army camp in Donegal. As a result of these events, Boland and Blaney left Fianna Fail. Haughey refused to leave the Party, consistently maintained his innocence, and finally succeeded Jack Lynch as Party leader and taoiseach in December 1979. Since 1970, Fianna Fail's dedication to constitutional rather than revolutionary means to bring peace to Northern Ireland and to achieve Irish unity has continued to be doubted by Northern unionists. The Party lost the 1973 general election (primarily, it seems, because there was a general feeling that after sixteen years of uninterrupted Fianna Fail government, it was time for a change), and Liam Cosgrave, taoiseach of a Fine Gael–Labour coalition government from 1973 to 1977, established what has become a bi-partisan policy of full cooperation with Britain against the IRA, as Fianna Fail, in power again from 1977 to 1981 under Lynch and then Haughey, demonstrated. The nagging worry of Eire governments and citizens, however, has been that the horrors taking place in the North would spill over to the South. The myths of Irish history, where gallant freedom-fighters through the ages have faced hopeless odds challenging the might and the authority of Britain in Ireland, has meant that amongst large sections of the community there has been a surrender to romance where the IRA is concerned. Eire governments have to talk a tightrope to contain this romance without being perceived by the electorate as British puppets.

Southern Ireland's interest in principle in the North, and its practical involvement as a propaganda base and place of escape for IRA men fleeing security forces, was early on recognized by British governments. In September 1971, Edward Heath held two meetings with Jack Lynch at Chequers (the British prime minister's country house), at one of which Brian Faulkner, Chichester-Clark's successor in March 1971 as Northern Ireland prime minister, was present, which established the principle of close consultation on Northern Ireland between London and Dublin. Security arrangements also began to be coordinated as a result of these meetings. The ever-increasing level of violence in the North, however, was forcing the deployment of more and more troops and more and more money (public expenditure per head in Northern Ireland rose from £239 in 1967–8 to £387 in 1971–2, compared to £223 in 1967–8 and £308 in 1971–2 in England. In 1988–89, the province was a net cost to the exchequer of about £1,900 million). The first soldier was killed by the IRA in February 1971, and Chichester-Clark resigned as prime minister when his demand for tougher security measures to curb violence was refused. Faulkner had more success in this respect, persuading Heath to allow internment without trial of all those suspected of terrorist violence.

Internment began on 9 August 1971 and lasted until 5 December 1975 during which time 2,158 people were interned. As a policy, it was disastrous, turning Northern Catholics completely against

Unionist government while simultaneously witnessing the high-point of horror and IRA activity. Of the 173 deaths from violence in Northern Ireland during 1971, only twenty-eight happened before internment was introduced. Catholic resentment at what was seen as yet another attack on the Catholic community led to more riots, culminating with 'Bloody Sunday', 30 January 1972, when in Londonderry soldiers killed thirteen people, some of whom may have been themselves firing at troops, but this was never proved.

'Bloody Sunday' was another turning point. The day's events, including scenes of troops being petrol-bombed and spat at and firing at suspected IRA snipers, like the previous three years' violence, were brought in colour to a world-wide television audience. Convinced that some new form of politics was essential to gain Catholic confidence, the Heath government decided to invoke its powers under section 75 of the 1920 Government of Ireland Act, proroguing Stormont and imposing direct rule from Westminster on the province in March 1972. William Whitelaw, secretary of state for employment, was appointed by Heath to become the first secretary of state for Northern Ireland.

William Whitelaw faced a double threat from unionists who deeply resented their loss of control and British lack of confidence in them, and from the Provisional IRA which mounted its most sustained effort to disrupt the province and bomb Britain out of Ireland. He tried hard to win broad support by announcing in May 1972 a £35 million expansion of the Belfast shipyards providing 4,000 new jobs in a traditionally Protestant industry. He demonstrated his willingness to compromise by meeting Provisional IRA leaders in London in July (it came to nothing: the IRA would not compromise). Having failed to stop the IRA campaign, he launched 'Operation Motorman' on 31 July when he sent the army into 'No Go' areas, finally ending them. In 1973 he began interning 'loyalist' terror suspects (in the nine months following direct rule, eighty Catholics and thirty-eight Protestants were killed), showing Catholics that security measures were not aimed at them alone. In the twelve months after 'Motorman', the number of shooting incidents was halved, and the number of explosions fell by one-third compared to the previous twelve months.

In the decade before direct rule, the Unionist Party had found itself increasingly divided between those who favoured reforms and concessions to the nationalist community, and those amongst the predominantly rural and working-class rank-and-file unionists who felt that their upper-class leaders were no longer in touch with their feelings or problems. The populist Rev. Ian Paisley gradually was coming to speak for many unionists as violence and IRA activity drove them back to their first principles: that Catholics were nationalists out to subvert Unionist government. In the conservative, rural society of Northern Ireland such perceptions have great influence since in significant sections of society, information is transmitted primarily by word of mouth rather than by books and newspapers, and opinions are formed by personal experience of being caught up in the troubles – of having a friend killed; being questioned by police, army, illegal organizations etc. Class politics never took hold in the North because political and sectarian loyalties were always stronger.

In April 1970, standing as a Protestant Unionist, Paisley won O'Neill's old Stormont constituency in a by-election, catching the popular drift with his comment on O'Neill that he was 'a man beneath contempt who talked of progress and who every day on his way to Stormont passed 200 houses with no water and never thought to do anything about them'. The 'big house' Unionist leadership, represented by O'Neill and Chichester-Clark, able to fraternize with British politicians on an equal social footing, increasingly concerned to preserve democratic processes in the face of violence, was easily portrayed as out of touch and out of step with traditional Northern Irish unionism, the basic unionism of Sir Basil Brooke and Ian Paisley.

The facts of Paisley's religious–political career are simple. In 1951 at the age of twenty-five, he founded his own virulently anti-Catholic Free Presbyterian Church, and has been its head as Moderator ever since. He quickly established himself in the populist proselytizing tradition of earlier Free Church clergymen. In 1962 he was arrested in Rome demonstrating against the opening of the Second Vatican Council. He built up an organization, Ulster Protestant Action, 'to keep Protestant and Loyal workers in employment in times of depression, in preference to their Catholic fellow workers'. After O'Neill met Lemass, Paisley launched a campaign against him, jibing at the 'big house' and the 'fur-coat brigade' and predicting that 'O'Neillism' would mean the end of 'Protestant supremacy'. Events then began to play into his hands, and as violence increased, so did votes for the Democratic Unionist Party, founded in 1971 by Paisley. After the imposition of direct rule, Brian Faulkner led moderate Unionists in cooperating with Whitelaw, finally splitting the Unionist Party in 1974, forming his own minority Unionist Party of Northern Ireland (UPNI). Faulkner's Party enjoyed some success to begin with, but by 1979 had ceased to be of electoral significance. The Official Unionist Party (as the old Unionist Party distinguished itself from 1974 and into the 1980s), while maintaining a willingness to reform Northern Irish society and political institutions, refused to accept Whitelaw's most important proposal – power-sharing with nationalists – and formed the United Ulster Unionist Council (UUUC) as a loose cooperative arrangement with the Democratic Unionist Party and the Vanguard Party (launched in 1972 by an ex-Unionist minister, William Craig, to oppose direct rule). the UUUC won eleven of the twelve Northern Irish Westminster seats in the February 1974 United Kingdom general election: unionist and Protestant Northern Ireland had clearly opted to uphold, albeit with moderation, the principle of Protestant supremacy in the province.

On the nationalist side, politics changed too. The Nationalist Party (no longer regarded by Catholics as capable of enunciating their interests) was swept aside by the civil rights campaign of 1968–9. Austin Currie, Nationalist Party Stormont MP for East Tyrone, took a lead in the civil rights movement and was a founder-member in 1970 of the Social Democratic and Labour Party (SDLP), along with Gerald ('Gerry') Fitt, Republican Labour Party Westminster MP for West Belfast since 1966, who became Party leader, John Hume, a Londonderry Catholic community leader and NICRA activist, and Patrick Devlin, a Belfast politician and ex-chairman of the Northern Irish Labour Party. The SDLP rapidly gained the full support of Catholic voters, throughout the 1970s successfully competing with the Provisional IRA's appeal to Catholics that violence would secure justice, maintaining a basic support for constitutional and political procedures. This has been a very difficult political path, leading the SDLP at times into contradictory positions. Thus in 1974 the SDLP shared (limited) power with Unionists under Brian Faulkner, but refused to offer unconditional support to the security services. Nevertheless, its part in fighting for democratic methods to resolve differences commands respect.

Northern Ireland's fourth major Party was also founded in 1970:

the Alliance Party. It was formed by a group of moderate unionists previously uninvolved in politics, its leader, Oliver Napier, having been a liberal Catholic Belfast solicitor. The stated aim of the Party has been to attract unionist and nationalist support to break away from sectarian divisions in the province. Its electoral support has come principally from the North's middle class and has hovered around 10 per cent throughout the 1970s, compared to the 15 to 30 per cent for the DUP, the 20 to 30 per cent for the Official Unionists, and the SDLP's average of 25 per cent.

Against this backdrop of political changes William Whitelaw in October 1972 published a statement of his objectives. His concentrated purpose was to devise a new form of government in the province which would 'seek a wider consensus than has hitherto existed' and 'to be such as will work efficiently and will be capable of providing the concrete results of good government'. He publicly recognized that the question of Irish unity was a central issue, and on 8 March 1973 he held a referendum in the North on the question. The SDLP, establishing its own nationalist credentials, boycotted the poll (in July 1971 the SDLP had withdrawn from Stormont in protest at the 'institutions of government' and, echoing the creation of the first dail in 1919, had established a short-lived alternative 'Assembly of the Northern Irish People'). In a 59 per cent poll, 58 per cent of eligible voters (i.e. 99 per cent of the poll) voted to stay within the United Kingdom. Catholics abstained (and were advised to do so by the SDLP and the IRA). In May 1973, Whitelaw piloted a Constitution Act through Parliament which repealed the 1920 Government of Ireland Act and set up a proportionally elected unicameral seventy-eight member assembly with an executive to be appointed from it by the secretary of state for Northern Ireland. This executive and assembly were to enjoy powers similar to those of Stormont, but not including sole control of the judicial system or the police. The SDLP, the Alliance Party and Unionists under Brian Faulkner lent broad support to the Act. A minority of Unionists broke with Faulkner at this stage, joining Paisley's Democratic Unionists and Craig's Vanguard Party in opposing it on the grounds that the SDLP (who they still perceived as Catholics disloyal to the union with Britain) could have a place in the executive, and that the Act left the secretary of state with too much power (i.e. that Unionist supremacy was not guaranteed). These Unionists also felt that since

Unionist candidates commanded majority electoral support, any arrangements that did not result in Unionist government were undemocratic. In elections for the assembly in June, Faulkner's Unionists won twenty-two seats; the anti-Act Unionists won twenty-seven seats between them, and the SDLP consolidated their position as representatives of the Catholic community with nineteen seats.

On 21 November 1973, Faulkner's Unionists, the SDLP and the Alliance Party agreed with Whitelaw to cooperate in an assembly power-sharing executive. Brian Faulkner was designated chief executive with Gerry Fitt as deputy chief executive. Whitelaw was moved at the end of November to become once again secretary of state for employment, being succeeded in Northern Ireland by Francis Pym. On 6–9 December a tripartite conference between the British and Irish governments and the Northern Ireland executive-designate was held at the Sunningdale, Berkshire, Civil Service College. A wide measure of agreement was reached at Sunningdale. The Irish government agreed that Northern Ireland would remain part of the United Kingdom until a majority of the electorate in the province decided otherwise. It was agreed to set up a Council of Ireland with certain executive functions, and it was agreed to improve anti-terrorist cooperation between North and South. On 1 January 1974, the Northern Ireland Executive took office. On 4 January the Unionist Party made its deep reservations about the executive and Sunningdale clear to Faulkner, and he resigned as Party leader, then forming his own Party, the UPNI. The IRA made plain its opposition to the new constitutional initiative of the executive by stepping up its attacks on troops and police, hoping to force the SDLP to take sides with the forces of law and order and so risk being seen as 'traitors' by the Catholic community. Before anything was resolved, the United Kingdom general election in February 1974, called by Edward Heath on the issue of trade-union power, resulted in a change of government at Westminster and a clear statement by unionist voters in Northern Ireland that they rejected the executive and power-sharing. In an attempt to win credibility, Faulkner decided to seek modifications to the Sunningdale agreement, emasculating the proposed Council of Ireland. The agreement was by then rapidly becoming a dead-letter because hard-line nationalists in the South had challenged it in Eire courts on the grounds that it implied a surrender of the Eire constitution's claim to sovereignty over the whole of Ireland, forcing Liam Cosgrave's government to defend itself by stating that the government supported the all-Ireland constitutional claim. This meant that Dublin could not recognize the North's existence legally, and so was not able to implement the Sunningdale agreement to extradite people wanted in the North for terrorist crimes. It also meant that unionist suspicion of the South as a sanctuary for terrorists was reinforced.

While negotiations were beginning on modifications to Sunningdale between the executive, the Eire government and the new British Labour government, a new organization, the Ulster Workers' Council (UWC), called a province-wide strike against the executive and the Sunningdale agreement. The UWC had been formed by the leaders of the three main Unionist Parties – Harry West (Faulkner's successor as leader of the Official Unionists), Ian Paisley and William Craig – combining with Protestant defence and terrorist groups – the Ulster Defence Association (a vigilante coordinating body, organized on military lines, and the largest Protestant paramilitary force), the Ulster Volunteer Force (the counterpart of the Provisional IRA), sometimes illegal and heavily involved in assassinating Catholics), and the Orange Volunteers (Orange ex-servicemen, closely linked to the Vanguard Party). Their strike, which began on 14 May 1974, lasted for fifteen days and brought the province to a halt. On 29 May, faced by a complete shutdown of all services, the Unionist members of the executive resigned, forced to accept that power-sharing and Eire involvement in the North was unacceptable to nearly all unionists. After only five months, the executive had collapsed.

At the time, many people thought that the February 1974 general election, coming so soon and so unexpectedly after the start of the power-sharing experiment (Heath's government could have continued in office without an election until mid 1975), was responsible for the executive's failure. However, in retrospect it seems that unionist fears and antagonism to Sunningdale were as deep-rooted then as they have been ever since, and that while the executive alone might have gathered support, linked as it was in Sunningdale to a Council of Ireland, it was destined to fail.

In the two decades since the Sunningdale experiment, successive British governments have followed a dual policy of battling terrorism while seeking political arrangements that will reduce terrorist activity and condition the more extreme unionists to be more flexible about compromises British governments make with nationalists and the Republic. In turn, this has generated responses in the South, not least because the wellbeing of the Republic is affected by the state of the North.

Common ground for effective compromise between unionists and nationalists in the North narrowed after 1974. Unionists came to reject power-sharing; nationalists came to insist upon it. In March 1976, Merlyn Rees, secretary of state 1974–6, publicly recognized that compromises were unlikely, saying in the House of Commons that while direct rule was not intended to be permanent, the government 'does not contemplate any major new initiative for some time to come'. The consequence of this was a *de facto* policy of administration in the hands of unionists. Roy Mason, Rees' successor from 1976 to 1979, determinedly continued this policy – 'positive' direct rule, he called it – and had success: the number of people murdered in terrorist attacks dropped and arrests of terrorists increased. In May 1977 Mason faced down a 'loyalist' strike against direct rule that sought to echo the effect of the 1974 Ulster Workers' Council strike. His handling of the strike, constant refusal to deal with the IRA or 'loyalist' terrorists, and insistence that the United Kingdom government would not withdraw from the North, promised stability and thus reassured most people. It also meant that direct rule was proving to be the system that least exacerbated divisions in the North. Within ten years, the logic of this situation – full integration of the North with Britain – was to become Unionist policy.

Direct rule has lasted more than twenty years, from 1972–4 under the 1920 Act, and since 1974 under the Northern Ireland (Temporary Provisions) Act, renewable annually, endowing the secretary of state with the considerable executive functions permitted by the 1973 constitution Act. Labour and Conservative governments in Westminster have maintained a broad agreement on the government of the North, although Labour, in opposition throughout the 1980s, in 1981 changed from straightforward support of democratic majority wishes in the North to a policy of seeking withdrawal by actively campaigning for a united Ireland. This was to energize and make explicit what has been implicit in

British policy since 1972. Labour's 1988 policy document, *Towards a United Ireland – Labour's Plan for Peace*, detailed steps by which the administration of the North would be increasingly harmonized with the South so as eventually to weave a pragmatic unionist acceptance of Irish unity. 'While consent must, by definition, be freely given', Labour declared in the document, 'no group or party will be allowed to exercise a veto on policies designed to win consent for unification.' In 1989 at the Labour Party Conference, the Party leadership defeated a resolution calling for withdrawal from the North, but the Party's preponderant desire for withdrawal was clear.

Following the 1979 United Kingdom general election that saw Margaret Thatcher become prime minister for the first time, her Conservative government attempted unsuccessfully to replace direct rule with a new devolved government in the North. Humphrey Atkins, Mason's successor as secretary of state 1979–81, chaired a Constitutional Convention in 1980 that foundered on the intransigence of Parties in the North. Thatcher and the Irish taoiseach, Charles Haughey, then met in Dublin in December and took an important step to improve dealings between Britain and the Republic. Amid much speculation and profound unionist suspicion, the two leaders agreed on still closer cooperation on security matters, the establishment of joint civil service working parties on matters of mutual interest, and on regular meetings between British prime ministers and Irish taoiseachs (in Irish, the plural is taoisigh). In a phrase that stirred hopes and fears, the two leaders referred to the 'totality of relationships within these islands'. This was the start of a major shift in nationalist awareness, signalling a move away from traditionalist anti-British positions, and the jettisoning of a nationalist sense of being patronised by Britain. Extreme nationalists and 'loyalists' correctly feared that Britain and the Republic recognized that their common interests were greater than historical antipathies. Three years later, the main political Parties in the Republic – Labour, Fianna Fail and Fine Gael – joined with the SDLP in a review of nationalist attitudes. Meeting in Dublin as the New Ireland Forum, they published a report in May 1984 reaffirming the objective of a united Ireland to be obtained by peaceful means, but adopting a principle already at the heart of British policy: that the consent of a majority of the people in

Northern Ireland was a precondition to any change in the status of the North. 'The political arrangements for a new and sovereign Ireland', said the report, 'would have to be freely negotiated and agreed by the people of the North and by the people of the South.' It was a very important step for nationalist politicians to take.

Acceptance by constitutional nationalists North and South of the principle of consent in Northern Ireland represented an unequivocal success for British policy (and thus a considerable political and personal risk for nationalists). It also removed a strong unionist argument against dealing with nationalists. Furthermore, it clearly placed the SDLP and the Parties of the Republic on the side of democratic progress, against Sinn Fein and the IRA. In 1985, Garret FitzGerald frankly stated the new nationalist position (and alluded to the background Southern fear that Northern violence would spill over into the Republic):

No sane person could wish to change the status of Northern Ireland without the consent of the majority of its people. That would be a recipe for disaster and could, I believe, lead only to a civil war, that would be destructive of the life of people throughout our island. (*Irish Times*, 20 November 1985)

The change within mainstream Irish nationalism was not met by unionists or the IRA. Unionists considered that agreeing to political compromises with nationalists in the North and to any acknowledgement that the Republic had an interest in the affairs of the North would risk a real surrender of their British citizenship and identity. To most unionists, every change after 1969 seemed to threaten their status, and they viewed every step taken by governments in Westminster and Dublin as possible stealthy erosion of their position. Because of direct rule, elections have become, in effect, plebiscitary, demonstrating support within and between unionist and nationalist Parties, in the process squeezing out the Alliance Party. Traditional unionism decayed, and a large number of unionists felt politically homeless after the introduction of direct rule. As a result abstentionism grew, and apparent electoral gains were often less substantial than appeared. Unionist votes in the decade after Sunningdale steadily drifted towards hardliners, especially Ian Paisley. Between 1983 and 1985, votes for Paisley's Democratic Unionists grew from 20 per cent of those cast in the 1983 Westminster general election to 23.4 per cent in the 1985 local government elections (which, uniquely in the United Kingdom, are conducted under a proportional representational system in line with elections in the Republic), while Ulster Unionist (as the Official Unionist/old Unionist Party was now termed) support fell from 34 to 29.8 per cent. On the nationalist side, Sinn Fein won 13.4 per cent of the votes in the 1983 election compared to 17.9 per cent for the SDLP, and 11.8 per cent compared to 17.6 per cent in 1985.

For the IRA, violence increasingly became an end in itself. Sinn Fein's electoral performance was seen as an endorsement of violence, and the party's connection with the IRA (made apparent in 1981 by Danny Morrison, Sinn Fein's publicity director, who asked at the Party's annual conference, 'Will anyone here object if, with a ballot paper in this hand and an Armalite in this hand, we take power in Ireland?'), was used to provide respectability for IRA violence, especially in the United States. Spectacular terrorist acts designed to attract publicity and generate support, particularly among Irish–Americans, became a feature of IRA activity. Noraid, a US-based organization ostensibly gathering support for the nationalist community in the North, has been linked to funding for the IRA. In October 1984, at the British Conservative Party conference in Brighton, the IRA detonated a bomb in the Grand Hotel where Margaret Thatcher and most of her Cabinet were staying. Five people were killed and more than thirty were injured. Among the dead were an MP, Sir Anthony Berry, and Anne Wakeham, wife of the chief whip. Norman Tebbit, secretary of state for trade and industry, was severely injured and his wife, Margaret, was crippled. Claiming responsibility, the IRA declared: 'Thatcher will now realize that Britain cannot occupy our country, torture our prisoners and shoot our people in their own streets and get away with it. Today we were unlucky. But remember, we have only to be lucky once. You will have to be lucky always' (*Time*, 22 October 1984).

Marie Wilson was killed by an IRA bomb in Enniskillen on Remembrance Day, 1987. Her father, Gordon, publicly forgave Marie's killers and devoted himself to the cause of peace in the North. He was appointed an Eire senator as a taioseach's nominee in February 1993, and in April met two IRA spokesmen and confronted their absolute dedication to violence.

I was there to say, for God's sake, boys, enough is enough. And I got a point blank response. Nothing.

There was one man and one woman. The man never took his cap off. He answered yes, no, he passed the shades of grey to the young lady, who was the most articulate. I'll swear she was a graduate. I could raise an odd wee smile from her, but not from him. He was a hard man. But they were utterly polite. We drank tea and orange juice.

They presented me with a typed sheet of paper stating again that they were sorry about Enniskillen and my daughter, and repeated they were not the aggressors, but responded to British aggression.

In two words, what they said was, Brits out. And I said, do you mean Protestants out? and they said oh no, we would hope to win Protestants over to our way of thinking. I said, but you have driven Protestants away, you haven't won over a single Protestant in 24 years and 3,000 dead.

I challenged them why, if their targets were the army and the police, they had killed, in Enniskillen, 11 gentle folk? It was the only time I raised my voice in anger. In Warrington, I said, you killed two little boys, on a Saturday morning, where there was no army or police.

And they said, that was a mistake. I said, I am tired of hearing the IRA talking about their mistakes. And really, it was then that we agreed that we weren't getting anywhere . . . I did not expect them to say, 'Okay, Gordon Wilson, we will do as your say.' Some called me naive, and said I was made a fool of, and maybe they were right. God knows. But I had hopes. People had told me they couldn't think of anybody more likely to get something from the IRA, in the way of a little peace. I thought I might, if only a change of emphasis. I was wrong. (*The Times*, 5 November 1993)

Terrorism and unionist unwillingness to make any more concessions, however, did not prevent Margaret Thatcher's government, first with Charles Haughey and then with Garret FitzGerald, negotiating steps to strengthen the fight against terrorism and improve stability in the North. On 15 November 1985, at Hillsborough Castle, near Belfast, the residence of the secretary of state for Northern Ireland, Thatcher and FitzGerald signed the Anglo-Irish agreement. With the force of international treaty, the agreement gave the Irish Republic the right, within the principle of consent, 'to put forward views and proposals' about the government and administration of the North, especially on security, prisons, law and order, individual cases of prisoners, and the composition and role of the Police Complaints Board and the Police Authority for Northern Ireland. The Westminster government's motive was to affirm and improve the Republic's support against terrorism and to demonstrate to unionists that the Republic could be a friend. The Republic's interest was to show that diplomacy could advance nationalist ideals, and to try to keep terrorism locked up in the North.

The common ground between the two governments resulted in a formal acceptance by the Republic of Northern Ireland as part of the United Kingdom. This was the first time since the creation of the Republic that such a statement was given by an Irish government, and it went a long way to counteract traditional unionist objections to the Republic's claims in its Constitution to the whole island of Ireland. 'Any change in the status of Northern Ireland', the Republic formally acknowledged, 'would only come about with the consent of the majority of the people of Northern Ireland [and] the present wish of a majority of the people of Northern Ireland is for no change.' The Republic also undertook further anti-terrorist measures, including adherence to the 1976 European Convention on the Suppression of Terrorism which made easier the extradition between North and South of those accused of terrorist offences. In exchange, the Republic's interest in the North was accepted in the series of practical agreements about the police and prisons, etc. Garret FitzGerald summed up the change in nationalist attitudes that the Anglo-Irish agreement represented:

Twenty years ago it would have been unthinkable that any Irish government could have got public support for the proposition that unification would not come without the consent of the majority in Northern Ireland. Twenty years ago politicians in the Republic were still espousing the untenable and provocative thesis that unification was a matter that should be decided by a majority in the island as a whole, over the heads of, and against the wishes of, a majority in Northern Ireland. (*The Irish Post*, 8 November 1986)

The agreement was immediately condemned by the overwhelming majority of unionist leaders who, despite assurances, were convinced that the Republic's formal involvement in Northern affairs was a major erosion of the North's position within the United Kingdom. In the Republic, Fianna Fail opposed the agreement in the dail on the grounds that it diluted national claims, but subsequently accepted it. Terrorists hit out against the agreement, and over the next twelve months the indices of terrorist violence increased. However, in later years the agreement saw greater efficiency in the war against terrorism, notably in increased arrests of terrorists as a result of cross-border military and police cooperation, and a gentle reduction in unionist fears. Democratic Unionist support fell to 17.8 per cent in the 1989 local government elections, while Ulster Unionists obtained 31 per cent. In the 1989 elections to the European parliament (which, in Northern Ireland, are also conducted under a proportional representation system), the DUP did better, obtaining 29.9 per cent of the vote compared to the Ulster Unionists 22.2 per cent. Sinn Fein's support in local elections was 11.4 per cent in 1987 and 11.1 per cent in 1989, and in the European election 9.2 per cent, while the SDLP's position improved: 21.1 per cent and 20.9 per cent in the 1987 and 1989 local elections, and 25.5 per cent in the European election. With the 1990 Broadcasting Act, Thatcher's government banned the direct transmission of the words spoken by Sinn Fein representatives and by spokesmen for the IRA, thus hampering their access to radio and television. In the Republic, where the IRA had faced such a ban under section 31 of the 1960 Broadcasting Authority Act, amended and reinforced in 1976, Sinn Fein, hoping to capitalise on what it considered would be the unpopularity of the Anglo-Irish agreement, in 1986 ceased its boycott of elections in the Republic. But in the Republic's 1987 general election, Sinn Fein received only 1.9 per cent of the vote; in the Republic's 1989 general election, its vote fell to 1.2 per cent.

The reduction in tension was not met by greater Unionist flexibility or by less determined terrorism. Humphrey Atkins' successors as secretary of state – James Prior, 1981–4, Douglas Hurd, 1984–5, Tom King, 1985–9, Peter Brooke, 1989–91, and Sir Patrick Mayhew since 1991 – continued the effort to secure some form of devolved government in the North to replace direct rule. Prior called it 'rolling devolution' and established an elected Assembly in 1982 with consultative powers, continued by Hurd and King, which sat until 1986 when the SDLP walked out. Despite clear Unionist hostility, Peter Brooke attempted to revive Nationalist–Unionist dialogue and cooperation in the North. In April 1991 he announced talks about the future of the North and the prospect of a restoration of limited self-government. Three months later, however, Unionist politicians boycotted the talks in order to emphasize their objection to the Anglo-Irish agreement's acceptance of the Republic's involvement in the North. In October

1993, against a backdrop of extensive IRA bombings in England and IRA and 'loyalist' murders in the North, John Hume, the leader of the SDLP, following secret talks with Gerry Adams, president of Sinn Fein, made private proposals to the United Kingdom and Irish governments that, said Hume, would bring peace to the North 'in a week'. John Major, prime minister since November 1991, met Hume but rejected his proposals. At the same time, Major and the Irish taoiseach, Albert Reynolds, in public hinted at proposals for a Northern Ireland settlement involving both governments and Sinn Fein as long as the Party and the IRA renounced violence. At the Lord Mayor's banquet in London on 15 November 1993, Major unambiguously invited Sinn Fein to participate in settling the future of Northern Ireland:

If the IRA end violence for good, then – after a sufficient interval to ensure the permanence of their intent – Sinn Fein can enter the political arena as a democratic party and join the dialogue on the way ahead . . . Some would deny them that path on account of their past and present misdeeds. I understand that feeling, but I do not share it . . . There can be no secret deals, no rewards for terrorism, no abandonment of the vital principle of majority consent.

The following day, Albert Reynolds gave Major's initiative a boost by dropping the Republic's precondition that there had to be an end to violence before there could be all-Party talks on the future of the North. This precondition had previously given the IRA, in effect, a veto on talks involving the South. London and Dublin, said Reynolds, were following 'parallel' policies.

All these efforts to end direct rule and start a process that would convince terrorists to end their bombings and murders, foundered on the intransigencies of Nationalists and Unionists in the North. Initiatives, if they were to be undertaken, were forced into the hands of Westminster and Dublin, thus confirming a *de facto* preference for direct rule in both communities in the North. Terrorists refused to end their terror as a precondition to political negotiations; Nationalists insisted on participation in the government and administration of the North; full integration with Britain had become a formal Unionist objective, providing a strong argument to reject further compromise with Nationalists and the Republic. After all, Unionists pointed out, if Northern Ireland is part of the United Kingdom, why should it not be governed in the same way as Wales and Scotland, with the same rights and protections as the Scots and Welsh enjoy?

These developments have played against a steady unfolding of horror in the North. Civil rights protests in the late 1960s met RUC and 'B' Special violence which together brought the army in, which encouraged the IRA's violence which fanned 'loyalist' terror groups. The year 1972, following direct rule, was the most violent in Northern Ireland's history in the half century since partition. The IRA and their 'loyalist' counterparts' dedication to violence is absolute. Gerry Adams in 1990 stated starkly: 'The onus is on those who claim that there is an alternative to the IRA's armed struggle to prove that this is the case.' Referring to unionists in the North, he declared: 'The argument that the consent of this national minority, elevated into a majority within an undemocratic, artificially created state, is necessary before any constitutional change can occur, is a nonsense' (*The Irish Times*, 17 November 1990). In the minds of Mr Adams and his supporters, the only alternative to the unionists' immediate consent to a united Ireland is that the IRA should terrorise them into it.

IRA men are prepared to die for this belief and their overall objective of a united Ireland free of Britain. In 1981, ten IRA prisoners starved themselves to death in the H-blocks of the Maze prison outside Belfast. Their leader and the first to die, Bobby Sands, had been elected MP for Fermanagh and South Tyrone in a by-election four weeks before his death. The hunger strikers were attempting to force the British government to let them wear civilian clothes instead of prison uniform: everyone recognized that their real protest was against the division of Ireland. Whatever their reason and the actions that had placed them in the Maze in the first place, Sands and his colleagues had demonstrated extraordinary bravery and determination, revealing intransigent dedication to their cause. Perhaps advances of technology, the spread of mass communication, and a growing habit of terrorism all over the world have enormously increased the destructive capabilities and effects of terrorist actions, making them more shocking and indiscriminate, and making ever clearer the inefficious wickedness of terrorism: a catastrophic impasse highlighted by the sacrifice and dedication of the absolutists on both sides in the North.

Between the revival of murder in 1969 and the end of 1990, more

Terrorism in Northern Ireland

	1972[a]	1981	1982	1983	1984	1985	1986	1987	1988	1989	1990
Deaths											
RUC	17	21	12	18	9	23	12	16	6	9	12
army	129	23	29	15	19	6	12	11	33	14	15
civilian[b]	321	57	57	44	36	25	37	66	54	39	49
Total	467	101	97	77	64	54	61	93	93	62	76
Injured											
RUC	485	332	99	142	267	415	622	246	218	163	195
army	578	140	98	88	86	33	55	104	229	190	180
civilian[b]	3813	878	328	280	513	468	774	780	600	606	423
Total	4876	1350	515	510	866	916	1451	1130	1047	959	798

[a] 1972: the year of most violence.

[b] civilian: the category into which terrorist casualties fall. In the case of injuries most are innocent bystanders affected by terrorist violence – wounded by bombings and so on; in the case of deaths, most are terrorists killed by the army and RUC, and by terrorist assassinations and reprisals.

than 2,800 people had been killed. In the same period, nearly 32,000 people had been injured. The violence has come to England with periodic IRA bombing campaigns and assassinations. In November 1974, immediately after the deaths of nineteen people by IRA bombings of a pub in Birmingham, the government passed the Northern Ireland (Temporary Provisions) Act making the IRA illegal and granting the home secretary powers to exclude from Britain (but not Northern Ireland) persons suspected of terrorist involvement.

The events of the 1960s onwards in Northern Ireland, let alone the history of Ireland over the previous 800 years, show that Ireland and Britain are inextricably bound to each other. Geography, at least as important as history, makes this so.

Select bibliography

Aalen, F. H. A. *Man and the landscape in Ireland*. London and New York, 1978

Akenson, D. H. *The United States and Ireland*. Cambridge, Mass., 1973

Arthur, Paul, *Government and politics of Northern Ireland*. London, 1980

Bardon, Jonathan, *A history of Ulster*. Belfast, 1992

Beckett, J. C. *The making of modern Ireland, 1603–1923*. London, 1966
Anglo–Irish tradition. London, 1976

Bell, J. Bowyer. *The secret army: a history of the IRA, 1916–79*. Dublin, 1979
The Irish Troubles. A generation of violence 1967–1992. Dublin, 1993

Bew, Paul. *C. S. Parnell*. Dublin, 1980

Bew, Paul, Gibbon, P. and Patterson, H. *The state in Northern Ireland 1921–72. Political forces and social classes*. Manchester, 1979
Conflict and conciliation in Ireland: Parnellites and radical agrarians. Oxford, 1987
(ed.). *The Revolution in Ireland, 1879–1923*. London, 1988

Bieler, Ludwig. *Ireland, harbinger of the Middle Ages*. London, New York and Toronto, 1966

Bolton, G. C. *The passing of the Irish Act of Union*. Oxford, 1966

Bowman, John. *De Valera and the Ulster Question, 1917–73*. Oxford, 1982

Boyce, D. George. *Englishmen and Irish troubles*. London, 1972
Nationalism in Ireland. London, 1982
Ireland 1828–1923: from ascendancy to democracy. Oxford and Cambridge, Mass., 1992

Boylan, Henry. *A dictionary of Irish biography*. Dublin, 1978

de Breffny, Brian. *The land of Ireland*. London and New York, 1979

Brown, Malcolm. *The politics of Irish literature*. London, 1972

Brown, Terence. *Ireland: a social and cultural history 1922–79*. Second edition, London, 1985

Buckland, P. *The factory of grievances: devolved government in Northern Ireland 1921–39*. Dublin, 1979

Canny, Nicholas. *From Reformation to restoration: Ireland 1534–1660.* Dublin, 1987

Chubb, Basil. *The government and politics of Ireland.* Third edition, Harlow, 1992

Colum, Padraic (ed.). *A treasury of Irish folklore.* New York, 1954

Comerford, R. V. *The Fenians in context: Irish politics and society 1848–82.* Dublin, 1985

Coogan, Tim Pat. *The IRA.* London, 1980
  Michael Collins: a biography. London, 1990
  De Valera: long fellow, long shadow. London, 1993

Cooke, Alistair B. *Ulster: the origins of the problem.* London, 1988
  Ulster: the Unionist options. London, 1990

Corish, Patrick J. *The Catholic community in the seventeenth and eighteenth centuries.* Dublin, 1981

Corkery, Daniel. *The hidden Ireland.* Dublin, 1924

Cosgrove, Art (ed.). *A new history of Ireland, vol. II: Medieval Ireland 1169–1534.* Second impression, Oxford, 1993

Cosgrove, Art and McCartney, Donal (eds.). *Studies in Irish history presented to R. Dudley Edwards.* Dublin, 1979

Costigan, Giovanni. *A history of modern Ireland.* New York, 1969

Cronin, Sean. *The McGarrity papers.* Tralee, 1972
  Frank Ryan: the search for the Republic. Dublin, 1980
  Irish nationalism. Dublin, 1980

Dillon, Myles. *Early Irish literature.* Chicago, 1948

Daly, Mary E. *Social and economic history of Ireland since 1800.* Dublin, 1981

Dangerfield, George. *The damnable question.* London, 1977

Davies, R. R. (ed.). *The British Isles 1100–1500.* Edinburgh, 1988

Dickson, David. *New foundations: Ireland 1660–1800.* Dublin, 1987

Dolley, Michael. *Anglo-Norman Ireland.* Dublin, 1972

Donnelly, James. *The land and people of nineteenth-century Cork.* London, 1975

Doyle, David Noel. *Ireland, Irishmen and revolutionary America 1780–1820.* Dublin, 1981

Dudley Edwards, Owen. *The sins of our fathers: roots of conflict in Northern Ireland.* Dublin, 1970

Dudley Edwards, R. *A new history of Ireland.* Dublin, 1975
  Ireland in the age of the Tudors. London, 1977

Dudley Edwards, Ruth. *Atlas of Irish history.* Second edition, London, 1981
  Patrick Pearse: the triumph of failure. London, 1977
  James Connolly. Dublin, 1981

Ellis, Steven. *Tudor Ireland.* Harlow, 1985

Fallis, Richard. *The Irish renaissance.* Dublin, 1978

Falls, Cyril. *Elizabeth's Irish wars.* London, 1950

Fanning, Ronan. *The Irish Department of Finance.* Dublin, 1978

Independent Ireland. Dublin, 1983
Faulkner, Brian. *Memoirs of a statesman*. London, 1978
Fisk, Robert. *The point of no return*. London, 1975
   In time of war: Ireland, Ulster and the price of neutrality 1939–45. London, 1983
Fitzpatrick, David. *Politics and Irish life, 1913–21*. Dublin, 1977
Foster, Roy. *Charles Stewart Parnell, the man and his family*. Sussex and New Jersey, 1976
   Modern Ireland 1600–1972. London, 1988
Frame, Robin. *Colonial Ireland 1169–1369*. Dublin, 1981
   The political development of the British Isles 1100–1400. Oxford, 1990
Gailey, Andrew. *Ireland and the death of kindness: the experience of constructive Unionism 1890–1905*. Cork, 1987
Gaughan, J. Anthony. *Memoirs of Constable Jeremiah Mee R.I.C.* Naas, 1975
   Austin Stack: portrait of a separatist. Dublin, 1977
Goldstrom, J. M. and Clarkson, L. A. (eds.). *Irish population, economy and society. Essays in honour of K. H. Connell*. Oxford, 1981
Guinness, Desmond, and W. Ryan. *Irish houses and castles*. London, 1971
Harbison, Peter. *The archaeology of Ireland*. London, 1976
Harkness, D. W. *The restless dominion*. Dublin, 1969
   Northern Ireland since 1920. Dublin, 1983
Herity, Michael, and Eogan, George. *Ireland in prehistory*. Dublin, 1977
Hickey, D. J., and Doherty, J. E. *A dictionary of Irish history since 1800*. Dublin, 1980
Hopkinson, Michael. *Green against green: the Irish civil war*. Dublin, 1988
Hoppen, K. T. *Elections, politics and society in Ireland, 1832–85*. Oxford, 1984
Hyde, Douglas. *A literary history of Ireland*, ed. Brian O'Cuiv. London, 1980
Johnson, Paul. *Ireland: land of troubles*. London, 1980
Johnston, Edith Mary. *Ireland in the eighteenth century*. Dublin, 1974
Joyce, J., and Murtagh, P. *The boss*. Dublin, 1983
Kee, Robert. *The green flag*. London, 1972
Kennedy, Kieran A., Giblin, Thomas and McHugh, Deirdre (eds.). *The economic development of Ireland in the twentieth century*. London, 1988
Laing, L., and Laing, J. *Celtic Britain and Ireland AD 200–800: the myth of the dark ages*. Dublin, 1990
Lawlor, Sheila M. *Britain and Ireland 1914–23*. Dublin, 1983
Lecky, W. E. A. *History of Ireland in the eighteenth century*. London, 1892
Lee, Joseph. *The modernisation of Irish society, 1848–1918*. Dublin, 1973
   Ireland, 1945–70. Dublin, 1979
   Ireland: towards a sense of place. Cork, 1985
   Ireland, 1912–1985, politics and society. Cambridge, 1989
Litton, Frank (ed.). *Unequal achievement*. Dublin, 1982

Longford, Earl of, and O'Neill, Thomas P. *Eamon de Valera*. London and Dublin, 1970

Lucas, A. T. *Treasures of Ireland*. Dublin, 1973

Lydon, J. F. *The lordship of Ireland in the Middle Ages*. Dublin, 1972

Lyons, F. S. L. *Ireland since the famine*. London, 1971
   Charles Stewart Parnell. London, 1977
   Culture and anarchy in Ireland, 1880–1939. Oxford, 1980

Lyons, F. S. L., and Hawkins, R. (eds.). *Ireland under the Union: varieties of tension. Essays in honour of T. W. Moody*. Oxford, 1980

Macardle, Dorothy. *The Irish Republic*. London, 1937

McCaffrey, Lawrence J. *The Irish question, 1800–1922*. Lexington, 1968

McCartney, Donal. *The dawning of democracy: Ireland 1800–1870*. Dublin, 1987

MacCurtain, Margaret. *Tudor and Stuart Ireland*. Dublin, 1972

MacDonagh, Oliver. *Ireland: the Union and its aftermath*. London, 1977
   Ireland since the Union. Second edition, London, 1979
   States of mind. London, 1983

McDowell, R. B. *Ireland in the age of imperialism and revolution 1760–1801*. Oxford, 1979

MacEoin, Uinseann. *Survivors*. Dublin, 1980

MacLysaght, Edward. *Irish life in the seventeenth century*. Cork, 1939

McMahon, Deirdre. *Republicans and imperialists: Anglo-Irish relations in the 1930s*. London, 1984

MacNiocaill, Gearoid. *Ireland before the Vikings*. Dublin, 1972

MacStiofain, Sean. *Memoirs of a revolutionary*. London, 1975

Mansergh, Nicholas. *The Irish question, 1840–1921*. London, 1965
   The unresolved question: the Anglo-Irish settlement and its undoing, 1912–72. New Haven and London, 1992

Martin, F. X. (ed.). *Leaders and men of the Easter Rising: Dublin 1916*. London, 1967

Miller, David W. *Church, state and nation in Ireland, 1898–1921*. Pittsburgh, 1973
   Queen's rebels: Ulster loyalism in historical perspective. Dublin, 1980

Miller, Kerby. *Emigrants and exiles: Ireland and the Irish exodus to North America*. Oxford, 1985

Moody, T. W. *The Ulster question, 1603–1973*. Dublin and Cork, 1974
   Michael Davitt. Oxford, 1982

Moody, T. W., and Beckett, J. C. (eds.). *Ulster since 1800*. London, 1955 and 1957

Moody, T. W., Martin F. X., and Byrne, F. J. (eds.). *A new history of Ireland*, vol. III. Oxford, 1976
   A new history of Ireland, vol. IV. *Eighteenth century Ireland 1691–1800*. Oxford, 1986

Morton, Grenfell. *Elizabethan Ireland*. London, 1971

Murphy, John A. *Ireland in the twentieth century*. Dublin, 1976

Nicholls, Kenneth. *Gaelic and gaelicised Ireland in the middle ages*. Dublin, 1972

Norman, E. R. *The Catholic Church and Ireland in the age of rebellion, 1859–73*. London, 1965

A history of modern Ireland. London, 1971

Norman, E. R., and St Joseph, J. K. S. *The early development of Irish society*. Cambridge, 1969

Nowlan, Kevin B. (ed.). *The making of 1916: studies in the history of the Rising*. Dublin, 1969

Nowlan, Kevin B., and O'Connell, M. R. (eds.). *Daniel O'Connell: portrait of a radical*. Belfast, 1984

Nowlan, Kevin B., and Williams, T. Desmond (eds.). *Ireland in the war years and after, 1939–51*. Dublin, 1969

O'Brien, Conor Cruise. *States of Ireland*. London, 1972

O'Broin, Leon. *Revolutionary underground: the story of the Irish Republican Brotherhood 1858–1924*. Dublin, 1976

Michael Collins. Dublin, 1980

O'Carroll, J. P., and Murphy, John A. (eds.). *De Valera and his times*. Cork, 1983

O'Connor, Frank. *The big fellow – Michael Collins and the Irish revolution*. London, 1969

O'Connor, Ulick. *The Troubles: Ireland 1912–1922*. Indianapolis, 1975

Ó Corráin, Donncha. *Ireland before the Normans*. Dublin, 1972

O'Dubhghaill, M. *Insurrection fires at Eastertide*. Dublin, 1966

O'Farrell, P. *Ireland's English question*. London, 1971

England and Ireland since 1800. Oxford, 1975

O'Ferrall, Fergus. *Daniel O'Connell*. Dublin, 1981

O'Halloran, C. *Partition and the limits of Irish nationalism*. Dublin, 1987

O'Halpin, Eunan. *The decline of the Union: British government in Ireland 1892–1920*. Dublin, 1987

O'Neill, Terence. *Ulster at the crossroads*. London, 1969

O'Neill, Thomas P., and Longford, Earl of. *Eamon de Valera*. Dublin, 1970

O'Neill, Tomas, and Ó Fiannachta, Padraig. *De Valera* (in Irish). Dublin, 1968

Ó Tuathaigh, Gearoid. *Ireland before the famine, 1798–1848*. Dublin, 1974

Ó Tuathaigh, M. A. G., and Lee, J. J. *The age of de Valera*. Dublin, 1982

Pakenham, Frank. *Peace by ordeal*. London, 1935

de Paor, Liam. *Divided Ulster*. Harmondsworth, 1970

de Paor, Maire and Liam. *Early Christian Ireland*. London, 1958

Peck, J. *Dublin from Downing Street*. Dublin, 1978

Ranelagh, John. *Ireland – an illustrated history*. London, 1981

Rees, Merlyn. *Northern Ireland: a personal perspective*. London, 1985

Rose, Richard. *Governing without consensus: an Irish perspective*. London, 1971

Northern Ireland: a time of choice. London, 1976
Ryle Dwyer, T. *Irish neutrality and the USA 1939–47.* Dublin, 1977
  Eamon de Valera. Dublin, 1980
  Michael Collins and the Treaty. Dublin, 1981
Shannon, William V. *The American Irish.* New York, 1964
Sheehy, J. *Discovering Ireland's past, the Celtic revival.* London, 1979
Smith, Howard. *Ireland, some episodes from her past.* London, 1974
Staples, Hugh B. (ed.). *The Ireland of Sir Jonah Barrington (1832).* London, 1967
Stewart, A. T. Q. *The Ulster crisis.* London, 1969
  The narrow ground: aspects of Ulster, 1609–1969. London, 1977
  Edward Carson. Dublin, 1981
Sunday Times Insight Team. Ulster. Harmondsworth, 1972
Thatcher, Margaret. *The Downing Street years.* London, 1993
Thompson, W. I. *The imagination of an insurrection: Dublin, Easter 1916.* New York, 1967
Townshend, Charles. *The British campaign in Ireland 1919–21.* Oxford, 1978
  Political violence in Ireland: government and resistance since 1848. Oxford, 1983
Travers, Pauric. *Settlements and divisions: Ireland 1870–1922.* Dublin, 1988
Utley, T. E. *Lessons of Ulster.* London, 1975
de Vere White, Terence. *The Anglo-Irish.* London, 1972
Wallace, Martin. *British government in Northern Ireland: from devolution to direct rule.* Newton Abbot, 1982
Walsh, Dick. *The party: inside Fianna Fail.* Dublin, 1986
Watt, John. *The church in medieval Ireland.* Dublin, 1972
Whitaker, T. K. *Interests.* Dublin, 1983
Whyte, John H. *Church and state in modern Ireland 1923–1970.* Dublin, 1971
  Interpreting Northern Ireland. Oxford, 1990
Williams, T. Desmond (ed.). *The Irish struggle 1916–26.* London, 1966
  Secret societies in Ireland. Dublin, 1973
Williams, T. Desmond, and Edwards, R. Dudley. *The great famine.* Dublin, 1956
Winstanley, M. J. *Ireland and the land question 1800–1922.* London, 1984
Woodham-Smith, Cecil. *The great hunger.* London, 1962
Younger, Carlton. *Ireland's civil war.* London, 1970

Index